JOURNEY TO LIVINGSTONE

Map by Thomas Kitchin showing European knowledge of Southern Africa before Livingstone's journeys.

Timothy Holmes

JOURNEY TO LIVINGSTONE

EXPLORATION OF AN IMPERIAL MYTH

CANONGATE PRESS

First published in Great Britain in 1993 by
Canongate Press Ltd, 14 Frederick Street,
Edinburgh EH2 2HB

ISBN 0 86241 402 4

British Library Cataloguing-in-Publication Data
A catalogue record for this book is available on request
from the British Library

The publishers gratefully acknowledge subsidy from the
Scottish Arts Council towards the publication of this
book.

Photoset by Falcon Graphic Art Ltd, Wallington, Surrey
Printed and bound in Great Britain by Biddles,
Guildford, Surrey

To
Randolph Vigne

Author's Note on sources, and Acknowledgments

This study is based to a considerable extent on only recently revealed Livingstone manuscripts, mainly letters. All letters quoted or cited are identified by date and the name of the recipient: the provenance of the letters can be established in I C Cunningham and G W Clendennen's *David Livingstone, a Catalogue of Documents* (1979) and its *Supplement* (1985, National Library of Scotland, Edinburgh), or in the author's *David Livingstone Letters and Documents* 1841–1872 (1990, London).

Extracts from Livingstone's Journals are taken from published sources. Other works, whether earlier biographies or sources of general information, are named where appropriate.

I wish to thank first my wife, Nadia Holmes, and children, Daniel and Jane Holmes, for their patience and wide-ranging help in preparing this volume. Invaluable assistance has come too from Mr Bill Cunningham (Scottish National Memorial to David Livingstone, Blantyre), Dr J S McGrath and Professor Tom Devine (Strathclyde University, Glasgow), Mr I C Cunningham (National Library of Scotland, Edinburgh), Mr Randolph Vigne, Mr James and Mrs Clare Currey, Mrs Kufekisa-Laugery, Mr Mick and Mrs Joan Pilcher, Mr John Fynn. Professor Emeritus George Shepperson gave the manuscript a sympathetic reading, and offered comprehensive suggestions for its improvement, while Dr Hugh Macmillan (University of Zambia) helped greatly in matters of fact, interpretation, and style. To all, my gratitude.

Any errors are attributable solely to the author.

CONTENTS

Prologue *Saint of Empire*   xi

Part One 1813–1851 From Blantyre to Ngami
1 First steps   3
2 Brave new world   11
3 Chosen path   18
4 Colonies, imagined or real   26
5 Noble objects   34
6 'Plucky little devil'   45

Part Two 1852–1856 Across Africa
7 Forward policies   57
8 Slave rivers   69
9 Destinies   80
10 Seek and ye shall find   86
11 'The greatest triumph'   95

Part Three 1857–1858 Fame
12 'Undoubtedly the Hero will arrive'   107
13 'Missionary Travels'   117
14 Apogee   131

Part Four 1858–1864 Disaster on the Zambezi
15 Into the valley   145
16 'Shall faith oust fact?'   159
17 Lake of Stars   173
18 Onward Christian Soldiers   187
19 Family matters   202
20 *Lady Nyassa*   215

Part Five 1864–1865 *Recuperation*

21   Necessary business   231
22   Quiet among friends   243
23   To start the world anew   255

Part Six 1866–1874 *Towards the City of God*

24   'We have been very slow'   269
25   'There is a river . . .'   281
26   '. . . the streams whereof shall make glad to City of God'   294
27   'The impression of being in Hell'   305
28   'You have brought me new life'   314
29   'How many days is it to the Luapula?'   324
30   Born again   333

Epilogue

31   In his name   343

Bibliography   353
Index   358

I am quite sure that (bar one) I have no race prejudices, and I think I have no color prejudices, nor caste prejudices, nor creed prejudices. Indeed, I know it. I can stand any society. All that I care to know is that a man is a human being – that is enough for me; he can't be any worse.

Mark Twain
(*Notebook*, ed. A.B. Paine, New York 1935, p.277)

PROLOGUE: SAINT OF EMPIRE

A massive bronze statue of David Livingstone overlooks the Victoria Falls (a mile wide, three hundred feet high) from the south bank of the River Zambezi. On the plinth that supports the giant figure, one arm outstretched towards the north, a plaque credits him with being the light of Africa, bringer of the gospel, unshackler of slaves. The unceasing roar of the great waterfall, the swirling spray that plumes up from its chasm, the slight, constant tremble of the ground beneath the feet, the rainbows that form and dissolve, give the place a magic air. But as the spirit rises with the clouds, the falling of the waters, never stopping, draws the body downwards, down to destruction in the foaming abyss. With a longing for immortality, for incorporeal life among the rainbows, many a person will grasp a tree to forestall suicide, even when standing at a safe distance from the fissure's slippery edge.

A few miles north of the Falls the town of Livingstone lies on a sandy slope that rises abruptly from the flat plain of the Zambezi valley. From the top of the main street the cloud thrown up by the cataract can be seen rising, silent and billowing, into the tropical sky. At most times of the year the heat of the day is overwhelming, people move with the economy of slugs, pausing in the shade of trees to break the relentlessness of the sun, or edging along the shadow of buildings, east side of the street in the morning, west after meridian. Many of the buildings have survived from the early days of the town, façades in Edwardian colonial pomposity, unofficial national monuments saved by legislation from demolition. The town was established in 1905 and was given its name in honour of the man who was – it is still believed – the first European to visit the magnificent Mosi-oa-Tunya (the Smoke that Thunders) which he christened after his monarch, in 1855 the still young, Queen Victoria.

In choosing to name the town after Livingstone, its founders with due deliberation placed themselves within the aura of a man who was regarded throughout the British empire as a saint. His life had been, so it seemed, a paradigm of Christian fortitude, his death in misery at a remote African village a martyrdom to godly ideals. At the south of the main street – called Mosi-oa-Tunya Avenue – where the slope down to the valley becomes pronounced, a building in Spanish-Mexican style, with a four-storey clock tower (the clock has rarely worked) and tiled roof looks out across the plain towards the Falls. This is the Livingstone Museum, erected in the 1930s by the colonial authorities. Four large galleries surround a square, verandahed, patio with a fountain at the centre, and in one of the four is a small Livingstone shrine – his jacket and braided peaked cap, surgical chest, medals (one of three missing, presumed stolen) notebooks, a Greek New Testament, photographs, page-proofs of his best-seller *Missionary Travels and Researches in South Africa*, photostats of holograph letters. The institution is the national museum of Zambia, the country called Northern Rhodesia after it became a British colony at the turn of the century.

Soon after independence in 1964, Zambia changed the names of towns and streets which recalled British rule. Fort Jameson became Chipata; Abercorn, Mbala; Fort Rosebery, Mansa. But Livingstone remains Livingstone's, and the place of his death, a thousand miles to the north, is hallowed as a national monument in the form of a cross-crowned obelisk. His name is remembered in those of churches, schools and colleges, and in a mountain pass. Children in Zambian classrooms learn that Livingstone was born in poverty, dedicated his life to spreading the gospel and ending slavery; his journeys across Africa made him a great explorer, his adventures and sufferings a hero, a Christian hero and exemplar.

Until a few years ago, my knowledge of the man derived from the sort of osmosis that issues from forgotten lessons at school, from histories of southern Africa, from the generalized hearsay that filters down to the present from the past; then in the early part of 1986 I found myself spending a few days at the Museum trying, with the help of the Keeper of History, to arrive at a satisfactory understanding of the transition from Stone Age to Iron Age in central Africa. After a great deal of reading and discussion, my head as full of as much as it could absorb, I found myself with an afternoon to spare. I decided to stay in the Museum as I couldn't face the walk through the melting heat to where I was lodging. When I had spent twenty minutes examining the Livingstone exhibits, I learned that I could read his handwriting and asked the librarian if I might see the originals of the photostats: he showed me into a small and blessedly air-conditioned upstairs room where four teak cabinets held holographs between sheets of glass in vertical pull-out drawers.

Reading was not easy as light from the window was reflected off the glass panels. The handwriting was more difficult than it had at first seemed, and in some letters impossible without a lens as it was so small and faded (clearly only the most legible texts had been chosen for public display). My curiosity would probably have been satisfied by a quick examination had I not come across this, addressed to Professor Adam Sedgwick of Cambridge University on 6th February 1858:

> ... That you may have a clear idea of my objectives I may state that they have something more than meets the eye. They are not merely exploratory, for I go with the intention of benefitting both the African and my own countryman. I take a practical mining geologist from the School of Mines to tell us of the mineral resources of the country, then an economic botanist to give a full report on the vegetable productions – fibrous, gummy and medicinal substances together with the dye stuffs – everything which may be useful in commerce. An artist to give the scenery, a naval officer to tell of the capacity of the river communications and a moral agent to lay the foundation for knowing that aim fully. All this machinery has for its ostensible object the development of African trade and the promotion of civilisation *but what I tell to none but such as you in whom I have confidence is thus* I hope it may result in an English colony in the healthy highlands of Central Africa – I have told it only to the Duke of Argyll ...

and further on:

> ... With this short statement you may perceive our ulterior objects. I want you to have some idea of them. I shall always remember you at Trinity with fond affection. Pray remember me kindly and say farewell to Prof. Whewell. Your auditor has given me two dozen of light ale and I hope to drink to your health and prosperity to your colleagues on the banks of the Zambezi.

I was startled. Livingstone had ulterior motives. He was a liar, a colonialist, interested in Trade! Not a teetotaller! The Devil's Advocate could make much of this. I copied the letter into a notebook, and was subsequently able to compare it with transcripts that had appeared in two authoritative studies of Livingstone; in both, the words in italic in the first paragraph, and the entire last paragraph had been omitted, without any indication that cuts had been made. This small point aroused my interest. Enquiries at the Museum (on a later visit) revealed that very few of the letters in its collection had been either transcribed or published; the Director kindly gave me permission to perform the first task and to try to accomplish the second (successfully, as it happened). While working on the transcriptions it became clear that even the small proportion of the collection that had seen print had in most cases been doctored to remove anything that might stain Livingstone's image or that of the civilisation of which he had been presented as a model.

Later, a reading of a host of Livingstone biographies showed that he was hardly the greatest explorer of his age, that as a missionary he was a failure, that he freed very few slaves: but people's myths are not always created around powerful and successful figures. One of the roots from which his grew is the apparent parallel between his life and that of Christ: birth to poor but pious parents, childhood in a workshop, sojourn in a desert, preaching and healing, love of the poor, agony and death, commending himself to God. Add to this the sudden re-appearance of Livingstone's dead body from the depths of Africa, and we have something so closely resembling a miracle as to make the analogy between him and Christ palpable. No stronger myth could have been found to justify the ways of God to man, or the ways of British colonial governors, Christian, clerical, or lay, to a conquered Africa.

Livingstone was finally buried in a modest tomb beneath the floor of Westminster Abbey, at the heart of the British Empire. This undemonstrative resting-place gives a spiritual dimension to the Victorian age, something lacking in the greatest surviving monument to the epoch, the Albert Memorial in Kensington, with its glorification of world conquest by British Industry, Trade, and Science – a world represented in the sculptured friezes of symbolic continents crouching at the four corners of the edifice. Across Kensington Gore the egg-shaped Royal Albert Hall lies with its portico facing the steepling Memorial as if it were expecting fecundity from there. A short way along the street, on the corner of the Royal Geographical Society building (once the residence of William Wilberforce, the abolitionist) a statue of Livingstone complements the scene as if to remind us that he was part of its ethos.

When Livingstone left Britain for the last time, in 1865, for the journey that would end with his death in Africa, the establishment had all but rejected him, and he them, but by the time he died he had been seated among the saints, his tomb engraved with an inscription that reads:

Brought by faithful hands
over land and sea
here rests
DAVID LIVINGSTONE
MISSIONARY, TRAVELLER, PHILANTHROPIST
Born March 19, 1813
at Blantyre, Lanarkshire
Died May 4, 1873
at Chitambo's Village, Ilala

For thirty years his life was spent in an unwearied effort to evangelize the native races, to explore the undiscovered secrets, and abolish the desolating slave-trade of Central Africa, where, with his last words he wrote:

'*All I can say in my solitude is, may Heaven's rich blessing come down on every one – American, English, Turk – who will help to heal this open sore of the world*'

TANTUS AMOR VERI, NIHIL EST QUOD NOSCERE MALIM
QUAM FLUVII CAUSAS PER SAECULA TANTA LATENTES
OTHER SHEEP I HAVE WHICH ARE NOT OF THIS FOLD, THEM
ALSO MUST I BRING, AND THEY SHALL HEAR MY VOICE

The clauses beginning 'For thirty years . . .' are given as statements of fact, the words in italics presented as Livingstone's own; and the emotive plea epitomizes what those who buried him wished him to be remembered for – the hero who gave his life to the great cause of abolition, the cause through which Great Britain liked to believe it had achieved the moral triumph of the nineteenth century.

The statue by the Falls had yet to be cast and erected, but the making of the maquette had started even on Livingstone's tombstone, for he did not use the word 'solitude' in his prayer, he wrote 'loneliness'. As an attribute of saint or hero there lies between these two words a difference of concept; the difference between strength and weakness, between fortitude and pathos.

Such a palimpsest demands investigation.

Part One

1813–1851
From Blantyre to Ngami

I

FIRST STEPS

More than a simple tombstone honours Livingstone in the land of his birth. The Scottish National Memorial to David Livingstone lies a few minutes' walk from Blantyre station, itself a short train journey from central Glasgow. The Memorial stands on the site of the Blantyre Works, the cotton spinning mill where for forty years from the final decade of the eighteenth century, three generations of the Livingstone family lived and laboured. Only two buildings of the old mill complex survive, one of them a three-storey tenement block which used to be staff housing: it is called Shuttle Row, and Livingstone was born there in his grandparents' apartment.

Shuttle Row is the centrepiece of the Memorial. The tiny apartment has been restored and furnished to its early nineteenth-century form, while the rest of the building has been made into a museum, where the exhibits illustrate Livingstone's career from beginning to end. Among the relics is a cast of the bone of his upper left arm, broken by a lion in Botswana. A tour through the galleries is a one-way journey past memorabilia which emphasise again and again Livingstone's struggle against slavery, with chains, shackles and neck-yokes in profusion. Finally, the visitor enters a darkened chamber. The press of a switch lights up, one by one, a series of dioramas which romantically – some might say sentimentally – portray Livingstone's life in Africa in the form of a Catholic church's Stations of the Cross. We see him first seated under a tree in the Kalahari instructing a circle of attentive blacks: the sky glows red along the horizon, the picture is called The Dawn. One after the other, in a programmed succession, with sound effects appropriate to each, the icons come alight in the gloom of the chamber until finally the pilgrim sees Livingstone giving up his soul to God.

The surrounds of Shuttle Row have been turned into a park sloping down to the river whose flow used to power the mill. Visitors to the shrine can relax and picnic there on sunny days, children enjoy the playground and cavort in the freshness and open air of the countryside. Livingstone's own childhood gave him little opportunity for that: from the age of ten he was working in Monteith and Company's factory from six in the morning to eight at night.

The first Livingstone of his family to find employment there was his grandfather Neil, a crofter from the island of Ulva who had been forced off his farm in the course of the Clearances, the deliberate depopulation of the Highlands that began in the wake of the defeat of the Jacobites at Culloden in 1746. Neil's father had fought in that battle on the side of Bonnie Prince Charlie, the Stuart Pretender to the thrones of Scotland and England, who hoped to restore the ancient line of kings that had been removed by the Glorious Revolution of 1688. Charles Stuart failed and his Highland supporters suffered the full fury of the English crown in a campaign of murder and repression which today would be called genocide. On the lordly estates, owned by supporters of King George II, most tenants who had not been killed, shipped in bondage to the sugar plantations of the West Indies or pressed into the colonial armies, were forced off the land. The landlords found that sheep were more profitable than potentially rebellious tenants; peasants found themselves crowded into the teeming slums of mushrooming industrial cities such as Glasgow. Gaelic-speaking Highlanders became part of the half-starved sweated labour of the Clyde's industrial revolution.

Neil Livingstone was fortunate in that he knew English (his wife liked the Bible to be read to her in Gaelic, and may have been both illiterate and monolingual): he had benefitted from the Reformed Church's passion for education, which would have been available to him after Ulva had been forcibly converted from Catholicism, if not from the ancient pre-Christian faith of the Celts. After migrating to Glasgow, he got work as a clerk (no doubt helped by being bi-lingual) at Monteith's Blantyre Works and stayed there for the rest of his life, rising to a position of trust in handling the firm's cash.

Besides its adult workers, the mill enjoyed the services of orphan children who worked in return for their keep and a basic education. To provide for the needs of this captive labour force, the mill owners provided a school with a paid teacher, and also a full-time tailor to make the children's clothes. In Neil Livingstone senior's time this post was occupied by David Hunter who had had to find employment (or perhaps, had had employment found for him) when he could no longer earn a living as a farmer. The Hunters were Lowlanders and Covenanters by religious and political conviction, suspicious of the State and of the established churches, believing in the Bible as the direct line between man and God, and hostile to the English establishment which ruled the United Kingdom.

Neil Livingstone's youngest son, named after him and whom we will call Neil junior for the time being, was born in 1788 and when he was old enough started work at the mill as a clerk, no doubt under his father's surveillance. He escaped that by becoming an apprentice tailor with David Hunter, but even if he married the Hunters' daughter

Agnes he liked tailoring no more than clerking, and spent the rest of his life as a self-employed commercial traveller in tea. In Neil junior and Agnes were united the two main, if contradictory, strands of Scottish national feeling: Jacobite and Covenanter. Neil junior was a zealous Reformed Christian, and used to take the opportunities his sales trips provided to distribute religious tracts; in 1830 he left the established Church of Scotland and joined a stricter, if unhierarchical, independent congregation at Hamilton, three miles from Blantyre.

Neil junior and Agnes Livingstone had seven children, of whom five survived: three boys, John, David, and Charles, and two daughters, Agnes and Janet. The family lived in Shuttle Row for many years, crowded into the tiny top-floor apartment which they had inherited from the Hunters when they moved to a cottage of their own. The Livingstones were not well off, but they were a good number of notches above the bottom of the social scale; by 1839 Neil junior was able to move the family to a rented cottage in Hamilton, and a dozen years later, into a house of their own, in Burnbank Road. But things were not easy for the family, and perhaps as a condition of the tenancy of Shuttle Row (after all, workers' quarters when Neil junior was not a mill worker) perhaps because of naked need, John and David both started work in the factory at an early age, David in 1823 when he was ten years old.

Child labour – for orphans or anyone else – was the order of the day at that time, and did not seem wrong either to employers or to working people who had recently moved to the cities from a life on the land where children helped on the farm from an early age. In the mill David worked first as a piecer and constantly moved above below and around the spinning machines to repair thread that was damaged or broken. It was exhausting work in the noisy and overheated factory and went on for fourteen hours a day with a short break for food. When the mill finally closed at 8 p.m. two hours of lessons started for youngsters in the company school. The Monteiths grew rich, but could salve their souls with the thought that they were providing education.

For the children, it took determination, spurred by necessity, to endure a day like that. When David had grown enough to be able to manage a machine he was promoted to spinner. Although the work was lighter, the hours remained as long, but the night school was not for him, as it was for others in his position, an additional burden. It was an opportunity of which he took every advantage, not only for the lessons, but for the access it gave to the library which the company maintained for its staff. For a young Scot of David's time and background, education was not a mere social grace, as it might be to the child of a landowner, but the pathway to the fulfilment of ambition: while it may well be true that many working children were resigned to their position in life, David was not.

Neil junior (who had revived his own Gaelic so as to be able to read to his mother) gave David his first schooling. By the time he started formal classes he was literate in English and able to go on to the classical languages. Gaelic was not taught; it was regarded by the establishment as the language of barbarians and rebels, fit only for extinction (a policy pursued not only in Scotland and Ireland, but later, vis-a-vis Afrikaans, in the aftermath of the second Boer War). We are told that David used part of his first pay packet, when he was ten years old, to buy a Latin grammar: by the time he left the mill in 1836 he knew that language very well, and had the rudiments of Greek.

As a piecer in the mill, David used to study on the job, propping his book against a machine and glancing at it whenever he passed: as a spinner, he had the book in front of him constantly. We are told that other youngsters used to tease him by throwing spindles at the book to knock it down. It is difficult to believe that David would have found this game a joke, and we see here the beginnings of the self-sufficiency, obstinacy and isolation that were to characterize him for the rest of his life, not to mention his extreme sensitivity to criticism.

His position at the mill was peculiar; his contemporaries were the orphan-apprentices whose status came close to serfdom, while he was a wage-earner who could afford to buy books and was free to spend his days off poaching salmon in the river or earning pocketmoney tending a nearby farmer's cattle. He had a father and a mother, and lived a family life in privileged accommodation, while his grandfathers both held important offices in the world of the mill, especially Neil senior who handled the money. The spindle-throwers' resentment of David was not only for being a swot: it was resentment for being a member of a higher social class, going to church on Sundays with his family in immaculately genteel clothes which annoyed the mill owner's wife by their presumption.

As David's later life would show, this ambiguity in status – one moment master, another servant – during his formative years, was destined to give rise to his determination at all times to keep ahead of the crowd, as well as to make it extremely difficult for him to collaborate with anyone who questioned his position: he would prove able to lead teams of African servants successfully on journeys of enormous distances, but often unable to work with whites, whether fellow missionaries or members of his Zambezi Expedition, without disastrous quarrels that rankled for decades.

David worked for sixteen years in the mill, while his father tried to make a success of his tea business, a difficult task during those years of extreme economic distress for the majority of the population. The lower-lower middle class to which the Livingstones belonged was terrified of being re-pauperised, and often embraced religion with blinding

[6]

enthusiasm to hide the fear. Neil junior was no exception to this generalisation, and as a believer was also hostile to any intellectual currents
that might undermine the foundations of faith. David on the other hand
was sceptical. He was possessed by a scientific curiosity which led him
to collect plants and study rock formations. The latter pastime was a
perilous occupation at the time for a believing Christian, for the science of geology – an important handmaiden of the burgeoning mining
industry which was fuelling the industrial revolution – was throwing
light on the structure of the world which called into question not only
Noah's Flood, but the whole doctrine of the six days' Divine creation
enshrined in the Book of Genesis. The ideas which would produce
Charles Darwin's theory of evolution were in the air – even in the
air of Shuttle Row – and those ideas were held to be incompatible
with, indeed inimical to, Christianity.

The Science and Religion debate was brought to a head in Scotland
– arguably the best educated country in Europe at the time – and
throughout Christendom by two of the brightest stars of the Scottish
Enlightenment in the latter part of the eighteenth century. David Hume
the philosopher used to ask whether knowledge could be confirmed
by any means other than a person's own experience, thus calling into
question the validity of many Christian 'truths'. Hume's contemporary
James Hutton had been a student at Edinburgh, and became a geologist,
laying the foundations of modern geological science by predicating that
the earth was constantly in a state of natural change, with heat as the
prime factor. When he rejected the creationist dogma in his statement
'We see no vestige of a beginning – no prospect of an end' he was accused
of Atheism. Unfortunately, Hutton's impenetrable writing style made it
impossible for many to follow his arguments and it was not until after
his death in 1795 that the Scottish mathematician John Playfair (this is
a name we will meet again in David's life) produced the clear explanation of Hutton's thinking which was to feed into Darwin's analysis of
natural phenomena. Any intelligent Christian, such as Neil undoubtedly
was, took an interest in these matters, and as a Scot especially as the
debate emanated from Scotland; he opposed them with the fervour of
a Spanish Inquisitor faced with heresy.

David is said to have refused to read the pious devotional works
his father pressed on him and in the years after his adolescence seems
to have gone through a period when he felt he had lost his faith, suffering the despair of the soul that fears it has been abandoned by
God. It took a secure and confident person in those days to make a
formal break with Christianity, or else a reckless one, especially where
Church, Kirk, or Chapel was the centre of social life and indispensable
to economic survival, as it was in Neil Livingstone's case, even if he
were self-employed. Some mill owners insisted that every one of their

workers be a member of a church, and would go to the expense themselves of building a place of worship in a new working class area where none had existed before.

David's crisis of faith ended after reading Thomas Dick's *Philosophy of a Future State*. In the book, Dick, a minister in the Scottish Church, confronted the supposed conflict between science and Christianity with the argument that science, by explaining the workings of the world, in all their complexity, showed how supreme God must be to have created such a miracle, and to keep it in operation: science would thus reinforce rather than weaken belief in the Creator. Dick's thesis satisfied David, and formed the basis of his approach to the matter for the rest of his days.

After undergoing a searing conversion – some people today might be inclined to see it more as a young man's reconciliation with a dominant father – David was admitted to membership of the Independent Church at Hamilton to which his parents belonged. If this step brought peace with God, it was also a first step on his path to fame. As he approached maturity, David could see that there was little future for him where he was unless he were to work his way up through the mill, a limited prospect for which his temperament did not suit him. Besides, his father's tea business was too small to provide two livings, and David had no capital with which to start on his own in anything. His adherence to an Independent Church excluded him from the patronage posts available from the ecclesiastical establishment, which he would not join even when he was offered a teaching position.

Neil jnr forbade his children to read novels, but travel books were allowed, and these were the main form of literary escapism available to David. Two Scots had won fame by exploring in Africa: Mungo Park along the River Niger, James Bruce at the other shoulder of the continent in Ethiopia, where he identified the source of the Blue Nile. Both had published successful accounts of their adventures. Bruce's *Travels to Discover the Source of the Nile* came out in five volumes in Edinburgh in the 1790s, and Park's *Travels in Africa* appeared in 1799, followed posthumously by his *Journal of a Mission to the Interior of Africa* in 1815.

Apart from these two Scots, the amount of travel literature that poured from Britain's presses before and during David's boyhood and adolescence was more than enough to satisfy the most curious mind or to quicken the imagination of anyone who believed he or his country had a destiny world-wide: British travellers were penetrating every continent, just as British seafarers had crossed every ocean during the previous centuries. It is not possible to know which travel books David read, but a few titles from the genre give an idea of what would be available to anyone with the means to lay hands on them. During his formative years, the following titles appeared: Hugh Clapperton's *Journal of a Second Expedition to the Interior of Africa*, John Franklin's *Narrative of a Journey to the Shores of the Polar Sea* (Livingstone was to meet Franklin's widow in Bombay in 1865), Basil Hall's *Travels in North America* and *Fragments of Voyages and Travels* (in nine volumes), Francis Head's *Journeys across the Pampas*, the two volumes of Matthew Flinders, *Voyage to Terra Australia*, William Burchell's *Travels in the Interior of South Africa*, Edward Clarke's *Travels in Various Countries of Europe, Asia and Africa* (in six volumes), Charles Darwin's *Journal of Researches during the Voyage of the Beagle*.

From before Livingstone's time, but no doubt still available, were his fellow Scot, Tobias Smollett's seven volume *A Compendium of Authentic and Entertaining Voyages*, John Newbery's *The World displayed, or a Curious Collection of Voyages and Travels* in twenty volumes, reprinted three times, and William Mayor's *Historical Account of the Most Celebrated Voyages, Travels and Discoveries* issued in twenty-five volumes between 1796 and 1801. The first part of Daniel Defoe's *Robinson Crusoe* would probably pass Neil's inspection as a travel book, since it was based on the true and well known story of a Scottish mariner, Alexander Selkirk, and his sojourn on an uninhabited island in the Pacific.

The two commodities upon which the Livingstones depended, cotton spun at the mill and tea sold from door to door, were both imported from distant lands; the former from America, the latter from China. Worlds beyond the seas had a fascination, and emigration was an appealing alternative to the constrictions of early nineteenth-century Scotland. Eventually, like himself, David's brothers went abroad, John to be a farmer (with at least one unsuccessful business venture) in Ontario, Canada, Charles to study for and enter the ministry in the United States.

After moving to Africa David regularly urged his sisters to emigrate, suggesting in one instance domestic service in Australia, but they stayed at home and set up a milliners in Hamilton where one of the family friends in the Independent Church was a lace maker: before going to Canada, John had tried the lace business too, but apparently without enough success to keep him in Scotland.

We do not know precisely when David decided that he would become a physician, but it seems to have been some time before 1833, when he was twenty. At nineteen he had been promoted to spinner in the mill, a position for which, as he himself has said, the pay was good, so that he was able to save. At first, however, Neil jnr was totally opposed to David's entering medicine, on the grounds that he did not want his son to earn a living from science. If this reason seems slight, Neil's objections may have been backed by economic considerations, such as the need to keep tenure of the Shuttle Row apartment which might be lost if none of the family was working in the mill.

It was a missionary-traveller who came to David's rescue. Karl Friedrich Augustus von Gutzlaff, ten years older than David, had become famous for his work in China, where while scarcely thirty years of age, he had translated the Bible into Chinese in the course of his energetic (if not notably successful) evangelical work. In 1834 he published his *Journal of Three Voyages along the Coast of China*: the book was issued with an enthusiastic Foreword and seal of approval from the London Missionary Society. The year before this volume appeared, Von Gutzlaff had issued an appeal to churches in Britain for medical missionaries to serve in China in the belief that the ministrations of Christian doctors would render the Chinese more open to the Gospel. This appeal enabled David to persuade Neil that the combination of medical practice with evangelisation was not inconsistent with his faith. Neil gave his permission, but it was several years before David started his studies at Anderson's College, Glasgow, in 1836. He made an arrangement with the mill whereby he worked as a spinner there during the vacations to earn enough for his upkeep and fees at Anderson's. The mill cancelled the arrangement two years later. Neil jnr and the family moved to a rented cottage, 46 Almada Street, Hamilton. David, with no income, applied to join the London Missionary Society, hoping to go to China.

2

BRAVE NEW WORLD

In Scotland the universities and technical colleges such as Anderson's were open to all men who could pay the fees. There was no religious bar as was the case at Oxford and Cambridge in England. David, with some financial assistance from his family, enrolled at Anderson's College (now the University of Strathclyde) in the centre of Glasgow, to study the basic disciplines of medicine: anatomy and chemistry. In the 1830s medicine as a science was still in its infancy and the causes of disease were only vaguely understood. An appreciation of the role of 'germs', for example, did not emerge until after the work of Louis Pasteur and Joseph Lister later in the century, and even then their findings were not generally accepted for many years. Many thought that diseases were induced by changes of weather or of temperature, or by the invasion of the body by poisons as happens in the case of snake bite: medicines were seen as antidotes to venom not as means with which to attack micro-organisms such as bacteria. Even while vaccination was practised successfully against smallpox, its workings were a mystery. Surgery was a gruesome business; with no effective anaesthetics until the mid 1840s (when ether and then chloroform came into use) the surgeon's greatest attribute was the speed with which he could remove a tumour or saw off a limb. And with no disinfectants, death often followed, not from the operation itself but from gangrene.

Livingstone, however, entered medicine at a time when the scientific approach was beginning to take hold, and when the transformations already wrought by the industrial revolution in Britain, and to a lesser extent in Europe and the United States, were ushering in a new age, an era epitomised in the figures of his contemporaries. A selection of people of his own generation – those born twelve years either side of him – could include, from Britain: Queen Victoria, Charles Dickens, Charles Darwin, Florence Nightingale, the Brontë sisters, Richard Burton and James Young; from Russia: Feodor Dostoyevski, Turgenev, Alexander II; from France: Louis Pasteur, Louis Napoleon and Charles Baudelaire; from Italy: Guiseppi Garibaldi; from Germany: Richard Wagner, Karl Marx, Otto von Bismarck, Alfred Krupp; from the United States: Abraham Lincoln, Herman Melville, Ira Aldridge,

Harriet Beecher Stowe. Among these names, we recognise the persons who moulded the new age into the forms we know today in all fields of human activity – science, literature, music, politics. Among them we find both the progenitors of socialist internationalism and of the multi-national corporation; of the creators and dissolvers of empires; of the elevation of race to an ideology and its demolition.

Livingstone hated Richard Burton, read Charles Darwin and Harriet Beecher Stowe, loved and admired Abraham Lincoln, moved for a short while in Dickens's circle, became the lifelong friend and to some extent protégé of James Young and would eventually be received by Queen Victoria. Young, who was born two years before Livingstone, was the son of a small-scale, self-employed Glasgow carpenter and coffin maker; by the time he was twenty he had acquired enough education to enter Anderson's, and with a borrowed ticket started attending the eminent Professor Thomas Graham's lessons in chemistry. Young was so brilliant a student that by 1832 he had become Professor Graham's assistant. After enrolling at the college in 1836, Livingstone was taught by Young for a short while, but the latter left Glasgow with Graham for University College, London in 1838. He did not stay on Graham's staff for long, deciding instead to go into industry in order to increase his earnings.

Young worked in a number of chemical firms, including Tennants, Clow & Co, which in the 1840s was the largest chemicals producer in Europe and, thus, in the world. By this time, Young had begun to take out patents of his own, and in 1847 was invited to the Riddings coal mines in Derbyshire where petroleum had been found dripping through the roof of the workings. Within a short time, Young had established a refinery which sold lamp oil and lubricants through an agent in Manchester, as well as naphtha to gasworks, where it was used to enrich the product. In 1850, Young registered his patent for the extraction of oil from coal and the following year set up a partnership to establish a refinery at Bathgate, near Glasgow, where a suitable type of coal was available. During the 1850s production increased steadily; lubricants for industry and the railways, naphtha, illuminating oil for use in mass-produced lamps, wax for candles.

Young's processes were used in the United States when the first oil wells came on stream in 1859 and although he had some difficulty in collecting his American royalties, the Bathgate works were fabulously profitable. A later plant at Addiewell (the foundation stone for which was laid by Livingstone in 1866) made Young a millionaire. By 1871 he had all but retired from active business, and can justifiably be acknowledged as the founder of the modern petroleum and petro-chemical industry, the first of the oil barons: if he had moved to the United States he would be as well remembered today as a Rockefeller or Andrew Carnegie, the emigrant Scot who became America's greatest steel lord. But Young was content to rest on his millions at home, lavishing large amounts of money on research projects and technical education, and endowing Anderson's College, of which he became a trustee in 1858 and served as president from 1868 to 1877. He was a proponent of science and technology as the key to his country's future success, just as Britain was beginning to be overtaken by Germany, especially in chemicals. He was also far sighted enough to see the importance of trade, and as early as 1857 was speaking in favour of a tunnel under the sea between England and the continent of Europe. He also liked Livingstone's thesis that in Africa, at any rate, Christianity and commerce went hand in hand with civilisation, and after his friend's death Young supported the partly-commercial Livingstonia Mission which in 1875 ushered in British rule over what is today Malawi. He also supported Livingstone himself, both morally and financially, and paid for a search party to travel up the Congo river in 1872 when no word had been received from David for several years. Young died in 1883, ten years after his friend, who had remembered him thus in a letter of 24th August 1866 to Adam Sedgwick:

> It is possible you know Mr Young by report – formerly my teacher in chemistry – has made a fortune by Paraffin oil and is a fine, straightforward good man.

James Young was to serve for many years as one of Livingstone's trustees, like another friend of university days, Dr Andrew Buchanan, Professor of Medicine. One of Livingstone's classmates at Anderson's was Lyon Playfair, who later became Professor of Chemistry at Edinburgh, a Member of Parliament and distinguished public figure. His younger brother Robert joined the army in India and was appointed Consul at Zanzibar in 1865, serving there during the first years of Livingstone's last expedition, when he was particularly concerned with Zanzibar's role in the slave trade.

In Glasgow, David took rooms where he lodged during the week when he was attending classes. At weekends he went home to Blantyre, doing the eight-mile journey on foot. The Glasgow he inhabited was a city in the process of free-for-all industrialisation well on its way to becoming – as the city of the Clyde – the world's greatest shipyard and, after London, the largest city in Britain. An appropriate destiny for a centre that had devoted itself to long-distance trade across the seas, particularly as the largest port of entry for tobacco into western Europe. The tobacco came from Virginia, while other merchandise such as sugar, rum and cotton were brought in from the Caribbean area or the southern United States. On the profits of this trade, the foundations of industry were capitalised, with much of its labour force coming, as we have seen, from the cleared Highlands. Three generations of the Livingstone family may have found adequate livings under the paternalistic aegis of the Blantyre mill, but under the naked capitalism of Glasgow, so short a distance away, conditions for the working people were vastly different from the cramped cosiness of Shuttle Row. A government report on Glasgow at the time states:

> In all districts of the burgh, and in the suburbs, there is want of sewerage and drainage ... the streets, or rather the lanes and alleys, in which the poor live, are filthy beyond measure ... The houses, in the disease-haunted areas, are ruinous, ill-constructed, and, to an incredible extent, destitute of furniture. In many, there is not a single article of bedding, and the body clothes of the inmates are of the most revolting description: in fact, in Glasgow, there are hundreds who never enjoy the luxury of the meanest kind of bed, and who, if they attempted to put off their clothes, would find it difficult to resume ...

The report, by Professor Robert Gowan, an expert on epidemic diseases, was made in 1844, and conditions would not have been much different in the late 1830s when Livingstone was at college.

Apart from his medical courses, Livingstone studied religious subjects: Greek, for example, to be able to read the New Testament in the original, and basic theology, the latter at the feet of Dr Wardlaw, the Congregationalist divine who attempted to soften the harsh determinism of Calvinism. Wardlaw allowed that salvation might be available not only to those forechosen by God, but also to those who opened their hearts to Him. But Wardlaw's influence extended beyond the field of theology (where he seems to have helped Livingstone finally to overcome his doubts); he was also a campaigner for the abolition of slavery.

The Abolitionist cause in Britain after the empire-wide emancipation of 1833 was directed at other slave economies, particularly the southern United States. In this, it was given inspiration and vigour by black Americans studying in Britain, and especially at Glasgow, where a constant stream of ex-slaves and freemen passed through the university doors, generally with the financial support of Christian abolitionists, both in America and in Scotland. One of these, an example of the sort of black person with whom Livingstone had first contact, was James McCune Smith, of the Free African School, New York, who graduated as physician at Glasgow in 1836. On returning home, Dr Smith went into medical practice, and extended his interests to become a pioneer actuary in the life insurance business. He was a leader of the anti-slavery movement in the United States.

Glasgow had not been a slave-trading port like Liverpool, Bristol or London, but it had benefitted greatly from its links with the slave colonies of the western hemisphere, where a number of Glaswegians made fortunes as planters in the Caribbean. In Livingstone's time, a few years after the 1833 emancipation, Glasgow continued to benefit from trans-Atlantic trade, especially tobacco from Virginia and cotton from the Mississippi, both of which commodities were produced by slave labour. Slavery, even five thousand miles away, was a factor which Scots of conscience could not ignore, especially as it was less than a generation since the feudal enslavement of Scottish miners and salters had come to an end. (It was miners and salters in Fife who had helped win the freedom of an African slave baptized David Spens in 1769; Spens settled in Scotland and worked for a farmer at Wemyss.) And it was less than a century since Highlanders taken prisoner after Culloden had been shipped to the colonies.

The arguments of Christian abolitionists were based on the premise that slavery was abominably cruel and a denial of God-given human rights – slavery was a sin and, like all sins, contaminated everyone who condoned it. More utilitarian minds saw slavery as wasteful, inefficient and incompatible with the mechanical methods of production that were becoming dominant in advanced economies, and that moneyless slaves could not become purchasers of factory-made goods: even the most miserable Glasgow slum dweller could aspire to ownership of Sheffield cutlery or Bradford woollens, something beyond the power of slaves.

Bearing all these factors in mind, Livingstone was a natural abolitionist, though it was not until the 1850s that he became an active campaigner himself, and then for reasons only indirectly concerned with the alleviation of misery. If this objective had been his prime concern, there would have been no better place to start than in Scotland. The fact is that he was determined to go abroad. He could have taken up the offer made to him in Glasgow of a teaching post under Church of Scotland patronage after the church waived its objections to his being an Independent, but he turned it down. Besides, the prospects in Britain for a doctor who could not afford to buy his own practice were not good, and the status of army or navy surgeons was low. And Livingstone as a propertyless Scot (and a member of a dissenting church) would come up against all the prejudices and social bars that supported a body politic dominated by the English aristocracy. His physician-explorer predecessor Mungo Park remarked after returning home from his first Niger journey that 'he would rather brave Africa and its horrors than wear his life out in toilsome rides amongst (Scottish) hills for the scanty remuneration of a country surgeon.'

The position of medical men is examined in the career of Mr Woodcourt as he moves through the pages of Charles Dickens's novel *Bleak House*, which is set in the 1840s.

> All his widowed mother could spare [Dickens writes of Woodcourt] had been spent in qualifying him for his profession. It was not lucrative for a young practitioner, with very little influence in London, and although he was night and day, at the service of numbers of poor people, and did wonders of gentleness and skill for them, he gained very little by it in money.

Although Woodcourt works for an established and moderately prosperous doctor in London, he decides to become a ship's surgeon even though, as Dickens's Mr Boythorn declares:

> By all that is base and despicable, the treatment of Surgeons aboard ship is such that I would submit the legs – both legs – of every member of the Admiralty Board to a compound fracture, and render it a transportable offence in any qualified practitioner to set them, if the whole system were not wholly changed in eight-and-forty hours.

The system *was* changed, and when Livingstone went aboard a Royal Navy ship in Luanda, Angola, in 1853, he was pleased to see that ships' doctors enjoyed the position they deserved.

But despite Boythorn's caveats, Woodcourt has no alternative to going to China and to India: '. . . he had no fortune or private means, so he was going away.' On the voyage, Woodcourt wins the admiration of officers and crew when he behaves like a hero after an accident at sea, and is able to return home respected. He marries the sweetheart he had left behind and is put in a position to begin a successful professional life when his wife's wealthy guardian buys him a comfortable practice.

Livingstone could hardly look forward to a prospect like that and, indeed, at the end of the second year of his three-year course at Anderson's he faced a financial crisis when the Blantyre mill refused to allow him to continue earning his fees by vacation work. (His parents too were affected by the mill's decision, for it was now that they moved to Hamilton.) David decided to solve his problem by short-circuiting his training and applying immediately for admission to the London Missionary Society before he had completed his medical course.

The LMS sent David a lengthy questionnaire which was designed to discover his motives for wanting to join the society. David filled it in with an effusiveness we shall meet later, but no reply came for months, not until Neil himself had written to London on David's behalf. In due course, the Society invited David for interview, and with his fare paid by Henry Drummond, the Hamilton lace maker, he departed Scotland for the English capital.

3
CHOSEN PATH

After being interviewed twice, Livingstone was admitted on probation to the London Missionary Society on 20th August, 1838 and started his training at the Society's seminary at Chipping Ongar, a small town east of London. The LMS had several attractions for Livingstone: on the doctrinal side it was non-denominational, though since its foundation in 1795 had become largely Congregationalist. Congregationalism was essentially a Calvinist movement, but maintained independence from the established Calvinist churches, such as the Church of Scotland: the movement was founded on the premise that each congregation should choose its own method of church government, without interference or imposition from any other authority; the movement was democratic and anti-hierarchical.

Congregationalism was introduced to Scotland in 1799 by Robert Haldane, the Reformed revivalist who also worked among the protestants of France and Switzerland; many of his Scottish followers with an eye to mission work abroad had joined the LMS, and many of its leading figures were Scots. The Society appealed to Livingstone both for its congregationalism and for its Scottishness. Moreover, by drawing on the vigour of the middle-class non-conformism which was transforming Britain economically, the LMS was the most successful of all British missionary societies, active in Asia, the Pacific, Africa, and the Caribbean. It offered wide scope for a young man who wanted to go to distant places.

The training provided at Ongar included study of the scriptures and the scriptural languages, Greek and Hebrew; theology and preaching practice. As a future pastor Livingstone was by no means a brilliant pupil: his lack of a solid formal education made him seem slow, while his dislike of public speaking made him a poor preacher. One of his difficulties in the latter respect seems to have been his voice which had a peculiar clotted quality, a characteristic he attributed to having an uvula that was too large. But even after he had had the offending organ removed by surgery, he never became a fluent speaker. His speeches came out in staccato gobbets, as if he were performing under some choking constraint.

And this is noticeable, too, in many of his letters to family and friends and has led to considerable misinterpretation. Livingstone had some appreciation of these limitations of his, and once said to James Young in the course of a letter on 12th December, 1862 on touchy subjects:

> . . . I can write (to you more) easily than to the others partly because I suppose you will make any allowance for mistakes or for the tone which may seem wrong when nothing is intended . . .

And he goes on to express the exasperation he was often to feel with others throughout his life who were not on his wavelength:

> . . . and partly because writing to Dr and Mrs Hannan is like confessing to the corner of a confessional box or conversing with a man as deaf as a door nail.

Some students of human nature might see Livingstone's verbal costiveness related to his continual concern for bowel movements, whether metaphysical or actual: receiving news after a long interval from his friend the Rev William Fairbrother, former Shanghai missionary, LMS official, and later a pastor in Derby, Livingstone began his lengthy reply of 14th January, 1851 with these sentences:

> My Dear Friend,
> I had almost concluded that your bowels of compassion for us poor Hottentots . . . had got into a state of hopeless constipation when I was cheered by some small symptoms of amendment in the shape of a note, you dared not call it a letter and I am glad of it for if you had I should have set you down among the great potbellies who modestly say 'I shall give my mite' and the mite means the same thing as it did in the case of the old man you and I saw at the missionary meeting at Brentwood (or ford) so carefully fishing out five shillings from among the sovereigns – But you promise amendment, very well, better late than never.

On 16th April 1858, issuing instructions to members of his Zambezi Expedition, Livingstone concluded his letter to the geologist, Richard Thornton, with this injunction:

> 10. Finally you are enjoined to take the greatest care of your health – avoid all exposure to night exhalations, and should you be troubled with drowsiness, constipation or shivering, apply promptly to Dr Kirk for medical advice.

Ironical advice in that with malaria, as Livingstone knew, the commonest affliction to be expected in the tropics was dysentery from which in fact, Thornton died.

At times Livingstone's cloacal imagery could turn scatological. Commenting to James Young on the reaction in the United States to remarks he had made at the 1864 meeting of the British Association, when Livingstone had said in effect that the Civil War was God's punishment for evil ways, he wrote: 'The gas I emitted in Bath sounded in America. Ugh!'

Livingstone's tutor at Ongar, the Congregationalist minister Richard Cecil, was doubtful about his suitability for mission life, but the LMS overcame what reservations existed, admitted him to full membership of the Society and paid for him to complete his interrupted medical studies. Livingstone moved into lodgings in London and resumed work for his degree. He made two good new friends in the course of his work, Richard Owen, who taught anatomy at the Hunterian Museum, and James Risdon Bennet, who lectured in pathology at the Charing Cross Hospital and who arranged for Livingstone to attend classes free of charge. Bennet was the son of the minister of the Congregationalist church where Livingstone worshipped. James Young was in London too, for the time being still with Professor Graham at University College.

Towards the end of 1840 Livingstone returned to Scotland to sit examinations and graduate at Glasgow. With that successfully behind him, he said farewell to his family, for he was to sail to south Africa in December, after being ordained on 20th November at the Albion Chapel, London. As we have seen, he had hoped that the LMS would send him to China, but events intervened to make this impossible just at the time he was getting ready to go abroad. The intervention took the form of the Opium War; a sordid incident paradigmatic of much of the ethos of imperial expansion during the nineteenth century which affected British social life profoundly.

The tea which Neil Livingstone traded for a livelihood came from China: it had become cheap enough to be affordable by the Clydeside milieu in which Neil moved after starting its career in Britain as a luxury beverage in the circles of the wealthy, as Alexander Pope observed in the *Rape of the Lock*. During the latter half of the eighteenth century, the price of tea began to fall with increased supplies from China available to be brought to Britain in the holds of ships of the London-based East India Company, which monopolised the trade.

If drink was the curse of the British working classes, a curse which the Temperance movement tried to exorcise by replacing alcohol with tea, opium was the bane of China, which the Chinese government tried to neutralise by forbidding its import. Opium, however, was the foundation of the East India Company's tea business.

The drug was produced on the Company's own plantations in India and bartered, illegally, for tea in China. The Company developed a highly profitable triangular trading system – opium from India to China, tea from China to Britain, manufactured goods from Britain to India (or hard cash straight into the Company's treasury, including that from the sale of Chinese crockery, even the cheapest of which, used as ballast in the tea ships, was so superior to the native British product that 'china' became, and remains, the English word for such tableware).

In the late 1830s, the Chinese government tried to meet the problem head on by closing the country to foreigners. The Company opposed this policy by force, and in 1840, war broke out. After a year's sporadic fighting, the Chinese were humbled by British firepower, compelled to sign away Hong Kong, and to re-open the country. On the British side during the negotiations, such as they were at gun point, was Karl von Gutzlaff, Livingstone's inspiration. When the treaty had been signed, missionary activity gathered pace; opium poured into China, producing a social catastrophe. Cheap tea became Britain's national beverage, and a small British shipping line, Peninsula and Oriental, rose to greatness on the narcotics trade.

With the Opium War threatening in 1839, the LMS offered Livingstone a posting in the West Indies, but he had his eye on another target and rejected it: his letter of 2nd July 1839 to his employers is couched in the effusive style we have mentioned earlier, and that is in such contrast to the tone of his letters to friends:

> When I first felt the expansive benevolence of the Gospel in my heart, it became an interesting question to me, how I could spend the remainder of my days in bringing my fellowmen to the enjoyment of the same happiness and peace? After much prayer for the Divine direction it appeared to be in accordance [with] the will of Providence that I should attempt to obtain a medical education in order to render service to the cause of missions by that means; after much exertion and overcoming considerable difficulties, in which I was sensibly assisted by the good hand of Providence, I spent two years in that study, all which in the event of my being sent to the West Indies might be considered as lost. For I would not use the knowledge which I have obtained without in all probability incurring the displeasure of medical men who have gone thither for the sake of gain, and it is well known how easily medical men can destroy each other's influence and usefulness, when an unsuccessful case occurs, as many hundred men have experienced in this and other lands.

Livingstone is making two points: he can only serve the missions as a doctor if he completes his studies, and he refuses to go to the West

Indies where he would be under the scrutiny of an established medical profession, if not in direct competition with it. His remark that he was becoming a doctor, 'in order to render service to the cause of the missions', is less than a full commitment to work as a missionary, and foreshadows the many difficulties that the LMS and its members in the field would have with him over the years when he would appear to be more an impresario of missions rather than a missionary proper.

By the time of this letter, with China off the map, his thoughts were on Africa, and he decided that that was where he would go when Robert Moffat, the 45-year-old Scot, and LMS pioneer on the fringes of the Kalahari, took a liking to him, when they met through the LMS in London, and thought he would be suitable for work in the region. Moffat recognised Livingstone's independent spirit, and his recommendation that he should not be attached to an established mission but should rather work on his own farther into the interior coincided exactly with Livingstone's own ambitions: not for him pastoral (or medical) work in the social deserts of proletarian Britain, or on the fringe of colonial society in the West Indies. In Africa he would be able to make his own path. He could emulate Stamford Raffles, who had turned the swampy island of Singapore into a flourishing outpost of civilisation by abolishing slavery and imposing government on Christian principles.

Even after emancipation in 1833, throughout the empire, the question of African slavery remained a lively topic in Britain, for slaves continued to be taken from Africa to the Americas, south and north, helping to maintain the 'peculiar institution' in the United States. The transatlantic trade had been in existence for so long that it had become a vested interest on both sides of the ocean: in Africa itself, many rulers had come to depend on it for foreign exchange and, like King Pepel of Bonny on the Niger, were indignant when it was outlawed by their best customers, the British. British abolitionists for their part realised that the work would not be completed until the African trade was ended. This they thought they could effect by stimulating economic development on the slave coasts of west Africa, enabling foreign exchange to be earned by the export of produce rather than human beings. These ideas were eloquently presented in Thomas Fowell Buxton's treatise *The African Slave Trade and its Remedy*. Christianity and commerce, Buxton declared, would end slavery within and from Africa.

A grand public gathering, celebrating this theme, was held at the abolitionists' London meeting place, Exeter Hall in the Strand, on 1st June 1840. The meeting was graced by the presence of Queen Victoria's husband, Prince Albert, with Buxton as the main speaker. His purpose was to stimulate public support for an expedition up the River Niger with the object of finding a site for a Buxtonite colony where Christianised

Africans, under (British) Christian discipline would grow tropical crops such as cotton for export. Livingstone was one of the Exeter Hall audience: he would, as we shall see, incorporate Buxton's ideas, with their Raffles-like echoes, into his thinking about Africa and his ideology of colonisation. As it turned out, the 1841–1842 Niger Expedition, financed by the government, was a disaster, with most of its members dying of malaria. But the idea lived on and subsequent expeditions had sufficient success to lead to the establishment of Christianity in the country today known as Nigeria.

A considerable segment of that part of British public opinion which was concerned with improving the world thought, unlike Livingstone, that Buxtonian ventures in Africa were a waste of money and effort (not to mention life) when so many people in Britain itself were living in the poverty, filth and misery that we have seen in Glasgow. And London was no better. Livingstone was to take hard knocks from this body of opinion later in his life; neither would he have enjoyed Charles Dickens's satirical treatment of Mrs Jellyby, in *Bleak House*, the 1840s Buxtonian with her brood of neglected children and a husband nearly bankrupted by her activities:

> You find me, my dears as usual very busy; but that you will excuse. The African project at present employs my whole time. It involves me in correspondence with public bodies and private individuals anxious for the welfare of their species all over the country. I am happy to say it is advancing. We hope by this time next year to have a hundred and fifty to two hundred healthy families cultivating coffee and educating the natives of Borrioboola-Gha on the left bank of the Niger.

Although Dickens abhorred slavery, as he made clear during his first visit to the United States, an element of racialism lies behind this passage and reflects the prejudice that lay within much British thinking about Africa and Africans which was, in due course, to evolve into the full-blown doctrine of white supremacy. Even the reformer, Dickens, was later to come to the defence of the notorious Governor Eyre of Jamaica whose method of dealing with blacks struggling against white supremacy included the disembowelling of pregnant women. Livingstone, for his part, and for all his belief in a British destiny, did not judge people by colour: his criteria were cultural, using the word in its broadest sense, a point of view that was to put him out of tune with his times both in Britain and abroad.

Livingstone may have been a tough morsel for the LMS to swallow, but he made good friends while he was at Ongar. Among them were Joseph Moore, who became a missionary in Tahiti, and Benjamin and Elizabeth Pyne (the Livingstone's fourth child, who died in infancy in

1850, was named after Mrs Pyne), with whom he exchanged letters for many years, as he did too with Margaret Sewell, the widow who kept the LMS boarding house in London where Livingstone stayed while completing his medical studies.

One friendship, however, ended in bitterness and recrimination on Livingstone's part which lasted until his death. This friendship was with Thomas Lomas Prentice, student at Ongar, and the son of a middle-class, probably merchant, family of Stowmarket about forty miles away. Both he and Livingstone were interested in the same young woman, Catherine Ridley, who came presumably from a similar social background to Prentice's. She was certainly not from Livingstone's, and she would have been one of the first English middle class girls he had met, one who, as he put it, had been a lady all her life and had always slept in a soft bed. Livingstone fell in love with her, but it is not likely that she could have married him, in spite of her interest in missionary life and no matter what she felt for him. In the 1840s English middle class families were careful with their daughters, and could control their wishes with the weapon of the settlement. Besides, Livingstone was by any measure an unconventional figure, almost a foreigner, and not only without property but largely without visible prospects, not even the prospect of leading a moderately safe life. The interior of Africa to which he was determined to go was to the 1840s English mind a frightening mystery and a land of horrors. Look what had happened to Mungo Park, killed on the banks of the Niger. A godly calling was no guarantee of longevity:

> There was a new-made grave
> On a far heathen shore
> Where lonely slept a man of God,
> His mission service o'er;
> There when the setting sun
> Had tinged the west with flame,
> A tender infant in her arms,
> A mournful woman came . . .

This stanza opens a poem called *Wife of a Missionary at the Grave of her Husband*; the same author also produced *Funeral of a Physician*:

> . . . the sense of loss
> Weighed heavy on each bosom. Aged men
> Bowed down their reverend heads in wondering woe,
> That he who so retained the ardent smile
> And step elastic of life's morning prime,
> Should fall before them . . .

These verses are by Harriet Lydia Sigourney, the Scottish-American poet who campaigned for abolition and for the missions to Africa. Judging by the number of her collections published in the 1840s she enjoyed a considerable readership, and Livingstone gave a copy of her *Lays from the West* to Catherine Ridley. In a letter to his brother John, dated 5th May, 1839, Livingstone said of the book, 'There are some very good pieces in it, and all religious.' She in turn presented him with a copy of Charles Bridges's *Reflections on the* 119th *Psalm* before he left England for Africa. In his one surviving letter to Catherine, Livingstone mentions that he was reading the book on the voyage, but even before he sailed, it must have been clear to him that his suit was lost and that she would marry Thomas Prentice.

Livingstone, however, continued to hope that he would see her again, married or not, trusting that Prentice would bring her with him to the south African mission field: as he wrote to Prentice on 5th March 1841 while approaching the Cape:

> I hope C has recovered from her indisposition. Indeed I feel almost confident she has. I have thought it would be well for her if she has recovered to look a little into the Sitchuana Testament. I think it would be of great advantage to her afterwards, for there are many gutterals and aspirates in the language which though no difficulty to a Scotsman are a plague to those who have not been accustomed to them. 'G' is always guttural, 'h' is pronounced as the spiritus asper of the Greeks . . . the other letters are sounded as in Dutch . . . Every letter is sounded and she might very soon read the testament by comparing it with the English. I mention this because I should like her to get the language well, and not merely be able to say such sentences in it as a Cockney in our language 'Bring me the Hegg of the 'en', or 'You 'eet me 'ard' for 'you hit me hard'. I should like her to practice the gutturals and aspirates although she learnt none of the language. You can get Testaments at the Bible Society house . . .

If Prentice showed Catherine his passage it is not difficult to imagine the anti-Livingstone propaganda he could make of it: Livingstone's expecting, even demanding that she learn a language which only the Tswana themselves or Scots, Dutch, Hebrew or Greek could pronounce. A combination of these instructions and Mrs Sigourney would be enough to deter any eligible young Englishwoman with no desire for martyrdom from marrying a person like Livingstone, no matter how much she might be dedicated to missions. Livingstone, far across the sea, faded from her life, but not she from his.

4

COLONIES, IMAGINED AND REAL

Livingstone was approaching twenty-eight years of age when he boarded a sailing ship, the barque *George*, at the end of December 1840 for the long voyage to the Cape. He was the first of the three Livingstone brothers to go abroad, and unlike many emigrants was fortunate in being able to look forward to a regular salary. Long lines of Scots had been shipped overseas as bondsmen after the disaster of Culloden, and streams were taking ship in the aftermath of the Highland clearances. Many others went willingly, to settle in the United States, in British colonies such as Canada, Australia and New Zealand, and to India to serve in the administration; as missionaries all over the world.

In the late seventeenth century, while it still had an independent parliament, Scotland had tried to establish a colony of its own, at Darien on the isthmus of Panama. Capital for the venture was raised by public subscription in Scotland, and money was handed over to the Company with an enthusiasm equal to that which had been shown for the National Covenant. But everything was lost, capital, ships, most of the settlers: the Scots had planned badly, while the English and the Spanish would allow no upstart encroachment on their territory or trade. A first act of Britain's Union Parliament, after it was established in London in 1707, was to dissolve the Darien company and place all colonial trade in the hands of London-based corporations such as the East India Company. But while Scotland as a nation may have lost her independent role on the world stage, the influence of individual Scots continued in the making of the British Empire. The Duke of Argyll, for example, esconced himself firmly in the directorate of the East India Company, and a Scottish seaman, Alexander Selkirk, provided the most enduring story to stimulate the British imperial imagination.

In 1703, Selkirk was quartermaster aboard a ship reconnoitring the Pacific. He quarrelled with the ship's captain and put himself ashore on a small uninhabited island called Mas-a-Tierra off the coast of Chile. Four years later he was rescued – wild-looking, clad in goatskins and hardly able to speak his own language – and arrived back in London in 1711. His rescuer, Captain Woodes-Rogers told the story in his book *Cruising around the World*, which immediately caught the imagination of Daniel

Defoe, a London-born journalist and pamphleteer. Defoe is thought to have interviewed Selkirk before sitting down to write *Robinson Crusoe* which he published in 1719. The book was an immediate success, and Defoe wrote several sequels, though it is only the first part, based on Selkirk, that is generally remembered today. It has attained that status of English prose classic enjoyed otherwise by the King James Bible and John Bunyan's *Pilgrim's Progress*. When Livingstone refers to one of his servants as 'our Man Friday' no footnote is needed to explain what he meant: when he compares himself with Selkirk what comes to mind is not only Cowper's line 'I am monarch of all I survey', but Robinson Crusoe himself.

Defoe's story is brief in the telling: a young man named Crusoe (the name is an anglicisation of his German-born father's Kreutznaer, and both are a reflection of the Cross) looking for adventure, goes to sea. He is shipwrecked on the English coast, but survives and joins a trading voyage to Africa where he is captured and enslaved by Moors. He escapes and makes his way to Brazil where he starts a farm. After some years he embarks on a slaving voyage to Africa, is shipwrecked again: the only survivor, he swims ashore on to what seems an uninhabited island in the Caribbean.

Most of Defoe's narrative is devoted to Crusoe's stay on the island; how he survived and flourished thanks to his native wit and the workings of providence. After undergoing a deep conversion to Christianity, his prosperity increases until it reaches the stage where the economic development of the island cannot go further without help, help which materializes in Friday, a young Carib whom Crusoe rescues from 'savages' who use the island from time to time for feasting on their prisoners of war. Friday becomes Crusoe's slave, but is enabled to embrace Christianity and obtain the chance of salvation.

With his slave's labour at his disposal, Crusoe becomes powerful enough to feel that he is the king of the island, able to defend it against attack and to turn it into a colony – with the crew of a captured pirate ship as settlers – and to make his way back to London. Meanwhile, his plantation in Brazil and his savings have made him a wealthy man: he continues to invest in his colony, sending supplies and wives for the settlers. The colony is attacked and overrun by Caribs, but they are defeated by a providential storm, after which the settlement is safe.

This scant outline shows the ideological skeleton of the romance: English Protestants with their direct relation with God, by being adventurous and prepared to face temporary deprivations, have the power to make good. This requires both initiative (supported by providence) and labour: when the individual's own labour is inadequate, servant or slave is needed, and though the slave might work for nothing, receives a great reward in being given the opportunity of salvation through Christ. This part of the story is a moral and economic justification for slavery, while the final part – dealing with Crusoe's establishment of a Christian colony, saved by providence from destruction – is an equal justification for imperial conquest.

Two other elements form part of the skeleton: one is the elite status of the English, acquired by their being independent Christians (unlike the Spaniards and the Portuguese in the tale, who need priests), and by their being simply English by 'race'. Crusoe's Spanish settlers get as wives whatever women he can find them in Brazil, while the English receive their wives from England.

The other element concerns Friday, whose appearance impressed Crusoe at first inspection:

> He was a comely handsome fellow, perfectly well made ... He had a very good countenance, not a fierce and surly aspect; but seemed to have something very manly in his face; and yet he had all the sweetness and softness of an European in his countenance too, especially when he smiled. His hair was long and black, not curled like wool; ... the colour of his skin was not quite black, but very tawny; yet not of an ugly yellow tawny as the Brasilians, and Virginians, and other natives of America are; but of a bright kind of dun olive colour, that had in it something very agreeable, tho' not very easy to describe. His face was round and plump, his nose small, not flat like the negroes, a very good mouth, thin lips, and his fine teeth well set, and white as ivory ...

Though Friday is by origin a 'cannibal' (whom Crusoe weans rapidly from the taste for human flesh) his very appearance, by approximating that of Europeans, sets him apart from the Africans, with their 'black skin', 'hair curled like wool', their flat noses, whom Crusoe was on his way from Brazil to enslave when he was stranded on the island. Thus apart from justifying slavery and colonial conquest, *Robinson Crusoe* contains the design of racial differentiation – whites at the top, blacks at the bottom – that has imbued the English worldview for centuries. Defoe did not create this worldview, nor is it specifically English (French colonial codes in the West Indies recognised one hundred and twenty eight 'degrees' of colour). He merely presented it in the readable and digestible form which would ensure that the book's metaphors would influence English thought for centuries.

The barque *George* with its young Scot seeking a future aboard, did not make easy passage at first. A few days out of English waters, as Livingstone wrote to Prentice on 27th January 1841:

> ... our little vessel went reeling and staggering over the waves as if she had been drunk, our trunks perpetually breaking from their lashings, were

tossed from one side of the cabin to the other, everything both pleasant and unpleasant huddled together in glorious confusion. You have been aboard a steamer; that is nothing to a little sailing vessel in a stormy sea such as we had about the Bay of Biscay, she writhed and twisted about terribly. Imagine if you can a ship in a fit of epilepsy. My nervous system not being oversensitive enabled me calmly to contemplate the whole scene and certainly I never beheld such a mess before, it might be called 'the world upside down'. The storm I won't attempt to describe.

After passing Madeira the cruise became pleasant, but off the Cape Verde Islands, the *George*'s foremast split, and the captain had to take her into Rio de Janeiro, then the capital of the Empire of Brazil, for repairs and fresh water. It was Livingstone's first visit to a truly foreign land, and a slave society at that. He enjoyed taking a naked bath under a waterfall in the hills above the city and having a meal with a peasant family despite the danger of being kidnapped by runaway slaves. He regretted not having any tracts in Portuguese to distribute, but tried out some pastoral work in the dock area. He wrote to Prentice on 5th March 1841:

I was much impressed with the need that exists for efforts on behalf of seamen. When in Rio they are always a disgrace to our country and to the cause of Christianity. You never find anyone drunk but an Englishman or American. Frequently they are stabbed or stript stark naked and sent so back to their ships. Yet these men consider themselves Christians. I went to two public houses where a great many seamen of both countries usually lodge and when giving some tracts to one to take on board to his shipmates whom he said were all drunkards, the American seaman who stood by said he was thankful that he was able to read tracts and requested one or two but added [to remember] we are not all drunkards.

A furious argument broke out about the definition of 'Christian', and Livingstone concludes the story: 'I confess I was afraid of my own countrymen although they treated me with the greatest respect.'

As time would show, it was his 'own countrymen' that Livingstone would find most disagreeable throughout his life, and who most often did not treat him as he thought he deserved. On the other hand, he had a manner and a sense of humour which many of his compatriots would find disagreeable. Two fellow passengers aboard the *George* were Mr and Mrs William Ross, he a former schoolmaster ten years older than Livingstone, and bound for the missions. Both Ross and his wife suffered badly from seasickness, and would not have been amused by Livingstone's jokes when he wrote to Prentice in January 1841 about it:

Seasickness ... is indeed a dolorous predicament to be in, a man and his wife and the stomachs of both making efforts to quit their bodies every time the head is elevated is really a melancholy spectacle. I pitied but could not cure – The only cruelty I was guilty of (and I am not quite sure but I should have done the same for you, if you, like my friend here, had rashly quoted the text to me before the sickness began 'Two [i.e. man with wife] are better than one') was quoting the same text to him when both he and his spouse were turning their stomachs out into one basin.

After fitting a new mast and filling the water tanks, the *George* sailed from Brazil, diagonally across the south Atlantic, around the Cape of Good Hope, to make landfall at Simon's Town, the British naval base on the south of the Cape peninsula. By the time Livingstone set foot in Africa, he had learned from the captain of the *George* a new skill – navigation – which was to prove of immeasurable value to his career. His shipboard study of Setswana might have prepared him for medical and pastoral work; his study of navigation suggests he had further objectives in mind. On 17th March, 1841 he was in Cape Town staying with Dr and Mrs John Philip, Cape superintendant of the London Missionary Society, and discovering that mission life in south Africa was less a contentedly humming beehive than a whirring nest of hornets.

At the time of Livingstone's arrival, Dr Philip was sixty five, and had been with the LMS in south Africa for twenty years: he was a Scot from Kirkcaldy and a Congregationalist. Philip had overseen the expansion of LMS activities in the territory, been responsible for bringing in French Huguenot missionaries to work in Lesotho and other northern areas, and had helped with the establishment of Congregationalists from the American Board (the equivalent of the LMS) in Natal.

When Philip came to the Cape, the colony had been under British rule for fourteen years – it had been taken over from the Dutch in 1806 during the Napoleonic wars when the Netherlands was a satellite of France. At the time of the annexation, the Cape was a slave colony, where all the rigours of the old Dutch code applied, including punishments such as mutilation. Slaves had been imported from Indonesia, Madagascar and other parts of Africa. A further source of labour for the settler-farmers (known as the Boers) was the indigenous Khoi population, which had been dispossessed and enserfed.

From the outset of British rule, the administration was prodded towards reform by the missionaries, with the result that the Khoi were given civil equality: slavery was abolished in rapid steps following the British 1833 emancipation act. Equality before the law for the 'coloured' Khoi and ex-slaves was more than many Boers could stomach, and in 1838 the Great Trek began, with thousands of Dutch families, especially from the interior of the colony, migrating north across the Orange River to find lebensraum in the territory beyond the reach of British law. All settlers, except the very small minority which supported the British measures, blamed the missionaries for upsetting the well-established slave-serf social order, and their anger was directed particularly at Dr Philip. He was the leader of the largest missionary group, the LMS, was the Cape heir of Wilberforce. Moreover, Philip regarded not only slavery and serfdom, but also racial discrimination as wrong. By the time Livingstone met him, Philip was a political figure loved by those who stood for equal rights, reviled and hated by those who took race as a determinant.

Livingstone had heard discussion and gossip about Philip among the missionary circle in London, and had formed a prejudice against him, that he was overweening and dictatorial, interfering constantly in the running of individual missions, accusations that would weigh heavily on Livingstone's independent mind. In Cape Town, however, he found that the missionary gossip against Philip had little to do with mission government: it was the echo of Cape political controversies of the day, with some missionaries siding with white settler opinion and its antagonism to Philip as a libertarian, and supporter of non-discriminatory suffrage. Emancipation might have been accepted in the colony as a fait accompli but the prospect of 'coloured' citizens gaining political influence was abhorrent to the majority of whites, just as the idea of allowing 'natives' any influence in the running of missions was resisted by many missionaries. A further dimension to these conflicts was the position on the borders of the colony, where settlers were attempting to take over more land. In the east there was a continuous state of war as the conquest moved into the territory of Bantu-speaking Africans. The government had brought in the British '1820 settlers' to increase the white presence in the area, but this only exacerbated the conflict. North of the Orange River the emigrant Boers were taking land from the Basotho, while further in the interior, beyond the Vaal, the trekkers were carving their own republic out of territory belonging mainly to the Tswana.

It was these Transvaal Boers, with their use of slave labour, whom Livingstone would most condemn, while they in turn would try to remove him from the scene. Livingstone, however, had a fair measure of sympathy for the Boers in general, condemning their 'stupid prejudice against colour', but appreciating the economic loss they had suffered as a result of the emancipation of slaves in the colony. This loss had two aspects. In the first place, the British government had promised compensation to the slave-owners, but claims had to be proved and the money collected in London: this might not be too difficult for those who resided in and around Cape Town, but was virtually impossible for the semi-literate farmers of the interior. The second aspect of the issue reminded Livingstone of what had been happening in Scotland, as he wrote on 29th July 1843 to his friend Henry Drummond, the lace maker of Hamilton:

> [The Boers] had the finest farms in the Colony: unprincipled Englishmen, seeing that these could be turned to their own benefit as sheep farms, took advantage of their discontent and ignorance, fanned the flame until they got them to sell their lands for almost nothing. The Boers believed everything they saw in print must be true, left the colony in thousands, determined no longer to submit to British rule. A worthless Tory journal, edited by a Wesleyan, has been the main instrument of this disaffection.

But Livingstone's sympathy did not turn into support, either for the Boers or for the 'colonial party' (missionary or otherwise) which denigrated John Philip. As he wrote to Prentice on 3rd August 1843 when he had had time to reflect on the complexities of the situation:

> [Dr and Mrs Philip] are eminently devoted and humble Christians. Their work will be known better when they have gone to reap the reward of their labours and when the name and memory of their calumniators shall be sunk in the shade of cold oblivion.
>
> He stated to me that he is only money agent of the Society and does not wish to interfere with the modes of operation or plans of any man, but the Society had compelled him frequently to act a part he had no inclination to, by referring disputes to his decision. Whichever he decided, generally one party has become his enemy – he appears most desirous to get the cause forward and if men will only work they may be sure of the co-operation and friendly regard of the Dr. He has been the means of saving from the most abject and cruel slavery all the Hottentots [i.e. Khoi] and not only them but all the Aborigines beyond the colony.

By the time Livingstone wrote this letter, for example, the presence of French missionaries in Lesotho had given the King, Moshoeshoe I, enough diplomatic influence with the British to prevent the emigrant Boers from destroying the kingdom. The letter continues:

> The Boers hate [Philip] cordially. Many think it would be doing God service to shoot him. They have an inveterate hatred of the coloured people and to him as their friend and advocate, you can't understand it, it is like caste in India. Can you believe it? Some of the missionaries have imbibed a portion of it. I name none, but you will find some of

that feeling amongst the friends of Dr Philip ... I am no partizan but
I am and always have been on the side of civil and religious liberty.

The fact that it was the British, under Christian influence, who had
abolished serfdom and slavery at the Cape (even if 'English' chicanery
had provided motives for the Great Trek) strengthened Livingstone's
belief that Christian British civilisation was the standard-bearer of
'civil and religious liberty'. But he defined that civilisation himself,
saw himself as its avatar, and realised that the social and political
complexities of the Cape made his message all but inaudible: many
missionaries were enmeshed in colonial society, and the colony was
no longer a place for pioneers. Fortunately he was being posted to
Kuruman, which lay north of the Orange River: but that would be
only a staging post on a journey which would take him, he hoped,
to virgin lands, inhabited by 'unspoiled' people, who would accept his
message.

5

NOBLE OBJECTS

Livingstone was not to be in Cape Town again for twelve years, but although he was to live during that time beyond the frontier of the Colony, the Colony, its politics and its racial attitudes, was a constant presence.

The country we today call South Africa was even in the 1840s in the process of becoming a union, a union brought about by migrations. The Great Trek of the Boers was one of these, but it had been preceded by an even greater dispersal known as the *mfecane*, an upheaval which had begun a generation before the Boers loaded their wagons (and their guns) and headed north. If the Trek was part of the momentum of colonization, the *mfecane* was a reaction to earlier European penetration.

In the first years of the nineteenth century the Zulu leader Dingiswayo began to build up Zulu power and after his death the work was carried on by his successor Shaka. Shaka created a Zulu empire by incorporating weaker tribes and expelling others which would not accept Zulu hegemony, hoping to establish a kingdom strong enough to deal with European power. This exercise gave rise to two types of migration. First, a number of peoples were forced out of the Zulu orbit, among them the Mfengu who sought refuge on the eastern fringe of the Cape Colony, and the Kololo, led by Sebitwane, who moved from what is today the Orange Free State to the Upper Zambezi. The second occurred when Zulu leaders, who for one reason or another disagreed with Shaka, went off on their own. The most prominent of these was Mzilikazi, who took over much of the Transvaal: when he was defeated by the Boers he moved north to Zimbabwe where he established the Ndebele kingdom. Other Nguni groups moved into Mozambique, and yet others crossed the Zambezi and took over large areas of modern Zambia and Malawi, and even reached Lake Victoria. The Kololo, the Ndebele, and the Nguni of the Zambia-Malawi-Mozambique salient were all to play important parts in their countries of adoption, while the Kololo, with their language closely related to the Setswana Livingstone spoke, were to give him his opening to central Africa. In South Africa itself, the *mfecane* both facilitated the Boer conquest of the Highveld, and planted the seeds from which in the twentieth century a general African national consciousness would grow within the borders of the white-ruled country.

Livingstone enjoyed the months'-long journey from Cape Town to Kuruman, albeit in the company of the long-suffering Mr and Mrs Ross. They went by sea to Port Elizabeth, and then by ox wagon through the Karroo and across the Orange to the Moffat mission at the source (a powerful spring) of the Kuruman River, in independent Tswana lands. The Tswana were not united under one king as were the Zulu and the Basotho, and consisted of a federation of chiefdoms. Much of their territory was semi-arid, the population small and scattered, as Livingstone found to his disappointment: Moffat's promise in London, of 'smoke rising from a thousand huts' was a mirage. Nevertheless, Kuruman itself was impressive, with its large church, neat houses and flourishing irrigated gardens watered from the spring which rose as if miraculously in the midst of the overall dryness. But Kuruman was no place for pioneers (as Moffat had hinted): in Livingstone's opinion it was overstaffed, with barely a thousand people in the vicinity 'awaiting conversion'.

Moffat was still in Britain when Livingstone arrived at Kuruman, but the place was, even in 1841, a monument to his personal endeavour. Moffat was eighteen years older than Livingstone, and like him came from a poor, strictly Calvinist Scottish background: his formal education had consisted of learning to read the Bible and to write, and as a young man he took a job as a gardener in Cheshire. After a brief spell of revivalist Methodism, he returned to the Scottish tradition, joined the LMS to be a missionary, and went to the Cape in 1816. During the five years he spent in the colony before going north to set Kuruman on its feet, he learned Dutch. Apart from the mission itself, Moffat's outstanding achievement was the translation of the scriptures into Setswana, a language he had to learn from scratch and reduce to writing. When Livingstone met him in London, he was there to see his Tswana New Testament printed (later, he installed a press at Kuruman itself) and to see to the publication of his memoirs, *Missionary Labours and Scenes in Southern Africa* which enjoyed a wide sale and consolidated his reputation. He did not, however, attempt to make anything of his renown, nor did he ever become a figure of controversy like Dr Philip or Livingstone. Once he had chosen his path he followed it quietly, his devout heart assured that he was doing God's will.

His instructions as to what Livingstone should do in his absence were imprecise enough, 'learn the language', for Livingstone to be able, in good conscience, to do very much as he pleased, and what pleased him most was to get away from Kuruman. His first journey was undertaken with Rogers Edwards, a middle-aged artisan missionary (what in a Catholic order would be called a lay brother) who was travelling north, at Moffat's suggestion, to find a site for a new mission. The return journey altogether covered some seven hundred miles, and they found a suitable location at Chonwane, two hundred and fifty miles north-east of Kuruman, and near the present town of Zeerust in the western Transvaal.

In 1842 and 1843 Livingstone made two more long treks, reaching as far north as the town of Chief Sekoma (Sekhomi) of the Mangwato Tswana, near the south-western border of Zimbabwe. On these journeys, his travelling companions were Tswana servants from Kuruman: the journeys were far too long to be a mere search for a mission site for himself, though in his reports Livingstone mentions which chiefs are friendly and which are not. His first objective seems to have been to isolate himself among Tswana speakers to learn the language with all possible speed. On these travels, Livingstone was able to make friends with Africans, whether Christian or not, something that would have been difficult in the formal, structured atmosphere of Kuruman, and, in making friends, to find out more about the lives of the Tswana than could ever be discovered at an established mission. In this respect, these early travels set Livingstone apart from Moffat, who was little interested in the Tswana way of life as such, and consequently could not, or would not see that customs such as initiation ceremonies and polygamy were the cement of the social fabric. Nor would Moffat admit that the Tswana religion was worthy of study: for him the barrier between Christianity and 'heathenism' was inflexible and impervious: it could be crossed, but must not be bent or seeped through. Although he never broke with Moffat, on the contrary remained on good terms throughout his life, Livingstone's approach to Africans distanced him further and further from the majority of his missionary colleagues.

In those early years, the crux of the matter was the question of 'native agency', the training and employment by the missions of African catechists. This was strongly opposed by many of the missionary old guard on the grounds that Africans were incapable of transmitting the Christian gospel without error: their opposition went deeper than that, however – a seminary for catechists would eventually become a seminary for African ordinands, from whom would come African ministers. Livingstone's own clearly expressed disappointment at there not being a single mission in south Africa under African control showed the destination to which 'native agency' led. But the scriptural injunction that among Christians there is 'neither Jew nor Greek' was anathema in colonial society in south Africa, since it threatened white supremacy. (Livingstone's ideas on these matters, Protestant though he was, are so similar to the policies of Francis Xavier and the Jesuits in India, China, Latin America, Japan, and Africa that it is hard to escape the conclusion that he was influenced far more by Jesuit mission policy than he would care to admit, though certainly he expressed admiration for the work of the Jesuits, as we shall see later.)

Moffat stayed above the controversy, though when he returned from London he brought news that the directors of the LMS had agreed to 'native agency': but this concession did not dampen the argument, and Livingstone's disillusionment with the missionaries continued to grow: if his democratic ideals could not prevail he would strike off on his own. It remains possible that if he had believed that his policies would be put into practice he would have been content to devote himself to missionary and medical work, but unlikely. From the outset, he was prepared to neglect his duties as a doctor for the sake of travelling, an activity totally incompatible with offering good medical care. Travelling he believed was part of his Destiny, and he saw his survival of the perils it involved (whether from the elements or from wild beasts) as a sign. He wrote to Prentice on 9th October 1843:

> Indeed [the dangers] have been so many in a short space of time I now feel that I am on the everlasting arms of my Shepherd as a little child is on the arms of its mother.

Apart from the reasons we have mentioned for his early journeys there was another motive: to be the first European to reach a large lake that was known to exist beyond the Kalahari. Moffat had mentioned in London that an expedition to find it would be a good idea – an idea that may have appealed to Livingstone as much, if not more, than the 'smoke rising from a thousand huts'. If Bruce had made his name by locating the source of the Blue Nile, and Mungo Park by his revelations about the Niger, why should Livingstone not make his own by allowing the arms of the Shepherd to carry him to a great, unmeasured lake? There was talk about the lake while Livingstone was staying with Dr Philip in Cape Town in 1841. Two of the French Huguenot missionaries, Thomas Arbousset and Francois Daumas, who had come to south Africa under Philip's auspices and who were stationed in Lesotho, had made a journey of exploration northwards from their mission and had written a book about it which was soon to be published in Paris under the title *Relation d'un voyage d'exploration au nord-est de la Colonie du Cap de Bonne-Esperance*. The book appeared in 1842, and so great was the interest it aroused in the Colony that an English translation was issued at the Cape a few years later.

Arbousset and Daumas mention the existence of a large lake somewhere in the interior, but are not specific about its location. Moffat, however, knew roughly where it was, and in Cape Town the unfortunate Ross seems to have 'blabbed' (Livingstone's word) about Moffat's knowledge. Livingstone wrote to his friend David Watt on 7th July

1841, shortly after leaving Cape Town, that all missionaries wanted to be the first to see the lake, that there was a danger of the French setting out first, but that if he, Livingstone, learned Tswana he might forestall them. In fact the French were too tied up in Lesotho to undertake any more long exploratory ventures, but Livingstone kept probing closer and closer. On his return journey from the Mangwato in 1843 he knew, from conversation, that he was only ten days' journey (an optimistic underestimate) from the lake and regretted that he was unable to go there for want of men and supplies. But he was now certain of his objective and was confident that it was only a matter of time before he reached it.

In a preface to *Relation d'un voyage* the committee of the Paris Missionary Society (to which the authors of the book belonged) inserted this cautionary sentence: 'A missionary is not by vocation either a naturalist or a philosopher; it is not in the service of science that he crosses the deep or traverses the desert; nobler objects are set before him . . .' Livingstone was able to set this dogma on its head because, as we have seen, he believed that everything he did was part of the 'nobler object', and that object he could achieve by being a naturalist, a philosopher, and a man of science, as he had learned from Thomas Dick's *Philosophy of the Future State*. Geography was a branch of science which he had prepared himself for by learning navigation, medicine he had studied and now practised (however fitfully), and there were other areas where he could make his contribution to Dick's 'philosophy' as he wrote to David Watt on 23rd May, 1845:

> I am trying to procure specimens of the entire geology of this region and will try to make a sort of chart . . . I sent a dissertation on the decrease of water in Africa . . . Ask if [Professor Owen of the Hunterian] wants anything in the four jars I still possess of either rhinoceros, camelopard etc . . .

In investigating the human order, Livingstone's attitude was as scientific as his study of the world of nature. As we have seen, he understood the place of initiation and polygamy in Tswana society, and of rainmaking. In describing economic activities he was equally free of superciliousness: he writes to Prentice on 2nd December 1841, about the first journey north of Kuruman:

> We travelled in a north easterly direction about 130 or 40 miles for the purpose of visiting a position of a tribe who live in a mountainous region there, a most industrious race who were busily engaged in the manufacture of wooden bowls, spoons etc, and some things iron for making picks, axes and spears.

Livingstone remarks that iron-working methods were basic and that the chemistry of smelting was not understood, but saw that a technological foundation existed which could be built on:

> The ore they extract from the mountains. A fine field for Manning [Prentice's brother, who wanted to become an artisan missionary] for the arts are in the most uncouth state . . . A furnace is built of clay similar in shape to a haycock in England, having an orifice at the top and two at each end low down, a place being excavated from below to allow the 'blastman' to sit on a level with it. Two leather bags open at the bottom with two straight sticks fastened along the orifice and the mouth of the bags fastened around tubes of clay which enter the orifice in the furnace, constitute what may be called the 'bellows in embryo'.

Livingstone describes the smelting process and remarks that much iron is lost because of its deficiencies:

> By a little knowledge of chemistry, Manning might save them a great deal of iron and labour too . . . After smelting they weld very well, but a huge stone grasped in both hands is the only hammer and another stone is the anvil.

Livingstone's attitude to the iron-workers may well be that of a person who thinks he knows more about the subject than they do, but he clearly regards their skill as something valuable in itself, and capable of extension. Other missionaries would condemn indigenous iron-working because it was accompanied by religious ritual (as Livingstone observed elsewhere in the letter) which they called 'superstition', and be happy to see locally made picks and axes replaced by hardware from British factories, a process which during the colonial period virtually destroyed Africa's metal-working technology. The area Livingstone visited on this journey became the site of South Africa's richest iron mine, Thabazimbi.

He failed, however, at this stage, to understand an important aspect of Tswana protocol, the presentation of gifts to a chief. He regarded the expectation of gifts as begging, while it was in fact an assertion of authority on the chief's part: but his remark that many Tswana chiefs were 'hereditary asses' has been misunderstood. He is harking back to Bagehot's remark, 'It was said in 1802 that all the hereditary monarchs in Europe were insane', and is attributing what he regarded as the mental deficiencies of the chiefs not to their being Tswana, but to their being hereditary, an upwelling of Livingstone's dislike of hierarchy. Not a subtle man himself, he had difficulty in comprehending other people's subtleties, using the word in its unpejorative sense, not only in custom but also in language. He found Tswana easy enough to understand when read from the page, but had difficulty in grasping what was spoken to him. This applied both to Tswana and later to the languages of the Zambezi valley, and we have to assume that he did not appreciate the importance of tone which, in the Bantu languages he encountered, is a semantic indicator. A word which might be transliterated, for example, *mabele* can have two or more meanings – millet or breasts – depending on whether the middle syllable is spoken with a high or low tone. He was dimly aware of this aspect of the language, but he saw it in terms of vowel length:

> ... we have words differing from each other in only a slight change in the central vowel 'o' as tlola, tlōla, tlŏla, tlola, tlola and meaning to create, to transgress, to jump, to spy, to remain, respectively. In writing, diacritic marks are not invariably used to indicate the power of the vowels.

Apart from this dull spot, Livingstone's study of African languages was original and perceptive. Moffat's approach to language was pragmatic as it was the only means by which he could transmit the word of God to the Tswana. Livingstone's was both pragmatic and scientific. He was an early practitioner of the discipline of linguistics (a word which came into English about his time) and could have made a reputation in it if his other ambitions had not been paramount. In starting to learn Tswana Livingstone, as we have seen, made use of Moffat's translation of the New Testament but, unlike Moffat, he had the advantage of knowing some Hebrew which had been part of the course at Ongar. He also knew Latin and Greek. Any comparison of Greek and Hebrew will show that the two languages differ, not only in vocabulary, but also in structure, while Greek and Latin are closely related in both respects. Livingstone perceived immediately that Tswana differed in structure from English, or from Greek and Latin, and that attempts to describe Tswana in the terms used in grammars of the classical languages were misguided (just as it would eventually be seen that English could not be bound in the classical straitjacket). To take but one example, nouns in the classical languages are classified by gender – masculine, feminine and neuter – which influences the form of adjectives. In Tswana, nouns have no gender and are grouped in classes, each group being identified by a prepositional affix which is carried over to both verb and adjective.

Livingstone was thus able to study Tswana on its own terms, and to prepare an *Analysis of the Language of the Bechuanas* which he had printed privately in 1858, less as an academic exercise than as a manual for his British colleagues on the Zambezi Expedition. In the *Analysis* Livingstone advanced the theory that Tswana was related to the Coptic of ancient Egypt.

The realization that languages which, at first hearing, seem totally different from each other could be related was growing rapidly in the early nineteenth century. In the 1790s a British official with the East India Company had shown that Bengali was related to western languages such as Latin and Greek. Some years later the German philologist Jacob Grimm proved the existence of an Indo-European family of languages which includes not only those we have mentioned, but Irish, English, German, Russian, Italian, Iranian, Hittite, Sanskrit and Singhalese, to name but a few. Livingstone soon started making comparative word lists of the African languages he came in contact with (a habit that stayed with him all his life) and was quickly aware that Tswana was part of an extensive language family. Ludwig Krapf, a German-born (but Anglican) missionary in east Africa at the same time saw, too, the existence of such a family and wrote in 1846 that all the African dialects from the Equator to the Cape formed one group. Livingstone, from his reading of Krapf and others, and from his own experience, was able to say confidently in the introduction to the *Analysis*:

> . . . there exists the closest relationship between primitive and almost perfect [Setswana] and the dialects spoken by the Caffres [i.e. Xhosa], Zulu, Matabele, Malokuane and Basuto. Indeed, the structure of all these is essentially the same. The Bakhoba or Banyeiyi of Lake Ngami; the Bashubea, Barotse, and Batoka of the Leeambye or Zambezi; the Bashukulompo, who live to the north-east of that river; and the Balojuzi, who inhabit countries far to the north-west of S.lat.14°; with the Bamoenye, Ambonda, Banyenko, Balonda &B&, all speak dialects which contain nearly as many Sechuana roots as English does Latin. The list of words furnished by Captain Tuckney in his *Voyage up the Zaire or Congo River*, and the communications of missionaries in the country adjacent to [Mombasa], with vocabularies furnished by the Baptist and Church Missionaries at Fernando Po and the West Coast, render almost certain that the groundwork of all south equatorial African tongues, except the Bush or Hottentot [i.e. San or Khoi] is of the same family . . .

Linguistics today has extended the boundaries of the African language families, relating the 'Bantu' group (which Livingstone outlines here) to groups extending across the whole breadth of sub-Saharan west Africa.

Livingstone's introduction to Coptic came through Chevalier Bunsen's *Egypt's Place in Universal History*, as he acknowledges in the *Analysis*:

> I have followed the clear arguments of the learned Chevalier Bunsen in his disquisition on the ancient Egyptian language, and have often been struck by the similarity the structure of that language bears to the Sechuana.

As an example of this, Livingstone writes:

> The Sechuana absolute verb, like that of the ancient Egyptian is often expressed by the same words which express the absolute noun: a peculiarity which, according to Bunsen, may be explained in a philosophical point of view by the inseparable union, and therefore apparent identity, of the two ideas of personality and existence.

On a more formal basis than was available to Livingstone, African linguists are today showing correspondences between the Wolof language of Senegal and Guinea and ancient Egyptian. Livingstone's hunch of a correspondence between Setswana and Coptic may in the course of time be shown to be correct. But even if the matter is not resolved, his assumption that ancient Egypt was an African civilisation – with the corollary that the Pharoahs were black – was not one readily accepted in the West which preferred to think of Egypt as essentially Mediterranean and therefore near-European. Nor would his assertion that Setswana is an 'almost perfect' language have endeared him to those who regarded African languages as a gibber of mumbo-jumbo. In both these insights Livingstone would have found himself out of harmony once again with the colonial party, for their implications denied white superiority, especially as he found that one of the great virtues of Setswana was that 'the lowest class of the population [speaks it] as correctly as the highest'. Certainly not the position with English in which usage was fast becoming a class indicator.

After many years' work, Livingstone completed an early draft of the *Analysis* in 1852 but, as we have seen, it was not published until six years later and then in a private printing of only twenty-five copies. A summary of the work was included with an edition of his Cambridge lectures of 1857, but though he never wrote again at any length on linguistic subjects, he corresponded with Wilhelm Bleek, the German scholar who became interpreter and librarian to the governor of the Cape, and who later laid the foundation for systematic comparative linguistics in southern Africa.

Language, the natural sciences, geographical exploration – the first three years of Livingstone's time in south Africa saw him beginning to display the versatility that characterised his entire later life. On the other hand he was discontented; unhappy with missionary society, doubtful about the value of mission work, unwilling to commit himself fully to medicine. In addition, his failure to win Catherine Ridley ached like an unhealed wound. It is not known whether he wrote to her again after a letter from Rio de Janeiro, but it is not likely. Since May 1840 when he told his Ongar friend Henry Dickson that, 'Mr Thomas Prentice . . . has now succeeded in his addresses to Miss Ridley', Catherine had to most intents and purposes been Prentice's, and even if Livingstone hoped that Prentice, who was sickly, would not be able to marry her, direct letters would have been ill-mannered. However, he kept her informed about his continuing interest through his letters to Prentice and presumably heard news of her from him. Much of Livingstone's comment on the salubriousness of the Botswana climate (much of it whitewash, as anyone who has lived there will know) was by way of an invitation to move from East Anglia to south Africa. But the move was never to be made, as Livingstone recorded to George Drummond, another Ongar friend in June 1843:

> Prentice is married to Catherine and has a child. I believe he got her because he intended to be a missionary. Now she is stuck up at his father's country house at Stowmarket.

Livingstone's conviction that Prentice deceived Catherine into marrying him by pretending that he was going to be a missionary (in fact he became a corn merchant) persisted all his life. In a letter of 1869 to his son Thomas, Livingstone was still harking on the matter. A few months after writing to Drummond a letter arrived from Prentice. Livingstone's reply on 9th October 1843 is the last known piece in their correspondence. The opening paragraph is redolent of distress:

> My Dear Friend Prentice,
> 'Hope deferred maketh the heart sick, but when the desire cometh it is a tree of life', is the passage which sprung into my mind when I saw your letter. I cannot tell you how much I longed for it nor how often I have thought of you and C. Then I became uncharitable – then angry then I don't know what, for I thought you must have written and then if you had not there must be some good cause for it. And then was that the illness of Catherine or what? But it would be endless to tell you all I have felt. But here you are at last. I got it on returning a few days ago from the erection of a hut at the Bakhatla a tribe situated a little more than 200 miles north of [Kuruman]. It is the nearest point in the Interior where an eligible spot can be found, and we have by this step taken possession of it for a station. A Lovelier spot you never saw, a hill in the rear is called Mabotsa (marriage feast).

In the following paragraph Livingstone comments on Catherine's illness:

> But what news you give me respecting C. Has it indeed been necessary for our Father to lay on his hand so heavily?

[43]

Livingstone answers his own question, suggesting that Catherine is being chastised:

> [God] has seen that this chastisement was really so, or he would not have afflicted it. He doth not afflict willingly nor grieve the children of men.

It is not difficult to understand Livingstone as meaning that Catherine was being punished for rejecting him in favour of the 'country house at Stowmarket'. Towards the end of the letter he says a painful indirect farewell to Catherine:

> May His presence be with your dear Catherine and comfort her as He only can. I hope your little boy will be a missionary [i.e. unlike his father]. Please give him a press to your heart for me. Please present my affectionate salutations to Catherine. I can't think of her as Mrs P. and will always name her as she was when I first saw her. [God's] presence supplies the loss of all we have left behind. Blessed Redeemer help us follow thee fully, for a kinder and better leader there never was.

The last sentence of the letter, cramped in the margin reads:

> I shall answer every letter of yours that reaches me.

We don't know if any ever did.

A few months after writing this, Livingstone had decided to marry Moffat's daughter Mary. Their first home would be at Mabotsa.

6

'PLUCKY LITTLE DEVIL'

Livingstone's 'marriage feast' took place at Kuruman on 2nd January 1845; the ceremony performed by the Rev. Prosper Lemue, a French Protestant missionary.

He had decided to find a wife soon after it had become apparent that Catherine Ridley was forever out of reach. Soon after this, in September 1843, he wrote to David Watt:

> There's no outlet for me when I begin to think of getting married but that of sending home an advertisement to the Evangelical Magazine . . .

But the outlet was found close at hand. Mary Moffat had returned to Kuruman with her parents at the beginning of 1844 and Livingstone came to know her while he was recuperating there from his mauling by a lion at Mabotsa in February of that year. This incident with the 'king of the beasts' has become a highlight in iconic versions of Livingstone's life though he played it down at the time, possibly because it reflected poorly upon his common sense, perhaps out of modesty for his endurance under pain. Livingstone shot and wounded a lion that had been taking livestock at Mabotsa. He had fired both barrels but the lion came after him, sprang on him and gripped his left upper arm between its jaws, shaking him furiously and breaking the bone. His life was saved when one of his assistants, Mebalwe, fired and killed the animal. Livingstone set the bone himself, without anaesthetic, but though it knitted, it did not set true. Livingstone was laid up at Mabotsa for several agonising months while his wounds healed, and then moved to Kuruman to complete his recovery in greater comfort than could be found in the rough accommodation of a mission station under construction.

There he made his proposal of marriage to Mary a few weeks later, was accepted, and returned to Mabotsa to finish building the house. This new mission station had been approved by the directors of the LMS on the understanding that it was to be run jointly by Livingstone and Rogers Edwards – though in secret Livingstone had no intention of staying there for long. He was determined to have a station of his own far to the north of established missions, and knew that the LMS would never allow a single man to do that: thus it was that he was expected to share Mabotsa. Livingstone also believed that relations with Tswana rulers would be easier if he had a wife, and more acceptable in a conservative, closely-regulated society. He may have been worried, too, by the strong emotional surges he sometimes felt for men he admired, such as a youth named Sehamy who accompanied him on several Kalahari journeys. Sehamy had been Livingstone's right-hand man, 'sharing hunger and thirst', anticipating Livingstone's 'every want', even sleeping beside him at night. When he died of fever, unconverted to Christ, Livingstone burst out: 'Poor Sehamy, where are thou now? Where lodges thy soul tonight? Did'st thou think of what I told thee as thou turnedst from side to side in distress? I could now do anything for thee. I could weep for thy soul. But now nothing can be done. Thy fate is fixed. Oh, am I guilty of the blood of thy soul, my poor dear Sehamy.'

Livingstone's beliefs told him that the non-believer Sehamy's 'fate was fixed': this was cause enough in itself for grief, but he was in no way responsible for the ways of God. How then could he be guilty of the blood of Sehamy's soul? Had he not tried hard enough to convert him? Beneath the piety of this passage lies a more personal and intimate emotion, which could only be consummated acceptably in family life.

But, above all, Livingstone needed a competent assistant, as he had seen in the aftermath of the lion incident when he had to rely on the care of Mr and Mrs Edwards, which he found lacking. (At a future date, Mrs Livingstone was to pull out a troublesome Livingstone tooth with a pair of pliers.) He needed a guardian of the hearth, a female Friday. In this respect he could be certain that Mary Moffat would be more suitable than any respondent to an advertisement in the *Evangelical Messenger*: she was used to Africa, understood how a mission and a household should be run, was accustomed to semi-poverty, and knew how to improvise. Even if she were a plain-looking woman, and plain in manner, she was the daughter of a well-known man who could be a useful ally.

As for Mary, she was twenty-three and nearing the age when permanent spinsterhood was in prospect, which would mean perpetual dependence upon her parents, both of them strong-willed, even domineering, persons. There was no possibility in those days of a woman in Mary's position having an independent life, and marriage provided the only opportunity of having a home of her own. Livingstone might not be the ideal choice but the choice at Kuruman was in any event limited in the extreme. The Moffats may have hoped that marriage would domesticate Livingstone, Mary may have looked forward to Livingstone's fulfilling his ambitions. Whatever the case, once she had married him her course was set. She followed her husband with a mixture of dutiful devotion and ill-expressed love, but little happiness, little contentment. Not even the sense of security a marriage for convenience was supposed to offer a woman and her children lay on the path ahead.

When Livingstone wrote to the directors of the LMS to announce his forthcoming marriage, he mentioned it as casually as if it concerned nothing more personal than the purchase of a horse:

> Various considerations ... having led me to the conclusion that it is my duty to enter into the marriage relation, I have made the necessary arrangements for union with Mary, the eldest daughter of Mr Moffat in the beginning of January, 1845. It was not without much serious consideration and earnest prayer, and if I have not deceived myself, I was in some measure guided by a desire that the Divine glory might be promoted in my increased usefulness. I hope this will be considered a sufficient notification of the change contemplated and that it will meet with the approbation of the Directors.

But Livingstone's written tone may be misleading here, as it often was on his own admission, when dealing with delicate matters: he clearly did not want the directors to think that he was marrying for his own advantage, either in anticipating the increased salary the LMS would have to pay a married man, or in his marrying the boss's daughter. Livingstone had brushed aside suggestions in London that he should marry before going to Africa (with no mention, presumably, of his hopes for Catherine), and his union with Mary, so shortly after she had returned to Kuruman, might be interpreted by missionary gossip as an indication that he had merely been waiting for the opportunity to advance his career by a dynastic marriage. It is more likely that the immediate availability of Mary so soon after the collapse of his earlier hopes was providential, it solved one problem and presented an opportunity. But to have made his announcement with any obvious pleasure would have added a lot of smoke to a very small fire.

A letter to Mary, on 1st August 1844, when he was on the way to Mabotsa to build their house before the wedding sets the tone for their fifteen years of marriage:

> And now, my dearest, farewell. May God bless you! Let your affection be towards Him much more than towards me, and kept by His mighty power and grace, I hope I shall never give you cause to regret that you have given me a part. Whatever friendship we feel towards each other, let us always look to Jesus as our common friend and guide, and may he shield you with His everlasting arms from every evil.

[47]

Livingstone may have given her cause to regret, but he never did so with conscious deliberation. He did so because he was what he was, a driven man. Later he confessed that he found little to recommend the married state, and perhaps it would have been better, at least for Mary, if he had not felt marriage to be necessary for the advancement of his ambitions. Perhaps it would even have been better if he had been a member of the Society of Jesus rather than the LMS.

Soon after the wedding the couple moved to Mabotsa, but their stay there was short. As we have seen, the mission there was established jointly by Livingstone and Rogers Edwards – by trade a carpenter, twenty years older than Livingstone – and who had spent many years at Kuruman as an artisan. The two men did not get on well and were unable to work together. There appear to have been two reasons for this. In the first place, Livingstone regarded Edwards as one of the 'colonial party', with a hierarchical attitude towards blacks. On the other, Edwards regarded Livingstone as an upstart who intended to take over Mabotsa for himself and keep Edwards in the subordinate position he had long suffered under Moffat. Edwards, at fifty, wanted to be his own man and Mabotsa was his last chance. Matters came to a head shortly after the Livingstones had taken up residence. If the men did not come to blows, they sublimated their antagonism in screeds of accusation and counter-accusation to the LMS – Livingstone's letter covered thirty-two pages. Edwards had the good sense not to post his own.

Livingstone having, he believed, shown that he and Edwards were quite incompatible, packed his wagon and trekked forty miles north to Chonwane where the chief of the Kwena clan, Sechele, (with whom Livingstone had made friends) was willing to have a station. It is possible that if Livingstone had told Edwards that he saw Mabotsa as a mere stepping stone, the quarrels would have been avoided, but he did not. Livingstone needed the quarrels to justify his move northwards. He may have intimated to the LMS that he did not see Mabotsa as a permanent posting but he had no authorisation from the directors for a move. Not for the last time, Livingstone presented the LMS with a fait accompli. His connection with the Moffats put him in a stronger position than if he had been on his own, for they would not want him to be dismissed or, with their daughter, be transferred to another country. The latter was a step Livingstone was prepared to take if he did not get his way in south Africa and as early as June 1843 he had written to Arthur Tidman, Foreign Secretary of the LMS, to tell him so:

> I must also state that I have, since hearing of the delightful prospects opened in China, felt again the glowing of heart towards that country which was familiar when I dedicated myself to missionary work there.

[The Chinese, defeated in the Opium War, had been compelled to open the country to the opium trade – and to missionaries.]

In the event, the LMS acceded to Livingstone's insubordination over Chonwane, and from then on allowed him to do more or less as he pleased. He did not let the quarrel with Edwards die a natural death. A dozen years after it should have been buried Livingstone was to direct his spleen at the unfortunate carpenter's son, Samuel, who had become a trader, accusing him of the theft of the journal of his 1851 travels and of passing it on to James Chapman to plagiarise in his book *Travels in the Interior of South Africa*. Disturbing as the Edwards affair might have been in itself, it was no more than a foretaste of the stream of vindictiveness of which Livingstone was capable: his abiding sense of insecurity led him to turn viciously on anyone he felt to be a threat to his standing (or his ambition).

If Mary hoped for a settled life at Chonwane, she was disappointed. She was clear of the rancorous atmosphere of Mabotsa, she may have given birth to her first child (Robert, named after her father), but the Livingstones were at Chonwane for only a bare year, and during that period she and the baby were taken on two long wagon journeys through the central Transvaal. Livingstone wanted to establish catechists there, but came up against the Boers who would not entertain any British and London Missionary Society presence in the lands they had conquered, and whose inhabitants they were rapidly subjugating.

In 1847, with Mary pregnant again, the Livingstones followed Sechele and his Bakwena from Chonwane, where the water supply was unreliable, to Kolobeng, eighty miles to the north (near Gaborone, the capital of present-day Botswana). It took Livingstone eleven months to build a proper house there but the four years at Kolobeng were to prove the longest period in her whole life during which Mary had a home of her own. Some idea of life at Kolobeng comes in a letter to Livingstone's physician friend James Risdon Bennet, whom he had met and been helped by in London:

> ... We have been so fully occupied since our removal to this locality in erecting temporary dwellings and then more permanent buildings – clearing land for corn and teaching, I could not allow myself the pleasure of correspondence. Every day is spent in somewhat the following manner. We rise early and hold school, then manual labour as we can; work continues up to the time when the sun goes down. I then go to the town to spend an hour or so in conversation with any one willing to be taught. We have three week evening meetings as soon as it is dark and a prayer meeting in the Chief's house somewhat later.
>
> My better half has an Infant and Sewing School immediately after dinner attended by from 60 to 80 children ... the only intermission of

my duties through the day is about 15 minutes for dinner . . . the manual labour will be less severe by and by. It is easy to build a castle in the air but no joke to build a cottage on the ground . . .

The reason of our removal hither was the want of water at Chonuane for irrigation. Here we have excellent water – a great blessing indeed and should we have peace for a few years we shall be surrounded with many comforts in consequence. Nearly all the English vegetables grow well in our winter, and peaches, apricots, oranges, apples, grapes, figs flourish in summer. [Livingstone is obviously thinking largely of the gardens at Kuruman.] I have seeds of all these in the ground and some are two feet high – there are some native fruit trees worth transplanting and I mean to try. We have an olive tree about a foot high and ginger (one plant). Some of the medicinal plants might succeed if we had fresh seed to try. Rhubarb would be of great value. Also jalap – none of the medicinal seeds though germinated . . . I have castor oil trees in the garden and use the seeds but they cause great nausea before they operate.

Livingstone could not resist the temptation to compare the apparent success of his (and Mary's) efforts with what had happened (or rather, what he said had happened) with Rogers Edwards. Thus he wrote on 23rd June 1848:

... The people behave with decorum in the chapel – seem to listen attentively – the numbers are from 100 to 150 on sabbath. Attendance at the infant school being in no way compulsory we hope good is being done, all who come do so simply because they like it and yet there are seldom fewer than 50 and sometimes they amount to twice that number. It is very different at Mabotsa. Soon after we left, some unpleasantness arose between the missionary and chief. The former had to pay a fine to be allowed to remain there and as a heathen does not readily forgive for many months afterwards a single Mokhatla never entered either school or chapel. The benefit of the mission has been ever since almost entirely confined to some failures we brought from Kuruman. It is a great pity for it is one of the finest localities in this country. Never send any artizans as assistant missionaries . . .

If any sentences appear nonsense from my ideas remaining in the Sitchwana idiom please transform them into sense. I shall do better or try to do so next time.

I never had time to take the latitude till a few days ago and that was in consequence of having given leg a cut with an axe. It is 24 degrees 38'S, and we are about a degree and a half west of the longitude of Mosega which you may see on maps. I have not the means of taking the longitude.

Livingstone had remembered his lessons in navigation and reports his latitude with satisfaction for, he believed, it placed him farther north than any other missionary in south Africa – some 250 miles from Kuruman as the crow flies.

He would have had no opportunity of English conversation except with Mary were it not for the passage of the occasional itinerant Cape hunter or trader, shooting game and bartering cloth and other manufactured goods, including guns and alcohol for local hides and skins, and if possible, ivory. The only whites permanently in the area were the Boers, who now no longer appeared to Livingstone as victims of English chicanery deserving of sympathy, as he wrote to William Fairbrother on 14th January 1851:

> They are great plagues to the progress of missions these same Boers. They are of Dutch extraction. Each has his big bible which he never reads. Each has his horse and gun with which he can kill blacks. They look upon themselves as the peculiar favourites of Heaven – that they resemble the children of Israel when led by Moses. And the blacks are the descendants of Cain and may be shot as so many baboons.

The Boers were at the time so intoxicated with the Old Testament that when they reached the north-flowing Mokalakwena river in the central Transvaal they thought it was the Nile and named their settlement on its banks Nylstroom.

With some justification they regarded Livingstone as an enemy, an agent of the British Pharoah from whose clutches they had made their exodus. In due course they would impinge heavily upon Kolobeng, but not before the Livingstone house had become the port of call of a third, and very different, type of white man, a type of person with whom Livingstone had never before been friendly. These were the well-moneyed upperclass Englishmen who came to south Africa to hunt 'big game'. Livingstone described the sport as itinerant butchery, but this scruple did not stand in the way of his making friends for life with several of these visitors.

The first on the scene was Thomas Montague Steele, aide-de-camp to the East India Company's Governor of Madras. At the time of his visit in 1843, when Livingstone was at Mabotsa, Steele was twenty-three. Livingstone helped him organize his hunting trips, and the two men discussed the problems of exploration, including that of reaching the Lake. When Steele returned to his post in India, he spread the good news about the hunting and about the helpful Livingstone (to whom he presented as an aid to exploration the sextant with which he took the latitude of Kolobeng to report to Bennet). The Livingstones named their second son after Steele, who remained an army man, and became a general.

He served in the Crimean war, was appointed commander-in-chief in Ireland and was knighted. In 1874 he was one of the pall-bearers at Livingstone's funeral.

Following Steele, Frank Vardon and William Cotton Oswell arrived to stay with David and Mary at Mabotsa in 1845. Both were on leave from India, where Vardon was in the army and Oswell in the tax department of the East India Company. Vardon made only this single trip to south Africa, for though he longed to return, he was not wealthy enough to do so. He and Livingstone got on well, and he characterized his host as a 'good and kind little fellow'. Livingstone conferred some kind of immortality upon him by naming a tropical antelope, the *puku, Kobus Vardoni* when he identified it as a new species some years later. Vardon's contribution to science was to take to England the first specimens of the south African tsetse fly. We don't know when he was born, but he died about 1864.

Unlike Vardon, Oswell was wealthy in his own right, apart from his Company salary of £640 a year – as a married man Livingstone earned £100 – and was to make two trips to south Africa. He has been described by Francis Galton, the British explorer of Namibia, as '. . . a living realization of the perfect and gentle knight of whom we read in old romances'. He was the grandson of Joseph Cotton, a ship's captain in the merchant marine of the East India Company, who made a fortune through his 'extraordinary commercial acumen'. Cotton's daughter Amelia married William Oswell, a merchant in the Russian trade, (grain and furs) who had investments yielding £1400 a year. The religious tone of the family may be gauged by the marriage of Amelia's sister, Phoebe to Thomas Bowdler, the Anglican clergyman who produced expurgated versions of the works of Shakespeare and who gave the English language a new word.

Young William, born with many a silver spoon in his mouth, was sent in 1818 to the foremost boys' boarding school of the day, Rugby. There, Dr Thomas Arnold was putting into practice his reforms in education which were to become the hallmark of the English public school system – taking the sons of merchants and manufacturers, giving them the accent and outlook of the aristocracy, producing the British ruling class of the nineteenth century and the 'muscular Christian' senior managers of the Empire. William excelled at school. He was a splendid athlete, nicknamed 'muscleman' and a writer of polished Greek and Latin verse.

When, at nineteen years of age, he finished at Rugby, his uncle John Cotton placed him in the civil (as opposed to the military) service of the East India Company, of which he was a director. William was sent to Madras, where he soon learned to speak Tamil so well that, unlike most of his colleagues, he was able to collect taxes without the aid of an interpreter. Apart from being athletic, devout, and intellectually brilliant, he was extremely good looking. However, he was not immune to malaria, and it was to recuperate from an attack which nearly killed him that he took up Steele's suggestion and went to south Africa in 1845. Livingstone had often spoken about the salubriousness of the Kalahari climate, and whatever its defects, the general dryness kept the area relatively free from mosquitoes. Oswell and Vardon based themselves at Mabotsa, and from there travelled, hunting and exploring to the north-east where Oswell was interested in mapping the course of the Limpopo river. At the end of the tour he returned to India, sending a present to Livingstone before sailing from the Cape. Livingstone wrote to him on 22nd March 1847:

> We found that the waggon arrived at Kuruman before us. It had got a turn over which damaged the tent but that will soon be mended. Yokes and everything that could be stripped off were gone except the sail, this I suppose occurred after you left. We were glad to get it as it is, we needed a waggon and but for your very great kindness should have been obliged to wait and save at least three years more. Please accept of our united and hearty thanks for the favour.

For several years Livingstone spelt the name 'Oswel'.

After this first visit, Oswell described Livingstone as 'the best, most intelligent and most modest (a rarer virtue is modesty than you suppose) of the missionaries,' but his voice is captured better in a remark he made some years later: 'To look at the man you would think nothing of him, but he is a plucky little devil.'

Livingstone and Oswell had discussed Lake Ngami and planned to visit it when Oswell could take leave again. Livingstone hoped that Steele would come as well and expected that Chief Sechele would also join the party. When Oswell arrived at Cape Town in the latter half of 1848 he set about equipping the expedition, buying everything from wagons to French brandy, spending £600 with the merchant Howson Edwards Rutherfoord, who besides being a businessman was also, as it happened, a local director of the LMS. Oswell also engaged servants for the journey, one of whom was a young Cape man named William John Thomas, freed from slavery in 1834. Steele did not come, but Oswell had with him a forty-five year old Scottish aristocrat, Mungo Murray of Lintrose. At Kuruman, they were joined by a trader, J H Wilson, who was interested in ivory. Towards the end of 1849, Livingstone joined the caravan at Kolobeng, with a party of Tswana – Sechele himself was not able to go. Mary stayed at the mission with the children.

This was not the first white expedition to the Lake; the first attempt had been made by Andrew Smith in 1834, the second by James

Alexander a few years later, but both had been defeated by the desert. The Kolobeng expedition had two advantages over its predecessors: one of the Tswana in the party had been to the lake before, while Livingstone himself knew both the language of the people whose territory they would be crossing and a good part of the territory itself.

The six-hundred mile journey took nine weeks, and Lake Ngami was seen by whites for the first time on 1st August 1849. It was then a large sheet of shallow water stretching to the horizon, but the expedition was not able to measure it as they did not have a boat and the shores were too marshy to walk around. Livingstone wanted to go further north, but the wide Botletle river, which flows eastwards out of the lake, could not be forded, or crossed without boats, so the party retraced its path to Kolobeng where it arrived at the end of September.

Whether Livingstone deserved the acclaim he attracted as the 'discoverer' of Lake Ngami is debatable but Oswell, whether deliberately or by default, made it possible for him to take the credit. Immediately on reaching Kolobeng, Livingstone sent the LMS in London a long report of the journey: the directors passed the letter to the Royal Geographical Society, which awarded Livingstone its Gold Medal as well as one half (twenty-five guineas) of the annual Royal Prize for geographical discovery. Mungo Murray, as far as we know, wrote nothing about the expedition and Oswell made no attempt to win honour for himself. As time passed, however, it was recognised that without him the journey would never have taken place, and he was given awards such as the Medal of the Paris Geographical Society.

Livingstone was to write that Moffat was jealous of his success and, whether this were true or not, Lake Ngami proved to have been an ambition worth aiming, and waiting, for. It brought Livingstone international fame, fame that lay outside the confines of the missionary world, and led him to realise that he would be able to look elsewhere than the LMS for a living. Before Ngami he might have been content to stay among the Tswana (the LMS wanted him to compile a Setswana dictionary, which would have taken years). After Ngami, he was convinced that his future lay further to the north. Once more, Oswell was to help him.

Part Two

1852–1856
Across Africa

7
FORWARD POLICIES

Lake Ngami was Oswell's gift to Livingstone, but both men knew that it had no value in itself as far as Livingstone's purposes were concerned. It was too remote for a mission, it lay in unhealthy looking territory which was sparsely peopled: an occasional trader might be able to deal in ivory, but the Kalahari was a formidable obstacle. Ngami, however, was not an isolated lake in a desert, but the extremity of a system of interconnected waterways. One, the Botletle river, flowed on through the Kalahari. Immediately beyond Ngami lies the delta of the Okavango river, which rises in a high-rainfall area of the Angola highlands and with its abundant tropical waters flows south into the Kalahari: the open swamps of the shallow basin in which it comes to rest are linked to the Chobe river, which runs out of the delta's north-eastern shoulder and joins the Zambezi.

If Livingstone had no more than a mental sketch of this geography before reaching the lake he was able to confirm from the people there that Ngami was within striking distance of the Zambezi. And any mental sketch he may have had came from verbal reports about the Zambezi kingdom of Sebitwane and his Kololo people. The southern African peoples of Livingstone's day lived by no means in splendid isolation from each other. Moshoeshoe I of the Basuto corresponded with Sechele of the Bakwena, three hundred miles to his north-west, while Sechele was a friend of Sebitwane, a further five hundred miles away. Any European explorer who, like Livingstone, spoke an African language was by no means going into the unknown when he travelled into the unmarked spaces on European maps. We can assume that Sebitwane knew what was happening in Lesotho and that Sechele at Kolobeng was aware of events on the banks of both the Zambezi and Caledon rivers. All three of these leaders were products of the *mfecane*. Moshoeshoe had gathered around him clans broken and dispersed by the Zulu empire and founded the Basotho nation; Sebitwane, born near Moshoeshoe in what is today the Orange Free State, a South African province, had led his people first westwards and then north along the Kalahari fringe across the Zambezi to the floodplain of the upper reaches of the river which he had conquered and settled.

On his way north, Sebitwane had intervened in a Bakwena dynastic dispute and ensured Sechele's victory. By the mid-nineteenth century the *mfecane* in southern Africa had all but run its course, though the coherence of regional geopolitics was now coming under direct threat from both Boer and Briton. Moshoeshoe was the elder statesman of the sub-continent and had met the challenge by using missionaries as moral armour against white aggression. Sechele used Livingstone in the same way. Sebitwane may have been beyond the range of white ambition at the time but he was under threat from one other aggressive offshoot of the *mfecane*, Mzilikazi and his Ndebele in western Zimbabwe: might not the Kololo neutralise this danger by installing a missionary of their own, especially one like Livingstone, part of the family of Robert Moffat, himself a friend of Mzilikazi?

By the time Livingstone and Oswell had arrived back at Kolobeng from Ngami they had decided to visit Sebitwane and the Zambezi. They could not undertake the journey until the following April – the Kalahari during the summer months was too hot and dangerous – and Oswell decided to employ the intervening six months going to the Cape to buy supplies and a boat which would enable them to use the Botletle and the Okavango waterways. By the time he returned in May 1850 with the boat (unfortunately made useless by the warping of the timbers) Livingstone had already left, 'unable', Oswell laconically remarked, 'to resist the desire and opportunity of being the first to visit Sebituane.' Oswell went off hunting with William John Thomas and other retainers. Oswell was right about Livingstone's motives but the expedition was a failure. Livingstone took with him Mary, as well as their children Robert who was four, Agnes, a year younger, and Thomas, a babe in arms. Mary was pregnant. Common sense might have dictated that this was not a suitable entourage for a twelve-hundred mile wagon journey through dangerous country, but it may be that common sense was overridden by Mary herself, not prepared to put up with another lengthy spell without her husband at Kolobeng. How the mission itself was expected to function during these absences we do not know but the casualness with which Livingstone went on these journeys reflects, even with the most generous interpretation, his disillusion with sedentary mission work. Livingstone had no permission from the LMS for the first Ngami trip, nor for the second, though he did keep Moffat informed.

Travelling by ox wagon through friendly country can be a great pleasure, with its rhythm of camping at watering places, outspanning and inspanning, covering up to twenty-five miles on a good day. The Livingstone family's Ngami journey had little of that, however. After a bad season water was scarce (if they had got used to eating frogs and locusts at Kolobeng they now had to drink, after two days' thirst, from fouled pools), the wagon fell into a pit trap, the oxen were in danger from tsetse; and at Ngami they were consumed by mosquitoes. What is more, fever struck and, for the first time, the Livingstones experienced malaria. A few days after the return to Kolobeng, with sickly children and Mary beyond her time, a daughter – Elizabeth Mary – was born, only to die six weeks later. Mary herself, stressed and exhausted to the point of collapse, developed a paralysis of one side of her body and was taken to Kuruman to recuperate.

If Livingstone did not reach Sebitwane, he collected information useful to his plans: Ngami was not a viable route to the Zambezi – tsetse formed a potential barrier to ox transport once the Kalahari had been crossed, fever was prevalent. With hindsight, it is strange that he did not make the remotest connection between fever and mosquitoes though he knew by now that cattle acquired infection from the bite of the tsetse fly which, he believed, 'injected a poison', as did a scorpion.

This second Ngami journey was not the last abortive and potentially disastrous expedition Livingstone was to make, but like those that lay in the future it did nothing to deflect him from his purpose and in the following year he and Oswell set off again northwards, accompanied once more, despite passionate pleas from the Moffats, by Mary (yet another time pregnant) and the children. Oswell, too, thought it unwise to take the family but could not prevent it. The expedition left towards the end of April 1851, and instead of going via Ngami, struck due north once it reached the Botletle, crossed the hundred-mile wide Makarikari salt pan and arrived at the edge of the swamps on 13th June. Livingstone and Oswell left Mary and the children outspanned there and took to canoes which carried them to the Chobe river. There they met emissaries sent by Sebitwane, and on 21st June, met the king himself who had boated four hundred miles down the Zambezi from his northern capital, Naliele, to welcome the visitors. That he knew they were coming, and when they were to be expected, says much for the efficacy of an intelligence system based on the 'bush telegraph'.

Sebitwane was an impressive figure. Oswell minced no muscular Christian words in remembering him:

> This really great Chief – far and away the finest Kafir I ever saw – he was the fastest runner and best fighter among [the Kololo]; just, though stern, with a wonderful power of attaching men to himself, he was a gentleman in thought and manner . . .
>
> In the dead of night he paid us a visit alone, and sat down very quietly and mournfully by the fire. Livingstone and I woke up and greeted him, and then he dreamily recounted the history of his life, his wars, escapes, successes and conquests, and the far distanced wandering in his raids.

Shortly after the first encounter, Sebitwane insisted on meeting Mary, and he, Livingstone and Oswell canoed to the outspan. There, the king noticed that the oxen were showing symptoms of tsetse infection, and promised to replace them from his own herds. Sebitwane and his retinue had been at the outspan only a few days when he fell ill with an infection of the lungs, which Livingstone attributed to an old spear wound in the chest. 'I saw his danger,' wrote Livingstone in *Missionary Travels*, 'but being a stranger feared to treat him medically lest in the event of his death I should be blamed by his people.' Sebitwane did indeed die, while being taken by his retainers to Linyanti, the southern capital of the kingdom, where he was buried. He was forty-five years old.

As with Sehamy, Livingstone's grief overflowed: 'Poor Sebituane,' he cried to his Journal in an entry of 6th July 1851:

> My heart bleeds for thee, and what would I not do for thee now that nothing can be done! Where art thou now! I will weep for thee till the day of my death . . . I will weep for thee, my brother, and I would cast forth my sorrows in despair for thy condition, for I know that thou wilt receive no injustice whither thou art gone . . . I do not wonder at the Roman Catholics praying for the dead. If I could believe as they do, I would pray for them too.

While it is interesting to see the modification in Livingstone's determinism – Sehamy's fate was 'fixed' (perhaps Oswell's Anglicanism had softened his views) – Livingstone was mourning for more than Sebitwane. He and Livingstone had discussed the establishment of the mission before death intervened, and Livingstone was afraid that without Sebitwane he would not be able to proceed. However, he failed to appreciate the political continuity of the Kololo state. Sebitwane was succeeded by his daughter Mamochisane, who at the time of his death was at Naliele. A few weeks after the funeral she sent a message downriver that her father's promises to Livingstone and Oswell were to be honoured, that fresh oxen were to be given them, and that they were to continue prospecting for a suitable mission site. The Livingstones were also provided with labourers to establish a garden.

When permission came from Mamochisane, Livingstone and Oswell travelled on horseback the eighty miles north-east of Linyanti to Sesheke on the Zambezi (Mary and the children stayed at the outspan). Livingstone was overwhelmed by the beauty and promise of the broad river, flowing steadily between wooded banks. A greater contrast to the scorching Kalahari and the swamps of Ngami and Chobe would be difficult to imagine, or to the puny Orange and the 'grey, green, greasy, Limpopo'.

After his years at Chonwane and Kolobeng on the fringes of the desert, Livingstone was obsessed by water and fascinated by rivers. He and Oswell prepared a detailed map of the waterways related to the upper Zambezi, using instruments to plot latitude and longitude for the stretches they visited, and verbal information from local people for what lay beyond the horizon. The map, remarkably accurate, is printed in Oswell's biography. They stayed only a few days at Sesheke, arriving on 4th August and returning to Mary in time to depart south for Kolobeng on the 13th. Livingstone had wanted to travel along the Zambezi but Oswell insisted on ending the expedition, as he foresaw difficulties in the tsetse-infested country, and had to be in England in 1852. Besides, any delay beyond August would entail crossing the Kalahari during the worst time of the year. The party reached the Botletle in September, and on its banks Mary gave birth to her fifth child who was named William Oswell. The Livingstones had to remain beside the Botletle for a month after the confinement, and Oswell went ahead to prepare the way to Kolobeng.

The last leg of the journey saw Livingstone making friends with another wealthy young Englishman, William Frederick Webb, a landowner. He had fallen ill while hunting, and was taken to Kolobeng to recover. When the Livingstones arrived home they found that Sechele and the Bakwena had moved away to a better-watered place. The mission was dead: but Livingstone did not grieve for his visit to the Zambezi, his discussions with Oswell (if not with Mary), his eager reception by the Kololo (who with the forthcoming rainy season would be planting a garden for him), had convinced him that his hopes could be realised in central Africa.

The Kololo kingdom's heartland was the valley of the upper Zambezi, most of which consists of a wide plain that floods every year towards the end of the rains. Sebitwane and the Kololo took over this fertile and tsetse-free area from the original Lui (or Lozi) kingdom, and also held sway over the high lands of the Batoka plateau to the east. Kololo rule started about 1840 and was based on the devolution of power to district chiefs. The Kololo, being Sotho speaking, introduced that language to the region, where it rapidly became the lingua franca: since Sotho is closely related to Tswana, Livingstone had no difficulty in conversing with Sebitwane or other Kololo, another factor in making the region attractive. In addition, the valley was, by contemporary standards, densely populated and the Kololo were interested in trade.

One of the first things that struck Livingstone and Oswell when they met Sebitwane and his retinue was the imported cloth they were wearing: it was obtained from Angolan Ovimbundu traders, known as 'Mambari' who had links with the Portuguese entrepôts on the Atlantic coast. Their contacts with the upper Zambezi dated from the end of the eighteenth century, but actual trade commenced only shortly before Livingstone and Oswell's visit – the pre-Kololo Lozi had not been interested. Two facets of Livingstone's hopeful vision thus existed there in 1851: 'smoke rising from a thousand huts', and a potential trading economy. The third, which provided the moral imperative, was that the Mambari exchanged their goods – cloth and firearms – for slaves.

As the slave trade was only just starting, Livingstone and Oswell agreed that it could best be stopped by putting into practice the Buxton remedy: Christianity, commerce, and civilisation, and that this could be done only by the establishment of Christian, and legitimate, trading enterprise through which local produce would be exchanged for manufactured imports. The slave trade would become uneconomic as the labour of potential export slaves would be needed for local production. The parameters of this vision went far beyond the policies of missionary societies. The LMS, for example, might agree to – even welcome – the establishment of trading posts alongside its stations, as was the case at Kuruman and consequently be supported by merchants such as Rutherfoord in Cape Town. But it would not allow its members to trade on their own account. Livingstone believed that commerce was essential to success, that the three 'Cs' were as inseparable as the three persons of the Holy Trinity. In time, as his ideas matured, he added another 'C' – colonisation – and was thinking seriously about its implications by 1852, as we know from his request to Moffat to send him a copy of the *Natal Times*, of 24th October 1851, containing a discussion of the labour problems of British settlers in that colony, many of whom had gone to Natal with the support of British 'Christian colonisation' societies.

Two practical problems had to be solved before Livingstone could cast any foundation for his establishment. First, he had to find a suitable site in Kololo territory (which henceforth we shall call Barotseland, the name by which it is best known today) away from the tsetse and fever-ridden swamps he and Oswell visited. Then he had to open a route to the coast less dangerous and more direct than the Kalahari crossing to the Cape. The ideal for this purpose would be a navigable river, but though the upper Zambezi looked propitious, he and Oswell learned that there was a large waterfall some hundred miles east of Sesheke which cut any water route there might be to the long navigable stretch of the lower river in Mozambique. Livingstone, while at Sesheke, therefore decided to go to the west coast, from whence the Mambari came; he hoped that the upper Zambezi would prove navigable far enough northwards to make a route to Luanda. It was obvious that Mary and the children could not possibly accompany him on a prospecting journey of such length and Livingstone decided to send them to Scotland to stay with his parents. Why Mary could not have stayed at Kuruman with her own parents we do not know. Perhaps the prospect for Mary of being once again under her mother's thumb was more than she could face, perhaps Oswell had persuaded the Livingstones that it was time for the elder children to start getting a proper education.

The Livingstones stayed only a few days at Kolobeng. Sechele came the ten miles from his new town to see them, and presented an ox. Oswell had not stopped but gone on direct to Cape Town. In the early days of December 1851 Mary, who was ill with a recurrence of the paralysis, said her final farewell to Kolobeng and the only home she would ever call her own. Ten years of nomadic misery and humiliation were all that remained of her short life. After breaking the journey south for a fortnight at Kuruman the family in its ox-wagon entered Cape Town in March 1852, a Crusoe caravan wearing bush clothes with Tswana speaking children and a troop of servants. It was the first time in more than a decade that Livingstone had been in 'civilisation'.

Oswell had arrived before them and set about making their life more comfortable. He supplied Livingstone with £200 (twice the amount of his LMS salary), smoothing his scruples about accepting charity by insisting that the money was not a handout but the proceeds from ivory that came from 'Livingstone's estate'. Part of the money was used to clothe the family for the voyage to Britain, and for Britain itself. When Mary's ship sailed on 23rd April Livingstone was to say goodbye to her and the children for four and a half years. The LMS had agreed to his trans-Zambezi expedition, and his salary would be used to pay for the family's upkeep in Britain. But even if Mary did not realise how long they would be apart (the LMS had provided for a two year absence) and even if she were apprehensive, her husband seems to have been confident both of his own survival and of the family's security under his parents' roof. We cannot know what David and Mary talked about before parting, but reading between the lines of a letter he wrote her, on 5th May 1852, soon after she sailed, we can imagine bitter painful words:

> My dearest Mary,
> How I miss you and the dear children! My heart yearns incessantly over you. How many thoughts of the past crowd into my mind. I feel as if I would treat you all much more tenderly and lovingly than ever. You have been a great blessing to me. You attended to my comfort in many ways.
>
> May God bless you for all your kindnesses. I see no face now to be compared with that sunburnt one which has so often greeted me with its kind looks. Let us do our duty to our Saviour and we shall meet again. I wish that time were now.
>
> You may read the letters over again which I wrote at Mabotsa, the sweet time you know. As I told you before, I tell you again, they are

true, true; there is not a bit of hypocrisy in them. I never show all my feelings; but I can say truly, my dearest, that I loved you when I married you and the longer I lived with you, I loved you the better [letter cut] . . . Let us do our duty to Christ and he will bring us through the world with honour and usefulness . . .

This letter was sent by steamship, which would reach England before Mary. Her husband's words may have consoled her somewhat but his expectation that she would settle in with his parents proved vain. The elder Livingstones and David's two sisters had been living in a cottage in Hamilton since 1839, when they had moved from Blantyre. Neil was sixty-five, his wife Agnes seventy-one, their daughters Janet and Agnes thirty-four and twenty-nine respectively. Janet and Agnes were trying to earn a living as milliners. At the time, Mary was thirty-one and her four children aged between six and one. A small cottage, which was also a place of business, with Neil's tea chests, packets, and scales, and his daughters' lace, cloth, pins, needles and thread, is a dwelling that calls for the greatest discipline and restraint from its inhabitants. The most heartfelt charity in the world would find it difficult to accommodate a single stranger, let alone a troupe arriving from the Kalahari with Mary used to running a house and giving orders to servants, the children accustomed to cavorting half-naked in the sunshine and sand and speaking English in a most peculiar way.

Mary and the children stayed at Hamilton for about six months, and then started four years of wandering across England, staying now with Livingstone's friends, now in lodging houses. Mary was always short of money and Livingstone alleges that the LMS did not pay her the full amounts due from his salary, and that after paying for the children, she was left with only £45. When she fell ill, doctors' fees had to be found by friends, and the LMS refused to let her have the fare to travel to Kuruman. She began to drink heavily, and her comments on the missionary fraternity were anything but flattering. Mary had been in Britain a year when Neil felt constrained to write to the LMS in June 1853: 'Mrs L does not write to us, nor are we anxious that she should.'

During his four and a half years of separation from his family, David was hardly aware of the misery they were enduring. From his few letters to them it seems that he assumed that all was well, financially at least: he later excoriated the LMS for what he considered its meanness but made little allowance for his own absence which lasted more than two years longer than he had originally arranged.

He was in Cape Town for three months between March and June 1852. Oswell was there for part of the time. As we have seen, he gave Livingstone money for Mary and the children, but also presumably for

David's own long trek across Africa to Luanda. Livingstone had no savings and was in fact in debt to the LMS as a result of his habit of drawing advances on salary, both for his own needs and to send subventions to his brother Charles – studying for the ministry at Oberlin, Ohio – and to his sisters whom David was trying to persuade to emigrate. Before Oswell sailed for England – he left before Mary – he and Livingstone wrote a twenty-four page report for the Royal Geographical Society on their journey to the Zambezi.

Oswell never returned to south Africa but he took with him to England the servant he had recruited there, the former slave William John Thomas: as Oswell was preparing to leave he asked Thomas what he could give him as a reward for his loyal service. Thomas asked to be given passage to England and Oswell, once they arrived, found him work as coachman to his country parson brother, with the recommendation that a man who could handle a span of oxen across the Kalahari and the Karroo was quite capable of driving a coach and four. Thomas did not stay at this job long as Oswell met him again in the course of the Crimean War of 1854–1856 when Oswell was serving in Intelligence and Thomas was manservant to an officer in the Rifle Brigade. After the war, Oswell helped him to get a post as butler, and Thomas spent the last years of his life in the service of Mr Nathaniel Powell of Buckhurst Hill, Essex, who was a magistrate, a wine merchant, a renowned maker of glass, and a friend of William Morris. When Thomas died in 1864, Oswell travelled a hundred and fifty miles 'to take a last look at the dead face of my friend', and then erected a tombstone at the grave in Buckhurst Hill churchyard. The lengthy epitaph, which outlines Thomas's life, concludes with these words:

> In early life he was the right hand of him who on this stone would record the unwavering fidelity, cheerfulness and truth of a most unselfish Companion, Servant and Friend, tried amidst many wanderings, much need and some danger. May God in His mercy, for Christ's sake pardon master and man, and grant that they may meet hereafter as brothers.

Thomas, nicknamed 'Bono Johnny', was a tall, impressively built man, and women found him attractive, but there is no known record of his having married or had children. He was one of the first South Africans – and by no means the last – to leave the country, for whatever reason, and may have been spurred on his way by the high tension that prevailed at the Cape at the time of his departure. In the east of the colony, the Eighth Frontier War was in progress, with the British authorities in severe difficulties. In addition, many of the Khoi within the colony had risen in rebellion, so great were their grievances twenty years after they were supposed to have been given civil equality.

Dr Philip, whose views on these matters would be easy to imagine, had died in 1851 and Livingstone stepped into his place as a voice of protest. He declared that the colonial authorities were wrong in their forward policy of conquest, epitomised in the long succession of wars on the eastern frontier; that African peoples were entitled to fight for their land and freedom, and that if the Khoi had rebelled, that was no more than a symptom of bad government: 'We are no advocates of war,' Livingstone wrote in an as yet unpublished seventy-eight page pamphlet now in the National Archives of Zimbabwe,

> ... but we would prefer perpetual war to perpetual slavery. No nation ever secured liberty without fighting for it. And every nation on earth worthy of freedom is ready to shed its blood in its defence. We sympathize with the Caffres [i.e. the Xhosa of the eastern frontier], we side with the weak against the strong ...

If this general comment were not forceful enough, his remarks about the Cape Town treason trial following the Kat River Rebellion, stabbed at the heart of colonial morality:

> It is probable that no worse example could be quoted, from any part of the world, than what I witnessed in Cape Town in 1852, when in a Government prosecution a poor black officer [Andries Botha, a 'hottentot' rebel] of forty years service, the [Chief Justice] frequently indulged in jokes and at last called for a wine bottle, from which he took frequent swills, screwing up his mouth after each swill as if he did not like it. He had the sentence of death prepared before the jury gave their verdict, and a more disgusting, diabolical spectacle could scarcely be imagined than to see this old man [Sir John Wylde 1781–1859] gloating over his victim and foaming at the mouth in pronouncing sentence of death.

Apart from these biting attacks on the British administration, Livingstone was involved in controversy with the Boers, who accused him of supplying firearms, including a cannon, to Sechele and the Bakwena, charges which Livingstone denied vigorously and sarcastically. The cannon, for example, was a Boer transmogrification of a cast iron cooking pot he had given Sechele. But the fact was that the Bakwena did possess guns, and Livingstone may well have helped them to get them from traders, while he had himself presented a rifle to the chief near Ngami.

And not even the renown he had won from the Ngami journey could save him from petty persecutions, such as the official refusal of a permit to buy gunpowder for his own rifles, or a libel action instituted by a rural postmaster whom Livingstone was said to have accused of overcharging on his mail. However, he prepared thoroughly for his expedition. On the personal side, he had his troublesome uvula removed by surgery. On the scientific side he made friends with the Astronomer Royal at the Cape, Thomas Maclear, a fellow Scot, and from him learned how to take latitude and longitude properly, using the sextant given him by Steele and a chronometer bought with the Ngami prize money. Maclear remained a friend for the rest of Livingstone's life, their correspondence virtually uninterrupted over twenty years. To test the validity of his suppositions about trade, Livingstone arranged with Rutherfoord the merchant for George Fleming, a freed West Indian slave who had moved to the Cape, to accompany him with a load of merchandise to barter with the Kololo. Livingstone was to be helped by him again, at the end of the transcontinental journey, in Mozambique in 1856.

Livingstone happily left Cape Town (he described colonial society as 'effluvia') at the beginning of June 1852 and reached Kuruman towards the end of August, where he was joined a few weeks later by Fleming. While there they learned that the Boers' antipathy to Livingstone had come to a head. By the Sand River Convention of 1852 the British had given de facto recognition to the independence of the Transvaal Boers, who proceeded to set about securing their frontiers – one element of this campaign was the crushing of Sechele. They attacked him and the Bakwena in mid-September, killing more than a hundred and taking scores of prisoners (including children of Sechele) who would be used as labour. After the raid, some of the Boers looted Livingstone's house at Kolobeng, smashing it up, destroying books and medicines, and stealing furniture. Livingstone advised Sechele to seek redress from the British but the Governor of the Cape washed his hands of the matter and refused the Chief permission to travel to London to present his case to the government.

The Boer raids and incursions caused so much fear that Livingstone was holed up at Kuruman for two months because he could not get drivers to accompany him and Fleming northwards. When they eventually departed, Livingstone left in Moffat's care the first full draft of *Analysis of the Language of the Bechuanas* which he had completed while waiting to travel. In mid-February he said goodbye to Kolobeng, and even if he thought he might one day return, he could feel that he was leaving with a clear conscience since it was, in all but name, destroyed. In his twelve years in the region he had made only one convert, Sechele (who later lapsed, caught on the thorny question of polygamy), but he had done the groundwork for future missionaries.

In the Cape Colony he had observed the implementation of a British colonial policy just as aggressive as that of the Boers and had seen how emancipation from the slavery of status had brought to people like William John Thomas and Andries Botha not civil liberty but the slavery of race. He had seen how ineffectual orthodox missionary effort could be and how easily dedicated Christians, such as the Scottish ministers Robertson and Murray, serving with the Boers, could absorb and strengthen the ethos of colonial society. His experience of south Africa gave him the background to formulate his ideas on how to put his 'Christianity Commerce and Civilisation' into practice.

When he and Fleming arrived at the Kololo capital on 23rd May 1853 – almost a year after they had left Cape Town – Livingstone was ready to endure any hardship to realize his ideals.

8

SLAVE RIVERS

A new king was on the Kololo throne when Livingstone arrived at Linyanti, Sekeletu, brother of Sebitwane's successor Mamochisane, who had abdicated in her brother's favour. He was eighteen years old, and the continuity between his policy towards Livingstone and his father's was symbolised in the garden which had been planted for Livingstone at Linyanti and which was yielding maize for him at the time of his return.

For the first time, Livingstone found himself the guest of a fully functioning African kingdom. The Kololo had taken over the structure of the Lozi state they had conquered, but had introduced a number of innovations. The most important of these, as far as Livingstone was concerned, was a readiness to trade – unlike the defeated Lozi who were content in the self-sufficiency of the upper Zambezi floodplain where the annual inundation at the end of the rainy season allowed the development of an economy far richer than that on the true African savannah. The phenomenon of the yearly flood made Livingstone think of Egypt and strengthened his hopes that Barotseland could become the centre of a great civilisation. He constantly made comparisons between the material culture of central Africa and the ancient Nile valley, besides, as we have seen, correlating the languages. In his last years he developed a passionate belief that the Nile and the Zambezi rose beside each other at the Fountains of Herodotus at a place yet to be discovered in equatorial Africa.

In Barotseland, Livingstone's first objective was to find a site for his mission and trading station. Linyanti was not suitable as it was in a swampy area, difficult of access, and fever-ridden. Livingstone had his first attack of malaria there. To examine prospects further north Sekeletu took him (and a retinue of one hundred and sixty) two hundred miles up the Zambezi in a flotilla of canoes to Naliele, his second capital, built on a mound in the middle of the floodplain. No suitable site was found en route so, while Sekeletu stayed at Naliele with his court, Livingstone continued upriver for another hundred miles, with equally disappointing results. He was looking for a place on high ground which, he assumed, would be free of fever and clear of the swamps and marshes which at that time of year, just after the flood recedes, are the most characteristic feature of the plain. On either side of the flat valley, which is up to twenty miles wide, the land rises a few hundred feet to the level of the central African plateau, but there is no true high ground in Barotseland and malaria is prevalent throughout the area. Livingstone suffered seven attacks of the disease during the nine weeks of touring before he and Sekeletu were back at Linyanti in September.

However, if Livingstone's idea of a settlement had to be put aside for the time being his ideas on trade persisted. As we have seen, he and Oswell had been struck by the Kololo's possession of goods brought by traders from the Atlantic coast: now, on his travels with Sekeletu, Livingstone had encountered parties of traders themselves, one from the east coast, the other from the west.

The Kololo desire to trade was not a policy developed in a vacuum, for they were on the perimeter of a central African commercial network that had been in existence for centuries. The first threads of this web were spun as many as a thousand years ago with the exchange of essential commodities between areas of differing productive capacities. Iron for salt, dried fish for grain, copper for pottery, are examples of the internal commerce of central Africa brought to light by archaeology. By the eleventh century, merchants from Asia and the middle east were operating on the east coast, joining the central network to that of the Indian Ocean; in the fifteenth century, the network was linked to the West through Portuguese establishments on the Atlantic coast. During the eighteenth and the first three-quarters of the nineteenth century, two export commodities were paramount, ivory and slaves. In earlier days copper going east had been important and later, rubber and beeswax going to Europe.

All long distance trade, including that in copper, depended on slavery; only human beings could carry goods to the coast, animal transport being impossible because of the tsetse fly. The tsetse detests the concentrated smell of humans but will readily attack a span of oxen; human sleeping sickness, which Livingstone never saw, is also carried by the fly.

Domestic slavery was an essential feature of the social structure of the kingdoms of central Africa, and in the course of time became the basis for the slave trade itself. Slaves had been exported from Africa since the rise of civilisations north and east of the Mediterranean and by the tenth century there was a flourishing trade between the Indian Ocean coast and the middle east. By the sixteenth century the Atlantic trade was well under way having started in Portuguese ships about 1450.

Livingstone had no illusions about ending domestic slavery and even benefitted from it. The system continued in Barotseland until the present century, and within living memory children could be frightened into obedience by being told that they would be 'sold to the Mambari'. Some of Livingstone's porters were no doubt Sekeletu's slaves. But he was determined to see the export trade brought to a halt, for it had created what remained the greatest blot on the English-speaking world's Christian conscience, the slave economy of the United States of America. Only when that blot was removed could his civilization justify its claim to world-wide moral ascendancy. Livingstone had a direct link with the United States through his brother Charles who, by the time David was in Barotseland, had completed his studies at Oberlin and was working as a pastor in New York state. Oberlin College, Ohio, was an Abolitionist centre during a period when American Protestant churches were splitting into pro- and anti-slavery factions. David knew the debate and on occasion rebuked Charles for repeating the argument that American slaves were no worse off than British industrial workers.

Although the import of slaves to the United States had been outlawed by the Federal government, smuggling from Cuba or Brazil continued and these countries were, in turn, importing from Africa despite British patrols in the Atlantic. The presence of west coast traders on the upper Zambezi thus formed a potential link between Sekeletu's river and the Mississippi. This is no doubt one reason why, while on his way to the Zambezi in 1853, Livingstone ordered from London a copy of a recently published novel, *Uncle Tom's Cabin*, by Harriet Beecher Stowe. He did not often read novels (one other he mentions is Thomas Hughes's *Tom Brown's Schooldays*, which is about Rugby, of which Oswell was an old boy) and would have wanted *Uncle Tom* less for entertainment than for its polemic: the book impressed him enough for him to quote from it.

The genius of Harriet Beecher Stowe's novel lies on one level, in the tenseness of its plot and sub-plots (despite its having been written as a serial) and at another, in the way in which the debate about slavery and (since American slaves were of African descent) about race grows so naturally out of the narrative. The author was a fervent Christian in the independent, Congregationalist tradition, a northerner who had lived long enough on the Mason-Dixon line to have seen slavery at first hand. Her novel is an ideologically Christian embodiment of Buxton's *African Slave Trade and its Remedy* throwing the questions into the American context she knew and answering them. Broadly speaking, the novel's questions are these: is slavery evil; how can it be abolished; what should happen to the freed slaves?

The first question may seem fatuous to a majority of people today, but in the 1850s of white America it lay at the heart of the debate. One group of Christians argued that slavery was part of God's plan and that, by bringing unbelievers into Christian society, it provided them with the opportunity of salvation: it was therefore good. Others stated that blacks were sub-human, did not have souls, and could therefore be used like animals. To this second argument Stowe replies by creating characters like the black Uncle Tom, his wife and children, who are all too obviously human, and saintly besides, in contrast to the white plantation owner Legree, who is eminently wicked. To the former question Stowe's answer is that slavery denies the slave freedom of choice and thus removes the chance of electing for Christ, while at the same time slavery engenders such a hatred for the slave-owner – and, by extension, his religion – that the slave sees Christianity as an evil itself. Additionally, slavery corrupts the slave-owner, enmeshing him in evil and making him incapable of salvation: Christians become or remain slave-owners at the peril of their souls.

Having established that slavery is evil, the novel examines methods of abolition. It allows that the system might come to an end as a result of economic forces, for example, if the market value of plantation crops were to fall below the level required to maintain a slave establishment (bearing in mind that slave labour was a permanent overhead, unlike the free labour force in British industry), or, if machinery were to prove cheaper than slaves in both capital and maintenance costs. But the author regards these factors as speculative and does not pursue them. Nor is there any sympathy for the idea that the slaves might free themselves by revolution – the overthrow of white rule in Haiti by Toussaint Louverture and his successors was still a lively memory and the novel would have lost the bulk of its white readership if that path had been advocated. No, slaves could be liberated only by true Christianity in action.

This proposition is advanced vigorously and three examples are given. In Uncle Tom's case one is negative, the other positive. After being sold by his owner, Shelby, Tom becomes the property of St Clair, a generous and good hearted man who treats the slave as 'one of the family'. But St Clair is sceptical about Christianity and his style of life is totally devoid of the Protestant work ethic; he promises to set Tom free, but dallies over having the manumission drawn up and dies before signing the papers. As a result of St Clair's negation of true Christianity, Tom remains a slave, is sold off as part of the deceased estate, finds himself the property of the diabolical Legree and is taken to his plantation. There, Tom refuses to act as Legree's flogger and, as a result, is flogged to death himself. Shelby's son, armed with manumission money arrives at Legree's just in time to be with Tom as he dies. Young Shelby is so moved by this martyrdom that he is converted and, as a true Christian, sets free the slaves on the estate he has inherited from his father. The ex-slaves are happy to continue working for Shelby as wage earners (as Livingstone would say, 'free labour replacing slave labour').

The third example concerns the novel's heroine, Eliza, and her husband George Harris. Both escape from their respective owners and are saved from recapture solely by the intervention of the true Christian Quakers of Ohio and delivered to Christian sanctuary in Canada where British law prevails and they are safe.

On the question of what is to happen to the freed slaves the novel offers two answers. As we have seen the Shelby slaves become employees but as the novel's readers would have known it was almost unheard of for manumitted slaves to carry on working for the previous owner so the Shelby case can be no more than an ideal. The novel's real solution is provided in the lives of Eliza and George Harris and their children who, by now all devout Christians, emigrate to Africa, participants in the 'colonisation' movement which had been launched to remove all blacks from the United States and resettle them west on the African littoral. (Livingstone opposed this idea, believing, perhaps from his time spent with George Fleming, that trans-Atlantic black people were as foreign to Africa as Europeans.)

Another American novelist of the period, Herman Melville, offers a rebuttal of the 'Uncle Tom' thesis in his story *Benito Cereno*, published three years after the Stowe novel. Slaves, 'transatlantic emigrants' as he ironically calls them, being transported by sea along the South American coast, stage a revolution, take over the ship, set up a government, hold the ship's master hostage and plan to return to their individual homes – not to a 'Liberia' – in Africa. Their plans are brought to nothing when a Yankee sea-captain who 'took to negroes not philanthropically, but genially' (that is to say, he was a sort of St Clair) intervenes: the outcome is that the hostage is able to escape, his ship is re-taken by the Americans, the slaves are sent back to the smith's to be reshackled, their leader is executed. The story suggests that only through revolution can slaves be made free and that intervention, by even the 'genial', causes re-enslavement. Enslavement, too, takes many forms, as the history of African-Americans since 1864 shows and as Livingstone saw in the post-emancipation Cape Colony.

The slave dealers Livingstone met on the upper Zambezi were a Portuguese, Silva Porto, with his Mambari followers from Angola, and a party of Swahili-Arabs from Zanzibar. Their presence was a shock because it showed that the area could no longer be regarded as Livingstone's alone, either as a place of trade or of discovery, for Silva Porto had already visited the upper Zambezi before Livingstone and Oswell made the journey. The Zanzibaris' objectives were commercial but Silva Porto had two concerns, commerce and empire; the extension of Portuguese authority across central Africa to link Angola with Mozambique.

The basis of trade was the exchange of manufactured goods –

mainly cloth-lengths used as currency – for ivory and slaves which were inextricably enmeshed. The export of slaves from Angola was illegal, which had reduced that market on the Atlantic coast, but trade in ivory had increased substantially since the Portuguese had relaxed the state monopoly in 1842. World demand for ivory seemed insatiable: supplies from Asia were becoming scarcer while those from West Africa (for example, the Ivory Coast) were drying up as a result of over-exploitation. By the mid-nineteenth century the central African interior contained the world's largest reserves, excellent both in the quality of the grain and the size of the tusks.

The uses of ivory have followed the development of the human economy. At first it was made into tools, simple ornaments, and votive pieces, then used as a medium for sculpture, for carving and inlays. Ivory's properties – a pleasant texture and colour, the accuracy with which it can be worked, its hardness, durability and resistance to splitting or warping – have enabled people to make pieces of great beauty and intricacy and have also given it important utilitarian uses. The keys of the spinet and harpsicord may originally have been veneered with ivory merely to stop the player's fingers being scratched by slivers in the wood it hides but in time it became an essential part of the harpsicord's direct descendant, that most versatile of all musical instruments, the pianoforte, as it enables the player to run the fingers uninterruptedly along the keyboard.

During the nineteenth century industrial techniques made it possible to manufacture pianos at a price which many of the emerging European and American middle classes could afford and the instrument became the cornerstone of home entertainment, as well as being, one suspects, a status symbol. In many a nineteenth-century novel only the poorest of families is without its piano prominently in place. This factor, together with the erection of innumerable new churches and chapels, each with its ivory-keyed organ, not to mention the spread of games like billiards, led to an enormous demand for tusks, one of which yielded three billiard balls, two of which were needed for each piano. Every keyboard entailed one elephant killed and at least two slaves to carry the tusks to Luanda, Benguela, Zanzibar, Mombasa, or Khartoum.

Livingstone saw the relation between the slave and ivory trades and believed he could legitimise the latter and, in consequence, bankrupt the former. If African rulers, whose prerogatives included a monopoly in ivory, could be supplied with their manufactured imports by 'legitimate' traders (like George Fleming, who bartered his goods for ivory at Linyanti), the slave trade itself would become redundant.

In 1851, Livingstone had decided that he should strike out west for the Atlantic coast. Fleming's refusal to return to Linyanti, because of the problems which beset the Kalahari route, strengthened Livingstone's determination to find an alternative. Silva Porto offered to take him to Benguela but Livingstone preferred to go to Luanda: despite its being further away, there was a British presence there. It took two months to work out a plan of action with Sekeletu and his councillors, then on 11th November 1853, Livingstone and his party set out from Linyanti for the Angolan capital.

It was a year and a half since he had left Cape Town and only six months remained of his paid furlough from the LMS. He was worried about his relations with his employers, for he had failed to find a suitable Barotseland mission site, which he was commissioned to do. And though he may have thought that one might be located on his travels he was uneasy enough about his source of income to write to Thomas Steele from Linyanti on 24th September 1853 to ask whether it was possible that the British government might support him. Livingstone was not unaware that his geographical exploits were of great interest to the secular authorities and worked assiduously to extend their scope. A few days after writing to Steele he sent Maclear a sketch map with a set of latitudes and longitudes which made it possible to produce, for the first time, an accurate map of the upper Zambezi as far north as Livingstone had been. With this, Livingstone won Maclear's respect and an increase in his own reputation. As Astronomer Royal, Maclear was in a position to ensure that Livingstone received recognition for his contributions to knowledge. Ngami was a dubious triumph but the mapping of the upper Zambezi was original scientific work which, besides its own value, showed up the deficiencies of earlier Portuguese charts and gave Britain the lead in the cartography of central Africa. Maclear published Livingstone's material in the Cape Town press and also sent it to the British Foreign Secretary, Lord John Russell, 'whose eyes,' Maclear wrote in May 1854 to the LMS agent at Cape Town, 'may perhaps be [distracted] for an instant from the sad scenes now in progress', the 'sad scenes' being the Crimean War.

Livingstone departed from Linyanti with twenty-seven porters pro-vided by the Barotseland government. His own contribution to the expenses of the expedition was minimal, little more than a box of trade beads, since money (even if he had any) would be useless. Sekeletu also supplied a number of oxen, one for Livingstone to ride – he named it Sinbad after the legendary Arab traveller – the others to be slaughtered for food, as well as ivory to be used as currency. Livingstone's own supplies included his scientific instruments, a box of clothing, a box for his papers, some tea and sugar, a bible and a magic lantern. This last piece of advanced nineteenth-century technology Livingstone used in attempts to blind his African audiences with science and Christianity.

The expedition expected to live off the hospitality of the people through whose territory it passed: Livingstone was not only financed by

Sekeletu, he was totally dependent on African goodwill at least until he reached Portuguese settlements. As long as the route lay through lands where Sekeletu's name was respected, all went well as far as hospitality was concerned. But Livingstone was travelling perforce during the rainy season when both ground conditions and disease were at their worst. His path crossed regions where seventy or eighty inches of rain might fall in a five month period, sometimes in downpours which would last a fortnight, and with an amazing efflorescence of insect life, from beetles the size of hamsters to mosquitoes in clouds, not to mention biting flies and a plethora of ticks. He was continually laid low with fever and dysentery (since he did not know that microbes cause illness, he did not boil drinking water), and often continually wet, day and night. '[I] Had a terrible attack of Rheumatic fever,' he wrote on 18th May, 1854, to R B Rawson in Cape Town, 'from sleeping some days on a plain on which the water was flowing ankle deep. We had trenches round our berths, but I had 25 days of it and am now very weak, having lost much time besides.'

As soon as the party left the grassy Barotse plain, it entered a different ecological zone, with high and dense forest which to this day seems to stretch endlessly to the horizon until it joins the true equatorial rain forest of the Zaire basin. The party also entered a different political zone, beyond the southern African influence which, as we have seen, had been extended as far north as the upper Zambezi by the Kololo. Once he reached the point where the Zambezi swings east towards its source, Livingstone was on the marches of the Lunda empire. This extensive state was centred on the high savannah of what is today the Shaba province of Zaire where the king, the Mwata Yamvo, had his capital (the empire was in one sense a dyarchy in that the Queen had her own capital and court and exercised considerable authority in her own right). Over the centuries, the empire had expanded from its heartland on the upper reaches of the Lualaba river: the Lozi whom Sebitwane conquered on the upper Zambezi are a Lunda offshoot, while to the east a further Lunda kingdom, that of Mwata Kazembe lies along the Luapula, in the north of modern Zambia. By Livingstone's time, the Mwata Yamvos had been trading with the Portuguese for several hundred years, mainly in slaves and ivory.

Livingstone met one of the young Lunda princesses shortly after leaving Barotseland. Her name was Manenko and she made a deep impression on him: she bossed him around, called him 'my little man', shocked him with her near-nudity, but provided food and canoes and led him to her uncle, Shinde, the powerful chief on the western border of the empire. Livingstone was given a royal welcome at Shinde's palace, which he repaid with a magic-lantern show. He tried to present the chief with one of Sekeletu's oxen, but Manenko claimed it for herself on the grounds that it was she who had brought Livingstone to the palace. Shinde capitulated to his niece, just as Livingstone had done. In an entry on 8th January 1854 in his *African Journal* he describes the formidable lady as:

> ... a tall strapping woman of about twenty, distinguished by a profusion of ornaments and medicines hung about her person ... in a state of frightful nudity. This was not from want of clothing, for, being a chief, she might have been as well clad as any of her subjects, but from her peculiar style of elegance in dress. In the course of a quarrel with her entourage she advanced and receded in true oratorical style ... and, as usual in more civilized feminine lectures, she leaned over the objects of her ire, and screamed forth all their faults and failings ever since they were born, and her despair at ever seeing them better ... My men succumbed sooner to this petticoat government than I felt inclined to do, and left me no power.

Livingstone, 'Unwilling to encounter her tongue', did as she told him to.

He does not tell us whether the self-possessed Manenko demanded more from him than obedience and the ox but, seventy years after Livingstone, a traveller in the same region, H F Varian, who was surveying the route of the Benguela railway in 1920 recalls in his book *Some African Milestones* the power of women rulers there and the privileges they expected:

> The Nhakatola [the Princess] was described to me as a good-looking woman, with refined features and small hands and feet, not unlike the ancient Egyptians ... On my way through, I stopped at her headquarters, where her dwelling-place [was], a well-built three-roomed brick house with a verandah ... There I left my tribute in the shape of a roll of white trade calico, spotted blue. I was somewhat relieved to learn that she was away superintending the fish harvest, which was her largest source of revenue. I had been warned that she was apt to attach herself and suite to any party travelling through her realm, and if she fancied, she was accustomed to exercise a royal prerogative, and share both board and bed during her visit. I did not stop to inquire into the truth of this but ... hastily dropped my tribute and sped northwards ... I was not looking for romance with dusky queens, no matter how attractive, and I was in a hurry to get through.

For good measure, the traveller adds '... Until recent years, the natives of this part of the world were not in the habit of wearing cloth, and consequently were very scantily clad.'

At Shinde's, Livingstone felt like 'a voice crying in the wilderness amidst the masses of heathenism'. His magic-lantern had aroused no interest in Christianity, and Manenko, whether or not she offered him more than food and canoes, was a far cry from the role prescribed for Christian women by St Paul. However, Shinde helped him on his way with gifts, including a valuable amulet made of cowrie shell, and when he returned, was equally friendly. Livingstone did not see Manenko again after leaving Shinde's: when he passed through on his way back to Linyanti, she claimed that lameness caused by a burn prevented her from accompanying the gift of food she sent him.

Soon after leaving Lunda territory, Livingstone and his party were in the lands of the Chokwe. Shinde was prepared to be on good terms with Sekeletu, but the Chokwe, relative newcomers to the area were busy carving out a territory for themselves, impinging on the Lunda and hostile to anyone who might block their ambition to become masters of the trade routes to Mwata Yamvo and his protegés or allies. For the first time in his experience, Livingstone found himself among Africans who treated him with the opposite of friendship and hospitality. Apart from the nightmare journey around the Kalahari with his family in 1850, when drought had been the enemy, the three hundred mile trek through the Chokwe domain was the worst Livingstone had so far made; incessant rain, vast tracts of swampy ground, dense forest, frequent bouts of illness, shortage of food and clothing, and the open, sometimes murderous, hostility of the Chokwe. The morale of his party fell so low that he only prevented a full-scale mutiny by threatening to shoot: it was not until the party fell in with a helpful Portuguese militiaman at the Kwango river that any sense of security returned.

A few days later Livingstone's half-starved caravan shuffled into Cassange (Kasanji), the Portuguese settlement deepest in the interior, three hundred miles from the coast. The Portuguese Commandant of the town, Da Silva Rega, took the Livingstone party into his care. Nourishing food and dry sleeping quarters did a world of good and selling Sekeletu's ivory raised cash to buy clothing and supplies for the rest of the journey, which was resumed after a week, fortified with a militia guard and letters of introduction to Cassange merchants' friends in Luanda.

They arrived there at the end of May 1854, six weeks after leaving Cassange. Despite assistance from Portuguese at other stations on the way, Livingstone reached Luanda in a state of collapse, suffering fever and a chronic diarrhoea which prevented him from riding Sinbad for more than ten minutes at a time. Fortunately, the one and only British resident in Luanda, Edmund Gabriel, was a man of great sympathy. He took Livingstone into his house and nursed him back to health, made sure that the Kololo porters were properly looked after and accommodated. Gabriel was Her Britannic Majesty's Commissioner for the Suppression of the Slave Trade; Livingstone was in a slave city, in a slave colony, from which millions of people had been shipped across the Atlantic.

9
DESTINIES

Livingstone spent over three months in Luanda, for much of the time ill and being cared for by Edmund Gabriel. Compared with the only other colonial city he knew – Cape Town – Luanda was an unimpressive place, beautiful though its setting might be on a wide sweeping bay with a long island offshore. Many of Luanda's twelve thousand inhabitants were slaves, it was garrisoned by men transported (permanently) from Portugal, its government hardly functioning. Yet this was the oldest Portuguese town in Africa, founded in 1495, and the capital of what the Portuguese claimed was a vast colony. In fact, Luanda had been established as a slave emporium and had remained so for three hundred and fifty years until, in the 1830s, the British government began enforcing treaties prohibiting the trans-Atlantic slave trade. Royal Navy ships of the Atlantic patrol were constantly present in Luanda harbour, blockading the city and serving as a living reminder of the international politics that had destroyed its commercial base.

In Portugal itself, slavery was being abolished with legislation against new recruitment, but Angola like the other colonies in Africa remained a legal slave economy. The enslaved captives Livingstone had met in Barotseland and at Shinde's were destined mainly for the Angolan domestic market where a plantation system based on sugar and coffee was getting under way. A considerable number, however, were being shipped illegally to Brazil from Angolan ports other than Luanda.

Portugal's first contact with what is today Angola took place in 1482 when an expedition landed near the mouth of the River Zaire, and established diplomatic relations with the King of Kongo, who converted to Catholicism and reciprocated by sending an ambassador to Lisbon. But relations on a basis of equality did not last for long; Portuguese technical superiority in the form of firearms and ocean-going ships soon gave them ascendancy, with Kongo reduced to vassalage, and the commencement of an orgy of slaving which spread southwards along the coast and inland. Between the sixteenth and nineteenth century more than four million persons were exported from Angola, with perhaps that number also dying while being transported from the slave source areas such as the Lunda empire to the coast and overseas.

Most Angolan slaves were destined for Brazil which was occupied by Portugal in the early sixteenth century and rapidly developed as their main region of overseas settlement. That south America rather than tropical Africa attracted the bulk of Portuguese colonists was the result of several factors:

Brazil is nearer to Europe and the discovery of gold gave it the glitter of an Eldorado. But more important than these attractions, when the Portuguese reached Brazil in 1500, the country was inhabited solely by stone age peoples (at a similar stage of development to the Khoi and San of south Africa) who could be subjugated – or exterminated – relatively easily with firearms. Tropical Africa was a different matter. Here the Portuguese came face to face with established states which had to be either subverted (as happened with Kongo) or defeated militarily. By mid-nineteenth century the Portuguese in Angola were still confined to coastal areas; all their attempts to conquer the interior had been repulsed, and they controlled only embattled settlements like Cassange and their tenuous routes to the coast.

If African rulers refused to be conquered, however, they were happy to trade, and their major item of commerce, slave labour, was precisely what an underpopulated Brazil needed for its sugar estates and mines. In the course of time the economies of Brazil and Angola became so intertwined that an amalgamation of the two territories became a possibility, especially as amalgamation would have made the slave trade between the two an internal matter and thus immune from British suppression under the terms of the treaty with Portugal. In the event, Brazil was not strong enough to fly in the face of British policy and the scheme was stillborn. When the trans-Atlantic trade was blocked, the Portuguese in Angola were little better off than they had been three centuries previously.

Livingstone was scathing about the lack of economic development in Angola, despite its wealth of resources. 'From Cassange down as far as I have come,' he wrote in his *African Journal*, 'we have a country equal if not superior to the valley of the Mississippi in fertility', and yet this area, which could have produced agricultural raw material for industry, did not have even a road to the coast, only the footpaths used by traders, the militia and the handful of inland settlers. Livingstone attributed the absence of development to the dearth of settlers – he must have been remembering the flourishing agricultural hinterland of Cape Town – and to the predominance of the slave system, which he saw not only as immoral, but more importantly, from the economic point of view, inefficient. Another factor he considered significant in the region's backwardness was the absence of Christian missionary effort. In the previous century the Jesuits had been active in the field, and their work still survived in a level of literacy he found surprising, but they had been expelled by the Portuguese government in 1759 and since then the Catholic church had confined itself almost exclusively to parish rather than evangelical work. The Jesuits, Catholic though they indeed were, had been too independent for the Portuguese authorities, especially when they began to work against slavery, but the Church itself was happy enough to operate symbiotically with the imperial system to the extent of sending priests to baptize and brand slaves as they were driven aboard ships for the journey to Brazil. In 1854, the Bishop of Luanda, Joaquim Moreira Reis, who befriended Livingstone, was serving as Acting Governor of the colony.

Livingstone's mordant view of the Portuguese was tempered in one respect: he found the apparent absence of colour prejudice admirable, and in great contrast to the colonial racialism of white Cape and Boer society, while the presence of an African Canon in Bishop Reis's diocese reminded him that no parish in the Cape, no mission in the whole of south Africa had a black minister-in-charge. Despite his hatred of slavery and his early dismissal of the Roman Church as the 'heathenism of Popery', his personal relations with the Portuguese in Angola were good and he saw considerable virtue in the Afro-European society that had arisen there. He started to learn Portuguese in Angola, and thanks to his knowledge of Latin rapidly acquired an adequate command of the language. His unquenchable curiosity would have led him to enquire about the history of Portugal, and how it had achieved its place in the world, and no doubt Edmund Gabriel and Bishop Reis were happy to enlighten him.

Livingstone did not directly attribute the difference between the status of blacks in Catholic lands and those in Protestant lands to the differences between the Catholic and Protestant (and more especially Calvinist) approaches, but he was aware that in the latter the status line was drawn at race or colour. He had seen it in South Africa. As to the 'free' United States, writing to his future sister-in-law Harriet Ingraham of Massachusetts in May 1849, he says circumspectly:

> ... I have imbibed a little prejudice against some people on your side of the Atlantic. Indeed I owe them a grudge on account of the monomania under which they labour touching the complexion of my adopted country ... Is that their way of 'going ahead'? Has the grievous loss we sustained [in the emigration of the Pilgrim Fathers] in the extraction of so much worth as went away with our Ironsides and sturdy Independents been all thrown away on their progeny? I feel quite crusty towards them when I remember their privileges and often wish they would recollect what is expected of them in the nineteenth century. But I am sure you are not one of their number.

The anti-slavery cause in the United States, which Miss Ingraham with her Massachusetts background and her education at Oberlin could be assumed to support, had its task complicated by the pervasive racialism which existed in the northern 'free' states, despite their Christian constitutions. The abolitionists were aware of the dilemma, and *Uncle Tom's Cabin* discusses it at some length. St Clair the New Orleans slave-owner is apparently free of colour feeling, while his New England cousin Ophelia has a deeply ingrained prejudice against, even revulsion for, blacks. White abolitionists might promise slaves freedom from formal bondage, but they could not offer them equal rights and civil liberty: the predominantly Calvinist ethos of white America drew the status line at colour. Calvinism, which divided the whole human race into the elect and the damned, saw no Christian contradiction in regarding whites as the Chosen, and blacks – to whom so much demonology had been attached by Christian slaveocracy – as the Lost. A black in slavery was no more a part of society than a pack-mule and therefore no threat to the white social order – a black in freedom had likewise to be excluded, so the colour line replaced the slave-status line. The line was drawn both horizontally and vertically, so 'free' blacks could become either helots without civil rights, or be separated territorially. American experience shows that after Lincoln's freeing of the southern slaves in 1864, the position of free blacks there began a sharp decline. In New Orleans free black musicians who, before emancipation, had moved easily through general society were, after the event, ghettoised and could play only with other blacks.

In *Uncle Tom's Cabin* the author compromises with racialism in two ways. First, she makes her heroine Eliza so fair-skinned that she (and her child) are able to 'pass for white' and thereby survive the scrutiny of her pursuers and reach the Ohio successfully. Her husband, George Harris, is also light enough to pretend to be a sun-tanned Spaniard and to make good his own escape. These deceits are more than incidental to the novel's plot, they are concessions to a racially prejudiced white readership which might be able to feel patronisingly sympathetic to a subservient and harmless African Uncle Tom, but would find the prospect of an enterprising, proud and articulate African Eliza or George Harris both unsympathetic and alarming.

The novel compromises with its white audience again by sending the Harrises off to Africa, to spread 'civilisation and Christianity', where they will be in no position to claim the full citizenship which is rightly theirs in the United States. If asked, Livingstone would have insisted that American blacks enjoyed civil liberty and equality in the land of their birth: and any scepticism he may have harboured about Protestant attitudes would have been sharpened by the case of Samuel Ajayi Crowther, a freed slave of Nigerian origin who was settled at Freetown, the British colony for emancipées. Crowther became the foremost

Anglican pioneer missionary in Nigeria from 1843 onwards: he was appointed bishop but had to resign when white clergy and colonial officials refused to work with him.

Livingstone would have found H B Stowe's resolution of the issues inherent in slavery and racialism less sympathetic than those put forward in the most influential of Brazilian abolitionist novels where the routes lead to Catholic integration rather than Calvinist exclusion. Bernardo Guimarães's *A Escrava Isaura* (Isaura the Slave) was published in 1875, thirteen years before Brazilian abolition, but is set in mid-century. The heroine, Isaura, is the daughter of a Portuguese estate manager and a mulatta slave, and because of the matrilinear inheritance of status, a slave herself. Like Eliza, Isaura is light-skinned and beautiful. The plot includes predatory white males, an invalid manumission, escape, recognition, recapture and humiliation. (There are numerous parallels with *Uncle Tom*, but the divergences are more revealing.) Early in the story, Isaura and the white hero, Alvaro, fall in love, and when they are eventually reunited after Isaura's travails through a slave society, Alvaro declares:

> Arise, you noble and sublime woman … Arise Isaura, it is not at my feet but in my arms, here close to my heart that you must throw yourself. Despite all the prejudices of the world, I regard myself as the happiest of mortals to be able to offer you the hand of a husband.

Isaura finds fulfilment in becoming a member of the national family, an outcome unthinkable for Eliza, but it is an outcome that also awaits Alvaro's freed slaves: they are allotted small farms on a sub-divided estate, which become their own property when they have paid Alvaro off.

It would be a travesty of the truth to suggest that nineteenth-century Brazil was free of race or class prejudice: quite the contrary, as can be seen in Aluisio Azevedo's 1881 novel *O Mulato*, where prejudice on both counts leads to tragedy. But as the introduction to the 1985 edition of *Isaura* states:

> Brazilian society, which in the nineteenth century felt so deeply for the misadventures of Isaura, accepted her because she was fair-skinned and educated. Being white and not having a slave character, she can show through her sufferings 'how vain and ridiculous is all discrimination based on birth or riches'.

The last of these sentiments coincides with views Livingstone expressed throughout his life, but which he found difficult to reconcile with the spirit of many British contemporaries. In social relations he preferred what he had seen in Angola to what he had seen at the Cape, and to what he understood about the United States. He wanted to build a Christian empire, but the type of empire he wanted must be free of both slavery and race discrimination. If he could not embrace Catholicism, if Calvinist elitism in action was unattractive, even repugnant, he would draw a blueprint of his own.

10

SEEK AND YE SHALL FIND

Livingstone's stay in Luanda was made easier by the fame that already surrounded him. His visit to Lake Ngami, his mapping of the Upper Zambezi, had brought recognition and were known in Luanda, where one English newspaper at least, *The Times*, arrived regularly. The *Official Bulletin* of Angola published the translation of a lengthy article he wrote about the country towards the end of his visit. He delighted in going aboard the Royal Navy ships in the bay, both to impress his Kololo porters with the wonders of British technology and to enjoy the hospitality of the officers. He was offered a free passage to England aboard one of the ships, *Forerunner* which he refused, providentially, as the vessel went down off Madeira. Less providential was his meeting with Captain Norman Bedingfeld, as we shall see. Bishop Reis gave Livingstone the freedom of the city, equipped the expedition for its return to Barotseland and sent presents to Sekeletu. He also gave Livingstone a letter of introduction to the Portuguese authorities in Mozambique. With Alfredo Schutz, a Luanda merchant, Livingstone discussed the possibility of the Portuguese setting up a chain of trading stations stretching across the continent from Cassange to Tete on the lower Zambezi.

At this stage, Livingstone was prepared to include the Portuguese in his plans but he would not do their work for them. Before he left Luanda he was asked by the bishop to help the Angolan government to extend its influence further into the interior where the visits of Silva Porto had left no more than an ephemeral impression. The bishop wanted Livingstone to take with him the Austrian botanist, Dr Federeich Welwitz, who had been sent by Lisbon to explore Angola. But Livingstone refused. He was determined that any honour for his own explorations should not be diminished by anyone who could report to Europe. He wrote in his *African Journal*:

> A project has been set afoot [in Luanda] for an embassy to Sekeletu, which would have deprived me of all credit due to my energy in opening up the path to Luanda . . . As it appeared evident to me this plan would afford Dr Welwitch an opportunity of availing himself of all my previous

labour, difficulties and dangers without acknowledging his obligations to me in Europe, I considered it would not be prudent to put such a temptation in his way . . .

Livingstone left Luanda in September 1854 and reached Linyanti a little less than a year later, in August 1855. Once again he travelled through the rainy season: the journey inland proved as difficult as that to the coast, and confirmed, if that were necessary, the unviability of the route for his purposes. He would follow the Zambezi to the east coast no matter that he had long overstretched his sabbatical from the LMS. In doing so he would become the first European to traverse the continent, beating Silva Porto; he would also prove that the Zambezi was 'God's Highway' and show that only Portuguese idleness had stopped them from making use of it. How Alfredo Schutz's trading stations would fit into Livingstone's design is not clear; either they would be ancilliary to Livingstone's establishment or, more possibly, they represented a scheme which Livingstone knew would never be realised but which won him goodwill from the Portuguese which he needed as they controlled both coastlines.

When Livingstone reached Linyanti there were lengthy discussions in the council about his next move and, eventually, the king decided to support Livingstone again on the understanding that he would return to establish his mission in Barotseland. Livingstone departed from Linyanti on 3rd November 1855 in the company of Sekeletu and two hundred retainers, some of whom were to travel on to Mozambique. Their first night out of Linyanti was enlivened by a ferocious thunderstorm, the type that occurs in the tropics at the start of the rains when the accumulated heat of the late dry season transforms itself into lightning so powerful and vivid it seems to have a voice of its own ahead of the thunder. Livingstone had set himself a path which would lead to psychic tempests just as terrifying.

After reaching Sesheke on the Zambezi the party travelled eastwards along the river, bringing Livingstone within a few days to the huge waterfall called by the Kololo Mosi-oa-Tunya, the smoke that thunders. This waterfall is doubly unique in that it is not only the largest curtain of vertical water in the world – a mile wide and three hundred feet deep – but it also falls into a narrow chasm both sides of which are at the same level. Thus the observer can enjoy an almost godlike view of the whole phenomenon, from above, below, and opposite. Livingstone gives the impression that his visit to the Falls was by way of a detour from the route to the coast (he intended to cut corners) but even if that were the case, it was a detour he would never regret. His first full description of the scene (which he edited for publication), from his journal, has never been bettered by later writers:

... The most wonderful sight I had seen in Africa.

In looking down into the fizzure on the right of the island [at mid-falls on the lip of the chasm] one sees nothing but a dense white cloud which at the time we visited the spot had two bright rainbows on it [the pre-Kololo name for the Falls was Shongwe, rainbow] (The sun was on the meridian and the declination equal to the latitude of the place). From this cloud rushed up a great jet of vapour exactly like steam and it mounted up 200 or 300 feet high. There it changed its hue to that of dark smoke and came back in a constant shower which soon wet us to the skin. This shower falls chiefly on the opposite side of the fizzure and a hedge of evergreen trees whose leaves are always wet. From their roots a number of little rills run back into the gulph but as they flow down, the column of vapour licks them up clean off the rock and away they mount again. They are constantly running down but never reach the bottom. On the left of the island we see the water a white boiling mass moving away to the prolongation of the fizzure near the left bank of the river.

The fizzure is said by the Makololo to be much deeper further to the eastwards ... They behold the stream like a white cord at the bottom and so far down (probably 300 feet) and they become giddy and were fain to go away holding on to the ground ...

On the left side of the island we have a good view of the mass of water which causes one of the columns of vapour to ascend, as it leaps quite clear off the rock and forms a thick unbroken fleece all the way to the bottom. The whiteness gave the idea of snow, a sight I had not seen for many a day. As it broke, wild pieces of water all rushing on in the same direction each gave off several rays of foam exactly as bits of steel when burned in oxygen gas give off rays of sparks.

The snow white sheet seemed like myriads of small comets rushing on in one direction each of which gave off (as they are represented on paper) from its nucleus streams of foam. I never saw the appearance referred to noticed elsewhere ...

I have mentioned that we saw five columns of vapour ascending from this strange abyss. They are evidently formed by the compression suffered by the force of the water's own fall into an unyielding wedge shaped space. The enormous mass coming down in the constant flow must batter that already there in somewhat the same way that air is compressed in a piston to produce fire ...

Apart from its clarity, what is remarkable about this passage is its use of scientific and industrial imagery: the small comets giving off streams of foam, the great jet of vapour exactly like steam which changed to the colour of dark smoke and produced a constant shower, the skyscape of an industrial city, any British Coketown, the pieces of water giving off rays of foam like bits of steel when burned in oxygen, the chasm itself the pistoned cylinder of some gigantic machine.

Livingstone realised that he had made a great 'discovery' and decided to use it for what can only be called political purposes. As he wrote to Robert Moffat in March 1856 a few months after his visit:

> I wish to name the Falls after our Queen, the 'Smoke Sounding Falls of Victoria,' as a proof of my loyalty. Some other things have taken well in quarters where I did not expect it, and the whole together may have a smack of the 'wisdom of the serpent', though I meant not so.

His fellow Scot, Moffat, would have understood what Livingstone meant by 'loyalty', a willingness to accept, even if in word only, the legitimacy of the Union of Scotland with England. This submission was essential to the furtherance of Livingstone's career. The second sentence of the passage must refer to the award of the Queen's prize for Lake Ngami. Now, with the Victoria Falls, Livingstone is deliberately capitalising on his geographical feats publicly. (How he must have blessed the day he left Welwitz behind in Luanda.)

The chasm of the Falls, visible in its entirety, is so enormous that an observer loses all sense of size or perspective and feels that it would be the easiest thing to bestride it. Livingstone may not have experienced this sensation, but he was only too conscious of bestriding a social chasm which he expected to be bridged by 'God's Highway'. Livingstone was a man of industrial society, Sebitwane his hero, and Sekeletu, were monarchs of an iron-age kingdom (the only functioning civilisation of the kind he was to see in Africa, since the Batswana and the African politics of Angola and Mozambique were being broken up by colonial forces). Livingstone felt particularly close to the Kololo kings because they reminded him of the lost realm of the Scottish Highland clans from which, on his father's side, he was sprung. When Livingstone remarks that the Kololo tradition of cattle-raiding was not regarded as real theft, he might be echoing the words written in the 1730s in *Letters from a Gentleman in the North of Scotland* by Captain Edward Burt, an English army officer stationed in the Highlands on road-building exercises: 'the stealing of cows they [the Highlanders] call *lifting*; a softening word for theft; as if it were only collecting their dues.' Other parallels were legion: on the material side, the Kololo like the Highlanders were — apart from cattle raiding — subsistence farmers who lived in small thatched dwellings. In religion (and medicine, part of the same cosmography) there was belief in spirits and magic; judicial punishments, if not arbitrary, were harsh; the political systems, centred on the head of the clan, were similar; domestic slavery in one form or another was a norm; individual ownership of land was unknown.

The years after grandfather Livingstone (or McLeigh the Gaelic name) moved from Ulva to Clydeside had seen the rapid and often brutal destruction of Highland society as the gridiron of capitalist modernisation was imposed upon it, a process which began with Captain Burt and his road builders. Livingstone hoped that his 'God's Highway' would bring modernisation to the Kololo, but without the disregard for human decency which had accompanied the Highland clearances. He did not feel for the Kololo, or for Africans in general, the morally superior disdain displayed by many Europeans, including missionaries such as Moffat and, even after Livingstone's time, by François Coillard, the French Huguenot evangelist of the upper Zambezi. (It was an attitude common too among the Lowland Scots Presbyterian missionaries amidst the Gaelic-speaking, hut-dwelling Highlanders.) Livingstone felt an innate sympathy, rather than a Calvinistic determination to extirpate any custom regarded as ungodly, as seen in the Lowlanders' attempts to kill the Gaelic language. Livingstone saw those he often called 'barbarians' as pre-Christians to whom faith would bring 'civilization', not as children of the damned. His use of the words 'barbarian' and 'civilized' (and he uses them often) is frequently caricatured as barbarian equals black African equals evil; civilization equals white European equals good. But this is a misunderstanding of his usage, for he employs the words quantitatively rather than morally, as can be seen again in a passage from the *Statistical Account of Scotland* compiled in the 1790s. Here barbarism can be equated with uncivilized people clothed in the coarsest garb, starving in the meanest huts, living in huts with cattle all of which equals poverty while civilization is equated with fields clothed in the richest harvests, herds fattening in luxurious pastures, the family decked in gay attire, enjoying manufactured conveniences of life, and a table loaded with solid fare all of which equals wealth.

Livingstone's ideas about what today would be called the 'development' of central Africa began to crystalize on his trek across the continent. The transition from barbarism to civilization described in the *Statistical Account of Scotland*, had been made possible by the agricultural revolution which took place during the eighteenth century, especially in Lowland Scotland, and which his maternal grandparents had experienced. It had been a generally benign process of modernization and the consolidation of land holdings, not accompanied, as had happened in the English 'Agrarian Revolution', by the forced eviction of peasant tenants. At the end of the eighteenth century, the Lowlands had the best agriculture in Europe.

Livingstone's search for a 'healthy Highlands' in central Africa, inspired as much by nostalgia for a misty Scottish past as by the need to find a place where his mission could be settled comfortably, seemed to him to have succeeded a few weeks after leaving the Victoria Falls.

He marched out of the Zambezi valley in a north-easterly direction that led him on to the Batoka Plateau. This area of what is now the Southern Province of Zambia, lies more than a thousand feet above the valley and the change of atmosphere between the two areas is quite tangible at all times of year. In December, when Livingstone passed across the plateau, the valley is densely humid, the temperature a steamy 100°F during most of the day. By comparison, plateau temperatures do not rise much above 80°F, thunderstorms break the heat of the afternoons, and on overcast days the weather is positively cool. Passengers on today's train who fall asleep half naked at Livingstone station call for blankets when the railway reaches Kalomo a few hours later. Until recently, the valley was infested with tsetse fly, which meant that in Livingstone's time cattle could not be kept there and the main domestic animal was the goat. On the Plateau, then as now, large areas are free of tsetse, and cattle the way of life for the Tonga inhabitants. Agriculture in the valley is difficult because of erratic rainfall and poor soils, whereas the Plateau is well watered and fertile.

When Livingstone saw the broad shallow valley of the Kaleya river on the undulating northern reaches of the upland, he thought he had found his place. Not only was it high, cool, and presumably less liable to fever than the Valley, but it was part of Kololo territory, and therefore a valid site for the mission he had promised Sekeletu. Livingstone's route across the Plateau anticipated that taken fifty years later by the railway, the chief engineer of which was H F Varian, the author of *Some African Milestones* whom we have already met.

Livingstone continued northwards until he reached the Kafue river, which he followed downstream until it joins the Zambezi, which at this point is a broad, smooth-flowing waterway. His passage through the area is commemorated today in the name 'Munali' given to a range of hills which marks the edge of the plateau flanking the Kafue valley. 'Munali' was the nickname given him by the Kololo, and though it is sometimes romantically said to mean 'the man with red hair', is in fact the lambdacized pronunciation of the Cape Dutch title 'Mijn Heer' (my lord) which was given to ministers of religion. It is easy to see how 'Mijn Heer' became 'Monare' and, eventually, 'Munali'. It was while he was on this part of the journey, too, that his own name was in the process of being changed.

His father decided to restore the 'e' at the end of the family surname which, until then, had been spelled 'Livingston' at his insistence. Why he removed and then brought back the 'e' we do not know. Neil once said that he had taken the 'e' off because the name was long enough without it but no comment survives on why he put it back. It is difficult to believe that the changes were merely a matter of whim.

The original Gaelic family name, McLeigh, meant 'son of the

physician'. In Highland tribal society the art of the healer was intricately bound up with religious beliefs and practices, which among pre-Christian Gaels, whether in Scotland or Ireland, included the veneration of stones, the most sacred of which were believed to be able to move of their own accord and were, thus, 'living'. The name Livingstone can hardly be a phonetic transformation of McLeigh as Munali is of Mijn Heer and, unless it was chosen at random during the forced anglicisation of the Highlands, it can only be a translation of the Gaelic name. Neil, the ardent Christian and opponent of all superstition, may initially have wanted to make his name less iconic by removing the 'e', restoring it only when it became clear after Ngami and the Luanda journey that his son was going to make his name as a Christian healer and pioneer. As it happened, the restored 'e' made it possible for the name itself to become an ingredient in the Livingstone myth: 'Meanwhile, may your name be propitious; in all your long and weary journeys may the *Living* half of your title outweigh the other; till after long and blessed labours, the white *Stone* is given you in the happy land.' Thus did Professor George Wilson of Edinburgh write to Livingstone in 1857, after his return to Britain following the transcontinental journey.

By cutting across the Plateau, and rejoining the Zambezi at the Kafue confluence, Livingstone came upon a part of the river which is navigable by small craft for many miles in either direction, upstream as far west as the Kariba gorge, downstream to Mpata gorge. By not following the course of the Zambezi between the Victoria Falls and the Kafue, Livingstone did not see Kariba and so deprived himself of the opportunity of grasping the nature of the Zambezi; that it is not, as he persuaded himself and others, an easy-flowing Mississippi rolling, with the exception of the Falls, solemnly to the sea, but a capricious stream whose even flow is regularly broken by dangerous and impassable gorges and cataracts. But seeing its broad sluggish expanse at the confluence, he was able to maintain his faith in God's Highway and dream of establishing his station near the Munali Hills. He made the same error of judgement downstream from the confluence as he was approaching the end of the navigable stretch: he writes in *Missionary Travels and Researches in South Africa*:

> The ranges of hills, which run parallel to the banks of the river above this, here come close up to it and form a narrow gorge which . . . is called Mupata. There is a narrow pathway by the side of the river, but we preferred a more open one in a pass among the hills.

Having skirted this obstacle, Livingstone and his party of a hundred and eleven porters went on to the confluence with the Luangwa, which flows into the Zambezi from the north. On its east bank, facing both rivers, are the ruins of a Portuguese settlement called Zumbo. It was from here that Portuguese had set off on expeditions to the interior; to Mwata Kazembe, the Lunda king of the Luapula, from where they hoped to reach Mwato Yamvo and then Luanda. Zumbo was the furthest up the Zambezi that the Portuguese had established themselves, though the position had soon to be abandoned because of African hostility. This hostility affected Livingstone and his party too, when Mburuma, the chief of the area, tried to stop them from crossing the Luangwa, though after explanations they became friends. Further down the Zambezi, only Livingstone's diplomacy saved him and his men from attack. Not since his first passage through Angola had this happened and for the same reason: Livingstone had arrived on the fringes of Portuguese slave-trading and, until he could prove that he was not leading a slave caravan, his foreignness branded him as an enemy.

By the time Livingstone reached this part of the Zambezi his health began to deteriorate again, both from malaria and, though he would not admit it, from exhaustion. Travelling on foot through the middle Zambezi valley is an ordeal to be well avoided. During the rainy season, when Livingstone was there, the humid heat is suffocating and unrelieved – on sunny days, the temperature can rise to 120°F. Not the conditions in which to tramp through rough terrain along footpaths clogged with vegetation, with the endless effort and constant sweating causing a debilitating dehydration, and with all discomforts of terrain and weather sharpened by swarms of mosquitoes, midges, and other insects eager for blood. When Livingstone published *Missionary Travels and Researches in South Africa* and *Expedition to the Zambezi*, he underplayed these aspects of God's Highway, partly from modesty, partly so as not to deter those who might follow him, English traders. But he did acknowledge that only 'swift passage' by boat on the river itself would make his proposed inland settlement viable.

The chief, Mpende, who had at first sight wanted to attack Livingstone was mollified when he found that he was not Portuguese and, therefore, not a slaver. He told Livingstone that the country downstream was extremely rough and mountainous but that he could avoid the worst difficulties by crossing to the south bank of the Zambezi and striking across country towards Tete, the nearest Portuguese town where he would join the river again. Not only was this an easier passage, it was shorter. In taking Mpende's advice, Livingstone missed seeing a third (after Kariba and Mpata) and this time, the most formidable, Zambezi gorge, Kebra Basa, or Cabora Basa as it is known today. The broad sweep of the river at Mpende's gave the impression that it was the potential waterway Livingstone had dreamed about: the thought that the terrain would turn it into impassable cataracts and raging torrents, as the mile-wide river squeezes through a fifty yard defile, made it a prospect to avoid.

When Livingstone approached Tete, a fortnight after leaving Mpende, he was worn out and ill, perhaps sufficient reason for by-passing the gorge. The authorities at the town sent out a detachment of militia to meet him; he was carried on a litter into Tete where Major Tito Augusto Sicard, the Commandant, took Livingstone into his house and nursed him back to health.

11

THE GREATEST TRIUMPH

E foi que, estando já da costa perto,
Onde as praias e vales bem se viam,
Num rio, que ali sai ao mar aberto
Bateis à vela entravam e saiam.

Luís de Camões: Os Lusíadas V, 75

(And it happened as we stood off near the coast that we could clearly
see the beaches and the valleys and a river which here joined the sea,
with sailing ships entering and leaving.)

This river harbour on the Indian Ocean in Mozambique which Vasco
da Gama visited in 1498 was Quelimane, Livingstone's destination when
he left Tete. The ships Da Gama saw were vehicles of the transoceanic
trade between the middle east, Asia and Africa: the rulers of the port,
as of the other trading cities along the whole length of the African coast
from Sofala in the south to Mogadishu in Somalia were the Afro-Arab
Muslims (for convenience we shall henceforth call them the Swahili)
who had controlled the African end of Indian Ocean traffic for centuries
before Da Gama arrived.

Portugal's interest in east Africa had been twofold: trade in ivory,
slaves, copper from the far interior, gold from Zimbabwe; and control
of the sea-lane to India. Considerations of strategy led them to inter-
vene in Ethiopia to save the Christian emperor from being conquered
by the Muslims, and to destroy sea-going mercantile competitors. In
the early years of the sixteenth century, the Portuguese sacked and
burned the Swahili cities, Mombasa and Kilwa among them, built
their own fortresses where they deemed them necessary, and took
over the trade with the East which for nearly a century brought them
unbelievable wealth. They also tried to conquer Zimbabwe and convert
the Monomotapa empire to Christianity, but had not the strength to do
so.

By Livingstone's day a Swahili confederation based at Zanzibar

[95]

and linked to Oman had recovered the African seaboard as far south as the Rovuma river, leaving the Portuguese in occupation of only the seaports along the coast of Mozambique and the towns along the lower Zambezi. Although the Portuguese claimed territory deep into the interior, as at the abandoned Zumbo, and hoped to link Mozambique with Angola, not even their occupation of the coast and the valley was secure either militarily or economically. In India, Goa was isolated from its hinterland while the Indian Ocean had become a British lake. Since the decline of gold mining in Zimbabwe – resulting equally from the exhaustion of shallow orebodies and the irruption of Mzilikazi and the Ndebele – the principal exports from Mozambique were ivory, small amounts of copper (brought by Bisa traders from Lundaland) and illegal slaves. Portugal had forbidden the slave trade but slavery was legal in Mozambique, as in Angola as we have seen, and this colonial slavery formed a reservoir from which exports could be drawn under the legal fiction of being voluntary labour: the main customers were French sugar planters on Reunion.

The hostility which had met Livingstone at Zumbo was only the smallest ripple of the storm the Portuguese faced in the valley and along the coast. African resistance to their presence south of the Zambezi had been reinforced by the arrival there in the 1820s by emigrant Ngoni from south Africa (part of the *mfecane*). In the valley itself the land-grant (prazo) system introduced by the Lisbon government in the seventeenth and eighteenth centuries was collapsing into anarchy as the prazeiros, many of them Afro-Portuguese, rebelled against colonial authority and became minor potentates in their own right. Moreover, indigenous people such as the Chikunda and the Manganja da Costa, many of them self-liberated slaves, were initiating a challenge which by the 1870s would lead to the formation of a state independent of the Portuguese.

Portugal itself was hardly able to finance its own garrisons but persisted in its dreams of future destiny, so well expressed in the sermon preached by Antonio Viera for the Feast of the Epiphany in 1662:

> God divided the waters and the Earth appeared: He made light and darkness ceased. This was the manner of the first creation of the world. And who does not see that God observed the same thing in the second creation, brought about by the Portuguese? The whole New World lay in darkness and obscurity because it was not known.

In Mozambique the Portuguese tried hopefully to bolster their position by keeping the colony closed to trade with third countries but this no more secured an economic autonomy than the advent of Mozambican independence in 1975 was prevented by the dream of Salazar's Estado Novo to settle a million Portuguese peasants in the lower Zambezi valley.

Livingstone attributed the failure of the Portuguese to open the Zambezi as a waterway to the interior to what he regarded as their decadence. But this did not bar him from making friends with individuals such as Major Sicard at Tete. The letter of introduction Livingstone brought from Bishop Reis of Luanda no doubt made him more acceptable than an ordinary foreign adventurer. But Livingstone's general feelings about the Portuguese led him into delusions of his own.

At this stage of the story, the most important of these concerns Kebra Basa or Cabora Basa. If a William Cotton Oswell had told him that the gorge was impassable, Livingstone would have taken him seriously enough to go and have a look himself. But when the Portuguese told him that it was totally unnavigable, he would have ignored them thinking they were making excuses for their own lack of enterprise by exaggerating the problem. Livingstone later explained his own neglect of an inspection of the gorge from Tete (a short trip of little difficulty) by claiming that the Portuguese had told him that it was merely a small cataract. He allowed his dreams to override common sense, a characteristic he shared with the Portuguese. But though they might have been irrational about their empire, they were right in not trying to sail through Kebra Basa – in either direction: the Zambezi was neither a Mississippi nor an Amazon. Livingstone came to belittle Portuguese geographical work when his own reputation was at stake but they knew the lower Zambezi well and they knew its main tributary, the Shire, which flows out of Lake Nyasa which Livingstone would claim to have discovered.

He rested at Tete for about six weeks. Apart from writing letters and reports he made a survey of the town and district, including a visit to an outcrop of coal at Moatize a few miles away (in the direction of the gorge). He solved the practical problem posed by his porters, whom he had promised to take back to Linyanti, by arranging with Major Sicard for them to be allocated land on which to settle and sustain themselves until Livingstone returned from Britain.

In late April, he set off down the Zambezi in a boat provided by Sicard, accompanied by sixteen of the porters – now paddlers – and escorted by a militiaman, Lieutenant Miranda. Also with Livingstone was Sekwebu, the much-travelled man who had proved himself outstandingly efficient as guide and interpreter on the journey from Linyanti. Livingstone planned to take him to Britain so that he could see 'civilisation' in action. Half the porters returned to Tete from Sena, half way down the river and, with the remainder, Livingstone went on to Quelimane, not through the Zambezi mouth but overland on foot until they reached the

Quelimane river where they boarded a Portuguese launch. Livingstone was ill with malaria at Sena and at a low ebb when he reached Quelimane but there he was given hospitality by Colonel Nunes, a friend of Sicard's, and soon recovered.

Livingstone arrived at his destination on 20th May 1856, almost exactly four years after he had left Cape Town. His friend Gabriel in Luanda had told the British authorities that Quelimane was his destination and had given an estimate of his time of arrival.

Livingstone had no doubt that his fame was a reality when he learned that Royal Navy ships had been interrupting their coastal patrols to call at the port to enquire about him and to leave presents and mail despite the fact that Quelimane was dangerous to enter because of the sandbar across the river – seven Royal Navy men trying to cross the bar on Livingstone business drowned when they capsized. Awaiting Livingstone on 20th May were a case of wine, medicines, newspapers and letters. Sir Roderick Murchison, President of the Royal Geographical Society, with only the Luanda journey in mind, saw fit to write:

> You will long ago I trust have received the cordial thanks of all British geographers for your unparalleled exertions and your successful accomplishment of the greatest triumph of geographical research which had been effected in our times.

So much the greater would be the praise when news of the successful completion of the second leg of the journey reached Britain. But Livingstone's satisfaction was tempered when he opened a long missive from his employers, the LMS, who told him, in effect, that while they admired his achievements (again only as far as Luanda) as a traveller-geographer, they did not regard what he was doing as missionary activity and could not support the establishment of a station in central Africa. Livingstone's reply elaborated the theme that 'the end of the geographical feat is the beginning of the missionary enterprise' (a memorable expression first used in a letter to Murchison from Tete). Yet he knew that even if he could not persuade the LMS to change its mind, he could place other irons in the fire. He had already written from Tete to the British Foreign Secretary, Lord Clarendon, drawing attention both to himself and to the suitability of the Zambezi valley for British expansion, and in the same vein to Murchison. To these powerful men, with access to funds, he suggested that the only barrier to free passage up the river was the Victoria Falls. Whatever the attitude of the LMS, Livingstone was confident that he would return to the Zambezi, and told his eight porters so when he sent them back to Tete with supplies bought with two elephant tusks, part of the load that Sekeletu had donated to pay for the journey: the remaining twenty he left in the care of Colonel Nunes.

Livingstone's importance was made plain in the newspapers he had been sent and then, tangibly, with the arrival at Quelimane of George Fleming who had been sent from Cape Town. He bore a letter of introduction to the Portuguese from William Thompson, the LMS agent at the Cape, and supplies for Livingstone himself. Fleming also had a considerable sum of money at his disposal in case Livingstone had not arrived and had to be looked for, and had instructions that if Livingstone were dead, he was to bring back his instruments and papers. This was the first of a number of expeditions sent to find Livingstone in the African interior, the most famous of them being that of H M Stanley in 1871. There are few things more flattering than being the personal object of a search expedition and to know that people are willing to risk their lives and spend their money to recover your papers. Livingstone would have been amused, too, to learn that his Luanda achievement had made him an accepted figure in colonial Cape Town. When Fleming returned, a public subscription was launched to celebrate the transcontinental journey and raised £800 for Livingstone.

On 12th July, Livingstone took ship for Mauritius, no ordinary ship but a Royal Navy brig, HMS *Frolic*, which sent two boats over the Quelimane bar to make sure he and his luggage were brought safely aboard. *Frolic* took a roundabout route to its destination, calling at St Augustine's Bay in Madagascar where Livingstone went ashore and made a word list from the language. In all, the voyage to Mauritius took a month. With Livingstone was Sekwebu, who became more and more distressed by the vastness of the sea. Eventually he broke down completely when they reached Port Louis and attacked one of the *Frolic*'s crew with a spear. Chains were brought out to bind him and he jumped from the ship, hauling himself under water by the anchor chain and drowning. Livingstone says that Sekwebu was 'a favourite with both men and officers' but the body of the 'sensible, worthy heathen' was not recovered, nor is any enquiry known to have been held. Many suicides are a mystery, and we can only suppose that the sight of the chains convinced him that he had been tricked into slavery. Livingstone was seriously ill at the time, and staying not aboard ship but as the guest of the Governor of Mauritius, Major General Hay, and in no position to do anything for Sekwebu or avert the final plunge.

In Mauritius for two months, Livingstone was celebrity enough to be invited to address meetings, to have a social round, to take an interest in, and give advice on, ladies' flower gardens, which gave him ample time to observe the economic experiment taking place before the governor's eyes, and under government direction: the replacement of slavery by the indenture system. At the heart of the matter was the need for manual labour, in large amounts, to work the tropical-zone plantations that were to produce raw material for Britain. As we have seen, Livingstone began to take an interest in the matter after his discussions with Oswell about the 'slave trade and its remedy' when they found evidence of slavery at Linyanti. On the way to Cape Town after the Zambezi journey Livingstone stopped at Kuruman and came across a newspaper, *The Natal Times*, of 24th October 1851, which contained a report of such interest to him that he wrote to Moffat to send the paper on to him. The core of the report reads:

Mr A W Evans rose to move the following Resolution.

That it is impossible to rely upon the Kafir population of this Colony, for a permanent and effective supply of labour, and that, successfully to raise tropical production, it is absolutely necessary to introduce free foreign labour . . .

At a season of the year when food was least plentiful among the Kafirs, labour was not to be obtained. The cry was universal, from the Quathlambas [Drakensberg Mountains] to the sea coast – the scarcity of labour – many were abandoning agricultural pursuits, many leaving the country in disgust, exports we had none, – the colony was being drained of its specie by thousands of pounds. In England, he had thought with others, that, by proper management, Kafir labour might be made available: he had lived to see the fallacy of this opinion: in proof of the aversion of African savages to work, he had known men in the Bechuana country to go into the fields and dig up roots for their subsistence, rather than take a spade in hand to earn 6d. a day for food . . .

. . . English emigrants were inexperienced in the culture of tropical productions, the work was unsuited to their habits, most of them aspired to be proprietors themselves, and the rest would expect £20 per annum wages with rations worth another £20; this was obtained in Australia but we could not afford to pay so much for labour here. Juvenile paupers had been tried at the Cape, until their maintenance in due subordination had been denounced as quasi slavery at Exeter Hall. The desired impetus to the prosperity of this colony must come from India or China: with the cheap labour which could be obtained from those countries, we should import an additional safeguard to the colony. Coolies and Chinese, from their difference in habits and religion, would . . . form no coalition with the Kafirs . . .

. . . He could positively state, that merchants in England were only waiting for a satisfactory settlement of the labour question to invest thousands of pounds in Natal. The soil must be made to yield a return for this money . . . labour and labour only was required . . .

Mr Moorewood, as an old colonist, felt himself entitled to deny that Kafir labour was unavailable. Thirteen or fourteen years ago, he had employed 30 or 40 Kafirs to land cargo from a wreck on this coast, and he had the same men in his service now, – treat the Kafirs properly, and colonists would have plenty of labour ... With regard to what had been stated by Mr Moorewood, [Mr Evans said] he was aware that certain old settlers possessed a kind of chieftain influence over the natives, but that was not available to newcomers nor to colonists generally.

Five years after the Durban speeches Livingstone could see in practice the system Evans had advocated. Mauritius was uninhabited when the Dutch discovered it in the seventeenth century. They used it as a stop-over and replenishment post on the sea route to Asia (exterminating the dodo meanwhile), then it was settled by the French in the eighteenth century. They turned it into a sugar colony worked by slaves from Madagascar and east Africa and remained in control until it was taken by the British in 1810 during the Napoleonic wars. The British used the island as a naval station, leaving the French settlers to continue producing sugar on their estates. When slavery was abolished in the 1830s workers were imported from India under contracts which gave the right either to remain in Mauritius or to be repatriated when the term expired. Reunion, the sister island of Mauritius, remained under French control and its sugar economy continued to rely on African slaves, largely from Mozambique, as Livingstone knew. Today, Reunion is a department of France, while Mauritius is independent.

The cultivation of sugar spread from the islands to Natal, where the inability of the British settlers to induce or force Africans to work on the estates led to the Durban speeches and Evans's resolution. A few years later, the indenture system was applied to Natal and Indian cane workers began to arrive, the first batch aboard the ship *Truro* in 1860, followed by others over the years. Few returned to India and today Natal has an Indian-descended citizenry of a million. It was in Natal that Mohandas Gandhi gained his first political experience in the early years of the present century as he strove to protect the Indian immigrants from racial discrimination.

Besides Mauritius and Natal, the indenture system was used in other sugar colonies of the British empire, resulting in the large Indian populations of Fiji, Trinidad and Guyana. Livingstone never advocated it for central Africa, though in the early nineteen hundreds the British South Africa Company put forward a scheme – soon to be abandoned – to settle the Luangwa Valley with Indian peasant families who under white supervision, were to grow food for the new mining towns of central Zambia. Livingstone's ideas on colonial settlement were based on the replacement of African slave labour by African 'free labour', thereby setting in motion a process of development which would 'benefit both his fellow countrymen and the Africans'. In Mauritius, his mind remained set on the settlement on the Batoka plateau, the seed from which his ideas would sprout and flourish, with him 'exercising a kind of chieftain influence over the natives' (to use Evans's words) like the 'improving' Scottish lairds who had initiated Scotland's agrarian revolution.

He was not going to allow the LMS to hinder him and on 8th August 1856 wrote to Thompson at the Cape telling him so:

> I will follow out the work in spite of the veto of the [LMS] Board. If it is according to the will of God, means will be provided from other quarters.

In a letter of thanks of October 1856 to Henry Trotter, commodore of the Cape naval station, for the free passage from Quelimane to Mauritius, Livingstone said that the potentiality of central Africa in terms of people and resources was considerable, and that if the LMS would not support his return to the Zambezi he would resign and continue privately. Trotter's was a sympathetic ear as he had commanded the Niger Expedition of 1841 launched at the Exeter Hall meeting Livingstone attended shortly before leaving for Africa. Meanwhile, Livingstone wrote another unsolicited letter in August 1856 to Lord Clarendon in which he included Lake Nyasa in his plan of things to come.

As he sailed for home aboard the SS *England* Livingstone knew what path he was to follow. The prospect of writing a book for the publisher John Murray (suggested by Murchison – and Murchison was too cautious a man to suggest what he could not arrange – and confirmed in a letter from Murray himself) offered Livingstone the chance of raising some capital while the fame that he knew was preceding him to London would place him in a strong enough position to get his way.

The *England* sailed from Port Louis to Aden and along the Red Sea to Egypt. Travellers then went overland to the Mediterranean to trans-ship for the second leg of the voyage, in Livingstone's case aboard the Peninsula and Orient liner SS *Candida*. In Egypt he learned that his father had died, and off Malta he was nearly shipwrecked (as had been St Paul). In the event he was delayed and wrote a regretful letter to his wife, from whom he had not heard since he saw her off at Cape Town in 1852:

P & O Coy. s s Candida
27 Novr 1856

My dear Mary,

I am sorry to find that your visit to Southampton to meet me on 11 (4) Decr. will be in vain, but I make ready this note in order that, should an opportunity occur of transmitting it, you may have the earliest intimation of the reasons for our detention.

We had very rough weather after leaving Malta, and yesterday at midday the shaft of the engine, an enormous mass of malleable iron, broke in a sort of oblique fracture, evidently from terrific strains which the tremendous seas inflicted as they thumped and tossed this gigantic vessel like a plaything ... The whole affair was managed by Captain Powell most admirably ... The Company ... will do everything in their power to forward us quickly and safely, and as they are remarkably liberal in the management of their affairs, I have no doubt of the best treatment. I am only sorry for your sake, but patience is a great virtue, you know. Captain Tregear has been six years away from his family, I only four and a half. If we can, I shall telegraph to you.

Ever affectionately yours,
David Livingston

6 December. We expect to reach Marseilles this evening. Will wait tomorrow (Sunday), then go to Paris on Monday, wait one day there, and be in London on Wednesday or Thursday. We are aboard the Elbeji, Tunisian steamer.

Send a note to the terminus of Dover railway at London Bridge with your address. If we leave on Monday morning as I intend, we shall be in Paris on Tuesday morning, then remain that day, leave on Wednesday morning and be in London the same night or next day. We have two ladies in the family way, and I don't like to run away as I may be needed.

You may publish an extract of this if you like to allay alarm. This is Saturday at noon.

Mary did not receive this letter in time, and instead of meeting him in London, went to Southampton, where the wrecked ship would have docked if it had completed the voyage. Livingstone went to Southampton to join her and the tone of their reunion is suggested in the verses she presented him:

A hundred thousand welcomes, and it's time for you to come
From the far land of the foreigner, to your country and
    your home.
Oh, as long as we were parted, ever since you went away,
I never passed an easy night, or knew an easy day.

Do you think I would reproach you with the sorrows that
    I bore?
Since the sorrow is all over now I have you here once more,
And there's nothing but the gladness and the love within
    my heart
And the hope so sweet and certain that again we'll never part.

A hundred thousand welcomes! How my heart is gushing o'er
With the love and joy and wonder thus to see your face once more.
How did I live without you these long long years of woe?
It seems as if 'twould kill me to be parted from you now.

You'll never part me darling, there's a promise in your eye;
I may tend you while I'm living, you will watch me when I die;
And if death but kindly lead me to the blessed home on high,
What a hundred thousand welcomes will await you in the sky.

The prophesy in the third last line would soon come true, but a hundred thousand welcomes Livingstone indeed received both from Mary, in the pathetic hopes expressed in the poem, and from the British public. Establishment and everyman alike were desperate for a national hero after the humiliating misery and squalor of the Crimean War.

Part Three

1857–1858
Fame

12

UNDOUBTEDLY THE HERO
WILL ARRIVE

In the sixteen years Livingstone had been away Britain had flowered in terms of Gross Domestic Product but in 1856 it was once again in a state of political unease. The London he left was the capital of a kingdom wracked by economic depression and political ferment, with the traditional ruling class of aristocrats, church and landed gentry struggling to maintain its ascendancy in the face of demands for democracy and the liberty, equality and fraternity which still echoed across the decades from the American and French revolutions – demands made vocal in the coalition of new proletariat and frustrated middle class which produced the 'People's Charter'. By the end of the 1840s the movement had all but evaporated. On one hand, police-state methods ate away like acid at its leadership and grassroots support, on the other, most of the middle class – mollified by the prospect of reform – came to see its survival in going about its business in the mottled shade of the tree of established order, with any discomfort incurred from living in a half-prone position soothed by the doctrine that inequalities were removable, that the tree could be climbed. The 1848 revolutions against autocracy which shook much of continental Europe to its roots, stirred hardly a branch, twig or leaf in Britain.

By 1850 the evidence that Britain was top nation was plain for all to see. London was the largest city in the western world. A boom in the construction of railways and the extension of towns was changing the country into a throbbing, integrated, industrial machine. Gold was pouring into the coffers from Australia and California; the Royal Navy, and the empire it protected, made London the virtual capital of the world.

The mood of the times, the optimism, self-confidence and anticipated glory (at least among the ruling coalition of old money and new) found expression in the most remarkable building of the age, the Crystal Palace, constructed of iron and glass, half a mile long, erected especially to house the Great Exhibition of 1851, the shining, tangible demonstration of Britain's primacy in the world. More than six million people, a quarter of the total population, bought tickets to enter and gaze in wonder at the products of native industry and seaborne empire.

What we today call economic growth was then thought of as progress. And for those who saw progress as a sign of God's blessing there was little doubt that Britain had been chosen to lead the world. 'Sugar Islands, Spice Islands, Indias, Canadas, – these by the real decree of Heaven, were ours,' wrote Thomas Carlyle, the Scottish sage and historico-philosopher, as he called for Heroes, strong-willed, brimming with divine purpose, to take the country forward. For several years after the Great Exhibition, Britain's onward march seemed unchallengeable. Even if in the distant Cape the frontier wars went on forever, even if Afghanistan was proving unconquerable, India was being subdued while at home the manufacturing economy moved steadily ahead to promising destinations, shedding new wealth (at least for the middle classes) in its wake as the new steamships ploughed the seas and steam locomotives charged along the new railways. Queen Victoria, her Prince Consort, her ministry of aristocrats, seemed to reign supreme over a flourishing land that they had made to flourish. And even if there were poverty, the poor could always emigrate or be assured that all but the most feckless of them could clamber, by their own efforts, aboard the ship of wealth which steamed imperturbably forward.

Then in 1854 disaster welled up from the depths of continental politics and Britain was thrown into war, a war whose causes were obscure and whose objectives were uncertain, fought in an equally obscure and uncertain place, the Russian Czar's Crimea. Livingstone first learned about it at Luanda after the first part of his transcontinental journey, reading about it in the pages of *The Times*, sending comment to his army friend Thomas Steele, then on the battlefield. And another friend, Thomas Maclear, writing from Cape Town to Lord Russell, the Foreign Secretary, about Livingstone's charting of the upper Zambezi expresses the hope that this latest feat of British enterprise would help to raise morale. British arms might be stuck in the Crimean morass but British grit was marching across Africa, a hint that Livingstone's work and name may be of wider value than his present reputation suggested. Livingstone was getting a good press in Britain and now, even at the Cape, was starting to be a figure to whom the British public could turn with relief.

The Crimean War gave us the Balaclava helmet and the world's first modern war correspondent, W H Russel, whose regular, up-to-date reports from the battle zones and their hinterland to *The Times* stunned his readers. Here, for the first time, in the clearest graphic prose, was revealed the horror, misery and squalor (no grand battle scenes presented as elegant games for gentlemen) of the lives and deaths of the men sent out to fight for incomprehensible ideals. The strongest point to emerge from Russel's despatches as a whole was the almost total incompetence of British generalship, on the battlefield, behind the lines, with thousands of men being lost through faulty strategy and logistics and through the appalling conditions in the military hospitals. The suffering of the wounded may have been alleviated by those 'Ladies of the Lamp', Florence Nightingale and Mary Seacole but the casualty lists were enormous and the stench of war hung over Britain in a foetid cloud for years, drizzling condemnation on the ruling class that had brought about such misery.

Russel's reporting was a journalistic triumph. It brought the war into his readers' clubs and drawing rooms and probably hastened its inconclusive end. But in the wider context his success – he went on to edit *The Times* – was no more than a symptom of the growing place that the daily press was to occupy in British life. Until 1855 the country's newspapers were heavily taxed by means of a stamp duty, the effect of which was to confine newspaper readership to the rich. In that year, in the middle of the war, the government, for some inexplicable reason – perhaps to dilute the influence of *The Times* and Russel's reporting – abolished the tax. An immediate effect of this move was the creation of a large new market for what at the time were called 'cheap' newspapers, selling for half the price. New titles sprang up across the land, while weeklies like the *Manchester Guardian* and *The Scotsman* became dailies. The mass press was born.

London publishers now also had the railways to carry their editions throughout the country and there were regional papers, such as those we have mentioned, to extend the market areas. The press changed both in scope and in character, became less dependent on political patronage, more on the tastes of its readers. For a paper to survive and flourish it had more to appeal to its audience than to impose itself, the latter a privilege which only the wealthiest publications such as *The Times* could enjoy. It is necessary to drag in this platitude as we consider the newspaper audience of the 1850s, the 'mass' beneficiaries of the abolition of the stamp – the rising middle class, the patriotic believers in self help, the proto-imperialists who might be expected to pour capital into colonies such as Natal: those who thought, not aristocratically but with money in mind, that Britain had received the call to bring progress to the world. The great majority of the four million people in Britain who could read fell into one or other, or several, of these categories. They took avidly to the press, giving Britain the highest per capita consumption of newspapers in the world, and would take just as avidly to newspaper 'personalities' that seemed to epitomise their aspirations.

For this public 1857 was a depressing year. Not only did the ghosts of the Crimea hover over the country, with Florence Nightingale providing constant reminders of their presence, but the great boom that had started half a dozen years before had come to a sudden end. Unemployment increased alarmingly, the gold-paved path to prosperity threatened to crumble, removable inequalities acquired renewed formidability. In March 1855, the London correspondent of the New York *Tribune*, Karl Marx, had given his American readers a typically blistering prognosis of the course of events, with a typically apocalyptic outcome:

> A few months more and the crisis will be at its height ... When its effects begin to be fully felt among the working classes, then will that political moment begin again ... Then will the working men of England rise anew, menacing the middle classes at the very time that the middle classes are finally driving the Aristocracy from power. Then will the mask be torn off which hitherto hid the real political features of Great Britain. Then will the two real contending parties in that country stand face to face – the middle class and the working classes ... and England will at last be compelled to share in the general social evolution of European society.

For the aristocracy, the ground seemed to tremble, for the middle class (from the upper to the lower lower) fears loomed for its ethic of respectability and independence, its two shibboleths.

The first of these concepts required a person to match the social tone, now taking its key note from the Christian virtuousness – family values, assumed modesty, sobriety, public spirit and so on – of Queen Victoria's court. In a hierarchical society dominated by the landed aristocracy, 'respectability' called for a desperate keeping-up of appearances, and a desperate drawing of distinctions between oneself and those even one twig lower on the tree. Possession of a piano was as much a dividing line between the middle and the lower class as possession of a billiard table was between 'real' wealth and the salariat; just as strict observance of the Sabbath in special clothes, the 'Sunday Best', separated the socially acceptable from the 'Great Unwashed' (a phrase that began to be applied to the 'lower orders' in the 1830s). Respectability required money, but since money was an unevenly distributed commodity, a person must be respectable within the funds available. If you could not afford a silver teapot, you could make sure that your china one was not cracked; and if you earned little, what you consumed must come from your own resources. You must be 'independent', must not rely on others for your well-being. If you lived on rents or dividends, your income must be assumed to derive from your own investment, and if you could not pay your debts, you must expect to be placed in prison as punishment for being 'dependent' on the credit of others.

Despite the hypocrisy to which these prerequisites for social status

Young Livingstone at the age of twenty seven at the outset of his life as a missionary.
David Livingstone Centre, Blantyre

Shuttle Row, Blantyre, in Scotland, where David Livingstone was born in 1813. *David Livingstone Centre*

David Livingstone's brother Robert. *David Livingstone Centre*

left: Robert Moffat, soon to be Livingstone's father-in-law, on his departure for Africa in 1843. *National Archives of Zimbabwe*

below left: Robert Moffat in his old age. *National Archives of Zimbabwe*

below: Mary Moffat, wife of Robert. *National Archives of Zimbabwe*

Livingstone's first surviving letter to William Cotton Oswell. *Livingstone Museum, Zambia*

ft William Cotton Oswell (1818–94), a wealthy friend and mentor of Livingstone who described him in the ..mous phrase 'a plucky little devil'. *Strathclyde University Archives, Glasgow.* James 'Paraffin' Young (1811–83), who became a friend of Livingstone when he was studying at the Anderson's College, Glasgow.

YOUNGS PARAFFIN LIGHT & MINERAL OIL COMPANY. LIMITED
ADDIEWELL WORKS. WEST CALDER. SCOTLAND

James Young's company remained Britain's largest public oil comany despite intense competition when his patent ended in 1864. *Strathclyde University Archives, Glasgow*

David Livingstone's daughter Anna Mary with her aunt Janet (?) *David Livingstone Centre*

Mary Livingstone, wearing a cameo of her husband David, circa 1859–1861. *David Livingstone Centre*

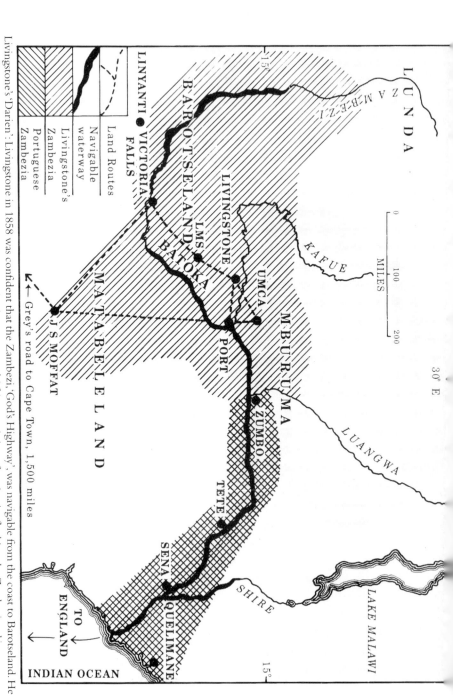

Livingstone's 'Darien': Livingstone in 1858 was confident that the Zambezi, 'God's Highway', was navigable from the coast to Barotseland. He dreamed of establishing a Christian-Scottish commercial colony in central Africa consisting of territories flanking the Zambezi and incorporating lands occupied or claimed by Portugal. Economic activity would spread out from his own centre and from the LMS, UMCA, and JS Moffat mission stations. The scheme came to nothing when the Cabora Basa gorge, a few miles west of Tete, was found to be impassable.

gave rise, they acted as a web that bound the political nation together (the unwashed were kept in their place by the police) and enabled it to shrug off the continental revolutions of 1848. But in the depression, psychic as well as economic, surrounding the Crimean War, the self-confidence of the political nation sank dangerously. Loss of faith in the hierarchy threatened to turn into a disease; it had not yet struck, but it lurked, lurked in the tenements where lived the alleged non-users of soap and scrubbing brush, erupted in the rash of burglaries, theft and muggings that terrorised the respectable and led them to erect hundreds of miles of iron railings to protect their privileged terraces and squares.

It is not by chance that the years in Britain immediately following 1848 saw a revival of interest in overseas exploration, or that this soon turned into a cult of the individual explorer. Livingstone had understood the mood when he strove to be the first European to reach Lake Ngami and the Upper Zambezi. Despite the grandeur of the Great Exhibition, perceptive people realised that Britain might have reached its zenith within the market it controlled. The loss of the United States had been offset by the gain of India and penetration of the Portuguese sphere of interest but China had been disappointing (a second Opium War had had to be started there in 1856 to tighten the British grip), and competition was beginning to appear from newly industrialising countries – Germany, France, Belgium, the northern USA, for example. Britain needed to broaden its portfolio, so to speak. And Britain needed paragons for the age. Within the living memory of the 1850s, two men achieved heroic status, both noble men of war, Horatio Nelson and the Duke of Wellington. But the Crimea had produced only aristocratic bunglers, its sole heroes the corporate six hundred of the Light Brigade charging 'half a league, half a league, half a league onwards into the Valley of Death'.

A new thrust of imperial expansion was bound to throw up men who, though not perhaps as memorable as Sir Francis Drake, would be in tune with the ethos of the political nation. A tune that could be orchestrated into paeans. This is not to suggest any conspiracy by the establishment, by the protagonists of greater empire, by the press, to manufacture new heroes. Merely that where there is a vacuum in the public mind something will flow in to fill it or, as Carlyle declared: 'Undoubtedly the Hero will arrive.' The first potential occupant of the plinth in the 1850s was Richard Burton. Born in 1821, son of a valetudinarian army officer who preferred half-pay to the parade ground, Burton became in 1855 the best known British explorer of the century when he published an account of the journey he had made over the previous year, in disguise, to the Moslem holy city of Mecca, had entered the Kaaba, touched the sacred stone, and returned unscathed to tell his tale. The journey itself was no great physical hardship –

Burton had money and joined a caravan of pilgrims – but the risk of discovery was great. And if he were discovered he faced the fate of all who, in fundamentalist Islam, blaspheme the Prophet. Burton survived by his wits and by possessing an extraordinary facility with languages, passing himself off as a Pathan who spoke Arabic with a Persian accent. The adventure would not have been possible had he not been born with dark eyes and black hair.

An extraordinary aspect of Burton's journey is that it was paid for by the Royal Geographical Society and subsidised further with paid leave from Burton's Bombay regiment, both of which knew that very little practical information would emerge from it. It was a gesture, a cocking of the snook, which told the world, if an Englishman can enter the Kaaba, England can enter anywhere. Burton's *Personal Narrative of a Pilgrimage to El-Medinah and Meccah* (the fifth word of the title is itself an insult to every Muslim) was a best seller, and he followed it in 1856 with his account, somewhat less awesome, of a further expedition, *First Footsteps in Africa; or an Exploration of Harar*. But somehow, Burton's reputation did not take off in the public mind. Perhaps because he made these journeys during the Crimean War, in which he as a British officer might have been expected to serve, perhaps because he was too clever – and liked to show it, perhaps because there was something shady about his spying activities in India, perhaps because he was not 'respectable' ('not married, you know, kept a Hindu woman in Baroda'), and not a Christian, except occasionally, for form's sake.

Soon Burton is away again – again on paid leave, again with RGS money – to find the source of the Nile, to solve a mystery that has fascinated Europeans for two thousand years, knowing that if he succeeds the reward (in financial terms at least) will be unbounded, while Sir Roderick Murchison's opinion that he is 'sound' and a 'gentleman' will drown out niggling puritan voices. But alas, it is not to be. For soon after he is on his way (with a promise, not fulfilled, of a further tranche from the RGS) Murchison is introducing to the Society, to the Press, and through it to an awestruck public, the achiever of the greatest geographical feat of the century, Dr David Livingstone, the 'e' now firmly attached to the name.

The occasion was the presentation to Livingstone of the Society's Gold Medal, and took place on 15th December 1856, just a few days after his side trip to Southampton to meet Mary, receive her poem, and bring her up to London. The RGS reception was a grand affair. Murchison spoke fulsomely, as did Sir Richard Owen, Livingstone's tutor in 1840. Both were distinguished men of science, Murchison as a geologist, Owen in anatomy. It was to Owen that Darwin sent for analysis the fossil bones he unearthed in South America during the voyage of the *Beagle*, and in Herman Melville's *Moby*

Dick it is to Owen that 'cetacean relics' are sent from Alabama for identification:

> some specimen bones of it being taken across the sea to Owen, the English anatomist ... he rechristened the monster Zeuglodon; and in his paper read before the London Geological Society, pronounced it, in substance, one of the most extraordinary creatures which the mutations of the globe have blotted out of existence.

William Cotton Oswell, back from the Crimea, was at Murchison's RGS reception as well: these were Livingstone's friends, giving him a welcome that established him as a public figure, but he was also being greeted by people outside his personal circle. Prince Albert received him, Admiral Sir George Back, explorer of the Arctic with Franklin in 1819 wrote a letter of congratulations and invited Livingstone and Mary to visit him: the ring was widening.

The night after the Gold Medal presentation, Livingstone attended a reception given for him by his employers, the London Missionary Society, presided over by Lord Shaftesbury. Because of Livingstone's misunderstandings with the LMS, the affair was not as happy an occasion as the previous day's, as he reported to Murchison, hinting in the same note that he might break with the LMS and turn to the government for a position. Within the week, he travelled by train to Scotland – a mode of transport that did not exist when he left home for London in 1839 – to visit his now widowed mother and his sisters at Hamilton. On the journey he wrote to *The Times* to argue that the cultivation of cotton in central Africa could be undertaken without slave labour on the American pattern, contrary to received opinion. After the family reunion (we do not know whether Mary accompanied him) Livingstone returned to London for another grand public event, the presentation of a Testimonial, that is to say, a donation of money, by the Lord Mayor of London at the Mansion House: more honour yet was to come from the financial centre of the world, the granting of the Freedom of the City a few months later.

If Burton received no similar adulation, one reason was that his ventures to Mecca and Harar were more a test of skill than explorations; the dangers were known in advance, the temperament of Islam was understood. Livingstone's transcontinental journey, on the other hand, was a revelation, one which seemed all the more extraordinary because of the ignorance in Britain of the physical nature of inner Africa (the Portuguese knew more) and because Livingstone had survived, not only the natural hazards presented by lion-infested, disease-ridden lands, but also that he, a white man, had survived the people who inhabited them. Where ignorance reigns supreme, stereotypes replace reality, and the stereotypes of 'darkest Africa' embodied all the demonism that Africans had been painted with during the centuries of the slave trade. We have seen traces of it in *Robinson Crusoe*, we see it solidly in the pages of Osborne's *Universal History* published in 1760, where Africans are described as

> ... proud, lazy, treacherous, thievish, hot and addicted to all kinds of lusts, and most ready to promote them in others, as pimps, panders, incestuous, brutish, and savage, cruel and revengeful, devourers of human flesh and quaffers of human blood, inconstant, base, treacherous and cowardly ... It is hardly possible to find in any African any quality but what is of the bad kind: they are inhuman, drunkards, deceitful, extremely covetous, and perfidious to the highest degree ...

For any white man to have spent three years among such people, to have come through with his blood unquaffed, his clothes on his back, his luggage and his virtue intact, must speak of divine protection 'of the highest degree'.

It would be wrong to suppose that Osborne's 1760 attitudes had died out in Britain in the 1850s. Quite the contrary. We have seen elements of them in Dickens's satire of the Jellybys. But the emphasis was changing: after all, what Osborne said about Africans had been said for a thousand years or more by Christians about Jews, and in 1857 a Jew sat in the British Parliament and was to become Prime Minister. Osbornian generalisations, even while they continued to feed popular prejudices, were seen, when examined, to be preposterous and, as far as Africans were concerned, moral slander was changing into intellectual denigration. (No one could doubt the morals of Mary Seacole, the African-Jamaican heroine of the Crimea veterans.) When Evans, in Natal, says in 1851 that Africans would rather eat roots than work for sixpence a day on a settler's farm, he is implying not that Africans are 'brutish, savage and cruel', but that they are congenitally stupid. In this view, Evans had the support of no less an intellectual giant than Thomas Carlyle in his *Occasional Discourse on the Nigger Question* published in 1849 and reprinted in 1853. Carlyle's 'Chosen Race', the British, governed by the 'strong silent men', who are his divinely-inspired heroes, have a mission to rule over those whose skins are dark. 'That,' he writes, 'you may depend on it, my obscure Black friends, is and was always the Law of the World, for you and for all men: To *be* servants, the more foolish of us to the more wise.'

Fortunately for Carlyle, and those who preached his world-view, support came from a most unexpected quarter, and gave their thinking a patina of scientific incontrovertibility. Charles Darwin's *The Origin of Species by Means of Natural Selection or The Preservation of Favoured*

Races in the Struggle for Life was published in 1859, but its theses had been under debate for at least a decade previously. The theory of evolution which Darwin presents, in the most meticulous detail (besides outlining and refuting the objections to it), supposes that all living things have developed from a single common ancestor by a process of natural selection in the face of environmental challenge: human beings form a single race, with a single common root. Darwin's failure, however, to explain what he means by race, and Herbert Spencer's coining of the phrase 'Survival of the Fittest' to explain evolution, allowed white supremacists to distort Darwin's theory and claim that whites were the 'fittest' and were thus doing no more than follow Carlyle's 'Law of the World' when they sought to dominate and, by implication, eventually replace, all other human varieties. Darwin's imprecise use of the word 'race' and his lack of curiosity about the operation of human societies, led him into a generalisation which provided ammunition for the Carlylite cannon for a century and more. Answering one objection to his Theory, Darwin wrote:

> Last, more than one writer has asked, Why have some animals had their mental powers more highly developed than others, as such development would be advantageous to all? Why have apes not acquired the intellectual power of man? Various causes could be assigned: but as they are conjectural, and their relative probability cannot be weighed, it would be useless to give them. A definite answer to the latter question ought not to be expected, seeing that no one can solve the simpler problem why, of two races of savages, one has risen higher in the scale of civilization than the other; and this apparently implies increased brain power.

The author of these obscure words was to claim that he did not understand what the racists were talking about when they propounded 'Social Darwinism', and opposed them openly in the Governor Eyre case of 1866, as we shall see. But he had undoubtedly, if unwittingly, contributed to the ideology of race; and would do so again more deliberately. This sort of venom fell not only on blacks, in general, but also on those who were seen to support them: 'Look at the Negro, so well known to you, and say, need I describe him? Is he shaped like any white person?' wrote Robert Knox in *The Races of Men*, published in 1850. '. . . Not in the least. What an innate hatred the Saxon has for him, and how I have laughed at the mock philanthropy of England!' And the great Carlyle himself could rant about the Exeter Hall people: '. . . Sunk in deep froth oceans of "Benevolence", "Fraternity", "Emancipation-principle", "Christian Philanthropy" and other most amiable looking, but most baseless . . . jargon.'

Livingstone possessed the gift of being able to take the measure of public attitudes with great rapidity, and was not deceived by the clouds of praise and enthusiasm that enveloped him at the RGS, in the voice of Lord Shaftesbury, at the Mansion House. He knew that in presenting himself, indeed, in furthering his own interests, in advocating Christianity, commerce and civilisation as a world-view he would have to take the Carlylites into account. And in doing so he would have to make himself fully acceptable to the less bigoted part – a potential majority – of the various political, ecclesiastical and commercial powers he would be appealing to for support in his next steps. In so far as he could go along with Carlyle's ideas about a British Christian destiny and the role of the strong silent man, he would do so. Inasmuch as he was descended from what many aristocrats regarded as the 'Lower Orders', he would show that he was as respectable as anyone could wish. As for independence, he would show that although he had lived for seventeen years on an exiguous salary, he was an exemplar of what self help and fortitude could achieve through Christ. And to the men of science, he would demonstrate that he was one of them.

After successful negotiations with John Murray (official publisher to the Royal Geographical Society), and after rejecting an offer from Macmillan Livingstone, with his wife beside him, sat down in lodgings at 57 Sloane Street, London on 22 January 1857, to write *Missionary Travels and Researches in South Africa* – adventure story, manifesto, prospectus.

13
MISSIONARY TRAVELS

In writing about south Africa and his travels further north, Livingstone had a number of immediate precedents to follow. A missionary perspective was given in Dr John Philip's *Researches in South Africa*, published in 1828; in his father-in-law Robert Moffat's *Missionary Labours and Scenes in Southern Africa* of 1842 from which, according to gossips at Kuruman, Moffat had made a fortune; and in Arbousset and Daumas's *Narrative of an Exploratory Tour to the North East Cape Colony*, issued in English in 1846. These three books were evangelical, suggesting the potential for the extension of Christianity beyond the established missionary stations. For the readers of the time they had an appeal as descriptions of 'new' and unknown lands, of strange peoples 'awaiting the gospel', of the probity and fortitude of the missionaries (indirectly they were soliciting support for the missionary societies).

A second genre was to be found in Burton's swashbuckling adventure stories interweaved with 'Believe it or Not' information and generally pejorative comment on the 'natives'. Burton wrote to establish a reputation and to make money, his only moral consideration to show how much cleverer was he – and by implication the white empire builder – than anyone else in India, Arabia, or Africa. Burton wrote like a gambler, throwing volume after volume at the public. His first books, about India, he staked at his own expense, and lost. He recovered with *Personal Narrative of a Pilgrimage to El-Medinah and Meccah* and *First Footsteps in Africa* with which he both made a name for himself and raised financial backing for further adventures, such as the expedition to the lake regions of central Africa.

A different work from any of these was Charles Darwin's now short titled *Voyage of the Beagle*, published in 1839 and re-issued in 1845. The *Beagle* set sail from England in 1832 on a journey of scientific investigation which took the ship around the world. One of the main tasks of the expedition – which was funded by the government – was to map long stretches of the South American coast. Darwin was taken aboard to investigate the flora and fauna of the lands that were visited, and was able to make lengthy tours into the interior. The discoveries he made – fossil seashells embedded in the rock of the high Andes, and the slightly different varieties of finch on each of the Galapagos islands – led him to question the biblical account of the origin of the world, and to start developing his theory of natural selection. He wrote up his journals into *The Voyage of the Beagle*, a classic account of the growth of scientific insight.

Livingstone, with Darwin, Burton and the south African missionaries behind him, with Friedrich von Humboldt's *Cosmos* – a copy of which was given him in 1854 by Lieutenant (later Sir) Anthony Hoskins of HMS *Philomel* in Luanda to entertain him on his way to Mozambique – with the travel books he had read as a youth, with Robinson Crusoe and Christian of *The Pilgrim's Progress* in the wings, was in a position to produce a work that would appeal to the various constituencies he had in mind. But he would not bracket himself exclusively with any one of them, nor make any concession to the Carlylites. Thrown out or, if not thrown out left safely locked in his journals, would be anything that might upset this delicate balancing act. He was preparing a curriculum vitae, just as he had done when he applied to join the LMS in 1839. Then he had been helped by his family and the Hamilton Independent Church. Now he had the support of Murchison, confidant of the government, of Professor Owen, of Oswell, Anglican gentleman par excellence, of John Murray (who knew the market inside out) and of Charles Livingstone, brother and minister of religion, who had come to Britain to see his recently widowed mother and became Livingstone's amanuensis.

It took a bare six months to complete a manuscript of nearly two hundred thousand words, to have forty-three illustrations commissioned, to have Arrowsmith's map drawn from Livingstone's observations – checked by Maclear. Writing at a rate of fifteen hundred words a day in longhand with steel pen and ink, rewriting and editing at the same rate while taking account of the comments of his advisors, this (even when the raw materials, notebooks and journals, lay before him, even with Charles to make the fair copy) was a monumental undertaking. But Murray wanted his deadline kept, publish the book before Christmas. Then even when all twenty-two chapters stood with their ink dry, he had not done enough. Something must be added, words must be said about the author himself, a personal dimension: and so it *was* done.

Livingstone opens the introduction with a disclaimer:

> My own inclination would lead me to say as little as possible about myself; but several friends have suggested that, as the reader likes to know something about the author, a short account of my origin and early life would lend additional interest to this book. Such is my excuse for the following egotism.

He gives a sketchy outline of the beginnings of the Livingstone family on the island of Ulva and mentions that his great-grandfather took part in the battle of Culloden, fighting for 'the ancient line of kings', then goes on rapidly to distance himself from his Highland background. At the same time he takes steps to protect himself from the English prejudice against the Celtic people of the United Kingdom, the 'Taffy was a Welshman, Taffy was a thief' syndrome, the belief that Irish and Highland Gaels were by nature untrustworthy and incurably rebellious, and announces himself a Protestant:

> My grandfather could give particulars of his ancestors for six generations before him; and the only point of the tradition I feel proud of is this. One of these poor islanders was renowned in the district for great wisdom; when he was on his deathbed, he called his children around him and said, 'I have searched carefully through all the traditions of our family, and I could never discover that there was a dishonest man among our forefathers. If therefore any of you should take to dishonest ways, it will not be because it runs in our blood. I leave this precept with you: Be honest.' Should I in the following pages per chance fall into errors, I hope they will be regarded as unintentional, and not that as indicating that I have forgotten our ancient motto. This event took place at a time when the Highlanders, according to Macauley, were much like the Cape Caffres, and any one could escape punishment for cattle stealing by presenting a share of the plunder to his chief. Our ancestors were Roman Catholics; they were made Protestants by the laird coming round with a man who carried a yellow staff, and the new religion went long afterwards, perhaps it does so still, by the name of 'the religion of the yellow stick.'

On the question of 'perchance falling into errors' Livingstone treads warily around the truth and, following the cue given in his opening sentence, says as little as possible about himself. Many aspects of his character he blurs or distorts, and where distortion would be too transparent, omits large and important aspects of his life. His descriptions of natural phenomena are usually wonderfully accurate, but personal matters and encounters which would muddy the clear flow of a Christian story are forgotten. The course of his life must be seen to spring from Christ and Christ alone:

> In the glow of love which Christianity inspires, I soon resolved to devote my life to the alleviation of human misery. I felt that to be a pioneer of Christianity in China might lead to the material benefit of some portions of that immense empire; and therefore set myself to obtain a medical education, in order to be qualified for that enterprise.

But at the same time he must show that he is not so fundamental a

Christian that his mind is closed, and must hint that from his early days science was a factor in his life:

> It is impossible to describe the wonder with which I began to collect the shells of the carboniferous limestone which crops out in High Blantyre and Cambuslang. A quarryman looked at me with that pitying eye which the benevolent assume when viewing the insane. 'How ever,' said I, 'did these shells come into these rocks?' 'When God made the rocks, He made the shells in them,' was the damping reply.

This story is told in the context of his countryside rambles with his brothers, an illustration of youthful curiosity and adventurousness.

Summing up his early years, which for him end when he joins the London Missionary Society, he stakes a claim to being a paragon of Samuel Smiles's self help (Smiles quotes the paragraph in his book), even if in doing so Livingstone must hurt those who had stood by him:

> Looking back now on that period of toil, I cannot but feel thankful that it formed such a material part of my early education; and were I to begin life over again, I should like to pass through the same hardy training. I never received a farthing from anyone, and should have accomplished my project of going to China as a medical missionary by my own efforts, had not some friends advised my joining the London Missionary Society on account of its unsectarian character ... This exactly agreed with my ideas of what a Missionary Society ought to do; but it was not without a pang that I offered myself, for it was not agreeable to one accustomed to work his own way to become in measure dependent on others.

In addition, he manages in the second part of the last sentence to suggest that his departure from the LMS – which his readers would have known about – was something for which the Society, by shackling his independence, was to blame.

Having made this point, and reassured anyone who might have wondered at his reasons for being, in his own word, so egotistic, he sought to reassure the establishment that he accepted the prevailing social order unreservedly. Rising with breathtaking patronage above the mill where he had grown up (and which here acquires the picturesqueness of a village) he presumes to speak for those he had 'left behind' and simultaneously submits his application – respectful, deferential – for membership of the 'safe' classes:

> Time and travel have not affected the feelings of respect I imbibed for the inhabitants of my native village. For morality, honesty and

intelligence, they were in general good specimens of the Scottish poor . . . Much intelligent interest was felt by the villagers in all public questions, and they furnished a proof that the possession of the means of education did not render them an unsafe portion of the population. They felt kindly towards each other and much respected those of the neighbouring gentry who, like the late Lord Douglas, placed some confidence in their sense of honour. Through the kindness of that nobleman, the poorest among us could stroll at pleasure over the ancient domains of Bothwell, and other spots hallowed by the venerable associations of which our work books and local traditions made us well aware, and few of us could view the dear memorials of the past without feeling that these carefully kept monuments were our own. The masses of the working people of Scotland have read history, and are no revolutionary levellers. They rejoice in the memories of 'Wallace and Bruce and a' the lave', who are still much revered as the former champions of freedom, and while foreigners imagine we want the spirit only to overturn capitalists and aristocracy, we are content to respect our laws till we can change them and hate those stupid revolutions which might sweep away time-honoured institutions, dear alike to rich and poor.

Having thus, he expected, said enough to show that he could present no possible danger to the governing class, he takes up again the matter of his 'independence' by omitting any reference to the part played by the LMS in his medical education. The Society, after all, as we have seen, paid for his final year of study in London, and the costs of his examination in Glasgow:

> Having finished the medical curriculum . . . I was admitted a Licentiate of Faculty of Physicians and Surgeons, and it was with unfeigned delight I became a member of a profession which with unwearied energy pursues from age to age its endeavours to lessen human woe.

As if this gratuitous rudeness to the LMS were not enough, he omits even to mention his theological training at Ongar, or his ordination under LMS auspices as an Independent minister. Indeed, one has to read *Missionary Travels* very carefully indeed to learn that Livingstone was a minister at all. Was he too independent (and Independent) to want to be known as an Independent? Or was he trying to disarm the snobbery of the overwhelmingly Anglican establishment? Moffat is mentioned as pointing Livingstone's way to Africa, and in later editions of *Missionary Travels* a chocolate-box Kuruman is added:

> The station is about seven hundred miles from Cape Town, and had been established, nearly thirty years before, by Messrs Hamilton and Moffat. The mission houses and church are built of stone. The gardens,

irrigated by a rivulet, are well stocked with fruit-trees and vines, and yield European vegetables and grain readily. The pleasantness of the place is enhanced by the contrast it presents to the surrounding scenery, and the fact that it owes all its beauty to the manual labour of the missionaries. Externally it presents a picture of civilised comfort to the adjacent tribes; and the printing press, worked by the original founders of the mission, and several younger men who have entered into their labours, gradually diffuses the light of Christianity through the neighbouring region.

Whoever may be the 'younger men' who have entered their labours, no mention is made of anything, such as Livingstone's abrasive relations with Messrs Ross and Edwards, which might disturb this idyllic mirror of mission life – an idyll which comes to include Livingstone's marriage:

> This oasis became doubly interesting to me, from being like a practical exposition of the text, Mark x.29 ('And Jesus answered and said, Verily I say unto you. There is no man that hath left house, or bretheren, or sisters, or father, or mother, or wife, or children, or lands, for my sake, and the gospel's, but he shall receive an hundredfold now in this time, houses and brethren, and sisters, and mothers, and children, and lands . . .') for after nearly four years of African life as a bachelor, I screwed up courage to put a question beneath one of the fruit-trees, the result of which was that in 1844 I became united in marriage with Mr Moffat's eldest daughter, Mary. Having been born in the country, and being expert in household matters, she was always the best spoke in the wheel at home; and when I took her with me on two occasions to Lake Ngami, and far beyond, she endured more than some who have written large books of travels.

Did Livingstone, one wonders, feel a pang for Catherine Ridley Prentice (a mere fifty miles from London, member now of the Plymouth Brethren) as he wrote these words, sounding as they do so like those of any anonymous 'satisfied customer' praising the efficacy of the Matrimonial Prospects column of the *Evangelical Magazine*? And did he have her in mind when he makes another concession to snobbery?

> In process of time our solitude was cheered by three boys and a girl, and I think it useful to mention that we never had the least difficulty in teaching them to speak English. We made it a rule never to talk to them, nor allow them to talk to us, except in our own tongue. Indeed they rarely attempted to use the native language, though they spoke it perfectly. When they went on board ship they refused to utter another word of it, and have now lost it entirely.

Strange words from one who considered Setswana a 'perfect' language, which his children would, inevitably, have spoken better than himself, whose skill he could not have failed to admire: but then accent and forms of speech were becoming touchstones of class in England.

The original introduction ends with these sentences:

> I spent ... the following sixteen years of my life, namely from 1840 to 1856 in medical and missionary labours there without cost to the inhabitants.
>
> As to those literary qualifications which are acquired by habits of writing, and which are so important to an author, my African life has not been favourable to the growth of such accomplishments but quite the reverse; it has made composition irksome and laborious. I think I would rather cross the African continent again than write another book. It is far easier to travel than to write about it. I intended on going to Africa to continue my studies; but as I could not brook the idea of simply entering into other men's labours made ready to my hands, I entailed on myself, in addition to teaching, manual labour in building and other handicraft work, which made me generally as much exhausted and unfit for study in the evenings as ever I had been when a cotton-spinner. The want of time for self-improvement was the only source of regret that I experienced during my African career. The reader remembering this will make allowances for the mere gropings for light of a student who has the vanity to think himself 'not yet too old to learn'.

And so he has to deny the extraordinary amount of knowledge he did acquire, from people, books, periodicals, observation, and pure reasoning – knowledge and an approach to the Cosmos that distinguish him as an outstanding intelligence, brought to light by the Scottish educational tradition from which he grew. The English did not like cleverness.

Like the five-year voyage of the *Beagle*, Livingstone's long journeys were made, as we have seen, for a multiplicity of purposes, even if he did not reveal them all in either the introduction or the text of *Missionary Travels*. The *Beagle*'s principal objectives were to chart the least known parts of the South American coast and to circumnavigate the world in order to fix longitudes with the latest equipment. A subsidiary, personal, motive of Captain Fitzroy was to take back to Tierra del Fuego four 'Fuegians' whom he had kidnapped on a previous voyage and brought to England in the hope that on their return they would form the nucleus of a 'civilised' Christian mission (one is reminded of Livingstone and Sekwebu).

Then there was Darwin. He was twenty-two when the *Beagle* sailed, and he paid his own way (or rather, his family did). His only qualification as 'naturalist' was the recommendation of Professor Henslow, the

Cambridge botanist, who had noticed the powers of observation and analysis possessed by the young theology student – for such Darwin had been.

Livingstone was in a sense a one-man 'Beagle', with his sextant and chronometer plotting charts, with his thermometer calculating altitudes. He journeyed like Darwin through unknown or little known places, recording in his notebooks and journals anything he thought was relevant to his ultimate purposes – and much about himself. When he quarried this mountain of paper for *Missionary Travels* he made public only his 'ostensible objects', as he called them. Darwin, on the other hand, had no ultimate purpose when he set out, besides the satisfaction of curiosity. A wealthy young man could afford non-utilitarian pursuits, Livingstone could not. Livingstone was concerned with facts, Darwin with questions.

Most of Livingstone's readers would be unaware of the errors, whether intentional or not, that he committed – post-dating his interest in going to Lake Ngami by five years, or stating that Silva Porto (whose name he does not mention) was not a European – and bought and read *Missionary Travels* keenly. It contains, as Livingstone intended, something for everyone. The Christian's faith in God is strengthened by the author's very survival of every imaginable danger. The missionary spirit is roused by descriptions of the people awaiting the Word. The abolitionist is inspired by the prospect of stopping the slave trade. Medical men are intrigued by Livingstone's approach to disease and the value of his treatment for fever. Empire-builders, millowners and engineers are excited by the prospect of untilled lands, fertile soils, the need for railways. The geographer, the naturalist, the geologist are fascinated by Livingstone's meticulousness in bringing unknown territory, with its unknown formations, plants and animals, into the realms of science. If the author says little about his wife and family, about his own sufferings and toils, so much the better, for the strong silent man does not discuss such things.

The narrative of the journeys is frequently interrupted with small gems of observation which shine in their own right and impart a truth-fulness to the panorama which the overall reality did not justify. Central Africa was not a rural paradise-in-waiting, requiring only a Prospero to wave a wand. But Livingstone's delightfully accurate descriptions have an enduring charm:

> In these forests, we first encountered the artificial beehives so commonly met with all the way from this to Angola; they consist of about five feet of the bark of a tree fifteen or eighteen inches in diameter. Two incisions or more right round the tree at points five feet apart, and then one longi-tudinal slit from one of these to the other; the workman next lifts up the

bark on each side of the slit, and detaches it from the trunk, taking care not to break it until the whole comes from the tree. The elasticity of the bark makes it assume the form it had before; the slit is sewed or pegged up with wooden pins, and ends made of coiled grass rope are inserted, one of which has a hole for the ingress of the bees in the centre, and the hive is complete. These hives are placed in a horizontal position on high trees in different parts of the forest, and in this way all the wax exported from Benguella and Luanda is collected.

(The same method is in use today in the forests of north-western Zambia.)

Or again, in another passage from *Missionary Travels*:

Ants surely are wiser than some men, for they learn by experience. They have established themselves even on these plains, where water stands so long annually, as to allow the lotus, and other aqueous plants to come to maturity. When all the ant horizon is submerged a foot deep, they manage to exist by ascending to little houses built of black tenacious loam on stalks of grass, and placed higher than the line of inundation. This must have been the result of experience, for if they had waited till the water actually invaded their terrestrial habitation, they would not have been able to procure material for their aerial quarters, unless they dived down to the bottom for every mouthful of clay. Some of these upper chambers are about the size of a bean, and others as large as a man's thumb. They must have built in anticipation, and if so, let us humbly hope that the sufferers by the late inundations in France, may be possessed of as much common sense as the little black ants of the Dilolo plains.

Pretty sketches such as these are sometimes developed in a way that reduces the imagination's distance between Europe and the African idyll:

The birds of the tropics have been described as generally wanting in power of song; I was decidedly of opinion that this was not applicable to many parts of Londa, though there birds are remarkably scarce. Here [in Mozambique], the chorus, or body of song, though, was not much smaller in volume than it is in England. It was not so harmonious and sounded always as if the birds were singing in a foreign tongue. Some resemble the lark, and indeed there are several of that family; two have notes not unlike those of the thrush. One brought the chaffinch to mind, and another the robin; but their songs are intermixed, with several curious abrupt notes unlike anything English. One utters deliberately 'puk, pak, pok'; another has a single note like a stroke on a violin string. The mokwa reza gives forth a screaming set of notes like our blackbird when disturbed, then concludes with what the natives say is 'pula, pula' (rain, rain), but more like 'weep, weep, weep.' Then we have the loud cry of the francolins, the 'pumpuru, pumpuru' of turtledoves, and the 'chiken, chiken, chik, churr, churr' of the honeyguide. Occasionally near villages we have a kind of mocking bird imitating the calls of domestic fowls. These African birds have not been wanting in song, they have only lacked poets to sing their praises, which ours have had from the time of Aristophanes downwards.

As we have seen in the description of the Victoria Falls – shortened for the book – Livingstone was as capable as anyone of writing as well as any 'poet'. But there is something lacking in *Missionary Travels*. In spite of the brilliance of hundreds of passages – and here we would include even the edited version of the Manenko incident – there is after the first reading an overriding flatness about the book, a lack of additional dimension. About Livingstone himself there is little personality, about the factors that formed his opinions in his south African days, almost nothing. Dr John Philip, in *Researches in South Africa* recorded incidents which made his condemnation of white rule at the Cape quite emphatic. But Livingstone, in *Missionary Travels*, avoids anything that might offend anyone whom he knew he was, or would be, dependent upon, whether British or Portuguese. How different a tone and impact the book would have had if Livingstone had included – as Dr Philip would have done – the sketch of Chief Justice Wylde, or pointed out that the 'convicts' manning the Luanda garrison were not criminals but political exiles, transported from Portugal. These were truths which Livingstone concealed for his own purposes. But the second factor contributing to the flatness of the book arises from the nature of the cosmography he derived from Dick's *Philosophy of the Future State*. Livingstone was unwilling, perhaps unable, to regard phenomena as more than individual products of the divine will, and not as parts of a natural order it was the purpose of science to investigate and explain. Livingstone went no further than to wonder at the power of God. The sagacity of his Dilolo ants was a gift of God, the amazing conduct of the honeyguide in leading people to a beehive need excite no speculation. A clear example of Livingstone's approach to a minor mystery comes in these sentences:

A great many fossil trees occur in this part of the country, some of them broken off horizontally and standing upright, others lying prone and shattered into a number of pieces. One was 4 feet 8 inches in diameter, and the wood must have been soft like that of the baobab, for there were only six concentric rings to the inch. As the semi-diameter was only 28 inches, this large tree could have been but 168 years old. I also found a piece of palm-tree transformed into oxide of iron, and the pores filled with pure silica. These fossil trees lie upon soft grey sandstone containing banks of shingle, which forms the underlying rock of the country all the way from Zumbo to near Luputa.

Darwin, without Livingstone's religious inhibitions, discusses a similar discovery in his *The Voyage of the Beagle*:

These were petrified trees, eleven being silicified and from thirty to forty converted into coarsely crystallized white calcareous spar. They were abruptly broken off and upright stumps projecting a few feet above the ground. The trunks measured from three to five feet in circumference . . .

This is as far as Livingstone would have gone, but Darwin continues:

It required little geological practice to interpret the marvellous story which this scene unfolded, though I confess I was at first so much astonished that I could scarcely believe the plainest evidence. I saw the spot where a cluster of fine trees once waved their branches on the shores of the Atlantic when the ocean (now driven back 700 miles) came to the foot of the Andes. I saw that they had sprung from a volcanic soil which had been raised above the level of the sea, and that subsequently this dry land, with its upright trees, had been let down into the depths of the ocean . . . but again the subterranean forces exerted themselves, and I now beheld the bed of that ocean forming a chain of mountains more than seven thousand feet in height.

Livingstone tells us what a phenomenon is, Darwin what it implies. Livingstone unearths fossil bones (tells John Smith Moffat to do so too) and sends them to Professor Owen (as did Darwin). But bones for Livingstone are bones, for Darwin they are the beginning of enquiry:

. . . the Toxodon, perhaps one of the strangest animals ever discovered: in size it equalled an elephant or megatherium, but the structure of its teeth proves indisputably that it was intimately related to the gnawers, the order which at the present day includes most of the smallest quadrupeds; in many details it is allied to the Pachyderms; judging from the position of its eyes, ears and nostrils, it was probably aquatic, like the dugong and manatee, to which it is also allied. How wonderful are the different orders, at the present time so well separated, blended together in different points of the structure of the Toxodon.

Darwin's flights of speculation give his narrative an aerial quality, an excitement of discovery, as does his determination to make comparisons, to find similarities which go beyond simile:

> Whenever I saw these little creatures [humming birds] buzzing around a flower, with their wings vibrating so rapidly as to be scarcely visible, I was reminded of the sphinx moths: their movements and habits are indeed in many respects very similar.

And he explains why he found the face of a snake hideous by likening it to that of the vampire bat, and uncovers the source of his horror in these words:

> I imagine this repulsive aspect originates from the features being placed in positions, with respect to each other, somewhat proportional to those of the human face; and thus we obtain a scale of hideousness.

Livingstone's frequent inability, or refusal, to relate one phenomenon to another, either as cause and effect or as analogy, characterised his approach. He was consequently able to pursue his objectives with undoubting certainty even if his certainties could, and did, lead him to sadly wrong conclusions. On the other hand, keeping his eyes on the ground was in the long run his greatest strength: for example, he had come to regard black people as 'men and brothers', and did not allow extraneous factors to lure him into white racial attitudes, even when his popularity was at stake. There were several reasons for his dislike of Burton – his flashiness, his overflowing talent for subjects as disparate as languages and swordmanship, his gifts as a writer. But above all Livingstone found Burton's negrophobia repulsive, even when expressed in its mildest form as in his *Lake Regions of Central Africa*:

> When a bullock is killed, one of us [Burton or his white companion] must be present. The porters receive about a quarter of the meat, over which they sit wrangling and screaming like hyaenas, till a fair division according to messes is arrived at. Then, unless watched, some strong and daring hand will suddenly break through the ring, snatch up half a dozen portions and disappear at a speed defying pursuit; others will follow his example, with the clatter and gestures of a troop of baboons.

It was not, as we have seen, for attitudes such as these that Burton was kept at arm's length by the establishment, where they were common coin. Darwin himself made a compromise in *The Descent of Man*, published in 1871, and gave his blessing to the notion that blacks were closer to apes than whites, and (reflecting a view held strongly by English males) that women were mentally inferior to men. Darwin made his peace, too, with Christian opinion, which initially *The Origin of Species* had outraged, by admitting God into natural selection, a concession given elegantly in the 1872 revision of the book:

> There is a grandeur in this view of life, with its several powers, having been originally breathed by the creator into a few forms or into one; and that, while this planet has gone cycling on according to the fixed law of gravity, from so simple a beginning, endless forms most beautiful and most wonderful, have been, and are being evolved.

Livingstone could have agreed with this: even more would he draw strength from the great scientist's words written in his journal towards the end of the voyage of the *Beagle*:

> The march of improvement consequent on the introduction of Christianity throughout the South Seas stands by itself in the records of history ... the changes have been effected by the philanthropic spirit of the British nation ... To hoist the British flag seems to draw with it, as a certain consequence, wealth, prosperity, and civilization.

Darwin, like Livingstone, was buried in Westminster Abbey.

When *Missionary Travels and Researches in South Africa* was published in November 1857, Livingstone saw his public standing reach new heights. Equally reassuring was the discovery that he had become a moderately wealthy man. Reprint after reprint, and a generous profit-sharing deal with John Murray enabled him to deposit over nine thousand pounds with Coutts & Co., bankers. James Young, then well on the way to making his own enormous fortune, tried to persuade Livingstone to buy a country estate at Dechmont – between Glasgow and Edinburgh – but Livingstone declined on the grounds that he did not want to appear to have made money out of being a missionary. Dechmont, besides, seemed unlikely to yield the income, about £500 a year, that Livingstone would need to support a secure social position. Instead, he placed the bulk of his royalties in a trust for his children's education. The rest he used, as we shall see, with openhanded generosity, to further his objectives in Africa.

Livingstone's literary seclusion during the months while he was writing *Missionary Travels*, first in Sloane Street, then at Barnet in the countryside north of London with his friend of Ongar days Wilbraham Taylor, came to an end in July 1857. The second phase of his triumphal march through the United Kingdom began, preaching – for that only can be the word – the power of the British trinity of Christianity, commerce and civilisation. No message could have been more welcome. Just as the odium of the Crimea started to dissipate, an even greater shock shattered British self-confidence, a threat to the very fountainhead of the country's overseas wealth. While Livingstone blotted the ink on the last manuscript pages of *Missionary Travels*, news began to come through of the full extent of the great uprising known as the Indian Mutiny.

14
APOGEE

Livingstone claimed that he would have returned to Mozambique a few months after his arrival in England, to take his porters back to Barotseland, had he not been persuaded to stay and write *Missionary Travels*. He had won high praise a few years before by refusing a passage from Angola to England, a refusal made, he said, because he had to return his first group of porters to Linyanti. In both instances he seems to be stretching the truth. At Luanda, he knew that he was going to Mozambique in any event; in Mozambique he had settled the porters with Major Sicard, an arrangement subsequently approved by the Portuguese government. As soon as Livingstone had read Murchison's letter of congratulations at Quelimane in 1856 (not to mention the newspapers that hailed him as a wonder), and had received the cold communication from the London Missionary Society, he knew that he had reached another crossroads in his life.

In England the period spent writing *Missionary Travels* made it possible for him to take his bearings and decide which route to follow. The most important factors to consider were the LMS, the Royal Geographical Society, public opinion, the establishment and the government that did its will. Family matters no doubt played a part in Livingstone's cogitations, but as Victorians knew: 'The ideally responsible man was not expected to involve a wife and children in his fate unless and until he had a good chance (under providence) of making that fate a good one.'

It is not difficult to imagine the talks with Mary on the options that faced him: to stay with the LMS, return to Africa and establish the Barotseland mission (there were no prospects in China where the new Opium War was under way); to take an office job at the Mission House (out of the question for either himself or the LMS); to settle in Britain as a country doctor or an Independent minister (not much promise in either, Livingstone would have thought). No, he must follow providence and complete his work in Africa, the Zambezi beckoned, and besides, another successful venture (it need not take more than a few years) would guarantee a respectable and comfortable future. Mary had no choice but to abandon the hopes of her welcoming poem: for Livingstone to be seen to be submitting to her wishes would be interpreted as weakness. She was under his command, women were 'other ranks'.

Livingstone's plans began to take definite shape when, early in May 1857, as a result of Murchison's negotiations with the Foreign Secretary, Lord Clarendon, he was told that a roving consulship to an amorphous area of Africa would be his if he wanted it. At the same time, Livingstone told the LMS that he would go ahead with fulfilling his promise to Sekeletu for a mission to Barotseland, and that an ancillary mission should be sent to Mzilikazi and the Ndebele in Zimbabwe. The LMS opened a public subscription for funds for central Africa, and there the matter rested for many months. The LMS was under the impression that Livingstone himself would head the Barotse mission, while Livingstone waited for firm news from the government about his official appointment – a question which Clarendon and the Foreign Office had to put aside when all their attention was claimed by the rebellion in India. Livingstone knew that the offer of a consulship was good, and would not be withdrawn unilaterally by Clarendon unless Livingstone showed himself quite unsuitable for the post. However, consulships were often little more than sinecures with which political services and grand adventurers in the British cause were rewarded, or into which otherwise unemployable members of the establishment were placed to get them out of the way. Thus Dickens satirised the upper-class Tite Barnacle clan in *Little Dorrit*, published in 1858 after being serialized during the previous year: these ticks knew the game well.

> And there was not a list, in all the Circumlocution Office, of places that might fall vacant anywhere within half a century, from a Lord of the Treasury to a Chinese consul ... but as applicants for such places, the names of some or every one of these hungry and adhesive Barnacles were down.

Livingstone wanted more than a Barnacalian Chinese Consulate. He was not going to Africa to wander about the savannah greeting chiefs in the name of Queen Victoria, nor sit in a Quelimane settling disputes about bills of lading and getting drunk British seamen out of gaol. No, he was going to 'open' central Africa with a flourish, and for that he needed more than an honorific with a salary, he needed public support, and support more influential than Murchison alone could muster.

In this respect he was at the right place at the right time, for the public wanted him too. He was mobbed in the streets of London and, at greater elevation, caused a sensation when his presence was noticed one Sunday at church. From across Britain (and from Ireland) invitations arrived in the post, to accept honours, to address meetings. The Indian war had sent a tremor throughout the land. A Day of National Self Abasement was organised by evangelical preachers. In London a crowd of twenty five thousand gathered in the Crystal Palace to have itself flagellated by the Reverend Charles Haddon Spurgeon, a fire and brimstone Baptist. Terror was spreading through many a boardroom, for the basis of Britain's export-led growth was cotton textiles, and India was becoming the country's single largest market, taking now over a hundred and eighty million yards of cotton cloth a year. The loss of that market, which the Mutiny presaged, would mean the loss of tens of thousands of jobs, and that could lead to rampaging socialism. Industry, church and state were under threat. Hence Livingstone's avowals of loyalty, hence the success of his preaching. All is not lost, he declared, and his analysis of the Indian crisis was appealing, even if wildly inaccurate. The uprising had taken place, he said, because the East India Company had been concerned only with commerce and had tried to exclude Christian missionaries. But if, over the previous century, India had been Christianised, the Indians would have accepted British civilisation, and no rebellion would have taken place. Combine commerce with Christianity, he stated again and again, and the world is yours. A secular proponent of British destiny at the time was Karl Marx. Writing, with Engels, before the Mutiny, he comments in *The First Indian War of Independence*:

> England ... in causing a social revolution in Hindustan, was actuated only by the vilest interests, and was stupid in her manner of enforcing them. But that is not the question. The question is, can mankind fulfil its destiny without a fundamental revolution in the social state of Asia? If not, whatever may have been the crimes of England she was the unconscious tool of history in bringing about that revolution.

Perspicacious people Livingstone spoke to were aware that events in India were not the only threat to Britain's export economy and all that flowed from it. Its major component, cotton textiles, depended on imported raw material, most of which came from the southern United States of America. But the north-eastern states were industrialising rapidly, imports from Britain that had run at two hundred million yards of cloth were declining, and their own cotton piece goods were beginning to challenge Britain's on the world market, in quantity and quality ('Merekani', i.e. 'American') was the most valued calico in east Africa, for example). Britain needed secure markets and secure supplies of raw cotton which America would cease to provide as more of its own production was absorbed by its own industry, and if southern production were to be disrupted. At the end of 1856 that disruption seemed imminent as the cotton industry heard of 'a great wave of slave unrest,' and learned that 'the bloodbath in Tennessee in which alleged slave conspirators had met a ghastly fate may in fact have been linked to a widespread plot throughout the western slave states,' a plot in which white southerners believed. The 'great wave of unrest' came in the wake of the Republican Party's emergence and the fierce presidential campaign of its candidate, Fremont, an abolitionist. A campaign which had led in 1856 to predictions of the civil war.

Livingstone's formula matched the mood of the masters of a manufacturing economy which needed to change its global approach, and he had offered a permanent solution to the cotton problem in his letter to *The Times* in January 1857, when he had held up central Africa as a glowing cotton prospect, where the crop could be grown by docile 'freemen' rather than by rebellious slaves. He repeated the point regularly in *Missionary Travels*. And millowners would know that he was addressing them too when he declared: 'I beg to direct your attention to Africa', as he did in what have come down to us as his Cambridge Lectures. Livingstone gave two lectures in the university city on 4th and 5th December 1857 which were an appeal for missionaries who would be more than evangelists, who would be an essential component in his economic masterplan, basing production on more reliable structures than British industry possessed in India or the slave states:

> My desire is to open a path to this district [Barotseland] that civilization, commerce and Christianity might find their way there. I consider we made a great mistake, when we carried commerce into India, in being ashamed of our Christianity . . . A prospect is now before us of opening Africa for commerce and the Gospel. Providence has been preparing the way, for even before I proceeded to the central basin it had been conquered and rendered safe by a chief named Sebituane . . . By encouraging the native propensity for trade, the advantages that might be derived in a commercial point of view are incalculable; nor should we lose sight of the inestimable blessings it is in our power to bestow upon the unenlightened African by giving him the light of Christianity. Those two pioneers of civilization – Christianity and Commerce – should ever be inseparable; and Englishmen should be warned by the fruits of neglecting that principle as exemplified in the management of Indian affairs. By trading with Africa, also, we should at length be independent of slave labour, and thus discountenance practices so obnoxious to every Englishman.

Having thus, in the span of a long discourse – which included biographical material and descriptions of the shining prospects of greater Zambezia – dispelled some of the doubts about British destiny,

Livingstone concluded his address to the assembled dons and under-graduates with a paragraph which filled the Senate House with applause and enthusiasm:

> I beg to direct your attention to Africa; – I know that in a few years I shall be cut off in that country, which is now open, do not let it be shut again! I go back to Africa to make an open path for commerce and Christianity; do you carry out the work, which I have begun. I LEAVE IT WITH YOU!

The second lecture took place in the Town Hall, where Livingstone stood in front of a large map of Africa. Speaking to an audience less clerical and academic than that which cheered him the day before. Livingstone's theme remains the same, but the tone is more personal:

> As an encouragement to those who think of being missionaries, I need say no more here than call to remembrance those Reformers who founded our colleges here. The missionary's work is one of the most honourable a man can desire . . . Indeed to be a missionary is a great privilege and honour . . .
>
> I propose on my next expedition to visit the Zambezi and propitiate the different chiefs along its banks, encouraging them to cultivate cotton and to abolish the slave trade; already they trade in ivory and gold-dust and are anxious to extend their commercial operations. There is thus a probability of their interests being linked to ours and thus the elevation of the African would be the result . . .
>
> I believe England is alive to her duty of civilizing and Christianizing the heathen. We cannot all go out as missionaries it is true; but we may all do something towards providing a substitute: moreover all may especially do that which every missionary prizes, namely commend the work in their prayers. I hope that those whom I now address will both pray for and help those who are their substitutes.

The Cambridge Lectures were edited by the Reverend William Monk – one of the organizers of the affair – and published in 1858. The volume runs to three hundred pages, of which a bare fifty suffice for the lectures themselves. Livingstone's life and work is summarised in a long introduction by Professor Adam Sedgwick (noted simultaneously as a divine and a geologist; he was a friend of Darwin's). The text of Livingstone's *Analysis of the Bechuana Language* is given in part, as well as a lengthy letter from him to Monk expatiating on the qualities required of a missionary in Africa. The compendium is a recruiting and a fund-raising tract which, together with the impact of the lectures them-selves, led to the formation of the Universities' Mission to Central

Africa. This organisation was supported by Cambridge and the other three 'ancient' universities – Oxford, which had already awarded Livingstone its highest honorary degree, Doctor of Civil Law, Durham, and Trinity College, Dublin, where Livingstone had the enthusiastic support of the Anglican archbishop, Richard Whately.

With the lectures, Livingstone broke out of the ecclesiastical isolation of the non-conformist churches – whose members were excluded from the ancient universities – and enlarged his constituency to include the Anglican establishment. By this time he had also been awarded such public honours as the Freedom of the City, not only of London, but of Edinburgh and Glasgow (where £2,000 was raised for him) besides being elected Fellow of the Royal Society, which made him a peer of the most distinguished scientific minds of the day. He was listened to closely by a substantial segment of the millocracy. Among the places he visited – besides those we have mentioned – between completing *Missionary Travels* and his apogee at Cambridge, were Manchester, Dundee, Halifax, Liverpool and Leeds, the most important centres of British industrial production and trade. He addressed Chambers of Commerce and Cotton Associations, his theme was consistent. Even at Kuruman, where Moffat's Christianity did not include commerce, trade in British goods through the hands of independent traders had grown from nothing to £60,000 a year. How much more promising than an isolated outpost in a sparsely-populated semi-desert would be the well-peopled, well-watered and fertile Zambezi basin. And if cotton was what they wanted, cotton they would get – Britain's own cotton. No loss of bullion that would finance industry in New England, no reliance on Southern slaves or rebellious Indians. Livingstone did not himself have to ask to be more than a Barnacle consul. Other people, including Archbishop Whately, did it for him, suggesting to the government that more was needed: a fully equipped expedition, with Livingstone as leader. A third attempt to open the Niger was on its way from England, why not the Zambezi as well? The government heard, from the churches, from the philanthropists, from commerce and industry, and presented a motion to the House of Commons proposing that Livingstone be granted £5,000 by the Treasury to do as he wanted. Approval came, unanimously, amid cheers and waving order papers. The Zambezi Expedition had been launched. On this issue at least, Palmerston, leader of a shaky ministry, could face the political nation with confidence, forget about wars and revolutions and smile with Christian benignity, welcome a new buttress to the tree of state. And the Queen had the new recruit to tea, flattered him graciously for an hour and a half, was amused at his joke: 'The Chief asked, if Her Majesty is so rich, how many cows does Her Majesty own?' And she said in parting, 'My best wishes will follow you'. Buckingham Palace

– a long way from Shuttle Row: such is the wisdom of the serpent.

Livingstone had been confident of his position as soon as his manuscript was on John Murray's desk at 50 Albemarle Street (a desk on which had lain the works of earlier, illustrious, and, let it be noted, successful writers, Sir Walter Scott, Lord Byron) and where would lie a couple of years hence *The Origin of Species*. Murray knew a seller when he saw one, and Livingstone was no exception. The orders that flowed in from bookshops and subscription libraries (one of which took 2,500 copies) were gratifying for Murray. For Livingstone they were a fulfilment and a confirmation of his destiny, even if its shape was not absolutely clear. But it was clear enough for him to have included in all the illustrations which showed him in person, his consul's cap, his trade mark – the lion that breaks his arm at Mabotsa has knocked the cap from his head; he wears the cap as he looks out across Lake Ngami; it remains firmly in place as buffaloes attack and scatter his caravan of porters. On 27th October 1857, a week or so before *Missionary Travels* was published, Livingstone broke with the LMS and left them holding the Barotseland baby, the mission that he himself was to have established. For he was to be not only a consul but the leader of a government expedition which would soon be announced – as it was in the Commons on 11th December. The official consular appointment, in the name of Her Majesty, came a few weeks later. With offices like these how could he be expected to tie himself down? For the LMS, Livingstone's defection had ended a period of embarrassment and uncertainty. He had undoubtedly grown too big for them, but his fame had brought them nothing but public support and helped in raising a small fortune – over £6,000 – for the Barotseland mission. The Society remained committed, even if reluctantly, to this venture, and Livingstone promised to help the mission as best he could. If it succeeded, the LMS would gain prestige, if it failed they could plead that they had been bullied into it by Livingstone and that he had let them down.

Livingstone had managed to give missions a good name even among the circle around the Carlylite hard core that opposed them on the grounds that the money would be better spent in Britain itself. Among these momentary converts to the cause was Charles Dickens, who wrote Livingstone up in an article on *Missionary Travels* in January 1858, some two months after the book was published:

> I have been following a narrative of great dangers and trials, encountered in a good cause, by as honest and courageous a man as ever lived . . .
>   Dr Livingstone's sensible independence of all those mischievous sectarian influences which fetter so lamentably the exertions of so many good men; and his fearless recognition of the absolute necessity of associating every legitimate aid which this world's wisdom can give with the work

of preaching the gospel to heathen listeners, are merits without parallel in the previous history of Missionary Literature.

Dickens's attitude here (when we remember the Jellybys) was influenced by his friendship with a rich and influential woman, Angela Georgina Coutts. Even if Miss Coutts did not own as many cows as Queen Victoria, she was one of the wealthiest persons in Britain, certainly the wealthiest woman in her own right, outside the aristocracy. She was an almost exact contemporary of Dickens and of Livingstone, born a year after the latter and like him of Scottish origin, grand-daughter of the Edinburgh founder of Coutts bank (in which Livingstone placed his money). The bank had opened in London towards the end of the eighteenth century and grown rich financing overseas trade, profiting from the opium boom enjoyed by the East India Company (of which another Scot, the Duke of Argyll, had been chairman). While in her twenties, Angela Coutts inherited the bulk of the bank's stock, making her a millionaire. She did not marry until she was sixty seven, perhaps because she was too independent, too rich, (few eligible men would be able to match her fortune) and when she did it was to a man much younger than herself. Queen Victoria placed her in the House of Lords as Baroness Burdett-Coutts.

Miss Coutts devoted her active life, and a good part of her wealth, to charities, in the administration of which she enjoyed for many years the services of Charles Dickens. In Britain, she supported the 'Ragged Schools' at a time when a state system did not exist, and provided an elementary, and strictly Christian, education (she was a fervent Anglican) for destitute children. Livingstone's friend Archbishop Whately of Dublin was an enthusiastic supporter of the programme, as was Dickens. Miss Coutts also put money into slum clearance, erasing squalid tenements in the east end of London, erecting in their place apartment blocks in which the previous alley dwellers could take flats at rents they could afford – with the proviso that they could be thrown out if they failed to keep the premises, and themselves, clean. Besides these expensive ventures, Miss Coutts established a refuge for 'fallen women', collected from the streets (London had more prostitutes per yard of pavement than seemed possible for a Christian city) and placed in a sort of convent where they were taught Anglican virtue, needlework and what is known today as home economics. As most of these women had little chance when graduating, reformed and scrubbed from the refuge, of earning a respectable living in London, Miss Coutts's plans included shipping them to the colonies to provide matrimonial services for male British settlers who needed to be saved from unthinkable cohabitations. One or two shiploads were despatched but on the whole the results did not come up to expectations and the scheme was dropped.

Her other foreign initiatives were more substantial. She provided the endowment for the Anglican diocese of Cape Town, where the incumbent from 1847 to 1872 – Bishop Robert Gray – was also Metropolitan of Africa and a firm supporter of the Universities' Mission to Central Africa. Another far-distant recipient of Miss Coutts's grace and favour was James Rajah Brooke – she bought him a ship. This English adventurer – Christian, abolitionist – nearly won her hand in marriage but, though he was unsuccessful, he enjoyed her continuing friendship and support in the role he had created for himself in the game of empire. Like Stamford Raffles who, a generation before him had founded Singapore, Brooke was seeking a fortune in the spice islands. In 1840 he was in Sarawak, a part of the Sultanate of Brunei on the northern flank of the great island of Borneo, when a revolt broke out against the Sultan. Brooke took the lead in suppressing the rebellion and, when it was over, the Sultan, in gratitude, appointed him Rajah Brooke of Sarawak. Brooke ruled the territory from 1841 to 1863 when he handed over to his son and retired. He suppressed slavery, introduced Christian missions (subsidised by Miss Coutts), drew his forty-seven thousand square mile domain into the world commercial system and on his estate created for himself as perfect a replica of an English garden as an equatorial climate would allow. He became a legendary figure (Robinson Crusoe and William Wilberforce rolled into one), paragon of Victorian benevolence, satisfactorily rewarded with the goods of this world and knighted by an admiring Queen. He was everything Livingstone dreamed of becoming, 'Monarch of all I survey'.

Miss Coutts invited Livingstone into her circle, had him at her dinner table, exchanged letters, ideas, hopes, colonial reveries, until Livingstone passed out of sight, beyond the reach of the mails, on his last journey. Through Miss Coutts, Livingstone met Earl Grey, an influential public figure in debate about British imperial policy, and through him his nephew, Sir George Grey, the new Governor of the Cape Colony. Miss Coutts gave Sir George backing in his plan to start a 'school for the sons of chiefs', a type of institution which became common during Britain's period of high empire in Africa. Also in Miss Coutts's orbit stood Samuel Wilberforce, son of William the abolitionist, and now Bishop of Oxford. Wilberforce put the weight of his influence behind the formation of the Universities' Mission but Livingstone's friendship does not seem to have survived the unhappy end the first mission came to. Or perhaps Wilberforce – nicknamed 'Soapy Sam' by his critics – after making a fool of himself in a public attack on *The Origin of Species* in 1860, found Livingstone insufficiently anti-Darwin.

Another philanthropist Livingstone made friends with at the time (not part of Miss Coutts's Anglican group) was Sir Samuel Morton Peto MP.

Livingstone lived in his house in London for a while. Peto was one of the new generation of self-made millionaires, his fortune accumulated from the building industry and the construction of railways, and spent on Baptist missions in foreign lands and on such domestic extravagance as the model village called Somerlyton, erected at his own expense near Norwich, his House of Commons constituency. Unfortunately for Sir Morton, neither ostentatious respectability nor good self help credentials could save him from the jeers of public disgrace when he went bankrupt in the late 1860s.

With these allies, not to mention the cotton fraternity, or James Young, Murchison, Clarendon and Palmerston, Livingstone was in almost as strong a position as he could hope for. All that remained was for his way to be made straight with the Portuguese, with whom relations at the time (as for some time past) were not of the best. Help was in sight, however, as Prince Albert was, through his Saxe-Coburg blood, the cousin of King Pedro of Portugal, and of Pedro's father Fernando II, king by marriage to Maria II who had died in childbirth in 1853, leaving Fernando as regent until Pedro was old enough at eighteen to occupy the throne. Prince Albert, who spoke English with a heavy German accent, was treated with some reserve by the British establishment but made a policy of supporting what he assumed were popular causes: the Crystal Palace and the Great Exhibition, the Niger Expedition launched at Exeter Hall in 1839 with Livingstone in the audience. He was prepared to use his influence now by giving Livingstone a letter of commendation to Pedro: perhaps royal patronage would overcome the distrust the Portuguese ministers felt for Britain.

They knew that the establishment of a permanent British station of whatever kind on the upper Zambezi (and Livingstone was quite specific about what he wanted to do) would frustrate their long-term ambition to create a new Brazil by linking Angola with Mozambique across the central plateau. They were also furious with Britain about the affair involving the French ship *Charles et Georges*. The vessel had been engaged in transporting slaves from Mozambique to Reunion: acting under British pressure to enforce the anti-slave-trade treaty, the Portuguese had seized and confiscated the ship in 1857, and arrested its captain. The French government had responded by demanding that the ship and captain be released, and when the Portuguese refused to comply, sent its navy into the mouth of the Tagus bearing the threat that Lisbon would be bombarded if French wishes were not met. Portugal called on Britain to come to its assistance. Britain, ignoring its obligations under the Treaty of Windsor, refused, not prepared to go to war with France over a slave ship. Portugal was left with no choice but to release the *Charles et Georges* and to pay France a huge indemnity. This sorry business, so fresh in the mind, was unlikely to endear Portuguese ministers to British abolitionists, but they were in no position to block the Zambezi Expedition even if they knew that the British would hardly allow a foreign flotilla to go steaming up a 'British' river – the Ganges or the Niger, for example – in search of colonial conquests in the interior. The fact was that Portugal was a semi-dependency of Britain's, and Britain had the power to make life as uncomfortable as it liked for the Portuguese government. If not by sending in the troops, then by disrupting Portugal's trade or putting pressure on her currency which was linked to the pound, by refusing new credits (the Lisbon to Porto railway was being built with British loans) or by raising the interest on Portugal's already large foreign debt to Britain.

Livingstone was not able to deliver Prince Albert's letter to King Pedro. The Portuguese said, diplomatically, that a yellow fever epidemic in Lisbon made a visit impossible, and Livingstone returned the letter to the Prince. On 15th January 1858, the British government appointed Livingstone consul to Quelimane, Sena and Tete but the Portuguese refused to accept so wide a brief, since having a British consul at Sena and Tete implied that the Zambezi was open to foreigners. On 7th February, however, they agreed to a commission for Quelimane alone. Livingstone protested at this limitation to his scope, but the Foreign Office was not prepared to put further pressure on Lisbon and conciliated Livingstone by extending his consulship to include Barotseland and other chieftaincies, such as Mburuma's, along the Zambezi, but beyond the limit of Portuguese claims. Livingstone retained this appointment from 22nd February 1858 until the Zambezi Expedition was finally wound up in 1864. The Portuguese, for their part, tried to pre-empt the abolitionist propaganda they knew would flow from the Zambezi once Livingstone arrived there. They passed a law emancipating all slaves in Portuguese territory, but stipulated that it would not come into effect for twenty years. That stipulation alone was enough to stoke Livingstone's temper, but the thought that the Portuguese had slighted him would turn them into enemies. It was too late to withdraw the friendly things he had said about them in *Missionary Travels*, but the time would come for them to feel the lash of his whip. Even Prince Albert, cousin of Portuguese kings, would feel its sting.

Part Four

1858–1864
Disaster on the Zambezi

15

INTO THE VALLEY

By the time Livingstone sat down with officials of the Foreign Office to plan the Zambezi Expedition he had set in motion two other ventures to the interior. The Barotseland Mission, as we have seen, he left in the unhappy hands of the LMS, but promised to help the mission party to get established once it reached the Zambezi from the south, the understanding being that it would make the approach through Kuruman. Its funds were to come from the public subscriptions raised for it by the Society. The second venture, the mission to the Ndebele in Zimbabwe, to be led by John Smith Moffat, was being funded in part by Livingstone himself. Livingstone made Moffat a capital grant of £500 and undertook to pay him a salary of £150 a year out of his own pocket. With these two missions in position, Livingstone would have placed both the Upper and Middle Zambezi valleys within missionary orbit. For if Sekeletu's writ ran from near the source of the river to below the Victoria Falls, the Ndebele controlled the south bank from the Falls for a considerable distance eastwards.

The Ndebele mission was essential to Livingstone's purposes now that he had decided not to lead the Barotseland mission himself. He was breaking his promise to Sebitwane, repeated to Sekeletu, that he and Mary would work in Barotseland and form the moral shield against the Ndebele. But if the Ndebele themselves were under the influence of a Moffat, their aggressiveness towards the Barotse could be tamed, Sekeletu could feel safe and sleep well at night. Livingstone's actual presence on the Upper Zambezi would not be needed, while the LMS mission would be able to get on with the evangelical work that Livingstone had put behind him. Livingstone's promise that Barotseland would be protected by missionaries would be fulfilled, even if not directly by himself. If Livingstone were to place the Universities' Mission north of the Zambezi, perhaps in Chief Mburuma's putative territory on the high ground that flanks the left bank of the river east of the Kafue confluence, he would have established a triangle of influence in the heart of central Africa. He knew that the Upper Zambezi valley was too unhealthy to be the permanent home of the LMS mission, but hoped to persuade Sekeletu to move his capital to the uplands

north of the Victoria Falls, made safe by the Moffat presence among
the Ndebele and hoped, too, that the LMS establishment would take
root there. Livingstone meanwhile would start his own settlement on
the Batoka plateau, within easy striking distance from each of the
three Christian outposts. George Grey, governor of the Cape, liked
these plans well enough to extract from the colony's legislature a sum
adequate to set up a regular postal service between Cape Town and the
Victoria Falls, passing through Kuruman and the Moffat Matabeleland
mission, avoiding the Kalahari crossing.

Livingstone did not envisage large-scale colonisation of the type
supported by Britain in Australia, New Zealand and south Africa and
which was causing in Australia the extermination of the Aborigines, in
New Zealand the displacement by war and conquest of Maoris and, in
south Africa, Africans from their lands. He wanted colonisation by a
small elite of dedicated Christians, not the settlers who in Natal were
unable to establish a sound working relation with Africans, and had
to import Indians to provide a labour force. He wanted stalwarts of
yeoman stock (not the type of men for whom Miss Coutts's reformed
ladies were being prepared), well enough educated for there to be a
clear division of labour between them and Africans:

> The idea of a colony in Africa, as the term 'colony' is usually understood,
> cannot be entertained. English races cannot compete in manual labour of
> any kind with the natives, but they can take a leading part in managing
> the land, improving the quality, creating the quantity and extending the
> varieties of the productions of the soil; and by taking a lead too in
> trade and in all public matters the Englishman would be an unmixed
> advantage to everyone below and around him, for he would fill a place
> now practically vacant.

Although he entered these words in his journal in 1864, towards the
end of the Zambezi Expedition, they are no more than an elaboration
of ideas he was nurturing in 1857 and 1858 when he outlined the 'ulterior
objects' of the expedition to Professor Sedgwick, the idea of a settlement
which would 'benefit' Livingstone's 'fellow countrymen' and Africans
alike. An objective which Livingstone said he wanted to keep secret,
but which was made public by Sedgwick in his introduction to the
printed version of the Cambridge Lectures, besides being aired at the
grand farewell dinner given for Livingstone in London shortly before
he sailed.

Elsewhere, Livingstone speaks of his settlement being like a mon-
astery (but without the celibacy) during the Dark Ages of Europe,
when monastic establishments were often centres of knowledge, of
agricultural and industrial development, of Christianity – that is to

say, of civilization – amidst the general heathenism. A more recent and relevant blueprint of his plans, however, can be found in the 'reductions' set up by Jesuit missionaries in Paraguay in the sixteenth century to protect the Guarani Indians from slave raiders and to save their territories from the Spanish colonisers' insatiable appetite for land and serfs. The 'reductions' were in fact industrial missions at which the Jesuits taught the Guarani, not only to read and write, but also a wide range of skills such as boatbuilding, blacksmithing, tanning and commercial farming. Over two centuries, these Jesuit establishments flourished but their very success in maintaining their independence eventually became too much for the colonisers to bear. The Jesuits were expelled and the 'reductions' destroyed with little effort, as the Jesuits' paternalism had deprived them of the will to stand on their own. In central Africa, Livingstone would establish a similar system. Free labour would replace slavery, a cash crop economy (especially cotton) would transform subsistence farmers into yeomen, trade would bring in the goods which make a respectable life possible, and the country would enter the world economic system as a nation of free men and women exchanging their productions in even handed commerce with the industrialised countries. Such a place Darien should have become; such a place Raffles' Singapore and Brooke's Sarawak were becoming; such a place central Africa would become, with Livingstone and Christian principle to guide it, and with the Zambezi Expedition to do the spadework.

In London in January 1858, the practical details of Livingstone's 'ostensible objects' had to be attended to. Once the £5,000 had been voted by the House of Commons, plans could be drawn up formally. The government, with the public mood in mind, wanted to put on a grandiose display of benevolence, with the Royal Navy and as many as two hundred men showing the flag up the Zambezi. Livingstone's first proposal had been modest, he had asked for little more than the means to take a few iron ploughs and a few items of machinery – a sugarcane crusher, an oilseed extractor – to Sekeletu. This was too puny a scheme for the government, and Livingstone – after rejecting the two hundred men idea (based on the shape of the Niger expeditions, the third of which was under way at the time), drew up a compromise which was large enough for the government but not too large, Livingstone hoped, for him to be able to manage himself. When this plan had been agreed by Clarendon, Livingstone was placed in the hands of Captain John Washington RN, Hydrographer to the Admiralty. Washington had planned the Niger Expedition and now acted as financial controller and chief supply officer for Livingstone. Assembling supplies for the expedition was a routine matter, handled with the Admiralty's time-tested efficiency, as were arrangements for the delivery of mail and replenishments to the mouth of the Zambezi. Ships of the Cape Naval Station were to call there regularly. Having a ship built for the expedition itself, a vessel suitable for use on the Zambezi, likewise presented no difficulty. Shipbuilders sprang to attention when Admiralty contracts were tendered. Livingstone suggested specifications – the question of draft was very important – left the matter to Washington and the navy and a steamer was commissioned from the Macgregor Laird shipyard at Birkenhead, which had just built the seventy-foot *Dayspring* for the Niger. Livingstone may have been pleased that the contract had gone to a fellow Scot, and one, moreover, who had been on the Niger, a man who would know what he was doing. But that pleasure would not last for long.

One aspect of the expedition over which Livingstone had complete control, where he had to rely on his own judgment even after taking advice, was the selection of his personnel. It went without saying that he was the leader. As second in command, he chose Captain Norman Bedingfeld RN, whom he had met in Angola, and of whom he said in the Cambridge Lectures: 'When I was at Loanda I was laid up with the fever of the country and, being very weak, Captain Bedingfeld, with whom I was on intimate terms, strongly persuaded me to go home.' After Angola, Bedingfeld served for two years on the royal yacht *Victoria and Albert*. He was devout, a keen anti-slaver, and had some experience of charting west African coastal rivers. He was ten years younger than Livingstone, and although Washington had doubts about him (he had a record of insubordination), Livingstone must have felt that youth and enthusiasm – even insubordination, a trait he had some sympathy for – could be directed to fulfilling the objectives of the expedition. He had enough confidence in Bedingfeld to delegate to him, a navy man, the final decision about the Macgregor Laird ship. If he were not satisfied, there was an alternative, the *Bann*, one of a pair of ironclad paddle gunboats built for the navy on Clydeside, and designed by the foremost naval architect of the day, John Scott Russel. The Birkenhead vessel was a seventy-five foot long paddle steamer with an eight-foot beam, with an engine that could be fuelled with wood. The ship's hull, in what was apparently an experiment, was built of steel sheets one sixteenth of an inch thick, the prime consideration being to keep the weight down to give the vessel a shallow draft. (Livingstone had been warned by the Portuguese Ambassador in London, the Count de Lavradio, that the lower Zambezi, with its sandbanks, could not be navigated by a steamer: Livingstone himself had travelled the river only in canoes.) In addition, the ship was designed so that she could be taken apart and transported in sections to the Zambezi. Bedingfeld travelled to Birkenhead to inspect her on her open-water trials, apparently without checking whether the boiler was being fired with wood or with coal, and accepted her.

Livingstone named the ship *Ma Robert* ('Mother of Robert', the title of honour given to Mary Livingstone by the Tswana at the birth of her first son), and after the trials she was split and loaded aboard the *Pearl*, the government-owned ship that was to take the expedition to the Zambezi. In spite of what transpired later, it is doubtful whether the *Bann* would have been suitable: with a heavy iron hull her draft was greater than the *Ma Robert*'s, besides which she could not be split and would have had to be sailed from the Clyde, around the Cape, to the Zambezi. Bedingfeld had chosen the vessel that he would command, a small affair compared to the warships he had grown accustomed to captain, and it is hard to see how he thought he would adjust to charting the Zambezi in a river boat, and to being subordinate to Livingstone. But if he were unhappy about these prospects he said nothing at the time. Perhaps he thought he could wipe his slate clean with the Admiralty by undergoing this penance; perhaps he believed that the ideals of the expedition would burn strongly enough to dispel any dark moments he might have to endure. Once a Captain RN, however, always a Captain RN. A sense of social exclusiveness is often reinforced by adherence to quirky doctrines, and Bedingfeld was not the only Captain RN in the nineteenth century to show this characteristic. Fitzroy of the *Beagle* was a follower of Johann Kasper Levanter, who taught that a person's inner being could be determined by the shape of his physical features and Fitzroy, so Darwin tells us, doubted 'whether anyone with my nose could possess sufficient energy and determination for the voyage'. For his part, Bedingfeld hoped to use the Zambezi Expedition to search for the Lost Tribes of Israel, which had not been heard of since the eighth century before Christ when they were carried away by the Assyrians. Even if Bedingfeld were not a fully-fledged British Israelite and did not subscribe to the movement started in 1837 by the Reverend John Wilson who taught that the Anglo-Saxons were God's Chosen People, he clearly hovered on its flanks. If Livingstone was unaware when he engaged Bedingfeld of the temperamental peculiarities the RN uniform concealed, he found them out on the Zambezi.

The second seaman in Livingstone's complement was a twenty-eight year old Scot named George Rae. He came from Clydeside, and had served as a ship's engineer on the routes between Britain and North America after working in the Tod and Macgregor shipyard at Glasgow. He was recommended to Livingstone by James Young and appointed the Expedition's engineer. Two other Scots were taken aboard the *Ma Robert* (and kept afloat and moving by Rae). Livingstone created a job for his brother Charles as photographer and moral agent. His qualifications for the first post were dubious, as was Livingstone's claim to Captain Washington that Charles was an expert on cotton – not a crop he would have been familiar with in his manse in New

York State. As for being a moral agent whose purpose it was to 'lay the Christian foundation' of the whole exercise, his influence was more often that of an Inquisitor than a pastor: besides, he was infuriatingly lazy, infuriatingly fastidious about his clothes and his food. He had complained about the inadequacy of the eight hundred dollars a year he was paid by his New York congregation and it is difficult not to think that he saw the expedition, with its salary of £350 ($1400), plus keep, as a sinecure in which he could advance himself. Livingstone had not seen his brother for seventeen years when they were reunited in 1857. He misjudged, or ignored, the way his character had developed, and came to regret bitterly that he had taken him along. But family feeling always overcame objectivity.

Also from Scotland was Dr John Kirk, born in Barry in 1832, son of a Church of Scotland minister. Kirk graduated in medicine at the University of Edinburgh in 1854, and during the Crimean War had served as assistant physician at a British hospital in the Dardanelles, where he spent his spare time collecting botanical specimens, ranging as far from base as the mountains of Greece. His strong interest in botany, which he shared with his father, took him after the war to Kew Gardens, where the Director, Sir William Hooker, was sufficiently impressed with him to recommend him to Livingstone for the Zambezi. Livingstone offered him the dual position of medical officer and economic botanist, which Kirk accepted, rather than pursue the application he had made for the chair of natural history at Queen's College, Kingston, Ontario. Even if Livingstone was pinching pennies by rolling two important posts into one, Hooker's confidence in Kirk was fully justified for, apart from his professional skills, he possessed a gift for diplomacy which enabled him to remain a neutral, if a sorely tried one, in the vicious quarrels that wracked the expedition.

It was not by chance that the three members of the party to be most affected by these quarrels were the Englishmen, Bedingfeld, Thomas Baines and Richard Thornton. Thornton was the youngest of the group, barely twenty years old, and a fresh graduate of the Royal School of Mines, where he had excelled in geology. He was the son of a country parson, and had been recommended to the expedition by Sir Roderick Murchison. Baines also came Livingstone's way through the Royal Geographical Society. He was thirty-seven, an adventurer born at Kings Lynn, Norfolk. He had started his professional life as a sign painter in Cape Town, then served as a soldier in, and artist to, a Scottish regiment during the Cape frontier war of 1850 to 1853. After that he went as artist-storekeeper (his sign painting talents had blossomed) to an expedition through north-western Australia, and when he returned to Britain the Zambezi Expedition was being launched. His work in Australia, both as an administrator and as an artist, impressed the RGS and he was elected fellow. After some hesitation, Livingstone took him on in the same capacity he had enjoyed in Australia but, knowing, as we do, Livingstone's feelings about the 1850–53 war, which had led to his virtual expulsion from Cape Town when he was preparing there for the journey to Luanda, knowing Baines's pride in having been a good 'Kaffer-shooter', Livingstone's decision to take Baines was wrong.

Livingstone seemed satisfied with the team he had assembled. Captain Bedingfeld, he told Miss Coutts, was a devout Christian, and most of the men were Scots, a clannish commendation which suggests that it was not by mere throw of the dice that it was only the Scotsmen who survived the expedition with their reputations intact. But it was not only men who were going aboard the *Ma Robert*. Mary Livingstone and six year old William Oswell were being taken as well. The male members of the party were unhappy about this decision of their leader's but Mary was determined, and it was too soon to send young Oswell to boarding school. Mary must have put up a strong fight to be included. Had she threatened to 'go to pieces' completely if she were left behind? Livingstone must have felt, in the end, that she could be useful, would not be a burden, and perhaps would help with tending the sick. Writing to Miss Coutts on 13th February 1858 he said that though Julius Caesar had called women 'impedimenta', Mary 'did her best'. The three other children, Robert, Agnes and Tom, were to remain in Britain under the ultimate care of Livingstone's trustees, James Young, Professor Andrew Buchanan (of Glasgow University), and James Hannan (a Glasgow businessman in the textile industry), who were to pay for their upkeep and education from the money Livingstone had earned from *Missionary Travels*. Livingstone's friend, the Quaker lawyer Bevan Braithwaite of Kendal was to act as a sort of unofficial trustee, and took a more personal interest in the children, particularly Agnes and Tom, than the others could. Agnes, now eleven, stayed with her aunts and grandmother at Burnbank Road, Hamilton. Robert, approaching twelve, and Tom at nine, were to be placed in schools.

On the face of it, Livingstone took a somewhat mechanical attitude towards his children: looked after by God and provided with nourishment for body and soul, they would make their way in life. His own childhood had been mechanical enough and, in plain material terms, his children were better off than he had been at their age. If Mary had been the one to insist on going to the Zambezi, then it was she who must carry the blame for their total lack of parental care at a crucial time in their lives.

Livingstone attended, too, to other family matters. He provided for his mother to be paid an allowance, and tried to help his elder brother John, by then settled in Canada, arranging for him to become the sole agent there for James Young's paraffin, on the understanding that John would put up the capital to get his end of the business going. Unfortunately, the agreement does not seem to have been prepared carefully enough and, as we shall see, the arrangement came to a messy end.

Family affairs aside, Livingstone had to deal with the details of personnel management with members of the Expedition itself, who, quite naturally, wanted to have their conditions of service made clear before they committed themselves finally. Baines, for example, demanded, and received, a higher salary than he was at first offered. Kirk, before his appointment was confirmed, tried to see Livingstone in Glasgow to discuss the details, but a dinner party intervened. Kirk left a letter, and Livingstone replied a few days later, on 4th January 1858:

> My Dear Sir,
> ... I saw you in the distance and the servant gave chase but she said that you suddenly vanished and your note of 1st January explained why.
> I was absent the whole of Saturday and now before starting for London (20 Bedford Square) answer your questions as far as I can. The passages out and home will be defrayed by Government, the contemplated length of the expedition is two years but there is a possibility of its being prolonged beyond that period by circumstances of which we are not at present aware.
> With regard to the 'necessary expenses' I am not quite clear as to what you mean; suppose you shoot a buffalo, there will be no expense incurred in cooking and eating it. There are no inns or hotels in the country. The lodging will all be free. The expedition will have supplies of plain food – coffee, sugar etc., and everything else I suppose will be got in the usual mess fashion, each member contributing a share of the expense of the extras. I shall not be answerable for luxuries of any kind whatsoever. An expedition of this kind cannot be successful unless all the members are willing to 'rough' it and it will be well if we all thoroughly understand this before setting out. The salary is £350 per annum. If you are prepared to rough it when necessary, I shall feel obliged by a note to that effect and will then recommend your name to Lord Clarendon.

Kirk was not happy about the salary (especially as he would have to pay income tax on it – perhaps as much as £5 a year) but he took Livingstone's offer and, by 14th January, began to receive instructions about what equipment to buy for his botanical work, and what medicines he would need as the expedition's physician to have in stock.

The expedition's terms of reference were worked out between Livingstone and Clarendon's Foreign Office, and with their authority to back him, he prepared a detailed 'job description' for each of the members, each adapted to the functions the recipient was expected to perform. These job descriptions give the clearest idea available of what the 'ostensible objects' of the expedition were, remembering that Livingstone's plans for a colony were meant to be a secret shared only by him, Alan Sedgwick and the Duke of Argyll (who was not enthusiastic). To Kirk, Livingstone wrote:

> The main object of the Expedition to which you are appointed Economic Botanist and Medical Officer is to extend the knowledge already attained of the geography and mineral and agricultural resources of Eastern and Central Africa, to improve our acquaintance with the inhabitants and to engage them to apply their energies to industrial pursuits and to the cultivation of their lands with a view to the production of raw material to be exported to England in exchange for British manufactures; and it may be hoped that by encouraging the natives to occupy themselves in the development of the resources of the country a considerable advance may be made towards the extinction of the slave trade, as the natives will not be long in discovering that the former will eventually become a more certain source of profit than the latter.

Livingstone makes it clear that apart from their professional duties, members of the party will be expected to join in the rough work – which he envisaged as little more than sailing the *Ma Robert* up the Zambezi to the Kafue confluence and then hauling stores, luggage and equipment up to the place on the plateau he had in mind. There a prefabricated iron house would be erected to act as headquarters and an agricultural station would be started with experimental crops of wheat and European vegetables.

Kirk was to investigate and identify local products of a 'fibrous or gummy' nature, sources of beeswax, dyes, and vegetable oils that might be exportable to Britain (Livingstone had high hopes for a shrub of the *Securidaca* family, called bwazi in Chichewa – he spelled it buaze – which was used for making string and fishing nets). The main emphasis on the botanical side, however, was cotton: '. . . it will be our duty to visit [the Chiefs along the Zambezi] and invite them to turn the attention of their people to the cultivation of cotton, by giving them a supply of better seed than that which they already possess.' Cotton, Livingstone knew, was no new crop to the region. The plant is indigenous to the drier parts of the Zambezi valley, and its fibre had been used for centuries there to make cloth, though local production had begun to die out as a result of the import of manufactured calico, first from India, and later from Britain and the United States. This economic process echoed what was happening in India itself, with a country which had been the greatest exporter of cotton cloth (the very word 'calico' is Indian and came into English at the end of the sixteenth century) turned into an importer of textiles manufactured in Britain from its own exported raw cotton. Livingstone laughed at the village handlooms he saw in Africa, knowing that they were doomed to extinction as the commercial production of cotton (made more profitable by the introduction of better seed) generated the exchange to make substantial imports of cloth a permanent part of trade.

Besides being economic botanist (and MO), Kirk found himself appointed ad hoc zoologist. In this field his instructions came through Livingstone from the famous Richard Owen, who gave Kirk a triple brief. Its first element was purely in the interests of science, Kirk being told to search the mudflats of the Zambezi for specimens of *Lepidosireus*, a type of lung-fish which seemed to represent a transitional stage between true 'gill' fish and land-living reptiles. It was a type of creature that aroused debate in the discussions of evolutionary theory then swirling around Darwin, Owen and others in Britain (Livingstone was to tell Owen that Darwin's theory was not upheld by his observations in Africa) but Livingstone seems not to have understood Darwin adequately, for he supports his remark to Owen by stating that there is no great struggle for existence in Africa, nor evidence of natural selection.

Owen's other directives to Kirk had clear economic, not to say political, objectives. The zoologist was to make a thorough study of the tsetse fly with a view to developing a method for 'the extirpation of the species'. Owen may have been told about Livingstone's colonial ambitions, but perhaps he was thinking of missionaries and traders when he wrote:

> From the concurrent testimonies of travellers in South Africa, it appears that the presence of the Tsetse fly is a barrier to progress by means of oxen or horses through the districts [infested] by it. The tsetse fly would prove a similar or greater obstacle to a settlement in the so infected districts by any colony depending upon cattle or horses for food or transport . . . [Kirk was to report on] the period and place of the [tsetse's] oviposition; the nature and course of its metamorphosis; the habitats of the larva and pupa; the ordinary food and period of existence of the insect in its perfect state; in short, as complete a Natural History of it as the time . . . and opportunity may allow.

The elimination of tsetse, Owen knew, lay in the future (more than a hundred and fifty years of research by Owen and his successors in this field is only now beginning to find solutions to tropical Africa's tsetse problem) but another concern of his, and of the business interests to which much scientific research was tied, was ivory:

The commercial value of ivory, the alleged large proportional size of the tusks and fine quality of the ivory supplied by the elephants of the Zambezi district, render all that relates to it and can be accurately ascertained respecting the food, haunts, and habits of that variety of elephant an object of great practical importance; especially in consideration of the scarcity and price of ivory during the last half of the century.

Owen's instructions to Kirk were additional to those from Dr Joseph Hooker of the Botanical Gardens at Kew, which specified how Kirk's research on plants was to be done.

Livingstone's general prescriptions as to the Christian element of the expedition are broad and vague, whether given to Kirk or the others:

> ... imparting to them [Africans] religious instruction as far as they are capable of receiving it – and inculcating peace and good will to each other ...

Kirk, as the medical officer, received an injunction to bear in mind when dealing with African patients:

> Never neglect the opportunity which the bed of sickness presents of saying a few kind words in a natural respectful manner and imitate in as far as you can the conduct of the Great Physician whose followers we profess to be.

Difficulties in verbal communication with Africans were to be overcome in advance by studying Livingstone's *Analysis* of Setswana, copies of which were printed especially for the expedition. Kirk seems to have been the only member of the party to have taken language study seriously at first.

Livingstone's instructions to him on 18th March 1858, ended with this inevitable advice:

> Finally, you are strictly enjoined to take the greatest care of your own health and that of the Expedition. My own experience teaches the necessity of more than ordinary attention to the state of the alimentary canal – constipation is sure to bring on fever – and it would be well if you kindly explain to the different members the necessity of timely, remedial aid to overcome any tendency to it ...

In the private letter of 15th April 1858, Livingstone promises Kirk that he will have his botanical specimens delivered to Dr Hooker at

Kew with the utmost speed as 'it is of importance to get them into the hands of our friend before the German of Angola.'

Thus would it be assured that any new African botanical species would bear the stamp of the Livingstone expedition, and not that of the competition, Dr Welwitsch of Luanda. (Today, Kirk's name is recalled in a forest tree of the Zambezi basin, *Kirkia acuminata*, but the 'German of Angola' enjoys the honour of being remembered in *Welwitschia*, the unique plant he found in the Namib Desert: not only does it flourish where, for lack of water, nothing else survives, but its leaves, like human hair, grow continuously until death.)

All members of the Zambezi Expedition received their instructions some weeks after sailing from Birkenhead. That took place aboard the *Pearl*, commanded by Captain John Duncan of the merchant marine, on 10th March 1858. Livingstone had said goodbye to the three children who were staying behind – a bitter parting, he told Miss Coutts – unaware that he would never see Robert again. While the ship was being got ready to sail, Livingstone paid a visit to Liverpool, across the Mersey, to see Dr Thomas Raffles, the seventy-year-old minister of Newington Chapel, cousin, and (while he was alive) confidant of Stamford Raffles, founder of Singapore. We can only guess at the conversation, but it would be surprising if it did not embrace Livingstone's own plans to establish his own slave-free outpost of Christian commercial civilisation.

It was a bright clear midday when the *Pearl* steamed out of Birkenhead. Livingstone had Queen Victoria's best wishes and the cheers of his farewell dinner following him, but a chill wind was blowing as the *Pearl* entered the Irish Sea, the Bay of Biscay was rough, but Livingstone's own clear bright prospects were to last until the muddy waters of the Zambezi delta were entered on 12th May. The *Pearl* called at Freetown, Sierra Leone, to take aboard twelve Kru seamen recruited for service on the *Ma Robert*, and the Livingstone party was given a grand dinner by the Governor of the Colony. The only jarring note during the short visit ashore was Kirk's discovery that the Creoles of Freetown were not the subservient 'yes massa' people he had expected freed slaves to be – hardly surprising considering that many of them were sprung from the loins of the indomitable Maroons of Jamaica. The Kru themselves were (and are), native to the coast between Freetown and Monrovia, renowned for their seamanship: many of their number served on British warships, not seeming to care that they were given nicknames like John Coffee or Long Will as long as they enjoyed due respect.

Livingstone established a routine for his party on the *Pearl*, which included lessons at 1 p.m. every day (except Sundays) in the Tswana language. Mary Livingstone, Thornton and (according to Livingstone)

Bedingfeld suffered from seasickness, though in Mary's case the sea-sickness was soon diagnosed as morning sickness, which Livingstone tried to keep secret from his colleagues. When the *Pearl* arrived at Cape Town he was able to hand Mary and young William Oswell over to the Moffats, who happened to be in the city at the time, expecting the arrival of both the *Pearl* and of the missionaries destined for Barotseland and Matabeleland. The Moffats would take Mary to Kuruman, and when she and the new baby were fit to travel, send them overland to join Livingstone on the Batoka plateau, where he was expected by then to have settled. John Smith Moffat's station in Matabeleland would be a place to stop and rest, and was only three hundred miles from the Victoria Falls. Mary would be able to bring with her the books and bits and pieces from Kolobeng which Livingstone had written about to Moffat from Tete in 1856. Her parents were not sorry that she and young William Oswell were being spared the rigours of the Lower Zambezi, no matter how inconvenient the pregnancy might be. Nor did Livingstone seem to be sorry to be relieved of his 'impedimenta': though why he at first tried to conceal the pregnancy, telling family and friends in Britain merely that Mary was 'ill' is a mystery. Was he ashamed of being thought of as weak or careless? Whatever the case, her miserable, wandering, life was spared for four years more.

As for Cape Town itself, Livingstone knew that his reception by 'society' would be very different from what it had been in 1852. There would be no libel actions this time, no obstruction by officials. Through Miss Coutts, the Governor was on his side, and Bishop Gray was an ally. The merchants, like Livingstone's old supporter Rutherfoord, were agog with prospects of sharing the Zambezian trade, sending onward the products of Britain's mills – and of Cape vineyards and distilleries – to the no-longer-dark interior. Governor Grey had had no difficulty in getting approval from their legislature to spend money on the over-land route to the Victoria Falls. State, church and commerce welcomed Livingstone and, to confirm their new recruit to the establishment, held a most splendid dinner to present their new star with an engraved silver casket containing the 800 guineas they had collected for him. The only thing that spoiled the celebration was Robert Moffat's speech, which lasted for forty minutes. So long that, as Thornton remarked, '. . . a lot of persons at the bottom end of the table had time to get elevated a little and became rather noisy.'

Livingstone banked the money, gave power of attorney to the government legal officer in case it was necessary to draw from it indirectly, and enjoyed a busy ten days before the voyage continued. He had old friends to see – Thomas Maclear especially – and new ones to confirm, Governor Grey, William Thompson of the LMS, Bishop Gray; acquaintances to make – Wilhelm Bleek, now the Governor's interpreter and librarian, Edgar Layard, new director of the Cape Museum, brother of Austin Layard, excavator of Nineveh, now a political figure of renown with easy access to 10 Downing Street; and old times and future promises to discuss with Rutherfoord. From Maclear's observatory on a buttress of Table Mountain, from the Governor's fine windows, Livingstone could look on Cape Town and rejoice, even indulge its leading citizens at Sir George's *conversazione*. And if people did not believe that his ideals could be achieved he could show them one, the conversion of slave labour to free labour, which had been fulfilled, here at the Cape. For was not young Richard Thornton pointing out the great benefits that had flowed when he said:

> Nearly all [the blacks] were slaves before the emancipation, but now from labour being dear in the Colony, many of them are well off, have houses as good as English cottages of their own, and they are now learning all the trades. In fact, throughout the Colony, they are far better off than the English poor.

And if one theory had become a theorem, and that theorem had been proved, why not the others, why not Batoka and the cotton fields of Zambezia? With God and God's government on his side, how could he fail?

The *Pearl* left the Cape from Simon's Town on 1st May, rounded Cape Agulhas, into the Indian Ocean, into the Mozambique Channel, into the mangroves at the mouth of the Zambezi.

16

'SHALL FAITH OUST FACT?'

If all goes according to plan the *Ma Robert*, assembled by Rae and the Kroomen at the delta, pilots the *Pearl* up the Zambezi to Tete, a distance of two hundred and fifty miles. There the *Pearl* offloads the expedition's stores, turns around, and resumes her voyage to Ceylon. The *Ma Robert* then takes the party aboard and delivers them from Tete to the Kafue confluence, a further three hundred and fifty miles upriver. A few days' march from there, the Batoka plateau lies waiting, salubrious, cool – even frosty – under the bright winter sky. The prefabricated house is erected, and members of the party commence the duties as laid down in their instructions, some along the Zambezi (Bedingfeld making charts, like Fitzroy of the *Beagle*), others on the highlands. Livingstone has brought his previous journey's porters up from Tete and takes them back to the Kololo capital where he persuades Sekeletu to move from Linyanti's swamps to the healthy highlands. Soon the LMS mission arrives, the overland route to the Cape is opened, Mary Livingstone, the baby, and young William Oswell come up from Kuruman, bringing what remains of Livingstone's belongings as well as orchard seedlings from the Moffats' nursery. A new Livingstone home is established, the cottonfields of free men begin to flourish, there dawns an age of prosperity, barbarism is transmuted into civilisation, produce flows to Britain, British goods flow back. And Livingstone? 'Monarch of all I survey', a redeemed Adam in a new Garden of Eden. 'Good times are coming', he used to chant to himself when things were going well, but he had little cause for joy as the *Pearl* made its entry to the Great River, Zambezi, 'za-mbezi', 'big water'.

He was just recovering from a prostrating attack of gastro-enteritis, so painful that Dr Kirk dosed him repeatedly with opium as an analgesic. Livingstone was the only person of the expedition to be attacked by the affliction, which suggests that his body harboured a type of amoebic dysentery, a disease that can lie dormant for years and suddenly erupt as a side effect of another infection, as a result of breakdown of immunity caused by general debilitation (neither of which Livingstone was suffering from at the time) or, perhaps, as a consequence of stress.

Tension there already was on the fringe of the expedition party, a lurking hostility between Bedingfeld and Captain Duncan of the *Pearl*: Bedingfeld, not only Captain RN, but recently officer on the *Victoria and Albert*, was chafing under the command of a common-born, common sailor who was, besides, such good friends with Consul Livingstone. But this symptom of a coming problem was not the main burden on Livingstone's mind, rather, it was the weight of uncertainty. He had promised so much that he could justly say, with Captain Ahab of the *Pequod*, 'I feel deadly faint, bowed and humped, as though I were Adam, staggering beneath the piled centuries since Paradise.' Livingstone felt that that Paradise lay beyond the mangroves of the Delta, but he did not know how to get there, did not know which channel led from the open sea to the river, did not know if the river offered clear passage and, worst of all, did not know for certain whether the gorge above Tete was an open gateway or a sealed portcullis. Promises lay piled like centuries on his mind. And the Conde de Lavradio had warned him, and the warning had been brushed aside.

In the event, it took six months to transport and assemble the whole party at Tete. Many hot days passed before a channel through the Delta was found, and not many days after that Captain Duncan realised that the Zambezi was too shallow and shoaly for his ship, offloaded all the stores a few miles up the mainstream on an elevated sandbank (which Livingstone named Expedition Island) and departed for Ceylon, leaving Livingstone to muse or glower over his little flotilla, the *Ma Robert*, a pinnace, and two whaling boats. Behind him on the dismal island lay the expedition's stores, which besides food and drink, scientific equipment, guns, ammunition, trade goods, tents, the half-erected prefab, included the small sugar mill for Sekeletu, and Captain Bedingfeld's harmonium.

By this time, Bedingfeld had quarreled with Captain Duncan, had had an open shouting match with Livingstone and threatened to resign. The hunt for access through the Delta, the preliminary survey of the river, the unloading of the *Pearl*, had taken from mid-May until nearly the end of June, and the party was only forty miles from the sea, more than two hundred from Tete. The only thing that had gone according to plan was the assembly of the *Ma Robert*, accomplished by Rae in three days. Now the level of the river was falling, and the brief cool season, such as it is at tropical sea level, would soon be over. The only achievement the expedition could chalk up was the finding of the deepwater Kongone channel through the Delta, but even then the channel was unsafe because of the sandbar at its mouth. Although the little *Ma Robert* had been the essential medium in the discovery of the Kongone outlet, even now it was becoming obvious that the vessel did not come up to expectations. Livingstone comments on the expedition's first five weeks' work in a letter, of 21st June 1858, to his millionaire friend Sir Morton Peto:

We have been for more than a month exploring the delta of this river in order to find a safe entrance and having succeeded beyond our expectations ... we find it prudent to send away the Pearl and go up by the steam launch Ma Robert ... we have set up the iron house on an island about 40 miles from the sea and when all our goods are in it, the Pearl will be sent off to Ceylon. We shall take them up to Tete by successive trips and the iron house last of all. Now if we had a sloop (paddle) ... such as you offered to build, we could even now go with ease up to Tete.

Livingstone is glossing over the predicament he is in, for even if Sir Morton's sloop is built (it never was) and sent to the Zambezi, he is now totally dependent on the *Ma Robert* (and the pinnace and whaleboats) to get the expedition's equipment – which had filled the *Pearl* – to Tete.

Although steamships were at the time the highest technological achievement of industrial civilisation, although the *Ma Robert* was a steamship, although she had looked beautiful on the drawing board, had satisfied Bedingfeld at her trials, was finely built (as Rae and his assembly crew could attest) she was a piece of science which rapidly wore down the morale of her complement, while the Zambezi laughed. The first fault to become apparent was that the ship was underpowered for the work it was required to do (perhaps because the current of the Zambezi was not taken into account in the design of the engine); the second that fuel was to be a constant and unremitting problem. The engine was specified to burn wood but the timber along the Zambezi had not been specified for the *Ma Robert*. Tropical softwoods, like the palms or the baobab, have a low thermal value (if they burn at all), while tropical hardwoods, which produce a fierce heat, are, as their name implies, hard, to a degree which no temperate hardwood – such as oak – approaches. Living trees are easy enough to fell with an axe, but once the wood has dried out, it is almost impossible with an axe to cut crossgrain or to split. The expedition found that the most suitable, and abundant, fuel tree on the Zambezi was *Combretum imberbe* (which Livingstone mistakenly names *lignum vitae*, a South American species), and its wood has been described as 'dark brown to blackish and extremely hard and heavy, hence its (English) name, Leadwood.' The tree grows up to a hundred feet tall, with a bole some twenty four inches in diameter. It is no wonder then that it took a day's cutting to get ready enough wood for a single day's steaming, or that in temperatures of 95° to 100°F, this labour soon became a curse, which could be relieved only occasionally by buying cut timber from villagers or from the Portuguese along the riverbank. In addition to the curse of the cutting, the leadwood had necessarily to be burned green, and this meant that it took the *Ma Robert* anything up to five hours to get up steam. Livingstone blamed the design of the boiler.

Livingstone could not admit that he was in any way responsible for the *Ma Robert*'s failings (or that he had omitted to investigate the fuel situation along the Zambezi). She had been custom built – even if with reference to the Niger steamer – on the basis of information about the Zambezi provided by him, and when she was first launched on the river (presumably burning coal from the *Pearl*), Livingstone was so pleased with her that he wrote Laird, her builder, a letter of congratulations. As Laird had worked to Livingstone's suggestions, he was in a way congratulating himself. But as soon as it became clear that the *Ma Robert* was going to be a disappointment, Livingstone turned venomously on Laird, the Admiralty and Bedingfeld. Laird was a 'Birkenhead Jew' who had schemed with John Washington to cheat Livingstone; Bedingfeld had rejected the *Bann* in favour of the *Ma Robert* because he would have had to sail the *Bann* out himself, which he was incapable of doing because he suffered from sea-sickness. Thus Livingstone in letters to friends. Never did he give the little ship credit for doing good service for thirty-two months, in spite of her main design fault, the sixteenth-inch steel hull which soon began to rust through in the hot humidity of the Zambezi.

Getting the stores up to Tete in the *Ma Robert* was a five months' agony as she was always overloaded (and overburdened towing the whaleboats which were also overloaded) and consequently went aground more often than necessary even in a river whose depth and navigability Livingstone had gravely overestimated. He cursed and kicked the little steamer, nicknaming her 'Asthmatic', but in kicking against her and all (except himself) concerned in her commissioning, he was kicking against his own hidden self: the first intimation to his ship's company of the monomania that was to keep everyone as uncomfortable as passengers in a lifeboat skirting a maelstrom. He took no notice of their fears, no more than Ahab heeded his Mate in *Moby Dick* when he cried: 'But let Ahab beware of Ahab; beware of thyself old man.'

Besides the state of the *Ma Robert* and the deceptiveness of the Zambezi, glinting so smoothly over the hidden sandbanks, there was another factor that Livingstone had not anticipated, not mechanical, not natural, but political – the lands of coastal Zambezia were in a state of war. On the right bank of the river there was stalemate: Ngoni (called by the Portuguese 'Landins') had invaded from the south, an offshoot of the *mfecane*, and taken possession, demanding and receiving, tribute from Lisbon's settlers. North of the Zambezi, from the Shire confluence to the coastal plains, there was a struggle for control between the Portuguese state and an Afro-Portuguese named Mariano, who had built up a following among Africans (escaped slaves and freemen) of the region and had become a Chief. At issue was the trade passing down the Zambezi valley to the port of Quelimane, mainly in ivory and slaves (a trade which, despite the affair of the *Jules et Georges* was increasing steadily, as we shall see) and, besides, the wish to be free of Portuguese rule.

Livingstone met the war on the *Ma Robert*'s first cruise up the Zambezi, with Bedingfeld surveying the river for a passage for the *Pearl*. They sailed into a gun battle at Mazaro (a few miles upstream from Expedition Island) between Mariano's men and those of the Governor of Quelimane. The latter Livingstone rescued under fire, at considerable risk to himself, but without, if he is to be believed, any help from Bedingfeld. Livingstone, adding cowardice to Bedingfeld's sea-sickness, sketches the incident to Sir Morton Peto in a letter of 17th September 1858:

> The people are at war with the Portuguese ... I landed once unin-
> tentionally on the battlefield – the sight of the dead sickened me and
> the Governor being very ill of fever his officers begged me to take him
> on board. The firing was resumed about as far off as the opposite side
> of the street from your house and all was confusion. I sent Bedingfeld to
> bring our men to carry the Governor – the fellow tried instead to get the
> steamer underweigh, but the Engineer [Rae] refused to set her agoing –
> seeing no one coming and not relishing the idea of a ball boring a hole in
> my precious body I took the Governor up and carried him off and cured
> his fever.

Livingstone and the *Ma Robert* were never deliberate targets of Mariano's army, and the Portuguese were grateful for the medical help they received from Livingstone, and especially from Dr Kirk. Kirk's services to the wounded were acknowledged publicly in the official government newspaper, the *Boletim de Moçambique*. But although Livingstone did not realise it at the time, his adventitious arrival on the battlefield was to prove the beginning of his serious problems with the Portuguese authorities. It was 'simply because we are English', Livingstone told Peto, that 'we pass and repass from one side to the other.' But this was not a mere passing from one bank of the river to the other, but between Mariano's territory and that held by the Portuguese. A notion of Livingstone's long-term hope that Britain would replace Portugal on the Zambezi had, almost undoubtedly, reached Mozambique (in 1858, to forestall the British, Lisbon proclaimed the whole stretch of territory from Zumbo to the coast the Province of Zambezia, a move we shall examine later); and undoubtedly, too, Mariano must have known of this hope when he offered Livingstone an alliance against the Portuguese. Livingstone turned this down, but received a party of Mariano's men aboard the *Ma Robert*, and Bedingfeld issued the 'rebels' with rum. A Portuguese trader, José da Cruz Coimbra, who on occasion supplied Livingstone with canoes, was Mariano's brother-in-law.

Mariano himself was in gaol in Quelimane during this war, and his brother Bonga had taken command of operations. The Portuguese militia, assisted by a settlers' private army of six hundred slaves, overran Bonga's fortress at the Shire-Zambezi confluence (and carried off large quantities of loot) but Bonga himself escaped without injury. The Portuguese would not have been pleased by the *Ma Robert*'s call at Bonga territory near the mouth of the Shire, a place named Shamo. Thornton records the visit in his journal in an entry of 14th/15th October 1858:

> ... came to what was Bonga's stockade = Shamo. Anchored for the night opposite it ... In an open space among the great trees was the citadel, surrounded by a strong stockade ... All was now in ruins ... Off pretty early up the river ... Spoke with lots of Mariano's people and gave several of them pieces of cloth to send word to Bonga that we were coming. About 10 [o'clock] came abreast of the first range of hills. Came up to Bonga. Anchored, landed, brought him on board to dinner, two of his men coming with him. One of them had been down in the launch to Expedition Island ... At first Bonga was not at all at his ease, but soon got more confidence. He had lost everything at Shamo. He asked if it had been safe (sic) for him to go in the launch to Senna to see the Portuguese, but the Dr. recommended him to send one of his men, as he could not promise him safety out of the launch.

It is difficult to see how this conduct of Livingstone's could be justified in terms of his appointment as HM Consul to Quelimane (where he had not even presented his credentials – unless he did so informally to the fever-stricken Governor rescued at Mazaro) nor for that matter how he could reconcile his later decision to establish an experimental farm at Tete with any of his three consulships. Livingstone had interfered in Zambezian politics (behaviour 'inconsistent with his diplomatic status') and his behaviour was equally inconsistent with his war on slavery, for Mariano and Bonga were undoubtedly engaged in the trade. He might have been trying to 'make the British presence felt', but the exercise in gunboat diplomacy (he had fitted firearms to the paddle-housings of the *Ma Robert*) backfired on him. Russell, once more British Foreign Secretary, replacing Clarendon, was furious. The King of Portugal complained to cousin Albert, who dissociated himself from Livingstone by refusing to become Patron of Livingstone's brainchild, the Universities' Mission to Central Africa. Livingstone had appointed José Nunes, English-educated son of the military commander of Quelimane as British Vice-Consul there to act as a link between the expedition and the Portuguese authorities, but this did not prevent a growing hostility between the Portuguese and Livingstone, at first perhaps political, but becoming more and more personal. This factor boded ill for the expedition.

The 1858 Mariano war had been started by the Portuguese on the pretext that Mariano and Bonga had been stealing slaves from the Portuguese (another way of saying that they had been giving refuge to runaways, even if the runaways then became slavers themselves, a common occurrence in all slave empires). The conflict had many of the characteristics of a maroon war, but with a major difference from the maroon wars that had raged in Jamaica and Guyana, for example, before emancipation. There, the slaves in revolt (for what is to run away but to rebel) could be isolated by colour from the white plantocracy, and, if it were convenient, accommodated to the power structure by being left alone provided they returned any *new* runaways. In Zambezia, on the other hand, Mariano and Bonga although by Anglo-Saxon norms 'black', were as much Portuguese as Tete's Goan parish priest or as José Nunes, or as Da Cruz Coimbra. The Portuguese colonial administration was dealing with people who presented a double problem. They could not be 'maroonised' and isolated, they were linked by blood and economics to 'loyal' settlers – hence the Governor's leniency to Mariano, set free to start all over again higher up the Shire when he had served his sentence. The 'rebels' might have to have their stockades destroyed from time to time, but they must not be driven so far that they turned completely against Portugal, drawing support from anti-Portuguese Africans (such as the Landins), from the general Portuguese slave population, and even from disaffected Portuguese themselves, such as the political exiles shipped from Lisbon to serve in the militia. Portugal could not afford to have petty squabbles turning into an anti-colonial struggle which Lisbon would find difficult, if not impossible, to suppress. At the same time, the Portuguese had to maintain a semblance of authority over Zambezia, or its occupation might be challenged by other European colonial powers. Such was the bouillabaisse into which Livingstone had tossed his consular cap. (If this imbroglio were to be turned into a Masque, the Portuguese might have cast the expedition as a Trojan Horse, and Livingstone as an icy Lucifer intruding into their tropical limbo. As for the Portuguese themselves, a xenophobic puritan script-writer could insert *dramatis personae* worthy of any Jacobean horror story.)

Livingstone, on the whole, dealt only with officials of the Portuguese government, whether military men or civilians occupying administrative posts, and had most contact with Major Sicard, landowner and commandant of Tete. The two men first met, as we have seen, on Livingstone's previous visit to the town in 1856, when Sicard nursed him back to health. Sicard was a slave owner (he made Thornton a present of a young man named Sekwati) and possibly a raider as well. Like Thornton, the other members of the expedition – except Charles Livingstone – made friends with the Portuguese all along the river. Charles began to reveal himself as the whispering serpent to the bearer of light, and his official position as moral agent to the expedition inspired him to try to enforce the most stringent astringent principles of respectability, as defined by New England puritanism (his wife, as we have seen, was from Massachusetts). For him, and through him for his brother, intercourse with the Portuguese was taboo, except on official business. For Livingstone himself, there were other grounds besides respectability for keeping his men from socialising. He regarded the Portuguese as enemies; fraternising leads to talk, and talk could compromise a Consul's secrets and strategies.

These considerations played only a small part in the dismissal of Captain Bedingfeld, but they were present nonetheless. The break between him and Livingstone became inevitable once the *Ma Robert* was launched and Bedingfeld had to place himself under Livingstone's command. By this stage of his life, Bedingfeld was not only constitutionally incapable of taking orders from anyone who was not a Royal Navy officer superior to himself, but also of performing the duties that on a man-of-war, such as he had commanded, fell to junior officers. Part of his arrogance arose from his own upbringing in the squirearchy, part from his caste status in the Royal Navy – even his wife was daughter of a naval officer – not to mention his service on the Royal Yacht. He objected vociferously to having to do the work of a 'lighterman' in having to issue rations to the crew and deal with the transhipment of stores. He neglected the hygiene of the *Ma Robert*, allowing her to become filthy, he could not handle the Kru seamen. He thought himself indispensable, and was furious when Livingstone proved that he could navigate the *Ma Robert* himself (and Bedingfeld's charts of the first stretch of the Zambezi were defective). The only job he could do properly was command. As Livingstone told James Young many years later, in a letter to him in January 1865, Bedingfeld wanted to 'ride roughshod over us all'. But, on the other hand, Bedingfeld must have been appalled by the slow progress of the expedition as it moved upriver from stage to stage, from Expedition Island to Shupanga, from Shupanga to Sena, from Sena to Tete. Apart from the delays caused by the fuel situation, it could take days of winching to drag the overloaded *Ma Robert* across a single sandbank.

If, as we have seen, things had turned out as Livingstone expected, Bedingfeld would have been very much his own man on the *Ma Robert* on the river while Livingstone busied himself on the highlands, and perhaps a mutual respect would have grown between the two men. But the frustrations (and extra work) of the reality as it was, meant that members of the expedition, with the exception of Rae as engineer and Kirk as MO, could not be slotted into their proper professional duties, could not (not even Kirk) work to their full instructions. Livingstone had no experience of coping with a contingency like this, tensions rose, personal idiosyncrasies came to the fore, and Bedingfeld took little trouble to suppress his own.

A number of Bedingfeld's quirks of character have come down to us in the journals of his companions of the Zambezi. One was his excessive piety; a fanatical performance of his own devotions in public view and a strong objection to working on Sundays. British ships' masters were often singularly religious, (from Fitzroy of the *Beagle*, driven to tantrums by Darwin's doubts and questionings, to John Newton, the captain of an eighteenth-century slave ship and composer of 'How Sweet the Name of Jesus Sounds', who had his 'cargo' kept silent below hatches on the Sabbath so that the crew's Divine Service could proceed undisturbed). Livingstone insisted that in the circumstances of the Zambezi, Sunday work was the Lord's work and, besides his scorn for Bedingfeld's piousness, found it no joke that Bedingfeld insisted that one of the purposes of the expedition was to search for the Lost Tribes (an irrationality that matched Livingstone's own search for the new Eden): two domineering men hunting white whales.

And Bedingfeld loved shooting (sea turtles in the Atlantic from the deck of the *Pearl*, birds on the Zambezi) a sport Livingstone abhorred – except in friends like Oswell. Bedingfeld loved, too, in Thornton's words, '. . . to astound the natives' by clicking and slipping his false teeth in and out of his mouth. And his harmonium! Cluttering the deck of the *Ma Robert* and then used for what Livingstone termed 'orgies with the Portuguese'. As Thornton records for 17th August 1858 at Shupanga, Bedingfeld had spent the morning shooting,

> . . . and returned about 12 – Capt B had shot a big brown eagle . . . Had a little lunch, after that Snr Azevedo's friend wished to hear Capt. B. play his harmonium, then we had music of all sorts. Our friend Snr Augusto commenced singing part of [Bellini's opera] the Norma. After dinner Capt. B. skinned his eagle.

A week later Bedingfeld – Livingstone's patience exhausted, the resignation confirmed – left the service of the expedition. Livingstone ordered Thornton (barely twenty years old) to write in support of his own charges against Bedingfeld, to add weight to the report Livingstone was composing to justify the termination of contract to the British government. And Livingstone told Thornton, on 25th August 1858, to get his own revenge on Bedingfeld for letting the expedition down:

> In making your copies of the chart [that first drawn by Bedingfeld] put in native names or those of your own invention rather than Bedingfeld's. To you belongs the honour of first laying down those portions of the river and your names ought to stand. Thus what he would call Arab point, from seeing an *East Indian* there call Nyuruka point.

This indirect insult had been preceded by a letter from Livingstone to Bedingfeld which the latter did not take kindly to. Written on 28th June 1858, barely a month after the expedition entered the Zambezi, Livingstone at his crass best states:

> A pretty extensive acquaintance with African expeditions, enables me to offer a hint for which, if you take it in the same frank and friendly spirit in which it is offered, you will on some future day thank me and smile at the puerilities which now afflict you. [Bedingfeld was thirty-three at the time!]. With the change of climate there is often a peculiar condition of the bowels which makes the individual imagine all manner of things in others. Now I earnestly and most respectfully recommend you to try a little aperient medicine occasionally.

Bedingfeld and Livingstone had to endure each other's company for several months after the final break as Bedingfeld had to wait for one of the Royal Navy ships to call at Kongone on its regular patrol, before leaving the Zambezi for good.

Livingstone, aware that Bedingfeld might start a row about his dismissal (and, indeed, he began to do so when he reached the Cape on his way home) supplemented his official report on the matter with references to the affair in letters to friends and acquaintances, beginning with Sir Morton Peto. To Captain the Honourable Joseph Denman, Commander of the *Victoria and Albert*, in a letter of 19th February 1959, Livingstone is discreet, mentioning only Bedingfeld's alleged sea-sickness. But Oswell was the recipient of a lengthy exposition of Livingstone's case:

> My naval officer thought we could move neither hand nor foot without him and resigned first, when we entered the Zambezi and subsequently when he thought I could not get rid of him. I was as mild as possible till I saw that he meant to ride rough shod over all authority [the remark repeated to James Young six years later] – but then I assumed the charge of the steamer, and when I made the first trip more successfully than

he had ever done I never saw human face lengthen as did Bedingfeld's. When I gave him notice to quit he began to dance and sing, but when he saw we got on better without him than with him, he tried to induce the other members to remonstrate with me. They gave me written declarations instead that I had acted quite right so off he was obliged to go. Not however before doing an immensity of harm – he overloaded the expedition with baggage [the operatic harmonium?].

Livingstone then expatiates on the *Bann* and the sea-sickness, blames Bedingfeld for the acceptance of the *Ma Robert*, mentions the stink with Captain Duncan, but says categorically 'I never quarrelled with him'. A dubious statement at best, which Thornton would contradict. In a letter of 2nd April 1859 Livingstone continues:

... and it is a relief to have done with him, though from my having turned skipper myself I have not been able to write to my friends. The vessel we have is such a botch of a job ...

I may tell you that between ourselves Bedingfeld was an awful bore from extra ostentatious piety – associated with a terrible forgetfulness of statement. His *private* devotions needs must be performed in the most public place in the vessel – and he tampered with the Kroomen – telling them he would soon be out again to Sierra Leone in command of another ship and would give jobs to those he knew etc – but they nobly declined to be led into mutiny by him. He told this himself – Proposed to the engineer also 'to lay our heads together and then we can do as we like.' If you have a war with such fellows in command woe betide our navy. Some Lord or other, pushes him on.

If there had been any substance in Livingstone's charge that Bedingfeld had incited the crew (and Rae) to mutiny – it is more likely that the Kru seamen grew mutinous under his arrogance – his career in the navy would have ended, even if he suffered nothing worse. In the event, the government accepted the justifications Livingstone had submitted formally for Bedingfeld's dismissal, but this had no effect on his prospects. He climbed uninterruptedly up the Royal Navy hierarchy, became Vice-Admiral in 1884 when he was sixty, ten years before he died. Perhaps there *was*, indeed, 'some Lord or other' behind him.

Livingstone, typically, could not let the matter rest, and some time after the letter to Oswell, on 7th February 1860(?) he wrote to James Young:

We hear that Bedingfeld has been shewing a letter written to him by Captain Gordon [of the *Hermes* which had escorted the *Pearl* from the Cape to the Zambezi] to everyone who will read it. Gordon tries to blacken Captain Duncan and me to the utmost – and in doing so asserts things on Bedingfeld's authority of which he has absolutely no personal knowledge ... Macgregor Laird and Bedingfeld, they have done us no end of harm.

More than four years after Bedingfeld had left the Zambezi, Livingstone writes about him again to Young, on 15th December 1862, finally revealing to his closest friend the factor which from the start was destined to make it difficult for there to be a good working relationship between the leader and the second-in-command:

> Bedingfeld had £600 while with me, and when I complained a little of this Lord Malmesbury [Foreign Secretary from February 1858 to June 1859] said in his Despatch to me that he thought I had far too little.

Livingstone had £500 a year, while Bedingfeld's salary as his deputy was supplemented by half-pay from the Navy. As the empire matured, and especially after the establishment of the Indian Civil Service, London created immutable rank/salary hierarchies for its imperial management structure. The need for such a system, which would minimise friction between officials – and such Livingstone and Bedingfeld were – can today be seen as the first important contribution the expedition made to British imperial thought. In any case, the days of the 'independent', like Livingstone, were drawing to a close.

The Bedingfeld affair did not affect the co-operation that the expedition received from the Royal Navy, which seconded two sailors, Walker and Rowe, to help, but even with their assistance the leap-frogging approach to Tete was not completed until 4th November, when the *Ma Robert* had the distinction of being the first steamer ever to be seen there. Exactly a week later, Livingstone's second daughter (and last child), named Anna Mary, was born at Kuruman. Mary had been two months pregnant when the *Pearl* sailed from Birkenhead, and Livingstone would have known to within a few weeks when the confinement could be expected. And would have known, too, that he did not now, in Tete, have infinity in which to set up house on the Plateau. There was an urgency too about two other matters. The Kololo porters – reduced though their number had been by violent death and disease – had to be taken back to Barotseland to fulfil the promise to Sekeletu, and Livingstone must be available on the upper Zambezi to give the LMS mission the help it would need to get established, diplomatic assistance vis à vis Sekeletu and material help in getting settled in a strange land.

Apart from these moral considerations, practicalities were pressing down on the expedition. November at Tete is infernally hot, the valley a steam bath awaiting the thunderstorms of the rainy season to bring relief, and that only momentary. Disease becomes a constant threat (Charles, Baines and Thornton were already ill) as do the nocturnal swarms of mosquitoes, whose scratched bites can rapidly ulcerate, as had happened to Thornton. Quinine taken against fever brings on dizziness and deafness, even dementia (as was happening to Baines), opium taken to relieve malaria's skull-cracking headache and aching joints brings lassitude and depression, if not worse. Tete in November is a place to escape from, fast, before the river falls yet further. Very life, it seems, now depends on getting the *Ma Robert* to the Kafue confluence, on getting the expedition on to the Plateau.

A short four days after the sickly, exhausted, party assembled at Tete – accommodated in a house provided by Major Sicard, but owned by the government – Livingstone headed the *Ma Robert* upstream towards Cabora Basa. On entering the gorge, the river bed narrows until the whole Zambezi is flowing between sheer rock faces less than forty yards apart, and yet the cliffs grow closer until the great river, a mile wide above and below the gorge, is compressed into a mere slit between high, almost perpendicular masses of rock, some climbing precipitately to the sky, some broken into enormous grey-black boulders that block the water's passage, splitting it into narrow, roaring, whirlpooly channels. The current is so strong here, the *Ma Robert* could not hold course and swung crashing into the base of the precipice. With that crash, all Livingstone's fears became reality, but yet his soul refused to accept: 'Let faith oust fact' cried Ahab's Mate aboard the *Pequod*, 'Let fancy oust memory', and so cried the master of the *Ma Robert*. He went ashore with Kirk and Rae, struggled over boulders the size of houses, hunting for the stretch of smooth water, flowing evenly, that would reassure him that the rocks at the entrance were small inconveniences, removable. But the higher upstream he clambered – the rocks so hot the naked hand could not keep a hold – the worse the prospect, as his companions could too easily see. Then he resolved to go further, alone, but Kirk insisted on going too, higher yet upstream, zigzagging up, over, down the buttresses of the gorge, climbing and descending three thousand yards of serpentine and granite, tearing clothes, blistering hands and feet, only to make a thousand yards forward. And what to find? God's Highway would not allow safe passage for even a canoe. Kirk and Livingstone found a true, living, thirty-foot waterfall, impassable, unclearable, even with all the world's artillery.

'Things look dark for our enterprise,' wrote Livingstone in his Journal. 'This Kebrabasa is what I never expected. No hint of its nature ever reached my ears.'

Can the third sentence be true? Had Livingstone forgotten that in *Missionary Travels* he had given the altitude of the river above the gorge, but not that at Tete. Had he forgotten what it implied when a huge river drops more than a thousand feet through forty miles of gorge? As much as living rock and living water, Livingstone had defeated Livingstone, fact ousting faith, memory, fancy. The Zambezi never had been, never could be, 'God's Highway'.

17
LAKE OF STARS

Faith ousted, hope survived, laced with self-deception. Livingstone tried to deflect the criticism that inevitably fell on his head because of his misjudgment of Cabora Basa by claiming that the gorge could be passed when the river was in flood, and if he had had a better launch than the *Ma Robert*. He wrote to Denman on 19th February 1859:

> In this groove there were some cataracts, but when the river is in flood, all disappear . . . But we need a strong steamer to go up . . . I felt inclined to drag [*Ma Robert*] up but feared a collapse as she is only 1/16 of an inch in thickness, and even if we succeeded, we should soon have been out of supplies after we had passed for she can carry but little cargo.

Since Livingstone knew that it was impossible even to walk along the gorge (forgetting for the moment the thirty foot waterfall), for he had been told by the Portuguese, St Ana, who had acted as guide, that the gorge was 'fearful when in flood', he knew that this dream was nonsense. But he had to massage away the doubts he had about himself, and which his backers would now have too. The only way to get the *Ma Robert* past Cabora Basa was to take her apart and carry her to the navigable water above, but as Livingstone had not inspected the other gorge, Mpata, which would have to be negotiated before reaching the Kafue, he could not be sure that even porterage would open the way to the Plateau, let alone convince anyone that the Zambezi was another Mississippi, even with the toughest-hulled steamer.

On his transcontinental journey, Livingstone had learned enough about the structural formation of central Africa to be able to draw an 'ideal section' of the landmass between the Atlantic and the Indian Ocean. This shows a plateau falling sharply to the western and eastern coastal plains. A river that left the plateau obliquely, rather than at right angles, like the Zambezi, might be navigable to the interior. Such a river was the Shire, flowing into the Zambezi from the north-west below Tete. The Portuguese knew about the Shire and that its source was a large lake. Candido Cardoso, a Tete trader-landowner who also served as magistrate and head of militia, told Livingstone in 1856 that he had visited the lake ten years previously and showed him a map he had made of the area.

Now, as 1858 drew to a close, Livingstone could not sit at Tete, enduring the doubts of his colleagues and the I-told-you-sos of the Portuguese (though he could be thankful that Bedingfeld was not there to give voice). A few weeks after Cabora Basa had swallowed one dream, he and Kirk set out aboard the *Ma Robert* in pursuit of another. They found the Shire to be navigable for nearly two hundred miles from its junction with the Zambezi to the foot of what Livingstone named the Murchison Cataracts. There they made friends with a Chewa (or Manganja) chief named Chibisa, who told them about the lake further upstream. Livingstone and Kirk returned to Tete and a proper expedition beyond the cataracts was set in motion. In mid-March (the expedition now entering its second year), Livingstone, Kirk, Charles, Walker and Rowe, with the crew, set out for Chibisa's (Rae, Baines and Thornton were left at Tete, Thornton with orders to investigate and if possible mine the exposed coal seam at Moatize nearby). Chibisa provided the party with guides, and leaving Walker and Rowe with the *Ma Robert*, Livingstone and his companions headed inland. With a palpable renewal of spirits, Livingstone describes the journey to Oswell in April and May 1859:

> In the interval of palaver about guides etc I write this to you.
>
> There is a high mountain near [the Shire's] entrance called Morambala. It is 4000 feet high and a fine point for a healthy station. It is well cultivated on the top having hills and dales and flowing fountains there – Lemon and orange trees grow well, so do pineapples . . . Above Morambala the country or valley of the Shire is marshy and the river winds, but not so much as the Chobe . . . There is plenty of game in the country but there is no hunting it – the grass is so tall one is lost and cannot get along except on paths . . . We left [Chibisa's] on the 4th and after a fortnight through a well peopled mountainous country came in sight of a high mountain called DZOMBA or Zomba in the East – We are now 1500 feet higher than the vessel and the Shire seemed coming round the north end of Zomba . . . We went south a little and crossed the spur of the mountains and first got a sight of Lake Shirwa on the 14th April; on 18th we were on its shores and a magnificent sight it is for it is surrounded with lofty mountains. Ngami is a mere pond compared to it.
>
> There is no outlet known – the water is bitter – a little like a very weak solution of epsom salts. We think it is sixty miles long . . . and the people told us that it is separated from the Lake Nyinyesi [lake of stars, i.e. Lake Nyasa or Malawi] by a narrow neck of land . . . We went down the Shirwa valley and [crossed] over the range which separates it from the Shire valley . . . Went down the Shire till we came to a branch

named Ruo which rises in that high range called Milanje – ascended it 7 or 8 miles and found we were about 30 miles of Lat. from Shirwa. If we don't get another vessel soon we soon go up the Ruo – carry a whaler over to Shirwa then go to Nyinyesi – this is for yourself only.

Livingstone is a discoverer once more, and immediately conscious of his great competitor, for his next sentence reads:

We could not hear a word of Burton – I have had no news from home – if he has discovered Nyassa first, thanks to my naval donkey I would have done all this last year – but we have got a lake of our own, and a short cut to his. Dr Kirk and 15 Makololo formed our party – country high and cold.

Livingstone realises – happily – that the Shire valley with its navigable river and the high ground that flanks it, cool, fertile, well-watered, can replace Batoka as the focus of his ambition. But first he must lay claim to it as his own 'discovery'. This entails both short-cutting Burton and discrediting the Portuguese – which he begins to do at the end of the letter to Oswell: 'The Portuguese are bent on shutting up what we open – they never went up the Shire and dare not now.' And for good measure repeats his refutation of the Portuguese claim that it was their citizens – the two Angolan pombeiros, or commercial travellers, (Amaro José and João Baptista) – who had crossed the continent first: 'An old lady of Tette distinctly remembers two black men coming to Tette and never went further – consequently the claim set up for them fails for 300 miles.'

Livingstone knew that Shirwa – 'the lake of his own' – was a mere puddle compared to Nyassa, but he could not go on to the latter immediately, expedition business had to be attended to, so after returning from the mountains to Chibisa's he took the *Ma Robert* down to the Delta to see if any Royal Navy supply ship had called. That not being the case, he went back to Tette at the end of June. On 11th July he set out again for the Delta with Kirk, Charles and the Sierra Leone seamen, who were being sent home – no longer needed now that Livingstone's Kololo were available, and anyway disgruntled with the treatment they had been getting from Walker, who was also leaving. To Kongone HMS *Persian* brought not only mail and supplies, but news of Burton's discoveries – Lake Tanganyika was one – and the news too that Albert Roscher, a young German geographer investigating Ptolemy's theory that the source of the Nile lies in a large lake (called Coloe by Ptolemy) in the deep African interior, had set out from Zanzibar for Nyasa.

Livingstone headed the *Ma Robert* upstream, now so eager to reach the lake that passion came to override judgment. For the first (and last) time on the expedition, he lost his temper with one of the crew he thought was idling and belaboured him with a billet of wood. For the first time he navigated so impatiently that one of the canoes (carrying porters) being towed behind the *Ma Robert* up the Shire capsized and a man was drowned. And Charles egged his brother on. After a night stop along the Zambezi Kirk, who had gone ashore to collect botanical specimens (Kirk took every small opportunity when not afloat to do his scientific work) was twenty minutes late back at the *Ma Robert*. Livingstone, persuaded, Kirk says, by Charles, set off without him, and only by running along the bank and hailing the ship did he save himself from being marooned. Charles accused Kirk of 'inconveniencing the expedition' by going off 'sporting' and said he had to be taught a lesson. Renewed faith and rising hope Livingstone may have had, but ambition's haste left little room for charity.

The *Ma Robert* docked at Chibisa's at the end of August. Livingstone and his colleagues immediately set out up along the Shire, had the first sight of the southern end of Nyasa on 17th September – six days, as it happened, before Roscher reached the north-east shore of the lake. Faith restored, hope justified, prospects unfold: Livingstone, discoverer yet once more, writes to Oswell on 1st November 1859:

> I propose to Government to place a small steamer on Nyassa – a common road could easily be constructed past the cataracts [which extend thirty miles] and the vessel made to be unscrewed and carried overland. We are going ahead in our ideas you see, but it is your own idea suggested long ago in the Kalahari that I am bent on carrying out. Look at it and see if I am visionary. Above or say abreast of the cataracts, the land East of Shire is in three terraces – the lower or valley of the river, strongly resembles that of the Nile at Cairo. This one is 1200 feet high – the next is over 2000 feet and 3 or 4 miles broad – then the third is over 3000 or about as high as Table Mountain. I never saw any part better supplied with rills of running water than these terraces and my companions Dr Kirk, C Livingstone and Mr Rae declare the same thing. Cotton is cultivated extensively over them all . . . We travelled in the hottest period of the year – that immediately preceding the rains – Shire valley was hot and stiffling [*sic*], but no sooner did we ascend to the second terrace than the air had a feeling of freshness. On the 3000 feet terrace it was delightfully cool, and on Zomba it was cold. We thus have changes of climate within a few miles of each other: Europeans without doubt could live here: the people have no cattle, but cultivate largely, and the trade in cotton could be developed I think by a small colony of our own . . . The field watered by the Lake and its feeders may be called cotton country of unlimited extent, which really seems superior

to the American, for here we have no frosts to cut off the crops – and instead of the unmerciful toil required in the slave states, one sowing of foreign (probably American) seed already introduced by the people serves for crops for three years, even though the plants should be burned down annually. There may be evils to counterbalance the advantages, but I don't know them yet.

The people are said by the Portuguese to be of quick apprehension.

We removed their suspicions ... by frankly telling them that we came to mark the paths for our traders, to come and buy cotton ...

Livingstone does not forbear to prove that the Portuguese are incapable of 'opening' the Shire (in fact, the Portuguese were not interested, their eyes still fixed on the gold of Zimbabwe, south of the Zambezi):

Nothing can be done with the Portuguese – they are an utterly effete, worn out, used up, syphlitic race; their establishments are not colonies, but very small penal settlements.

Kirk's observations confirm Livingstone's optimism about the economic potential of the Shire valley. His Diary entries for 3rd August to 5th September 1859 state:

Where is there better land for a colony? Fine soil, growing many crops now and fit to grow anything including wheat, with an abundance of water available for irrigation or water power. And below, a still richer valley where cotton and sugar would flourish.

Kirk believed that the inhabitants of the valley could with little trouble be brought into the market economy:

We always tell them that we are a great people who make cloth and guns and gunpowder and sell these to others for cotton and corn and other things: that this country seems good for growing such things as we wish; and that if we tell our countrymen that the people here are willing and able to give them cotton, they will come and sell goods regularly.

Livingstone's ideas on trade crystallised during this period in the form of the lake steamer, as he told Oswell. He did not know whether the government would support him in this project, and told Miss Coutts, in a letter of 10th October 1859, that he planned to build a steamer of his own and had no doubt that it would pay as a 'commercial specu-lation'. With the assistance of Rae, his engineering background and his experience of both the *Ma Robert* and the Zambezi, Livingstone drew up specifications for a ship that could steam from Britain to the Murchison

Cataracts, there to be taken apart, carried overland to the Lake, be reassembled and go into service. The commodities to be traded for the sort of British goods mentioned by Kirk, would include cotton, ivory, ebony, bwazi and lignum vitae – which has 'an attractive grain and an oily feel. The heartwood is very durable, especially underground . . . it would be suitable for turnery, fence posts, farm implements, construction work, railway sleepers and handicrafts.'

Also available at the lakeside market would be malachite and copper. These minerals, brought from Lundaland by Bisa traders, formed part of the slave-trade economy (as indeed did ivory), but Livingstone believed that legitimate trade, backed by his steamer, would make the slave trade (active though it was around the Lake) obsolete. Practical implementation of these ideas he had discussed with Oswell on the banks of the upper Zambezi. It was not Oswell, however, but James Young, industrialist, who now became the cornerstone of Livingstone's visionary edifice. Livingstone wrote on 28th January 1860, to tell him that Rae – his two-year expedition contract about to expire and at a loose end because the *Ma Robert* was beyond redemption – was on his way to Scotland to supervise the construction of 'a small steamer'. Young was asked to give what help he could and to extract £2-3,000 from Livingstone's trust fund to pay what Livingstone estimated the job would cost. Young was also asked to approach 'wellwishers' – Bevan Braithwaite, for example, and other 'persons who may be got to engage in the enterprise', who might be willing 'to supply provisions and seamen's pay and expenses out'.

There is little doubt that the Livingstone brothers intended to handle the 'commercial speculation' themselves and become merchants, a course of action decided upon after the visit to Lake Shirwa in 1859, before Nyasa had been reached, when David wrote to Young:

> My brother and I have concluded that it will be right to try and get up a trade in the produce of this country as we despair of the Portuguese ever doing anything except in ivory and gold dust. We are not men of business . . . and McOundle Shaw & Co of Glasgow know the proper things for African trade. The things must be strong generally, not flimsy dirt; though some of them are not such as can be used in England they will do for some things. A portion such as may be given or sold to chiefs may be in the form of 'Panno da Costa' [cloth of the coast, calico]. These panno da costa things are best for trade and so are imitation African cloths.
>
> We send £200 – half of which there is an order from my brother's agent, and the other half you must pay yourself from the money you may have in hand. I am supposing that another settlement may have been made with Murray [royalties]. I would have sent you an order on Coutts

[bank] at once but this goes through Portuguese hands three or four times and I don't trust them much . . . You are not bound to McOundle Shaw & Co, but they sent us a present of very proper goods for this trade and can serve us well if they liked. Excuse our presumption in trying to employ a landed proprietor for the benefit of our peddling. Had we possessed a proper ship we could have paid off the whole by lignum vitae and ebony.

In a later letter of February 1861, Livingstone suggests that Young expand his own business by sending some of his oil and oil lamps, presumably as samples.

The greatest of the 'evils that counterbalanced the advantages' in Livingstone's grand design were the Portuguese and the slave trade. The former he hoped to outflank – it was clear by now that the British government would do nothing to oust the Portuguese from Zambezia; there was far too great a danger that the French, England's colonialist rival, would move into the vacuum. As for the slave trade, Livingstone's mercantile activities would be supplemented by missionaries and then the much thought about Christian colony would come in to play its part.

There had been no missionary activity in the Zambezia region for seventy years, since the Jesuits had been expelled by the Portuguese. Protestant Christianity now had a fine opportunity.

Livingstone was ill with a recurrence of his dysentery when he returned to Chibisa's from Nyasa, and when he recovered he began directing his attention to the unfinished business of the Zambezi Expedition. While he, Kirk, Charles and Rae had been enjoying renewal of faith and hope at the sight of the lake, Baines and Thornton had been left behind at Tete. It was at them that Livingstone now pointed the accusing finger. Bedingfeld had been sacrificed to placate the demons of the shoaly Zambezi and the gremlins of the *Ma Robert*, Baines and Thornton were to be immolated to appease any malignant spirit that might plot the doom of the Nyasa venture. If Livingstone wanted merely to trim his personnel down to a size more appropriate to the new dimension of the expedition (neither an artist – Kirk was a good photographer – nor a geologist were needed in what was becoming a trading enterprise) he had only to notify Baines and Thornton that their contracts would not be extended when they expired on 31st January, four months ahead. But instead, both had to be disgraced. The memory of their easy-going ways, their friendships with Portuguese denizens of 'the slime pits of Siddim', their good natured acceptance of things as they were, must be erased with acid from Livingstone's image of the expedition, the vanguard of God's kingdom.

Baines, accused of theft, and subjected (while suffering the derangement that malaria and its remedies induce) to inquisition by Torquemada Charles, made a mumbled confession that perhaps he *did* dispose of a few cans of sardines and a loaf of sugar and did not record them in the out column of the stores book. Charles reported to his brother and refused to check stores or records in the presence of Baines, who is condemned as a thief, a sneak, an orgiast. Thornton's case was slightly different. He was not accused of sin, but of lack of virtue, of being a malingerer, a loafer, an idler, a time-waster, with his fever and ulcerated legs, and lacking in 'work ethic'. Livingstone does not even bother to ask to see his geological reports. But Thornton had laughed at the Livingstones' Scottish ways, he was not one of them – as were Scotsmen Kirk and Rae. He would have to go – but gently – for he was Murchison's protegé.

Neither of the Livingstones had the courage to do the dirty work, so David wrote:

River Shire
October 17th 1859

Dr. Kirk.

Sir,

You are hereby required to pass overland with Mr Rae to Tette in order to bring away two persons lately members of this Expedition, in order to send them home by the Man of War appointed to meet us at Kongone Harbour in the middle of November next.

As Mr Thornton, one of the persons referred to, has been honest, and failed in his duties as geologist chiefly from ignorance and want of energy, he is permitted to take his geological specimens with him . . .

The other individual, Mr Baines, referred to, having been guilty of gross breaches of trust in *secretly* making away with large quantities of public property, and having been in the habit of secreting Expedition property in his private boxes . . . It will be proper for you to ask him in the presence of Mr Rae, what he did with five jars of butter . . . what he did with five barrels of loaf sugar . . . Take possession of the [store-keeper's] book – of another book of mine in his boxes, 'The Plant' – specimens of brass rings and everything else you have reason to believe does not belong to him . . .

I am etc
David Livingstone

Thus does the strong silent man do business.

The hundred mile walk from Chibisa's to Tete, at the hottest time of the dry season, nearly killed Kirk and Rae of thirst and dehydration (the streams on the way were dry), but after spending a day recovering, they performed their unsavoury task, escorted Baines to Kongone. The Portuguese of Tete were so angered at Kirk (and, indirectly, at Livingstone) that at first they refused to provide canoes for the journey. Thornton was ill, and refused to go: he had money of his own and continued for a while, without expedition pay, with his geological work. Then, with his young slave, he went to Zanzibar where he joined Baron von der Decken's expedition to Mt Kilimanjaro. Later he returned to the Zambezi, as we shall see. Baines was taken to the Cape, where he tried in vain to have his name cleared officially. He became an artist-traveller and painted the first pictures of the Victoria Falls, some of which were published in a volume in London in 1864. Livingstone dismissed the book with a sneer but could not dismiss Baines so easily from his mind: Livingstone was still trying to justify himself into his dying days. But he seems to have remained unaware of, or to his credit not to have repeated, other comments on Baines's character. For example, one of the trader-explorers Baines joined after leaving the Zambezi was Charles John Andersson, he who had elicited from W C Oswell the remark that Livingstone was 'a plucky little devil'. Moving through Namibia in 1864, Andersson was exercised enough by Baines's reputation to record his impressions of the man in his journal. On 15th May 1864 he wrote:

> Baines in excellent humour this morning, and so he was last night. He has evidently fits of the blues. This morning he told me that several members of the Livingstone expedition were under the impression that he used mercury too freely; in short that it had affected his head. And I really fancy that there are moments when he is not all right, but it may also be attributed to absence of mind.
>
> ... Told Baines that old Nick himself would have the last word with him in argument.

A few months later Andersson had got to know Baines better. On 30th September the journal declares:

> I begin to think that there may really be some truth in Dr L[ivingstone]'s accusation against Baines for pe---n! Not that I believe he absolutely abstracted anything and concealed it or gave it away, but he eat [sic] it as he came in contact with the stores. Yes, eat [sic] it. I well remember there was one article in particular mentioned, viz sugar. Thus I have seen him eat it out of the sugar basin or the bag like the greediest child. Whole basins full have disappeared at a sitting. But I find he does the same with many other articles such as coffee, tea, milk, etc., of each of which and all he will consume large quantities when he has the run of them by himself. He buys gum, 'uintjes', etc. with my tobacco (of course not without my permission). The gum, he says, he wants for glue? Sometimes I detect him by it sticking in his teeth when

there is a peculiar clicking and smacking sound which tells a tale of itself.

At the end of 1859, Livingstone was waiting to hear whether the British government had agreed, firstly, to extend the expedition for a further two years, and secondly, to replace the *Ma Robert* with a new steamer, as the hull was now rusting through, and the vessel could be kept afloat only by sealing the holes with clay. When the mailbags containing the expected despatches were lost in the sea off Quelimane, Livingstone knew that he would hear nothing for a further six months, and decided to use the time to finish another piece of expedition business, to take the Kololo porters back to Barotseland and, at the same time, attend to the LMS mission, which should have arrived at Linyanti by then.

Of the a hundred and forty-odd porters Livingstone had left under Major Sicard's care in 1856, only about sixty were still alive. They had welcomed Livingstone with a great display of emotion when he arrived at Tete in November 1858, but that had not meant that they all wanted him to take them back to their homes. Some were Sekeletu's serfs, and felt that they had found freedom in Mozambique, others had married in Tete and started families, yet others saw opportunities for advancement where they were, and many were to become important in political developments along the Shire, establishing their own dynasties.

Livingstone, with Kirk and Charles (all that remained of the original expedition), and the few homeward-bound Kololo, left Tete for Barotseland in mid-May 1860. Charles thought the journey a waste of time, and Kirk did not want to go and complained that the constant tramping left him too little time for botanising. But, as he had decided to renew his contract, he had no choice but to comply with the leader's wishes. Livingstone estimated that the return journey of fourteen hundred miles would take six months.

Although no great physical hardships were encountered, it was not a happy trip. At Zumbo Livingstone learned that his friend Chief Mburuma, to whose realm Livingstone was Consul, and to whom he was bringing a letter from Lord Clarendon offering a commercial treaty (part of the original grand design), had been murdered by José de St Ana (nephew of Livingstone's friend Nunes) during an ivory expedition. Livingstone's hatred of the Portuguese grew, now that they were found impinging on what he still regarded as 'his' territory.

Livingstone led his party past the Kafue confluence and along the middle Zambezi valley. They inspected the Kariba gorge and then ascended the escarpment, arriving on the Batoka plateau in July, mid-winter, two years later than originally anticipated. Kirk was as impressed with the area as Livingstone had been: of the 'vast undulating plain' Kirk wrote,

The Batoka lands are the only ones suited for Europeans between the coast and the interior along the Zambezi. There are many places where people eager to make money might risk themselves, but this is the only European climate and here the thermometer sometimes falls to 30°. Sheep would succeed admirably.

This was the last time Livingstone was to see the lands that had engendered his visions. Now he put them behind him, avoided them on the return journey to Tete, travelling along the valley below.

When the party reached the Victoria Falls, they found there the first European tourist, a man named Baldwin, who had made his way by compass to look at Livingstone's discovery, timelessly magnificent enough for even the sour Charles to be inspired to describe it as 'better than Niagara'. But if Baldwin's presence was an encouraging sign of approaching 'civilisation', there was bad news as well. Livingstone learned that Sekeletu was seriously ill, and that the LMS mission to Barotseland had ended in disaster, that Livingstone's hopes for it and the civilising influence it was expected to exert had come to nothing – and he realised that his own reputation would be damaged again by this second (after Cabora Basa) obvious collapse of his plans.

The Barotseland mission was led by the Reverend Holloway Helmore, with an assistant named Roger Price, both straight out from Britain and neither conversant with either the Tswana or the Kololo language. Both men were married. The Helmores had four young children, the Prices an infant. Maclear had met them at the Cape en route to Kuruman in 1859. He had had a premonition about their fate, had felt that they were too naive for the undertaking they were embarking upon. When they arrived at Linyanti, with a small company of Kuruman acolytes, in April 1860, they found themselves totally unprepared for the situation they met. They lacked the diplomatic skill to persuade Sekeletu to accept them as substitutes, for the time being, for Livingstone and had probably expected to find Livingstone there waiting for them. They were treated as intruders and confined to their encampment. Moreover, they had no medical experience, let alone a doctor with them, and soon, inevitably, were struck down with malaria. Mr and Mrs Helmore, two of their children, Mrs Price and her child, all died. Roger Price and the Helmore orphans, with the African assistants, struggled back across the Kalahari to Kuruman.

Livingstone does not come well out of the affair. He had instigated the mission, more or less forced the LMS to send it, had deluded himself and the LMS into believing that he would be able to help it. His report on the matter to the LMS is cold and callous, with hardly a hint of remorse, only disgust at the incompetence of the missionaries (and by implication of the LMS itself). Once again he had been let down. Kirk tended to confirm this view:

> The blame, I think, lies much with the Society that sent them out. Surely if it is worth improving the heathen, it is imperatively necessary to provide those so employed with things and appliances necessary for their health. Instead of which a large body of Europeans ... are sent off without medical assistance into a notoriously unhealthy country.

The matter did not rest there. LMS officials in Britain, anxious to retain public confidence in the Society, blamed Livingstone for the disaster. Livingstone, for his part, transmuted any guilt he might have felt into hatred of the Society's administration, and kept the argument going for another decade. His case was strengthened by the success of the mission established in Matabeleland by John Smith Moffat (not a member of the LMS) and paid for, as we have seen, largely by Livingstone himself. Whether we accept Livingstone's version of events at Linyanti (that Price had made threats with a gun) derived entirely from the Kololo, or that of Roger Price (that his companions had been virtually murdered, the sick children even refused water), the venture was not an entire waste from the Christian missionary point of view. The widower Price married Mary Livingstone's sister Bessie Moffat and lived on for many years of evangelical work. Towards the end of the century he helped found the LMS stations on Lake Tanganyika and, as far as Barotseland is concerned, helped persuade François Coillard in the 1880s to resume Helmore's defeated work on the upper Zambezi. Coillard saw himself as Livingstone's successor, and the Paris Evangelical Missionary Society became the instrument through which Christianity was effectively established in what is today western Zambia.

Livingstone's feelings for LMS people were further exacerbated by a seemingly minor event. When he had last passed through Linyanti in 1855, he had left there two of his Journals with instructions that they were to be sent on to Kuruman. In the five years since they had not turned up, though Livingstone had been told that they had been given to a trader to take south for him. This trader was none other than Samuel Edwards, son of the very Rogers Edwards with whom Livingstone had quarrelled so violently at Mabotsa a dozen years previously. Samuel Edwards had denied ever receiving the journals, but Sekeletu's wife told Livingstone that she had given them to Edwards (Samo as he was called) herself. Livingstone had already accused Edwards of being a thief, his motive being to plagiarise the journals in a book of travels. His charge now seemed to be confirmed, especially as the Kololo had demonstrated their honesty in preserving intact the contents – books, medicines, tools, even the famous magic lantern – of the wagon he parked at Linyanti in 1853.

Besides the Helmore mission debâcle, there were other factors that convinced Livingstone that his Barotseland and Batoka dreams were over. Sekeletu was suffering from a skin disease, a type of leprosy perhaps, which Livingstone and Kirk knew would eventually kill him, even if they were able to relieve his pain for a while. The Kololo in general, weakened and reduced by malaria – to which, unlike their Lozi subjects, they had no immunity – were becoming a spent force. A Lozi pretender to the throne was waiting in exile, and it was only a matter of time before, to use Livingstone's expression in another context, 'the ancient line of kings' was restored, as indeed happened a few years later, shortly after the death of Sekeletu.

The atmosphere of depression, failed hopes, death, present or imminent, that engulfed the party was curdled further by the behaviour of Charles Livingstone. Whatever demons inhabited his soul burst out in furious quarrels with his brother, culminating in a physical attack and constant violent verbal whining, mocking abuse of the man whose grand strategy now lay in ruins. And when Charles, in paroxysm, attacked kicking the leading Kololo porter (Charles was saved in the nick of time from being speared to death) Kirk thought he had gone mad. The only light Kirk could see in this cloud of animosity was that David had at last realised that Charles had been the cause of much of the dissension in the expedition since it first entered the Zambezi.

With a handful of Kololo escorts – one of whom was to fetch medicines for Sekeletu from Tete – the party started back down the Zambezi. After a brief stop to examine an exposed coal seam at Sinazongwe below the Victoria Falls, Livingstone and his men sped eastwards (the despatches ought to be arriving) in canoes, but speed produced a mania of its own. In a last, fist-shaking gesture of defiance of Cabora Basa, Livingstone decided to descend the gorge *in the very canoes*. Fortunately, even at its approach to the head of the gorge, the Zambezi was so turbulent that the attempt had to be abandoned not, however, before several of the boats, if not their occupants, had been lost, including that containing all of Kirk's gear, and eight books of research notes covering his work during the previous two and a half years. As a result, Kirk was unable to complete a formal report on his findings. But he was lucky to escape with his life, as were the others. (Even in his last days, when he was approaching eighty, Kirk recalled his experience in Cabora Basa as the most terrifying of his long life.) With the remaining canoes now useless, the party had to clamber on foot through some of the roughest country in the world. Charles conducted himself with what had now become characteristic spite. He was ahead of and separated by some considerable distance from his brother and

Kirk and had with him the porters and the stores. Instead of waiting for, or searching for, David and Kirk he pressed on, left them without food to become, over a period of days, so weak that they could hardly drag themselves out of the gorge with its November temperature over 100°F and its rocks too hot to touch. Kirk's dislike of Charles had become so bitter that the editor of his diary saw fit to censor his remarks from the published version. Kirk had a dread even of Charles's company, and would have left the expedition had Livingstone himself not asked him to stay on. Kirk's recognition of David's strengths (flawed though they might be), his loyalty to him and to the expedition itself, were enough to persuade him, but he would soon begin to realise that the forces that drove David could be more dangerous than the imps and goblins that stoked Charles's vindictiveness. (There had been an example on this journey of David's courage-verging-on-madness when he had measured the depth of the Victoria Falls by taking a canoe across the current above the lip to an island in the middle which slightly overhangs the three hundred foot chasm, and there, leaning over the precipice, played out a piece of cord he was using as a tape.)

When they were back at Major Sicard's house – the trip, as Livingstone had predicted, had taken just six months – they found that the lost despatches had arrived. Lord John Russell, the new Foreign Secretary, had decided that the expedition was to continue but was to forget about Batoka, concentrate on Nyasa and the Shire highlands and try to find a new route there, perhaps up the Rovuma, which would by-pass the Portuguese. A new paddle steamer, the *Pioneer*, was on its way to replace the *Ma Robert* and with it was coming the advance party of the Universities' Mission to Central Africa, destined for the Shire. *Pioneer* and the missionaries were due at the Delta towards the end of January, in a month or so, and Livingstone must go to meet them.

As the *Ma Robert* steamed out of Tete for the coast, it was as if she knew that she had been 'declared redundant', like a discarded grandparent, no longer wanted or needed. On the approaches to Sena she grounded on a sandbank, her rust-riddled hull collapsed and she sank, once and for all.

18

ONWARD CHRISTIAN SOLDIERS

Running aground indeed at this stage of the expedition was Livingstone's wider reputation. The failure of the grand design – the opening of God's Highway – was epitomised in the Helmore mission's pathetic end, and even if the shock of Cabora Basa may have been to some extent lessened in the enthusiasm – echoed by Lord Russell – that had greeted the 'discovery' of Shirwa and Nyasa and the potential of the Shire valley, Livingstone's name still depended on his being, in fact, the discoverer. The Portuguese understood well that if Livingstone's claims concerning Shire and Nyasa were accepted internationally, their own claims over Zambezia would be considerably weakened and their ambitions for an African empire to replace Brazil would be put in jeopardy. Prince Albert may have withdrawn his support from Livingstone, but that was in a sense no more than a royal gesture arising from family feeling for King Pedro. As far as the Portuguese were concerned, Livingstone's colonisation scheme lay at the heart of the matter, and as its implementation depended on the strength of Livingstone's word, it would be politic for the Portuguese to call that word into question.

At the very time that Livingstone was travelling from Tete to the Delta to meet – and to take under his wing – the Universities' Mission, of whose progress the Portuguese could not but be well aware, the Marquês de Sá da Bandeira, Portugal's Minister of the Marine and the Colonies, issued in Lisbon a document entitled: 'Note concerning some lakes in East Africa, and the Zambezi and Shire Rivers'.

The Marquês's article (given here in a literal translation) is scholarly and unpolemical in tone, and starts with this apparently disinterested paragraph:

> Since the famous Doctor Livingstone, after travelling along the Shire River *in Zambezia* has written that it has not been navigated by the Portuguese, we were interested enough to examine certain books with a view to establishing what knowledge they contain about the lakes and rivers mentioned above, [recorded before Dr Livingstone's] recent journeys were undertaken . . .

The Marquês then gives five published examples of Portuguese discoveries in central Africa, dating from 1597 to the nineteenth century,
and expatiates on the geographical knowledge which these examples
display, especially in respect of Shire and Nyasa. In the third example,
the Marquês cites Livingstone against himself:

> Dr Livingstone, referring to a conversation which he had at Tete, in the
> house of the commandant of the town in February 1856, says on page
> 640 of his Travels [1857 edition. This passage was removed from later
> editions of the book]: 'One of the gentlemen present, Senhor Candido,
> had visited a lake 45 days to the NNW of Tete, which is probably the
> Lake Maravi of geographers, as in going thither they pass through a
> people of that name. The inhabitants of the southern coast are named
> Shiva [Chewa]; those on the north, Mujao; and they call the lake Nyanja
> or Nyanje, which simply means a large river. A high mountain shows in
> the middle of it, called Murómbo or Morumbola, which is inhabited by
> people who have much cattle. He states that he crossed the Nyanja at a
> narrow part, and was 36 hours in the passage. The canoes were punted
> the whole way, and if we take the rate about two miles per hour,
> it may be sixty or seventy miles in breadth ... From the southern
> extremity of the lake, two rivers issue forth; one, named after itself,
> the Nyanja, which passes into the sea on the east coast under another
> name; and the Shire, which flows into the Zambezi, a little below Sen-
> na.

The Marquês presents this extract as the culmination of evidence
from earlier years, such as that of Father Manoel Godinho, who
journeyed by land from India to Portugal in 1663, and published
a volume of *Travels*, from which the Marquês quotes Godinho's
words:

> According to a map I saw, made by a Portuguese who travelled for
> many years, in the kingdoms of Monomotapa, Manica, Butua and others
> in the lands of the Blacks, this lake is not far from Zimlaré [the hinterland
> of Quelimane] ... from it flows ... the river Shire, which after flowing
> through many lands ... joins the river Cuama [Zambezi] below Sena.
> That such a lake exists was told me not only by the Blacks but also
> by the Portuguese, who had already reached it by travelling along the
> above-mentioned river.

The Marquês ends his article with:

> It seems that the following conclusions may be drawn from these
> extracts —

1. That the river Shire had been navigated by the Portuguese in the 16th and 17th centuries
2. That the large lake called 'Nhanja Mucuro' i.e. 'Great Water', which exists in the country of the Maravi, had already been visited by them in the 17th century
3. That they made maps in which the said lake, the Shire, and other rivers were marked
4. That in their journeys between Tete and Cazembe they often crossed the river Zambeze or Coambeze
5. That Candido da Costa Cardozo had been at the place where the river Shire emerges from the lake, Shire having there the name Shirwa
6. That Doctor Livingstone, in visiting the Shire and fixing certain points by astronomical observation and making a description of the country, has added to existing geographical knowledge about this part of Zambezia.

Lisbon, January 1861 – Sá da Bandeira

There can be little doubt how dangerous to Livingstone's reputation as Discoverer of Nyasa was the Marquês's final point but, before the importance of that reputation became paramount, he was less than emphatic about it. In his letter to Oswell in April 1859, describing the visit to Lake Shirwa, he makes two remarks which show that he knew, in approaching Nyasa, that he was following Portuguese footsteps: 'The Shire ... really does come out of Lake Nyanja,' and he speculates that for a person on that lake the mountain Zomba, adjacent to Shirwa, would appear – like Cardoso's Murómbo – to be rising out of Nyasa (and it seems to us that 'Murómbo' is merely Cardoso's pronunciation of 'Zomba').

Sá da Bandeira's article was published in the *Boletim Official* of Mozambique in October 1861 but a year passed before Livingstone, prompted by a request for comment from Austin Layard, the under secretary for Foreign Affairs, on both the article and on the new Portuguese map of 'their' Zambezia, wrote a reply. Livingstone opens his counterblast with an ineffable sentence:

> This map, when taken with a paper by His Excellency in the Mosambique Boletim of 26 October 1861 affords pretty plain proof that the Viscount's geographical knowledge is by no means equal to his patriotism ...

He then mounts a point-by-point attack on map and article in general.

Regarding Nyasa, Livingstone bases his refutation on two main points – that the Marquês's early geographers were merely reporting hearsay, and that Cardoso was a liar (Livingstone does not mention the map shown him at Tete), and spices his assault with sarcastic jibes, such as, Cardoso 'asserts that the shores of his lake were covered with large cabbage-shaped trees with soft stems ... There are no soft-stemmed cabbage shaped trees on its shores.' Livingstone, the student of languages, has let his bile override his judgement, let alone his intelligence. Cardoso was talking about palm trees, abundant and a fine sight along the shores of the Lake. Darwin got it right in Brazil, 'Here' he wrote, on 18th April 1832:

> the woods were ornamented by the cabbage palm – one of the most beautiful of its family. With a stem so narrow it might be clasped with the two hands, it waves its elegant head at the height of forty or fifty feet above the ground.

The report of Father Godinho, Livingstone dismisses with an equal sneer:

> We read it as if it were said, someone in going to England in 1663 saw a map drawn by somebody else, who having travelled about many years in [the Algarve] had inserted a lake situated as if at Salamanca in Spain but placed it in the Alentejo.

But Livingstone's dismissiveness and sarcasm (he came to develop an obsession with what he called 'armchair geographers') concealed his own deep worries about his reputation and about the Portuguese claims in Zambezia which, if recognised, would enable Lisbon to throttle his colony in the Shire highlands. But beneath all his bluster, he elaborated what was to become the guiding principle in the imperialist scramble for Africa twenty years later – the principle that any imperial ambition in Africa must be supported by evidence of effective occupation of the territory claimed. As Livingstone pointed out, quite correctly, the Portuguese were not in control of any but a miniscule portion of the lands the Marquês's map said were theirs, and that its pretensions should be rejected: his case would have been supported at the African Conference at Berlin in 1884.

In February 1861, however, when Livingstone welcomed the vanguard of the UMCA at the Delta, the Portuguese were aware of this danger and were strengthening their tenuous grip on Zambezia: military posts were planned for Kongone, and Shamo, the entrance to the Shire. These moves could cause problems for the mission and the colony, but might be avoided by opening the new route to Nyasa, along the Rovuma, which entered the sea just beyond Cabo Delgado, the northern boundary of Mozambique. This was what the British government, speaking through

Lord Russell, wanted. But meanwhile other developments, only partly related to Portuguese manoeuvres, were becoming a far greater threat to the mission, and they were totally beyond Livingstone's control.

We have already noted the connection between the nineteenth-century slave trade in central Africa and the market for ivory in the industrial economies of Europe and America (and recall Owen's instruction to Kirk to investigate the ecology of the elephant). From mid-century, a wider range of tropical products was in demand as the industrial revolution moved forward and extended itself. East Africa, from the Zambezi in the south to Mombasa in the north, found that it could supply not only ivory, but cloves, gum copal, vegetable oilseeds and dyestuffs, as well as sugar from Reunion, the Comoros, and Mauritius. The markets seemed insatiable, and production rose to satisfy them. In 1856 Britain imported 463 tons of east African ivory; in 1864, 557 tons. Grain and oilseed exports from Zanzibar rose from £1750 in 1859/60 to £8000 in 1864; Zanzibar clove output increased from 2200 tons in 1856 to 3800 tons in 1866. And, despite increased production, prices remained high or even rose. Ivory showed an increment of 15% at Zanzibar between 1856 and 1865. The entire production, whether by Africans, Portuguese, British, French, or Arabs was, with the exception of Mauritius (as we have seen), based on slave labour; and the decade we are concerned with saw an increase of the slave trade which corresponded to the new demands for labour. Slave exports from Kilwa, the southern Zanzibari entrepôt, rose from 15,000 in 1859 to 22,344 in 1865. But even this figure does not show the real increase of the trade over the region as many transactions went unrecorded. Slaves from Zambezia, for instance, might be taken inland to be bartered for ivory as far away as the Lunda kingdom, Angola, or indeed Barotseland. Nor was this slave trade anyone's monopoly, those taking part in it showed no distinction of race, colour, or creed. There were independent Africans such as the Makonde and Yao; Arabs and their Swahili blood relations; Portuguese with their indigenised Marianos and Belchior do Nascimentos; Gujerat Hindus; British sugar barons on the islands (except Mauritius); Somalis; French.

Livingstone understood the real reason for the increase in slaving in the Zambezia-Nyasa area even, if for purposes of his own he laid most of the blame on the Portuguese settlers. On 31st May 1859 he wrote to his son Robert:

> We are guilty of keeping up slavery by giving increasing prices for slave grown cotton and sugar. We are the great supporters of slavery in the world, unwittingly often, but truly . . . I long to see our nation relieved from this guilt and stain . . .

He trusted that enterprises like the UMCA would help relieve the guilt and stain, but at the same time knew that he was taking the missionaries into an area where slave raiding had developed dramatically since he first went up the Shire in 1859: not only for the general economic reasons we have mentioned, but because by 1861 there was a new urgency among slave dealers. The Lisbon government, through Sá da Bandeira, was attempting to suppress the export of slaves from Mozambique (not very effectually, it may be said), while the French Emperor Napoleon III was moving (though at snail's pace) towards prohibition of the Free Labour Emigration scheme and Britain was applying stronger abolitionist pressure on the Sultan of Zanzibar. Slavers knew that business conditions were going to become more difficult, hence the haste to stockpile what would become a scarcer commodity. No rush for riches is an elegant affair, whether for yellow gold or black, but it would be in the middle of such a rush that the UMCA would find itself.

It is impossible to over-emphasise how important the UMCA was to Livingstone. Even without Prince Albert as patron, it had powerful establishment support. The fervour aroused by Livingstone's Cambridge lectures in 1857 had led to the holding of The Great Zambezi Meeting in the same place two years later, its purpose to launch the UMCA and raise subscriptions. This was no mere university affair, for now at the speakers' table sat William Gladstone, powerful politician destined to be Prime Minister, Samuel Wilberforce, Lord Bishop of Oxford, and Sir George Grey, now retired as governor of the Cape and preparing to go and rule New Zealand, all of whom gave unstinting support for the mission – £20,000 was raised for the UMCA. By comparison, the LMS collected £6000 for the Helmore mission; parliament voted £5000 for Livingstone's Zambezi Expedition, though in the end much more was spent.

The UMCA was not only a mission of the Church of England, but of that particular segment of the church, then on the ascendant, broadly reformist. This movement, born at Oxford University in the second quarter of the nineteenth century, was a response to the multiple crisis then facing Anglicanism. On the one hand, its hierarchy had become complacent, some would say corrupt (Bishops sitting by constitutional right in the House of Lords had, for example, consistently voted against the abolition of slavery, as the Bishop of Oxford's father, William Wilberforce, had found to his disgust). On the other, mass support for the church among the new industrial proletariat had been swept away in the tide of non-conformist evangelicalism and Wesleyan Methodism. Two further challenges threatened what the Oxford Movement believed was the historical Church of England: the most eloquent of its members, John Henry Newman, had taken the argument about the historicity of Anglicanism to its logical conclusion, had departed the Church of England and joined the Church of Rome, giving an intellectual respectability to Roman Catholicism which, at the time, was showing a resurgence in England (thanks largely to immigration from Ireland) and was re-establishing its own hierarchy. Then there was the challenge of science, in particular the theories of Darwin, which seemed to deny the very foundations of Christian belief: Bishop Wilberforce was to make the most famous attack on Darwin (at a meeting of the British Association held at Oxford) but did not emerge with any credit to his name, trounced by Darwin's friend, Thomas Huxley, who remarked that he would rather be descended from an ape than from a Bishop who prostituted his intelligence.

The mainstream Church of England was in fact attempting to come to terms with the changing, industrialising Britain, in both doctrine and practice. It was an effort that had to succeed if the church were not to become an irrelevant embarrassment to the power structure and suffer disestablishment (as would happen in largely Catholic Ireland and Methodist Wales. And Scotland was overwhelmingly Presbyterian). The doctrinal basis for the authority of the Church of England was the belief that it was a national church, founded not at the Reformation, but by St Augustine, who brought Christianity to the English in the sixth century. In its practice, the renascent church began to shake itself out of the comfortable life afforded by cathedral close and country vicarage, and engage in missionary work. At first its attention was directed at the new industrial slums, where its mission combined evangelisation with 'good works' – such as the Ragged Schools for pauper children, so much supported by Miss Coutts. But in 1857 the emergence of Livingstone at Cambridge, and his non-sectarian appeal for African missionaries, gave the reburnished Church of England an opportunity to show its mettle in foreign lands, to send out its own Victorian Augustines and, meanwhile, do itself good at home by outshining the non-conformists of the LMS, the Methodists and, even Anglicanism's own Church Missionary Society, tainted in the eyes of the mainstream by its puritanism. With few exceptions – one of whom was Livingstone's friend Archbishop Whately – the reformists were High Church.

The first two years of Livingstone's expedition had been so unrewarding, so opposite of successful, that it is difficult to see how the British government could have renewed his mandate unless it had been persuaded to do so in order to provide logistical support for the UMCA. Thus while Livingstone might see the mission as a renewed hope for his settlement scheme, he could also see that failure by the UMCA would be blamed on him, would spell the end of his second grand strategy and, besides, spell the end of support from the British establishment.

The UMCA forward party arrived at the Zambezi mouth in the first week of February 1861 (it was a little late, and Livingstone spent the time working on a dictionary of the languages of Sena and Tete), enjoying the services of two Royal Navy ships, HMS *Lyra* and HMS *Sidon*. With them was *Pioneer*, the *Ma Robert*'s timely replacement. A bare month before, the mission's leader, Charles Frederick Mackenzie, had been consecrated the Church of England's first missionary bishop by Robert Gray at Cape Town. Mackenzie was thirty-five at the time, tall, balding, genial, with traces of his Scottish origin in his accent. He had graduated brilliantly in mathematics at Cambridge, then taken orders and worked for some years as a curate in Natal. While on home leave in 1859 he attended the Great Zambezi Meeting, volunteered for the UMCA and was appointed its leader. Mackenzie was the youngest of twelve children; his mother had died while he was an infant and he had been brought up largely by his sisters. He had not married, and the only condition he made for joining the mission was that a sister should join him on the Shire. She was not in the forward party, which consisted of Mackenzie himself, Henry Scudamore and Lovell Proctor (both ordained), Horace Waller, a layman who would later take orders, a white carpenter, a white agriculturalist, and a number of black servants, including a cook, recruited at the Cape. If they had hoped to set to work immediately tilling the mission field, they were wrong. Livingstone insisted that February was not a good month to ascend the Shire, that they must use the time, until the valley would be safe from fever, in fulfilling Russell's instruction to explore the Rovuma. Mackenzie could not but agree. Bishop, and leader of the UMCA, he might be but he had no authority to command Livingstone. Livingstone, for his part, might not have been formally in charge of the mission, but he could show his power, and the mission's dependence on him.

Three months were spent on this Livingstonian peregrination. He sailed the *Pioneer*, loaded with the full mission and expedition contingents, as well as all the mission's stores, seven hundred miles up the Mozambique Channel to the Comoros, left the stores there, and steamed another four hundred miles to the mouth of the Rovuma. Shoals and sandbanks made it impossible for the *Pioneer* to proceed more than twenty miles upriver, no access to Nyasa by this route it seemed. Livingstone turned the *Pioneer* round and sailed back to the Comoros, but not before Mackenzie and his colleagues had had their first taste of malaria. Then, leaving half the mission's stores behind to make room for coal, Livingstone took the *Pioneer* seven hundred miles back to the Zambezi, and said that the journey upstream to the Shire cataracts would take three weeks. Instead, it took over two months, and not until 8th July, after being continually stuck on sandbanks or trapped in the Shire marshes, did the missionaries set foot on the lands they had been sent forth from England to sow.

If Livingstone and Mackenzie had not been drawn to each other – as fellow Scots, perhaps – from the start, it is unlikely that the party on the *Pioneer* could have held together, but not even Charles's patent antipathy to Anglicans, and especially High Churchmen as Mackenzie and Scudamore were, could break it up. Long dispassionate discussions about doctrinal matters passed the evenings away, aided by draughts from the cellar, interspersed with speculation about the latest scientific controversies. Mackenzie had brought a copy of *The Origin of Species* then just published. Though the *Pioneer* was just as uncomfortable and greedy for fuel as the *Ma Robert* had been, and though its engine was a poor performer, there was a unity of purpose aboard her which Livingstone, and especially the Bishop, were able to maintain. Mackenzie's success lay in his willingness to put his hand to anything that helped keep the *Pioneer* moving forward, from hauling and winching anchor chains, and pulling the ship across sandbanks, to working in the engine room. His very clumsiness, as when he put the engine into reverse, instead of forward gear, and grounded the vessel once again, became a virtue; his total lack of machismo, his almost-femininity, became a strength. But despite his undergraduate genius as a mathematician, he was possessed by a quality that was to prove fatal to this first UMCA mission, an enthusiastic naivety devoid of foresight or analytical practicability.

The upper Shire valley was a different place from that which Livingstone had described two years before the *Pioneer* arrived at the foot of the Murchison cataracts. The most immediate sign of change was that Chief Chibisa was no longer at his town; he had moved to a new place nearer Tete. Livingstone thus found himself without an interlocutor between the mission and other Manganja chiefs. In the second place, there had been a drought and, though July is harvest time, there was an obvious shortage of food. Drought and hunger place severe strains on a subsistence farming economy such as that of the Shire valley people, and this year the position was made worse by increased slaving activity – itself perhaps encouraged by the presence in the area of too many mouths to feed. Whatever the case, slaving had spread forcefully into the Shire area. It was only a few days after its arrival that the mission party, with Livingstone leading it to a permanent site he had selected for it near Lake Shirwa, met the first slave caravan. Amateurs these slave raiders must have been, for, challenged by 'the English' they fled, leaving their prisoners behind. The leader of the gang was named Katura, formerly a slave of Major Sicard of Tete, now turned slaver himself, whether on his own account or on commission from Sicard is not known, though Livingstone jumped to the conclusion that the Portuguese were behind the new slaving on the Shire. The eighty-four released captives were told that they could either return to their homes, or be taken in by the bishop and join his mission. They (or rather those who were not small children, too young to be offered choice) decided on the latter course. As Livingstone remarked, Mackenzie had found a congregation without having to look for one. Nobody seems to have asked how eighty-four destitutes were to be fed and cared for. What the mission party did ask itself was whether it should free other captives, and all agreed that it should, though Livingstone cautioned against the use of force, that is to say, firearms, and warned the bishop not to become involved in the conflict between the Manganja of the Valley and the Yao (he called them 'Ajawa'), who were disputing possession of the Shire highlands.

The agreement to free captives came as a licence for action, a relief from the strain and frustration of months of confinement in the *Pioneer*. Kirk went off in one direction in fruitless pursuit of a slave caravan; Charles raided the village of a headman named Mayazi, seized six slaves and told the chieftain that if he were caught slaving again, 'the English' would burn down his village and drive him from the land. The bishop, believing that the Manganja were the wronged party, declared war on the Yao, on one occasion marching, crozier in one hand, rifle in the other, at the head of a column of a thousand Manganja into the 'enemy country' of the Yao, and on one occasion at least, fired. The only positive result of this enthusiasm was an assembly of a hundred and sixty freed captives, among them two youngsters named Chuma and Wakatini, whom we shall meet later. The bishop established them with the missionaries at Magomero, the site chosen for the mission by Livingstone on a spit of land at the junction of two streams; the bishop fortified it with a stockade across the open approach.

As the price for supporting the Manganja, Mackenzie had exacted an anti-slavery oath from each chief but, when he came to take a census of his foundlings, he discovered to his dismay that three-quarters of them were Yao, taken into slavery by the Manganja. As if this blunder were not sufficient, he had antagonised the Yao to the extent that they became permanently hostile to the mission and to Christianity itself. Today the Yao people of Malawi (and the adjoining part of Mozambique) are predominantly Muslim. Mackenzie's 'Ajawa Wars' as he called them, doomed Magomero. Livingstone was later blamed for the mess, accused, quite wrongly the evidence shows, of encouraging the bishop to take up arms. But he is to blame in that Mackenzie's 'forward policy' sprang logically from the apparently successful liberation of the first eighty-four, and Livingstone's approval of it. Livingstone could never admit to himself that he could not change the world on his own, nor admit the extent to which he benefited from the status quo. In particular, he would have found it an impossible loss of face to confess to the enthusiastic bishop that in Zambezia slavery was a fact of life that had to be compromised with, as Livingstone had done, both for personal comfort and for the expedition's convenience. Katura the slave raider, for example, had attended to Livingstone in Major Sicard's house; slaves had starched Charles's collars and ironed his shirts; Tizora (known as Scissors), a slave on hire from Sicard did essential work as boat's pilot on the Zambezi and the Shire. Whenever possible, slaves were used to cut the enormous quantities of firewood the *Ma Robert* had needed (Thornton records that on one occasion a Portuguese loaned a hundred and twenty *bichos*, – 'animals', Portuguese pejorative – for this purpose). Slave wives of Livingstone's Kololo tended the garden that produced part of the expedition's fresh food and, if Thornton had had to be condemned at all, why not for owning a slave?

But what would Mackenzie, or his backers in England, have thought if Livingstone had let the caravan of eighty-four pass unchallenged and then told Mackenzie to do likewise with any others that he encountered? The uproar would have been great perhaps, but would soon have died away as the decision's good sense emerged, especially, as by freeing slaves in Portuguese territory, Portuguese law was being broken. As for taking sides in the struggle between the Manganja and the Yao – a dispute related more to land rights than to slaving – Mackenzie had allowed romantic notions to run away with him and had not analysed the circumstances adequately. He was not in the position of James Brooke in Borneo, where by supporting a powerful sultan against a pretender he was able to win from the victor both political authority and suppression of slavery in the area ceded to him. Mackenzie's only hope in the short term would have been to accept the offer of an alliance with Mariano, now out of gaol, who had moved with his followers on to the southern flank of the Shire highlands. But that was unthinkable, not only was Mariano a slaver himself, but both the Portuguese and the British governments would have been incensed.

A few weeks after depositing the UMCA at Magomero, and while Mackenzie prosecuted his wars and set about building a 'Bishop's Palace' and other housing for the mission, Livingstone, Charles and Kirk set out to examine Lake Nyasa. With them, apart from servants, was a young Irish seaman named Neill, one of the crew supplied with the *Pioneer*. The journey lasted three months, and Livingstone gives an account of it, and of his expectations, in a letter to James Young, on 7th or 9th November 1861, written after returning to the Shire:

> We have been up Lake Nyasa in a boat which we carried past Murchison's Cataracts, at the lowest of which I now write. We left this [place, Chibisa's old town] just three months ago and sailed some 250 miles, though the lake proper is but 200. In reaching [here] today I enquired anxiously if

the little steamer [Livingstone's own, named *Lady Nyassa*] had come. It seems as if other slow coaches existed besides the admiralty, but possibly she is detained waiting for a convoy at the Cape. If she is not strong she won't do for Nyassa; if we were to judge from our experience during the Equinoctial gales, we should it called [*sic*] the Lake of Storms. Tremendous seas get up in 20 minutes. We sat for days cowering and looking at the restless sea. Once caught we could neither advance nor recede and anchored in hopes we would ride it out. Really terrific rollers came across – but happily none broke over her or we should have been swamped. Our seaman, who has been in all seas of the world declared that in subsequent gales no open boat could have lived. The width of [the lake] is from 20 to 50 or sixty miles. Its shape is like the boot shape of Italy – 200 miles in length at least. No current. Depth unknown accurately . . . Plenty of fish and people innumerable. Slave trade brisk. An Arab dhow cut off from us twice to the East coast. We were on the West and could not cross. People civil, no dues levied nor fines imposed. Here is a field for benevolent enterprise. We are longing for the new vessel . . . We now go down to meet provisions and possibly the 'Nyassa'. 'Pioneer' sadly too long and deep, yet carries nothing.

Kirk's description of the trip is less sanguine about 'the field for benevolent enterprise'. The coast of the lake was fever-ridden, the inhabitants suspicious (though not aggressive), the climate – especially when sitting under the October sun in an open boat (they were using one of the *Ma Robert*'s whalers), near unbearable, the slave trade not 'brisk' but devastating, the northern reaches of the coast laid waste by Ngoni raiding (another offshoot of the *mfecane*).

Livingstone thought they had reached the northern end of the lake, but he was wrong, they had travelled little over two-thirds of the total length, and then only along the west coast – of which they made the first accurate survey, to be turned into a chart. They had turned back, mainly because supplies were running short, at a point where the mountains of the escarpments, looming over the waters, seem to be closing in from both sides. Livingstone's claim to having measured the lake was false, but unwittingly so. The trip had not been a waste of time, nor had it produced any disasters, even if the party was worn out and sickly when it arrived back at the *Pioneer*. Kirk's observation that some of the fishes in Nyasa resembled species in the Sea of Galilee gave a first hint to the world that the two lakes, four thousand miles apart, might bear some relationship to each other, as they were later found to do, both being phenomena of the Great Rift Valley.

Good news and bad news greeted Livingstone at the *Pioneer*. The bad news was about Mackenzie's Ajawa Wars, the good, brought by a new member of the UMCA who had travelled up from the coast by canoe (his name was Henry de Wint Burrup), being that a large party was expected at the Delta from England. More members of the mission, Mackenzie's sister, Mrs Burrup, James Stewart, a member of the Free Church of Scotland come to consult Livingstone about starting a mission of his own, Mary Livingstone herself, and presumably the steamer *Lady Nyassa*, with Rae as engineer. Soon after receiving this news, Livingstone wrote an optimistic letter, on 25th November 1861, to his friend Lord Kinnaird (a renowned agricultural reformer) extolling the productivity of the Shire area, claiming to have bought three hundred pounds of excellent cotton, and advancing again his plans for colonisation, anticipating that the government would reimburse him for the *Lady Nyassa* once she went into service on the lake.

But Livingstone was now, at the beginning of November, no longer in control of events. With the new arrivals expecting to be met at the Delta early in January, he had to get the *Pioneer* down to the coast without delay. He told Mackenzie and Burrup to make their way to the Ruo-Shire confluence and there await his return in January. But the *Pioneer* was not to reach the coast until the end of that month. It ran aground in the Shire marsh and was stuck for five weeks, the water level low because of the previous season's drought. The two ships bringing the newcomers had by then already called at Kongone, but finding Livingstone not there, had put to sea again for three weeks, returning on the last day of January. Livingstone reports to James Young on 19th February 1862:

> As I thought all would turn out right at last so it has come to pass – MS Gorgon with the brig in tow [the other ship was named *Hetty Ellen*] signalized us on 31st Jany 'I have – steam boat – in the – brig' then up went the flags again – 'Wife aboard' and my answer 'Accept best thanks.'

But all did not turn out right. Livingstone found that his badly twisted logistics had been given a further buckling wrench – the *Lady Nyassa*, instead of being sent out in one piece, towed by the warship, as he had insisted, was lying in sections in the brig. In the same letter he told Young:

> We towed in the brig and in a week Captain Wilson and his officers had all the shell and boilers on board Pioneer and two paddle box boats, but we can scarcely steam up river and we are creeping at snailspace and cutting wood of our own . . . Cutting wood for fuel prevents our cutting any to send by 'Hetty Ellen'.

But that is only the beginning of the story. Every piece of *Lady*

Nyassa, every ounce of stores had to be taken upstream to Shupanga, there offloaded, and the *Pioneer* sent back again to the Delta. Then Livingstone's steamer had to be assembled. The first stage of the operation, which included shipping the mission party – which Livingstone discovered to be larger than expected as Miss Mackenzie had brought two maids with her from England (and Mary one of her own too) – and its supplies to Shupanga, took three weeks. Livingstone was now nine weeks behind schedule. As the *Pioneer* was needed for the shuttle between the Delta and Shupanga, she could not be used to make the much delayed rendezvous with Mackenzie and Burrup at the Ruo (in January they had been alarmed to see the *Pioneer* sailing *down* the Shire at the time she was expected to be returning from the coast). So Livingstone sent Kirk, Miss Mackenzie and Mrs Burrup upriver in an open boat. They found neither the bishop nor Burrup at the Ruo, they struggled on to Chibisa's, there to learn that both men were dead. Mackenzie, canoeing down the Shire to the Ruo had lost the medicine chest and perished of fever, Burrup of dysentery. Soon Scudamore was dead too, and the mission, with the unordained Waller in de facto charge, moved from Magomero – which the Ajawa Wars had made untenable – to Chibisa's, there to await its fate. Miss Mackenzie, Mrs Burrup and their maids, returned to England.

Even after the death of the bishop and his two colleagues (Proctor, though often ill, survived, as did Waller) Livingstone had hope for the UMCA. But he knew, as his letter to Kinnaird shows, that the colonisation idea would have to be canvassed for. Even before the bishop's death, which Livingstone knew would weaken his cause, he had received a cold statement of opinion from Murchison, friendly but disinterested:

> Your colonisation scheme does not meet with supporters, it being thought that you must have much more hold on the country before you attract Scotch families to emigrate and settle there, and then die off, and become a burden to you and all concerned, like the settlers of old at Darien. [Murchison's use of this last phrase shows how well he understood Livingstone's ambitions.]

Russell was to be even more blunt: the British government, he said, was not prepared to underwrite colonies which entailed 'forcing steamers up cataracts'. Now Livingstone's most tangible hope lay in his own steamer, and even she was proving a frustrating item. It took three months, despite assistance from Captain Wilson and the crew of the *Gorgon*, to bring all her sections from the coast to Shupanga, and then another two months to assemble them.

By the time the *Lady Nyassa* was ready to steam the Zambezi, the Shire, and the lake whose name she bore, Mary Livingstone, whose name the foundered *Ma Robert* had borne, was in her grave.

19
FAMILY MATTERS

'With a sore and heavy heart,' Livingstone wrote to James Young on 5th May 1862,

> I have to tell you of the death of my dear bosom friend of eighteen years – she died on 27th [April] and I cannot tell you how greatly I feel the loss. It feels as if heart and strength were taken out of me – my horizon is all dark. I am distressed for the children.
> The disease was accompanied by continual vomiting, the most difficult form to treat as the remedies are rejected.

To his journal, in an entry of 8th May, 1862, Livingstone was more forthcoming:

> It is the first heavy stroke I have suffered, and quite takes away my strength. I wept over her who well deserved many tears. I loved her when I married her, and the longer I lived with her, I loved her more . . . Oh my Mary, my Mary! how often we have longed for a quiet home since you and I were cast adrift at Kolobeng.

Mary had come to join her husband in full expectation that they would soon be moving into a new Kolobeng in the Highlands but, before she arrived the situation along the Shire, as we have seen, had made that difficult, and as she refused to go back to Britain, she had no alternative but to ensconce herself on the *Pioneer* and await whatever promise the *Lady Nyassa* would bring of fulfilment.

When Livingstone left her at Cape Town in April 1858 to go to Kuruman for her confinement, it was planned that when the baby was old enough to travel, Mary would come north overland to join her husband at Batoka. When that scheme fell to pieces, she went to Scotland (but even if Livingstone had been able to settle at Batoka, communications with Kuruman would have been a serious problem – Sir George Grey's plan to connect the Zambezi to the Cape with a postal service had got no further than presenting Robert Moffat with a span of donkeys for a trial run; which never took place). In Scotland,

Mary placed the infant Anna Mary with David's mother and sisters at Hamilton, arranged with the Trustees for young William Oswell's schooling, then James Young organised a passage for her on the same ship that was taking Rae and the *Lady Nyassa* to Africa, joined, as we have seen, by James Stewart and the UMCA women.

Mary did not get on well with the missionary ladies, but became very fond of Stewart, who was often seen at her side in Cape Town. Stewart probably felt that he was doing no more in being solicitous to her than she deserved as the wife of the man he worshipped as the hero of the age. Stewart was ten years younger than Mary, then forty, and could not have imagined, in his Free Kirk high-mindedness, that his attentions to a plump, forbidding-looking woman, with what is today called a drinking problem, could cause scandal. But indeed that is what happened, especially after he was seen entering her cabin late one night. Stewart explained that he and Mary's maid, who had summoned him, were merely doing what they could to get an inebriate to sleep, but rumours of a liaison were spread by shipboard gossips, including Rae. In due course, Mary's visits to the saloon led her to borrow bottle money from Stewart and when, eventually, he felt obliged to refuse, she turned on him with hysterical abuse. By the time she arrived at Shupanga she was unhealthy in body and mind, greatly overweight, oscillating in mood between childish playfulness (challenging David not to be an old Fogey and to join in the fun, drawing cartoons in the margins of his letters) and despairing loss of faith. The, seemingly, endless process of getting the *Lady Nyassa*'s sections up to Shupanga – the *Pioneer*'s engine had been poorly maintained and often broke down – must have burned into Mary like the distillation of all the misery of her previous wanderings away from her husband: 1400 miles in wagons between Cape Town and Kuruman, 20,000 miles at sea; Cape Town to England twice, England to Shupanga. She might have sailed around the world, and here she was in a stinking-hot, cockroach infested, half-crippled paddle steamer. And the news from Magomero was bad. Besides, her husband seemed so incompetent: 'I never saw such constant vacillations, blunders, delays, and want of common thought and foresight,' commented an officer of the *Gorgon* on Livingstone's handling of the *Pioneer* and its cargoes.

Livingstone wanted to get Mary away from Shupanga, suggesting that she go up to the highlands, but she refused to leave. Apart from the presence of her husband, the makeshift dockyard at Shupanga with its bustle of activity, even life aboard the *Pioneer* with its comings and goings, were preferable to any embryonic Kuruman in the hills after years of life as an isolated nonentity. 'That's Dr Livingstone's wife, she's so . . . so . . . that he won't have her with him,' was the sort of Kuruman taunt she would no longer suffer. And perhaps, fed up with the prissiness of mission ladies and mission life, she felt able to express her independence and antipathy to missionaries by enjoying the presence of the seventy-two roughnecks from the *Gorgon* who were doing the hard work, and dissipating their prickly-heat-boredom with large quantities of Zambezian moonshine (kachasu to Africans, aguardiente to the Portuguese, gin to Thornton) – not to mention whoring with local ladies, one of whom, a horrified James Stewart records, 'was abused five times'. (How did he know?). They were behaving like the British seamen, those disgraces to Christianity, who had appalled and terrified Livingstone at Rio de Janeiro so long ago. And did those seamen pass Mary the occasional bottle of spirit, making it impossible for Livingstone to have obeyed his command that they themselves keep sober, or his wish that Mary go upstream?

At the end of March Livingstone took the *Pioneer*, with Mary aboard, to deliver the bereaved missionary ladies, their maids, and the seventy-two sailors, to the *Gorgon* for its journey to the Cape. At the Delta, Kirk rejoined the *Pioneer* for its return to Shupanga. He had accompanied the *Gorgon*'s gig, the open boat that had been to Chibisa's, back from the Shire to Kongone and had noted in his diary: 'Mrs L. is getting very stout; shipboard seems to agree with her,' but remarked that she suffered frequent 'febrile attacks' which lasted a few hours each. By the time the party reached Shupanga a fortnight later, Mary was becoming seriously ill. She was taken from the *Pioneer*, put to bed in the house on shore and treated for malaria, but she did not respond. Stewart attributed her sickness to drink and, given the total ineffectiveness of the quinine and the nature of her symptoms, vomiting, extreme weakness, yellowing of the skin, it would appear that she was suffering from hepatitis, which alcohol would have made fatal. She died at seven o'clock on the evening of 27th April, her husband sitting in tears at her bedside: 'The man,' Stewart wrote, 'who faced so many deaths, and braved so many dangers, was now utterly broken down and weeping like a child.' The following noon she was buried, in a coffin made by Rae, with a service led by Stewart, beneath a large baobab tree.

Livingstone sat down to write his grief away; a stream of letters to Mary's parents, to his children, confessions to his journal. But the grief was compounded by guilt, as had been his grief at the death of Sehamy. Livingstone had good reason to believe that Mary had gone to damnation. Ever since her exile in Britain during his transcontinental journeys, she had shown every sign that she was not in a state of grace – whether in her inability to get on with Livingstone's family at Hamilton, whether in her disparagement of missionaries, whether in her incipient alcoholism. Now, back with him, the distance she had put between herself and the Saviour had been alarming, for she seemed to have lost her faith altogether. Livingstone kept prompting her as she was dying to give some sign that she felt herself in the arms of the Lord and, having forgotten that she was deaf from quinine, berated himself later for not writing his words on pieces of paper for her to read and signal some response. A few years after Mary's death, Livingstone's mother received her own call. He was not present when she died, but knew from his sisters that all had gone well, that there need be no fear for the fate of the departed: Livingstone told James Young, in a letter of 30th June 1865,

> My mother died on Sunday at noon, was considerably better when I left and continued so till near the change.
>
> When that appeared, Agnes said, 'Jesus seems to be coming for you – can you lippen him?' 'Yes' – gave her last look to Anna Mary and said, 'Bonnie wee lassie' and fell asleep so gently the little thing is not in the least alarmed.
>
> There is a peculiar solemnity connected with a touch from the grim king to one so nearly related. I trust she soon felt the touch of Him who said, 'Fear not, I am he that liveth and was dead.'

But with Mary, as the touch of the grim king became an inescapable grip, she was in a weeping, half-conscious nightmare about her children, full of fear. Livingstone blamed himself for not counselling Mary enough while she was well, to bring her back to the true path, and tried to ease his conscience by clutching at straws. Going through Mary's papers he came across a short prayer – 'Accept me Lord as I am and make me such as Thou wouldst have me be' which he transcribed into his private journal. He convinced himself that Mary had been experiencing a dark night of the soul, that she had recovered from it, her faith restored. But he had only to look back on her life, deprived of so much, including his spiritual guidance, to know that he was responsible, in major part, for the depressed state he had seen her in at Shupanga. Mary's mother, Mrs Moffat, wrote Livingstone a kindly letter of condolence, but even she admitted that Mary had never been 'eminently pious', and implied that she had needed constant counselling. Much of Mary's depression had nothing to do with her Faith. She was worried about her children. All, except Anna Mary, were now well out of the nursery. Robert was approaching sixteen, Agnes was fourteen, Thomas thirteen, and William Oswell eleven. Though Agnes was all right in the more obvious respects Robert, in his adolescence, had become obstreperous, breaking every rule of God-fearing respectability his father had enjoined, in letter after letter, on all the children. Would David blame *her*? Had she failed as a mother? Was she in fact as useless as the Kuruman wives – no doubt remembering Livingstone's willingness to do without her for long periods – had whispered?

News of the children had been brought to Livingstone at the Delta by both Mary and Rae. The two younger boys were at school, there was a worry about their health, and Livingstone had written to James Young on 19th February 1862, to look into their well-being:

> Please keep Oswell at Brighton as his chest is tender – this is the case with all children from this country. If necessary to remove Thomas it would be well to send him there too, but he gets on so well at Kendal, if health fail not, keep him there.

Livingstone's hope for the three boys was that they would be able to take up middle class 'white collar' careers and he, understandably, had most ambition for the eldest, Robert. If news about Thomas and William were not absolutely reassuring, at least they were at school, any ailments could be coped with. But the news about Robert had brought alarm, and called for action. Hardly had Mary (and Rae) landed at the Delta than Livingstone wrote to Young on 2nd or 7th February 1862:

> Mr Rae has just added that in Edinburgh Robert associates with a bad boy named [J. Cormack]. This is an additional reason why he should be sent out. My pursuits have [pre]vented me giving that parental attention to him I ought, and it might be well to have some time with me. Please take the foregoing into account in forming [. . . judgment]. If doing well now of course no steps need be taken.

When he knew more about Robert's circumstances, presumably from Mary, he wrote again, hoping that an understanding of Robert's character would make it possible to get him back on track, and avoid the need to 'send him out' to the Zambezi. Livingstone, leading on from the remarks about Thomas and Oswell we have seen, says to Young in a letter of 19th February 1862:

> If Robert goes anywhere I beg you will remember his very excitable temperament. At St Andrews he complains that he is learning only what he had already acquired at Kendal, if so he would be better off at any of the medical classes. I suppose he has some of my nature and judging from myself placing him in a quiet family for lodging and allowing him to pursue his best in studies according to the advice of Dr Playfair [Lyon Playfair, classmate of Livingstone's at Anderson's College, was, at the time of this letter, Professor of Chemistry at Edinburgh] will prove more beneficial than he could be with Mr Hall as a cramming master. Of course I cannot understand or judge of the whole matter – but had Mr Hall threatened Robert's father with a thrashing as he did, a wholesome dread of threatening

would have been implanted through his hide for the term of his natural life.

Livingstone had obviously been discussing reports received earlier, for he continues:

Mrs [Hall?] wrote to me about it in great distress and advised me to reprove him for running away. I could not conceive what I should say, so said nothing. It was well he had the spirit not to submit to what you never authorized Mr Hall to do, but he ought to have escaped to you or to Dr Buchanan. I believe he went to Limehouse [the docklands of London]. Wine or spirits will never do for him. Pleasing his companions who are intended for the military profession [may] lead him into a love of them which we may have to deplore.

Was Livingstone thinking of Robert's mother's love of wine and spirits, as he wrote these last two sentences? The letter continues:

I think therefore he must be removed to lodgings and sent to some of the classes required in medicine – say chemistry, anatomy or natural philosophy. He had no fire at Mr Hall's. Let him have control over his own food and fire as we had in days of yore. I think it well to trust to the honour of boys to a certain extent. More will be done when they are aware of being trusted than if they are forced on by a cramming master. As for Mr Hall's [cram], he never once rendered any assistance in the lessons – was once or twice asked, but some excuse – 'somebody calling' or 'he was going to take a nap' [illegible] . . . scarcely fitted to secure the respect of any boy. Put your [son] John to Mr Hall, and if he does not pitch into him before three months John has not the pluck I take him to have. Robert feels sore that a letter of apology which Agnes saw before it was sent and says it was a good one, but never answered by Dr Buchanan.

(An attempt was made to destroy this letter, and it, like that containing Rae's report, has been re-assembled from scraps in the Livingstone Museum, Zambia.)

Things did not turn out with Robert as his parents, in this letter, had hoped. Even when Robert was a child in the Kalahari, William Cotton Oswell had noticed that he had an intractable side to his nature and, fortunately perhaps, for her, Mary did not live to see where that intractability would lead. Like his father, Robert would not be held down. He wanted to be a traveller, perhaps join the navy (an option Livingstone's trustees, Dr Buchanan and James Hannan – but not James Young – refused believing that they were doing as Livingstone would wish). Perhaps Robert's childhood years in the Kalahari had lasted long enough for him to have no taste for the suburban, frock-coated existence the respectable life held out for him. But his father found it difficult for a long time to come to terms with, let alone approve, what he recognised in Robert. He had less determined expectations for the younger boys and did not impose on them as heavily as he did on the firstborn.

After Mary's death, with Robert still unsettled and on the loose, Livingstone arranged for him to come to the Zambezi by way of Quelimane. Robert sailed to Port Elizabeth and then on to Natal, where he hoped to make contact with Robert Moffat (junior), his mother's brother. But Moffat had died on the journey from Kuruman (where he had a trading store beside the mission). Robert did, however, get help from his Moffat grandparents, which he acknowledged later to his father. By June 1863 Livingstone, again at the Shire cataracts, had heard that Robert was in Natal, and wrote on 2nd June 1863, to Kirk, then on his way home and possibly calling at Durban: 'If you see my boy Robert, say a kind word to him and advise him to work, for I fear he may turn out a "Ne'er do weel."'

For news to have reached Livingstone where he was, Robert must have arrived in Natal early in the year, and by June Livingstone knew that his expedition was in its last phase. On 5th July, however, he wrote to Kirk again: 'My son Robert is at Natal. Give him a kind word if you see him and may God bless you,' and also to George Cato, the mayor of Durban on 3rd July, asking him to find Robert work, if he came his way, and to give him a warning to avoid drink and 'evil company'.

The following month, on 8th August, Livingstone wrote to Kirk once more:

> Robert is said to be at Natal to join me, and I am sorry I cannot ask anyone save Captain Gardner [of HMS *Orestes*] to give him a passage, and he won't touch there. [Robert] would be useful in the 'L. Nyassa'. If you can drop a word about a passage to any likely skipper, I shall be obliged. If he cannot come, he must work his own way in Natal.

Shortly after writing this paragraph – part of a long letter – Livingstone heard that Robert, thanks to (now Sir) Thomas Maclear, was at the Cape, and told James Young:

> Robert came to Natal 'pennyless', one box without a key left on board was pillaged on his return to the ship so I suspect he had not been behaving himself. Sir Thomas Maclear, a real good friend sent for him to the Cape as he was idling his time away and running into debt in a hotel at Natal – got him lodgings at the Cape at 2/6 per day and I

suppose will get him employment at some manual labour. He seems fit for nothing else and must earn some money before any more is spent on him. I wished him to come up if he could do so before December [Expedition's end] but have told him if he could not that he must get work and stick to it. I must pay some £30 for him now. A hopeful youth certainly, and I cannot free myself from blame in his having so little of fatherly care. I am very heartsore about him.

And Livingstone now admits that to force children against their talents is wrong:

Should Thomas wish to go to sea in the Navy before I get home be sure please and let him follow his bent. I wish to give them all a good education as my legacy and they may take to any trade they feel inclined for after that. I shall feel it a great kindness if you will remember this without consulting your colleagues [the other trustees].

In October 1863, Mrs Moffat, Robert's grandmother, wrote him a long, gentle letter, giving news of Kuruman people, sending 'tender solicitude and affection' and 'longing to hear from you'. But if it took the usual two months for a letter to reach Cape Town from Kuruman, it is unlikely that Robert would have received it. He did not fancy whatever 'manual labour' Maclear may have found for him and, as Livingstone told Young from Zanzibar, sometime before 10th February 1864 and after the expedition was over: 'Robert has shipped into a brig that travels between Cape and New York – as a common sailor.' In July, Livingstone learned that Robert was in the American (civil war) army, and predicted that he would 'be made manure of for those bloody fields' and then no more was heard from him until October 1864, when Livingstone received a letter from him which must have caused him considerable anguish, both for its news of Robert's sufferings, so casually mentioned, and for its revelation of a mature and sensible young man (Robert was now eighteen):

My dear Sir, Hearing that you have returned to England I undertake to address a few lines to you, not with any hope that you will be interested in me but simply to explain the position. The agent of Mr McArthur of Port Natal said that he would write to him and inform him of my position and find me employment till I could find means to reach you. Mr Rutherfoord, Collector of HM Customs at Port Natal, interested himself in me for your sake and treated me with the greatest kindness. I believe that I owe some obligation to Mr McArthur. All he heard of me was that I was to come out in a certain vessel. Concluding that I had run away he would have nothing to do with me. I should have been very badly off had it not been for the kindness of Mrs Robert Moffat to whom, besides £1, I owe a great deal, perhaps more than I shall ever be able to repay.

From Port Natal I went to Cape Town where your agent Mr Rutherfoord advised me to find employment on board a brig which brought me to Boston, America. Here I was kidnapped and one morning, after going to be on board ship, I found myself enlisted in the U.S. army.

I have been in one battle and two skirmishes, and expect to be in another terrific battle before long. God in His mercy has spared me as yet. I have never hurt anyone knowingly in battle, have always fired high, and in that furious madness which accompanies a bayonet charge and which seems to possess every soldier, I controlled my passion and took the man who surrendered prisoner.

The rebels are not likely to hold out much longer as we have nearly all their railroads. My craving for travelling is not yet satisfied, though if I had the chance that I threw away of being educated, I should think myself only too much blessed. I have changed my name, for I am convinced that to bear your name here would lead to further dishonour to it. I am at present in this hospital, exposure and fatigue having given me ague fever. Your quondam son, Robert

Address: Rupert Vincent, N.H. Vols., 10th Army Corps, Virginia.

(How Livingstone must have regretted telling Thomas that Robert was only interested in making capital out of having a famous father.)

But when Robert left Cape Town in the brig bound for Boston, he knew that he was sailing to a country in arms. The American Civil War was the greatest conflict of the age, and by 1863, the Cape itself had become one of the battlefronts, with the Confederate warship *Alabama* raiding Northern commercial shipping in its waters during the period Robert was there. The *Alabama*, which used to replenish its stores at Cape Town, and which captured the Northern ship *Sea Bride* in Table Bay on 24th August 1863, was a sensation, its name surviving to this day in the Cape's most popular folk song 'Daar kom die Alabama'. (The fact that the 'Alabama' had been built at Birkenhead by Macgregor Laird, and handed over surreptitiously, in defiance of a British government embargo, to the Confederates, was not likely to make Livingstone feel any more tender towards the execrated builders of the *Ma Robert*.)

As for Robert's assertion that he was kidnapped in Boston, it is difficult not to suspect that he is concealing the truth, for the sake both of the family name and for his own. Shortly after the outbreak of the war, the British government declared neutrality and made it illegal for British subjects to join the forces of either side, but 'A few years later large numbers of immigrants were enlisted in the United States [the North] ...' There was no actual recruiting in foreign countries, but advertisements in the press encouraged immigrants to go to America and obtain bounties on enlistment.

Perhaps the immigrant Robert had taken the President's dollar, perhaps not. As far as his father was concerned, however, Robert was on the right side for, by the time he arrived in Boston, the war had become more than Lincoln's struggle 'to save the Union': it had taken on features of the abolitionist cause.

Livingstone learned later in 1864 that, after leaving hospital and returning to action, Robert had been taken prisoner by the Confederates in a skirmish near Richmond, Virginia, on 7th October. The American Ambassador in London, Charles Francis Adams, whom Livingstone met at a dinner party, put him in touch with the adjutant of Robert's regiment. The adjutant told him, as Livingstone reported to James Young on 4th January 1865, that an exchange of prisoners was being arranged, and that Robert would be given 'the consideration that his family merits'.

Livingstone's hope rose, and he began to talk about taking Robert with him on his next journey to Africa. However, relations between London and Washington were at a low ebb, thanks largely to the *Alabama* affair, and Livingstone had also upset the Americans when in a public speech he had commented on affairs in the United States. He reported to Oswell on 23rd March 1865,

> The Yankee adjutant of [Robert's] reg. said to Mr Adams the American minister, that in my speech ... I had not spoken well of their nation – What I said was that these terrible wars always taught terrible lessons and perhaps the lesson this one would teach would be that 'though on the side of oppression there is power, there be higher than they.' It is a line from Ecclesiastes – I did not answer this fault for fear I should make bad worse.

The Americans had interpreted Livingstone's remark to mean that they had brought the war on themselves by godlessly condoning slavery for so long. They may, too, have heard his even stronger view, noted later in his journal on 5th May 1865:

> If every drop shed by the lash must be atoned for by an equal number of white men's vital fluid – righteous O Lord are Thy judgements.

Livingstone heard no more from the adjutant except a repeated 'they are exchanging prisoners' and suspected that Adams had lost interest in the matter. Though he still hoped to take Robert to Africa, no word came from him, not even to Agnes, to whom he was very close.

In June 1865, Livingstone was told that Robert had been taken, wounded, to a Confederate prisoner-of-war camp at Salisbury, North Carolina, but it was not certain if he were alive.

'Robert we shall never hear of again in this world I fear;' wrote Livingstone, 'but the Lord is merciful and just and right in all his ways. He would hear the cry for mercy in the hospital at Salisbury'. He told a friend: 'I am proud of the boy. If I had been there I should have gone to fight for the north myself.' (Had he seen through the kidnap story?)

In August 1865, as Livingstone was leaving once more for Africa, still without any firm news from Salisbury, he told Oswell that Agnes was 'very much cut up' at parting from him, a sadness deepened because 'she was much attached to poor Bob, whose name I fear must be heard no more.' And a few months later on 1st January 1866, when well on his travels, he said to Oswell again:

> Nothing of Robert after his capture by the confederates – he was so fond of Agnes that he would have written to her had he been alive – it would be better if we knew but I fear we never shall.

In fact, Robert had died a prisoner on 5th December 1864, just before he turned nineteen. His name is remembered with his father's in Livingstone College, Salisbury NC, founded in 1879 by the African Methodist Episcopal Zion church. The college rapidly became one of the bastions in the battle for civil rights which the abolition of slavery had failed to secure for Americans of African descent, a battle in which the college's eponym would readily have joined.

On the Zambezi and Shire, in the midst of all the difficulties surrounding the expedition, even before the crisis of Mary's death, Livingstone had family matters constantly before him, and did his utmost to attend to them. Apart from the problems with his children, his sisters were finding it difficult to make a living as milliners, and his mother needed support. He asked Young, in February 1862, to 'give a little more to mother, say £50, but hint to sisters that if they can they ought to work, if only to baulk that gent who finds some mischief still.' Then there was the case of his brother John, who had run into trouble in Canada after a sound start, as agent for James Young's paraffin. On 28th January 1860, Livingstone had reported to Young: 'I got a letter from my Canadian brother, he seems likely to do well under your kind patronage, and he and I are both thankful for it.' But within a year things had gone badly wrong, and a dispute between John and Young's Paraffin Oil and Light Company threatened to go to court. Livingstone was asked to give his opinion, on a matter in which it was equally important for him, neither to impugn his brother's rectitude, nor to offend Young. Aboard the *Pioneer*, in intervals between work, theological arguments, and reading the latest issues of the *Quarterly Review, Chambers Journal* and *Punch*, while he was taking Mackenzie and his colleagues up to Magomero after the trip to the Rovuma, Livingstone had written at length to Young on 14th May 1861, starting with his peculiar personal vanities:

> I find I am in want of a new blue frock coat... I want it made in no particular fashion i.e. it must be made in the fashion of the day as it must serve for several years – buttons of the consular uniform ... Messrs Brownlow and Oliver have my measure ... I don't like it to hang flappingly.

Then, between news of the expedition and gossip about its members, he turns to the main business of the letter:

> In that unfortunate affair with my brother John I don't feel easy at not having given you an opinion, though by sending the documents you evidently intended me to form one. This I assure you was only because I did not wish to run the risk of endangering our friendship by writing, the tone of which might be read very differently from what was intended ... I avoided also giving my opinion to my brother or to anyone else.
>
> There can be no doubt that you are legally right. That is I think that you will have the law on your side, because you had a perfect right to sell the goods at a higher rate to him (as he believed), the sole importer into Canada than to customers at home. He spent all his little property in advertizing and would have come out well it seems had not umbrage been taken by your partners or self at the little he had, I suppose, without leave assumed.
>
> Then another party or parties in Canada were supplied with oil at so much a lower rate that they actually offered to supply him more cheaply than he could get it from you. When I say *you* I of course mean your firm. He might be misled by the Canadian parties making the offer, but he had the statement of one of your own agents at home that a larger price was demanded from him than from the others. My opinion then, in which I may be quite mistaken, is this. He relied too trustingly in the idea that by your friend[ship] he had secured not only the first but the sole right of importation for a time at least. This did not comport with your plan. In fact he had no right to assume so much and was let down by other agents being granted the privilege of importation and at a lower rate.
>
> In my own mind I explain this by supposing the lower rate to [have been] granted by another member of [the] firm without your knowledge. If your books show this, and no one else has a right to ask whether they do or not, I hope it may modify your law proceedings against him. I believe

him incapable of fraud. He has a very high character for integrity in upper Canada where he is known.

I feel that I led him into this unfortunate affair, you too thought it would be advantageous for both and must regret that it has turned out so differently from what we expected. All I presume to ask is to reconsider the case in view of the poor fellow being 'nursed' by other agents after he had spent his all in advertisements, and don't push your legal proceedings too hotly. If you take a wholly different view of the case from what I do, pray do not trouble to reply on the subject but let us continue our correspondence as heretofore.

As we hear no more of the matter, we may assume that it either lapsed or was settled amicably. Livingstone's display of diplomacy here is interesting. How lacking it had been in the air of acrimony that surrounded his treatment of Bedingfeld, Baines, and Thornton, in his branding Samuel Edwards a thief. But now Livingstone is dealing with the business of the clan, a clan in which James Young is coming to occupy the position of 'godfather-banker', as the sad story of the *Lady Nyassa* would show.

The little screw-steamer's hull was launched at Shupanga on 23rd June 1862, two months after Mary's death. But she was not to sail for the lake that season for, by the time she had been fitted out, the river was too low.

20

LADY NYASSA

After Mary's death, Livingstone's attitude towards his companions softened somewhat. He became more talkative and approachable, even if there were still times when he appeared consumed by his obsessions. When Richard Thornton arrived back at Shupanga in June 1862 Livingstone, thinking perhaps of his hopes that Robert would turn out well one day, gave Thornton his job back – for Thornton, barely twenty-four years old, had excelled himself since his dismissal from the expedition, had travelled to Zanzibar and joined the German Count Karl Klaus von der Decken's exploration of Mt Kilimanjaro, had made important geological discoveries in the Mombasa area, and had acquitted himself so well that the Count had taken his notes to incorporate in his own report. Back at Shupanga, Thornton was yet at work making a map of Kilimanjaro based on his observations (and copying out Livingstone's vocabulary of the local languages for his own use). Livingstone realised that he had been too harsh with Thornton and, in giving him a new commission, allowed him to follow much of his own path, just as he would now allow his own two younger sons to do.

Thornton records his negotiations with Livingstone in his diary, 14th July 1862:

> Then Livingstone read over the letter I wrote to him in May last year in answer to his letter of Jany 1st 1861, and said that my two charges therein were false and defied me to prove them.

[Thornton's charges against Livingstone were]

> *First*, that you condemned me mainly on the evidence of your brother C. Livingstone, without making a proper enquiry into the truth of that evidence, and without giving me an opportunity to defend myself. *Second* that you condemned me for having done no work without ever asking me what I had done. To this day you do not know what geology I did or did not whilst a member of the expedition.

Thornton's diary continues:

> Then after a long discussion [with Livingstone], I showed him I was
> right in my second charge. The Dr., whilst pressing home his charge of
> laziness, was very kind and gave me a very good character. At last he
> acknowledged my second charge and agreed to withdraw the charges he
> had made against me. Then he said he would give the recommendation
> for the restoration of my salary. But I told him that I did not want it, that
> I had very little work to show for the time and did not wish to receive
> pay for work I had not done. Then I told him I should be staying about
> 6 or 8 months longer to finish off my work here, and that I should like
> to get [from] the Government something for my work instead of working
> apparently in opposition to his expedition, and so supposed that I should
> become a sort of outer member of the expedition and receive my pay as
> before. He said he thought that it was a very good plan.

And there the matter rested, though Thornton's return to Livingstone
was not entirely disinterested. He wanted to clear his name, and he
wanted to increase his reputation as a geologist, in the hope of getting
a Government job when the expedition was over.

But despite Livingstone's new openness and willingness to be con-
ciliatory, the predominant mood of the party in mid-1862 was gloom.
Kirk was unhappy and eager to leave, his dislike of Charles as strong
as ever; James Stewart was whining his disillusionment with Livingstone
and preparing to abandon any Free Church plan for an industrial
mission; the new expedition doctor, Charles James Meller, sent out
with the *Pioneer* to fill the gap left by Kirk's botanical and zoologi-
cal researches, was ineffectual and sickly. And the news from the
Shire was bad. After transferring from Magomero to Chibisa's, the
UMCA was having to move again: fighting and slave raiding in the
valley were making its position at the cataracts impossible. Chibisa
and his people had returned, in flight from the Tete district where
they had been harassed by Belchior do Nascimento – described by
Kirk as a 'half-blind syphilitic' – and his slave marauders. And now
Chibisa wanted the missionaries to give him protection. To add to the
anarchy, and to Livingstone's distress, the Kololo he had left – armed
– in the valley, had become slave raiders themselves. The mission was
leaving the valley for the upland village of Mbame.

The Portuguese were incensed with Livingstone for 'stealing', that
is to say liberating, their slaves and handing them over to the missionaries, and were delighted when Livingstone sent Kirk to bring
the expedition's stores from Tete to Shupanga. The first sign that
Livingstone was retreating. On the other hand, the Portuguese were
beginning to implement the metropolitan slave code by which the

children of slaves were born free, and they had called Belchior to heel. Livingstone may have found a grain of encouragement in these small concessions, but he knew that the Portuguese could close the river whenever they wished, even if the chaos in the Shire did not itself make that route to the highlands and the lake too dangerous to travel. Once he had the *Lady Nyassa* on the lake, however, he would be beyond the Portuguese, and be able to start implementing his long-term anti-slavery policy, use the *Lady Nyassa* 'to get possession of the ivory trade . . . on the Lake and . . . render the trade in slaves unprofitable,' as he told George Frere, the anti-slavery commissioner at the Cape on 22nd December 1863. But the ship was taking a long time to build, far longer than anticipated even with the delays in fetching her in pieces from the delta. The delay rested, not in lack of effort, but in the vessel's very design:

> She is just the same size as the 'Pioneer', only of wood in place of iron, 111 tons in 22 sections and 3 watertight compartments. The sections are screwed together to a wrought-iron keel and by angle irons at the sides, strengthened by a strong angle iron along each bilge. . . She has 4 boilers and 2 screws, high pressure vertical engines.

Livingstone wrote this on 3rd June 1862; by the time she was ready for service it was July. The rivers were too low to take her to the Shire cataracts and Livingstone decided to use the six months that would elapse before the rainy season to make another expedition to the Rovuma, which he still hoped would give access, independent of the Portuguese, to the lake. That would suit his purposes, while the journey of exploration would also be a final fulfilment of John Russell's orders. Besides, he could collect stores at Johanna in the Comoros and buy the oxen he hoped would pull the *Lady Nyassa* up the Shire cataracts road (as yet unbuilt).

Kirk did not want to go on the Rovuma trip and so leave the company remaining at Shupanga without a doctor (Meller was away sick at the Cape) but Livingstone made it an order. Kirk was afraid that if he refused, Charles would persuade his brother to give him the Baines treatment for, as Kirk wrote on 29th July 1862: 'Dr L. though kind and considerate to me, still is not to be depended on.'

It was not a happy expedition, Livingstone was in his driven mood again. Kirk describes him aboard the *Pioneer* crossing from the delta to the Comoros, haunting the deck like Ahab:

> When the weather gets foul or anything begins to go wrong, it is well to give him a wide berth, most especially when he sings to himself. But the kind of air is some indication. If it is 'The Happy Land' then look out for

squalls and stand clear. If 'Scots wha hae' there is some grand vision of discovery before his mind . . . But on all occasions, humming of airs is a bad omen.

From Johanna in the Comoros, HMS *Orestes* (the ship that could not call at Durban to collect Robert) escorted the *Pioneer* to the Rovuma, where the party arrived on 7th September. Livingstone tried to cheer up his men with the thought that in a few weeks they might be 'rowing their boats into Lake Nyasa'. But that was not to happen: the river was low, shoals and rocky dykes made it impassable without constant winching. The party was several times attacked along the way (Kirk even shot and killed a man who was threatening him) and as the water was falling everyone, except Livingstone, was in mortal dread that they would be trapped unable to sail back to the estuary. As Livingstone forced the party on, Kirk wrote on 18th September 1862: 'I can come to no other conclusion than that Dr. L is out of his mind.' On 26th September, he wrote that they had reached

> . . . a field of rocks where the water came off in a rush. Yet Dr. L seems to intend taking up the boats. . . If he does, I can only say that his head is not quite of ordinary construction, but what is termed 'cracked'.

Fortunately, Livingstone's passion had worn itself out, there was to be no madness equivalent to sending canoes down the Cabora Basa, and the next day Kirk's diary entry, of 27th September 1862, reflects his relief: 'Began our return this morning.' They were a bare one hundred and forty miles inland. The last stage of the journey upstream had been forced on the party by Livingstone despite being told by a passing Kilwa merchant that there was no waterway to the lake, on the contrary in fact, only mountains. Livingstone ignored him, just as he had ignored warnings about Cabora Basa six years before.

'Things on board the *Pioneer*,' Kirk remarked as the party made its way back to Shupanga, 'are most uncomfortable.' Livingstone now knew for certain that there was only one waterway to the lake. The other members of the company wanted to leave the expedition. Even Meller, whom they had picked up at Johanna on his return from the Cape, was grumbly and still unwell. After a tedious passage up the Zambezi – its level had dropped further – with a gang of Comoran labourers and a team of oxen aboard, the *Pioneer* docked at Shupanga in mid-December. Later in life, Kirk described the Rovuma journey as the worst he had ever made, because of the physical danger; perhaps because he had had to kill; because of Livingstone. Again Kirk wanted to go home but 'Dr L' persuaded him to stay. And Livingstone, too, found nothing at Shupanga to counterbalance the disappointment of the Rovuma – quite the opposite. There was less water in the river than there had been in July. Its level pointed to the drought which had added another layer of devastation to the Shire valley. Even if by the end of December the Zambezi was beginning to rise, the *Lady Nyassa* would not be able to proceed upstream for several weeks, and now the ship itself – so trim on the water – looked as if it had become a burden. A letter from James Young told Livingstone that she had cost twice as much as Livingstone had estimated. The reply to Young opens:

> On perusal of your letter ... I thought it well to write a duplicate of the order to pay £5,589.59 ... and this I put into my despatch box in order that should death catch me ere I come down this river again, you and the Trustees may be all safe ... The only point in which my intentions were more than expected is I expected the cost would be about half, and the voyage out another £1000, or £4000 in all. But it is all right, we have the value of the money to shew, and if we succeed as we hope, never was money better spent.

But Livingstone begins to doubt this optimism:

> If Govt won't give a half – say £3000 I would not make a whine about it. I shall hand over whatever of my salary I can save to support the children [he adds, as an afterthought, 'and my mother'] and the interest of the £5000 that may remain [in the Trust] will do the rest. By giving you all I can out of £350 (that is £500 minus £150 for a missionary) [J S Moffat in Matabeleland] we shall get on very well.
>
> I think I shall not live very long, and if the children get all that was collected for them in Glasgow and elsewhere, they ought to get on.

Now the tone becomes bitter:

> Oh if I had looked sharper after my own interests I might have had a higher salary – Burton has £700 (Mr Layard's brother lately got a situation as commissioner at the Cape at £1000 not to be mentioned, and two slave commissioners at Luanda in our latitudes get one £1000 and the other £1500) ... Bedingfeld had £600 while with me ...

Then bitterness leads to depression:

> I may never see a home again. All my hopes of doing good in my home among the outcasts of Africa have been dispelled, but I shall do my duty notwithstanding.

His homelessness reminds him of Mary:

> I wish you to get me a gravestone of granite if it will stand the sun.
> If not then of iron or stone of at least five and a half or six inches
> of thickness. The shape neat without projecting angles that could be
> knocked off easily, of good size say 5 or 6 feet high, but not, with
> socket, above a ton and a half in weight. If you let me know the price I
> shall send an order to the three Trustees in due form. As also for a watch
> for Agnes . . .

Livingstone is worried about the attitude of Young's fellow trustees
and concludes (with a sentence we have seen before):

> I can write [to you] more easily than I could to the others partly because I
> suppose you will make allowance for mistakes or for the tone which may
> seem wrong when nothing is intended and partly because writing to Dr B
> and Mrs Hannan is like confessing to the corner of a confessional box or
> conversing with a man as deaf as a door nail. They never answer me the
> idewats. Love to Majames [Mrs Young].

Livingstone laid the letter aside for a while, and when it seemed
that he would be under way with the *Lady Nyassa*, added a few
words:

> PS: The water is rising fast and we shall have all the flood for our
> work . . . be joyful and drink your wine with a merry heart and send
> portions to those who are ready to perish, and may God's blessing rest
> on you and yours.

The letter is dated 15th December; on 11th January 1863 the *Lady
Nyassa* started upriver first towed by, and then tied alongside, the
Pioneer.

This upstream advance, Livingstone knew, was probably his last
chance (short of leaving the country altogether and starting afresh
elsewhere) to escape the grip of the Zambezian Portuguese. But he had
not lost all hope – perhaps the halting of Belchior had revived some –
that Portugal itself might respond to more pressure on slavery and thus
become more amenable to his activities. A few days before setting out
for the Shire, he dug out of his files and on 8th January 1863, replied
to, a letter he had received four years previously from Bishop Joaquim
Moreira Reis who had befriended him in Luanda in 1854. Livingstone
was looking for both moral and practical support, the former against
the slave trade, the latter for the UMCA:

My dear Bishop,

I thank you for your kind letter of 31st March 1857 which followed me to this country about two years after it was written.

After making excuses for not answering sooner, and explaining what he had been doing, Livingstone continues:

We are now about to carry a steamer past some cataracts on the Shire with a view to launch it on [the lake] and hope to do somewhat to stop the slave traffic of 20,000 annually who are taken from the Lake region to [Kilwa] and then to the Red Sea and Persian Gulph. If the Most High grants us success we shall have done some good in Africa. You can form no idea of the misery that the slave trade causes – for every one taken out of the country, two perish by the wars engendered or by the famine that succeeds.

A mission was sent out by a number of learned and pious men in the English Universities Oxford and Cambridge . . . they have been much troubled by the slave hunters. They are learning the native language and it is partly on their account that I trouble you with this letter. I believe that the Jesuit missionaries translated the Bible or other books into the language of Senna and Tette for I have heard old persons chanting the 'Pater Noster', creed etc in their own tongue. Now if we could get any of these books in the native language it would be of great assistance to the missionaries for it is exceedingly difficult to learn as it tumbles out of the mouths of the blacks. If any of your acquaintances knows of the existence of any books such as I mention in the old libraries of Portugal, I would cheerfully pay for copying them and will get them printed and will not forget to give all honour to the old authors.

The letter ends with a paragraph in Livingstone's imperfect Portuguese: 'Espera que VEa ter melhor [?] para trabalhar por ista Africa. Todas partes tem muita precisao de melhoramento pelo os servidores de Deus. . . As letras de recommendacao faze muito boa effecta quando chegou em ista Costa – muitas mil gracias.'

[I hope your excellency has better [?] to work for this Africa. All parts greatly need improvement by the servants of God . . . Your letters of recommendation were to good effect when I arrived on this Coast – many thousand thanks.]

A few days before this letter to the bishop, Livingstone had written to another Catholic clergyman, possibly a Jesuit, the Reverend James Russel asking for his help in tracing the old translations, but the note to Bishop Reis should be taken at more than its face value. As Livingstone suspected that his mail was being read by the Portuguese authorities, it could be seen as an 'open letter' designed to show the Portuguese in Zambezia that Livingstone had a friend in a high place in Portugal itself.

The Portuguese had set up a military post at the mouth of the Shire, and the *Pioneer* with the *Lady Nyassa* strapped to it, steamed past it, unchallenged, four days after leaving Shupanga, and entered the devastated valley. The river itself was hardly navigable, so shallow was it as a result of the drought, it took the clumsy catamaran two and a half months to cover the less than two hundred miles to Chibisa's, where it arrived on 1st April. The heat was appalling. January 23rd, Thornton remarks, was the hottest day he had experienced in Africa, so hot he felt he was losing the ability to breathe. The evidence of desolation lay on every side, fields without crops, starving people on the banks eating the roots of water lilies, corpses in the river being devoured by crocodiles. The party on the ships became exhausted and fractious or, as Kirk notes mildly, 'There seems to be a different feeling throughout the ship which does not make all work together with a will.'

The UMCA, however, despite all afflictions, was making a brave effort to survive, as Kirk records on 25th March 1863:

> I had a good chance to see the youngsters under the Mission – a nice set of boys and girls. Most of the women are married now to the men, so that things are getting in order.

But turning the freed slaves into a flock was not enough:

> ... there is much need to have them all engaged in cultivating lands which they can look on as a settlement. For this station is quite untenable. Drought cut off the crops and fever disables or kills the White men.

Kirk wrote this after leaving the grounded *Pioneer* to go overland to the Mission, now at Mbame, in the hope of saving the lives of two missionaries who were seriously ill. One of them, the newly arrived mission doctor, died before Kirk arrived, the other was nursed back to life.

There was such a shortage of food at Mbame that Thornton volunteered to go with the Reverend Henry Rowley, another new arrival at the mission, to Tete to buy sheep, goats and cattle for slaughter. The same journey had almost killed Kirk and Rae a few years before, but Thornton and Rowley returned successfully with the livestock. However, on 22nd April 1863, Livingstone had to write to Thornton's brother George:

> Dear Sir,
>   It is with sorrow that I have to convey the sad intelligence that your

brother Richard Thornton died yesterday morning about 10 o'clock. He became very ill on the 11th April – of dysentry and fever, and no remedy seemed to have much effect. On the 20th he was seriously ill but took some soup several times and drank claret and water with relish. We then hoped that his youth and unimpaired constitution would carry him through – the diarrhoea had nearly ceased – but about six o'clock in the evening his mind began to wander and continued so. His bodily powers continued gradually to sink till the period mentioned when he quietly expired . . . We buried him today by a large baobab tree about fifty yards from the first cataract and 300 from the right bank of the Shire – and there he rests in sure and certain hope of glorious Resurrection.

I enclose a lock of his hair. I had all his papers sealed up soon after his decease – and will endeavour to transmit all to you exactly as he left them.

The final paragraph deals with settling Richard's estate, paying his servants, getting his property back to England. Unfortunately, the Thornton family did not leave things there, on this dignified note. They blamed Livingstone for Richard's death, and embarked on a long and acrimonious correspondence, wrangling over money and property, which continued for more than two years.

Richard Thornton's name did not die with him: 'The five chief contributions to our knowledge of the geology of British East Africa are those of Thornton (1862), Beyrich (1878) . . . Sadebeck (1879) . . . Toula and Suess (1892),' wrote J W Gregory in his volume *The Great Rift Valley* which was published by John Murray in 1896. Although Livingstone does not mention it, (and, perhaps, was not aware of it) Thornton looked remarkably like his own son Robert.

While Thornton was on his deathbed, Kirk and Charles were also seriously ill, and on 27th April, with Richard's death in mind, Livingstone gave both of them permission to leave the expedition. Charles departed almost at once but, when Livingstone himself went down with his worst ever attack of dysentery, Kirk volunteered to stay on to look after him, and did not get away until 19th May. Livingstone ordered him to return to England by way of the Cape, no doubt hoping that while there he would be able to counteract the malice that was being spread about Livingstone's part in the Ajawa Wars (which Livingstone was rumoured to have started) and in Mackenzie's death. In the event, however, Kirk went home via Suez. Livingstone's notes to him from June onwards about Robert's progress in Natal were thus to no avail. But even if Kirk could not help Livingstone in these matters, he would have been gratified that 'Dr L' had at last recognised his long-suffering service and persistent endurance. Shortly after he left, Livingstone wrote, on 2nd June 1863: 'I am sure I wish you every success in your future life.

You were always a right hand to me, and I never trusted you in vain. God bless and prosper you.'

Livingstone was not so generous about Meller, who gave notice at the same time as Kirk and Charles were released: 'We shall soon be without a doctor for the "Pioneer",' Livingstone told James Young on 30th April 1863; 'for Meller has evidently got into a great funk by Thornton's death. . . . His departure . . . will be no loss. Kirk's is and no mistake.'

At this time, April and May, work was going ahead under Rae's direction with taking the *Lady Nyassa* apart so that she could be hauled in sections to the lake, using the road beside the cataracts which was then being cleared. But Livingstone was increasingly doubtful about the little steamer's prospects now that he knew that the Zambezi and Shire were the only access to Nyasa, and told Young:

> I sometimes fear that if these rivers are not to be opened and no effective restrictions put on the Portuguese, I shall yet have to screw our Lady Nyassa away to India and sell her there. I would not ask her price from Government – and only the half in being successful. I wished to make a thanks offering by devoting £3000 to that which promised to do the most good in the world.

In June, to get away from the foetid valley, Livingstone and Rae walked up to the lake to see if they could make a cruise in the small boat that had been left there after the 1859 exploration of the west coast. They found that the whaler had been destroyed in a bush fire, and walked back to the *Pioneer* tired yet refreshed by the break. But an avalanche of decisive news was about to descend.

The UMCA had a new leader, Bishop William George Tozer, and he had decided to move the mission from its site above the valley to Mt Morumbala at the Shire-Zambezi confluence. And there was a despatch from Earl Russell, recalling the expedition, promising free passages home for its members, saying salaries would cease at the end of the year. A letter, too, from Young stated that the Trustees had refused to pay for the *Lady Nyassa*, as a result of which Young had had to foot the bill himself in order to save Livingstone's credit.

Livingstone was enraged by Tozer's decision to move the mission, as it took it so far from the lake that it could no longer be part of Livingstone's plans (he was, at the time, intending to bring the 'iron house', originally destined for Batoka, to the UMCA station at Mbame) and he wrote scornfully to Young in July/August 1863:

> The mission is when we last heard of it on the top of Morumbala or 4000 feet high, quite among the clouds and no people near to teach –

I suppose the bishop is looking around maturing his plans, some think to bolt, but I would not say that [to] the public. Between ourselves the High Church missionaries of whom I fervently hoped better things are fit only for well-behaven ladies' boarding schools. They have no idea of what a missionary should do.

Young himself was a Reformed Presbyterian, a member of the 'Church of the Covenant', the most extreme of Scotland's non-established Presbyterians, most antipathetic towards High Churchmen. But Livingstone's respect for Mackenzie prevents him from suppressing all charity:

> However, remembering all our own failings, we cannot be harsh in our judgements on others.

The recall of the expedition could not have been unexpected, as after the previous year's exploration of the Rovuma, it had no more to do except aid the UMCA, and that had now established its own lines of communication through Quelimane. The British government had no intention of 'forcing steamers up cataracts' to fulfil Livingstone's ambitions on the lake, and took no interest at all in the *Lady Nyassa*. She was Livingstone's problem, with or without James Young. The expedition was being kept on the government payroll until the end of the year solely to allow Livingstone to get the *Pioneer* down to the coast with the next rainy season. Unhappy though it was about an alleged paucity of information from the expedition regarding the 'resources of the country' (the full value of the work it had done would not emerge for many years), there is no direct criticism of Livingstone himself; nevertheless, the British government was only too glad to get him out of its (and Portugal's) hair. On 1st January 1864, Livingstone was Consul no longer.

Livingstone knew that the dream had come to an end, that the *Lady Nyassa* was now no more than the expensive embodiment of a fantasy, that he had no choice but to sell her. To Kirk he says sadly on 8th August 1863:

> As for the 'Lady Nyassa' I would rather see her forming a second bar at Quelimane than that she should be a slaver or Portuguese property, which would be the same thing. We mean to take her to India when the hurricane season is over.

On the banks of the Shire, the ship lay in sections awaiting reassembly on the lake, to be screwed and bolted together again for the journey to the sea. Rae and the crew of the *Pioneer* who had taken her apart would now put her back together. Livingstone could not bear the thought of watching and waiting four months for the river to rise. Taking with him one of the *Pioneer* crew, who had been ill and needed a 'change of air', and a small party of Shupanga men as porters, Livingstone set out once more, with a small boat, for a trip on the lake. The boat was lost in an accident at the head of the cataracts, but no matter, he was used to walking, and exercise would do the anaemic ship's steward good. The journey took them along and above the lake to Kota Kota, the Zanzibari slave port on the west coast, then inland over the escarpment (which Livingstone named 'Kirk's Range') for about a hundred miles along the trade route between the lake and Katanga and the Lunda kingdom. Here, Livingstone had identified the main commercial artery between the heart of central Africa and Kilwa and had touched on the Zanzibari mercantile empire within whose confines he would end his days. He wanted to inspect the northern end of the lake to confirm his previous observations, but had to be back on the Shire in November, was short of time and had to leave that bit of business unfinished. The whole journey covered seven hundred and fifty miles. Livingstone, the ship's steward, the porters (except one, who had died of malaria) arrived back at the *Pioneer* fit and well, their 'muscles', he remarked, 'as hard as boards'.

The *Lady Nyassa* had been re-built, all was ready for the withdrawal but, as he waited for the river to rise, Livingstone's fear that Bishop Tozer was 'going to bolt' was confirmed. On 17th December, Livingstone said to Kirk: 'I received a note from the Bishop saying he "had determined to leave the Zambezi as early in the coming year as possible".' The entire missionary enterprise was now dying, for James Stewart had left too, earlier in the year, totally disillusioned with the country (which he had toured up the Zambezi as far as Cabora Basa, up the Shire to the highlands) disillusioned too, with Livingstone. Stewart threw his copy of *Missionary Travels* into the Zambezi, a pettish gesture of disgust at a god that had failed him. Livingstone reserved his bile for Tozer alone, leader of the 'first Protestant mission which in modern times has turned tail without being driven away. . .' In December 1863 he wrote to George Frere:

> With the mission departs the last ray of hope for the wretched downtrodden people of this region – and it has the not over creditable peculiarity that while the first party from a conscientious scruple of the late bishop, no teaching was attempted, the second party never went near the party to be taught . . . I cannot help feeling very sore at this . . .

Tozer took the Mackenzie mission's young freed slaves with him but left the older ones behind. To as many of the latter as so wished, Livingstone

offered sanctuary, took them aboard the *Pioneer* and the *Lady Nyassa* –
some forty in all, together with Waller, who had refused to accompany
Tozer. Waller then took most of them into his care. Tozer transferred
the mission to Zanzibar, an act Livingstone compared derisively to St
Augustine trying to convert England after settling in the Channel Islands.

On 19th January the two little ships set off downstream and in due
course entered the Indian Ocean. Near Quelimane they were taken in
tow by two British warships, fortuitously in the area, and delivered
through a violent cyclone that nearly sank them to Mozambique town.
From there the *Pioneer*, with Waller and most of the ex-slaves, was
escorted to the Cape, while Livingstone and Rae took the *Lady Nyassa*
under its own steam to Zanzibar. Rae parted from Livingstone there,
hoping to become partner on a sugar estate in the Comoros, notorious
slave islands. (His expectations came to nothing and he was soon to
die of a perforated stomach ulcer.)

The expedition was over, but not for Livingstone. He, now without
an engineer, was determined to take the *Lady Nyassa* with her high
pressure boilers and her vertical engine, to Bombay. He assembled a
crew of twelve, including two of the freed slaves from the Shire named
Chuma and Wakatini, his chief officer being a stoker named John Reid.
After taking on as much coal as the ship could carry, with barely a month
to spare before the Indian monsoon would make the voyage too perilous
to venture, they set out from Zanzibar. The two and a half thousand mile
journey, using steam and sail, took forty-five days and the *Lady Nyassa*
berthed in Bombay harbour just as the first storms of the monsoon
were breaking. Livingstone's early lessons in navigation, taken with the
captain of the barque *George* as she crossed the south Atlantic in 1840,
had proved their worth magnificently. The little steamer performed well,
though the engines gave some trouble. Chuma and Wakatini he placed
at a Protestant mission outside Bombay, paid off the rest of the crew
and found work for some of them at the docks. There, as he arrived,
Livingstone had seen a sight that symbolised his failed colonial dreams
and he made this entry in his journal on 13th June 1864:

> A great deal of cotton lying on the wharves, but in a woeful plight.
> It had been lying in the rain for some time and some bales lay right in
> puddles. The sparrows were hauling out portions to build their nests, and
> the goats were dancing on the bales as if their favourite rocks, defiling the
> while what is so costly. The slovenly way in which the bales had been put
> together were a strong contrast to the tidy bales of calicoes coming at the
> same time from England.

Livingstone was not at first recognised but when he was an invitation came from the Governor, Sir Bartle Frere, to be his guest, and

Livingstone stayed with him at his hill station for a week. Then with borrowed money he bought passages for himself and Reid to England, and on 23rd July 1864, stepped out of Charing Cross station into the streets of London and took a room at the Tavistock Hotel in Covent Garden. The *Lady Nyassa* was eventually sold not, as Livingstone had hoped, to the Khedive of Egypt to be used on anti-slavery patrols on the upper Nile, but locally in Bombay. The sum raised – a pitiful £2000 – Livingstone placed in the Agra Bank, which later collapsed – every penny lost.

Part Five

1864–1865

Recuperation

21

NECESSARY BUSINESS

'I am in a whirl at present,' wrote Livingstone to Kirk a few days after arriving in London, 'but hope to break off at a tangent.' Livingstone feared that he would be 'on the shelf' and had few clear ideas about his future except a determination to go back to Africa. Before his arrival, the *Morning Star* reported Sir Roderick Murchison as saying: 'Dr Livingstone intends to return to Africa after a stay in the country of some four months during which period he intends to consult his friends as to his future proceedings.'

The first friend Livingstone consulted was Murchison himself, and shortly afterwards he had tea with the Prime Minister: 'I had an opportunity of speaking to Lord Palmerston', Livingstone told Kirk in a letter of 28th July 1864. 'He takes a great interest in our work and so does Lady Palmerston. Indeed they are the great agents in what is done to put down slavery. It has been his life's work and aim to promote freedom and human happiness.'

But when Livingstone called on the Foreign Secretary, Earl Russell, to discuss his plans, he found him 'very cold in his manner'. Russell's under-secretary, Austin Layard, was, however, prepared to lend a more sympathetic ear and invited Livingstone to dinner to talk things over. Livingstone was given a warm welcome when he attended the Weigh House Congregational Church but, on the whole, his reception in London was far from rapturous and he was keen to get away to Scotland. The only thing that detained him, he told Kirk, was 'to let matters be known in the proper quarter'. He is very busy, he declares, and confesses to being very worried.

Livingstone had good reason to be concerned, just as Russell had reason to be cold. He had returned leaving a trail of corpses behind him, and if the death of Mary brought him the due measure of sympathy (one of the first letters he received in London was a condolence note from the widow of Henry Burrup) the fate of Burrup himself, of Scudamore, Mackenzie and other members of the UMCA left in their graves in Africa merely fuelled the controversy still exercising the Church of England about the whole conduct of the mission and Livingstone's part in the Ajawa Wars. Quite how many people died as a result of the Zambezi Expedition it is impossible to compute, but if British seamen drowned trying to deliver Livingstone's mail, porters dead in accidents or by disease, the Helmores and Prices in Barotseland, and Richard Thornton besides, an impressive total emerges. Apart from the expense in human lives, the expense in government money had been far higher than anticipated. The press knew these things, and so did Russell who could point the finger at Livingstone, and remained in no mood to look kindly at ventures up African rivers, even less so in view of what had happened with the Niger expedition which had set sail shortly before Livingstone's. Though it had succeeded in establishing an outpost of British interest at Lokoja, two hundred and fifty miles upriver from the coast, it had lost one steamer and become a severe embarrassment when its leader, Dr W B Baikie, appointed Consul, had taken to drink and women, fathering half a tribe of little Scots-Nigerians. These immediately salient matters aside, both Russell and Palmerston ('those two dreadful old men' as Queen Victoria called them) were in political disgrace, accused by their Tory opponents of cowardice for what was seen as their mishandling of the Schleswig-Holstein question, where the failure of their policy had allowed a formidable Prussian advance to the Danish front. Palmerston and Russell were indeed old, the former eighty, going deaf and slowly losing his sight, the latter (the super-Whig) seventy-two, age increasing his aloofness and disdain. Besides continental issues, the two veterans were in the midst of all the diplomatic and economic problems which the American Civil War had thrust upon Britain. Relations between London and Lincoln's Washington were on the verge of being broken off as a result of the supply of ships like the *Alabama* by Macgregor Laird to the Confederates. There was a fair amount of support in Britain for the Southerners, especially from the millocracy, which drew eighty per cent of its cotton from the slave states. When those supplies dried up at the end of 1861 there was a crisis in the cotton industry. The 'cotton famine' as it was called, threw half a million mill hands out of their jobs and indirectly affected hundreds of thousands of other workers, with all the dangers to the social order that unemployment on such a scale portended. Significantly, much of the working class supported the North, equating mill-owning capitalists with Southern slave drivers. Russell might well glare icily at Livingstone and ask, 'Where is all that Zambezian cotton you promised us?' and point out how greatly his tirades against the Portuguese had annoyed Lisbon and distressed Prince Albert who, although dead three years, remained very much alive in Victoria's mind. (Both Albert and Pedro V had died of typhoid, by coincidence within a few weeks of each other.) Russell however, could remember how Livingstone's exploits had cheered him during the Crimean War and was conscious that he did not deserve a complete brush-off, as did the *Morning Star* somewhat grudgingly: '. . . the government ought to leave [Livingstone] with only one alternative. Can they not make him an offer which may to a small extent mark the sense of his permanent public services and at the same time employ his great energy in some more practicable and useful enterprise.' Russell condescended, offered Livingstone a one-off lump sum, not immediately accepted, of £500 should he intend to return to Africa: but he must keep clear of the Portuguese.

While in London, Livingstone had rightly decided to keep out of the public eye as much as possible, had declined scores, if not hundreds, of invitations to speak, such as that reported in the *Hants Advertiser* in September 1864: 'Dr Livingstone has felt impelled to decline invitations [to speak in Southampton] on the grounds that he is most anxious to return to India, where he has left his steamer, the *Lady Nyassa* . . . He hopes however to return to England in about a year.'

There was one invitation, however, that Livingstone accepted: he agreed to address the annual conference, in Bath, of the British Association later in the year, his subject, in spite of Russell, to be the Portuguese slave trade. He also came to an agreement with John Murray for a new book. Other matters, too, he set in motion, such as clearing up the expedition's accounts, and straightening out the financial side of his involvement with the UMCA. He even took the trouble to see the execrated coward Meller, reported him to be 'sickly'; then, leaving his boxes in the care of his old friend Frederick Fitch, provision merchant to the expedition, he pulled himself out of his whirl and took the train to Scotland. He had been in London barely a week.

In Scotland he planned to see James Young at his country seat at Limefield, West Calder, and invited Kirk, who was in Edinburgh, to join him there. And so on to Hamilton where, on 2nd August, all the living members of his family, apart from John and 'poor Bob' in America, were brought together. He was reunited with mother and sisters, with Agnes, Tom and Oswell. He got to know little Anna Mary, five years old, born at Kuruman, who did not like the black doll her father gave her, nor his moustache when he kissed her. Livingstone's mother was eighty, she was not well, her mind failing; at times she thought that David was her favourite, Robert. Agnes was eighteen, the boys a few years younger, at school at Gilbertsfield nearby. David's sisters, Janet and Agnes, younger than himself were both unmarried and afraid of penury.

Livingstone knew that he would not be able to write his book in the crowded house in Burnbank Road and on that very 2nd August wrote to John Murray asking him to find a cottage near London, suggesting he might deal with Meller's brother, who was a property agent. Agnes would be Livingstone's housekeeper, and would require a piano teacher, while provision would have to be made for Tom, who was sickly.

After a fortnight at Hamilton, Livingstone went on a tour of the Highlands and Islands as the guest of the Duke of Argyll who was then just over forty and, as Lord Privy Seal, a senior member of Palmerston's ministry. Wherever Livingstone went, he was welcomed enthusiastically and his spirits rose. As he said to Kirk, in a letter of 1st September 1864:

> ... had a turn in the Highlands by Staffa and Iona and Ulva and Mull. The weather was delightful and my native air quite set me up again. I got a free passage and a ticket 'at any time to and from any place'. See what it is to come from rich ancestors.

This was Livingstone's first trip to the Highlands or to the island of Ulva, his father's place of origin:

> My ancestral Hall, presents walls only, which have never been high and the corn patches were small, but I was glad to see it.

There is no record of his visiting the Blantyre works to exhort the workers to respectability (as he had done during his stay in Scotland in 1857). Perhaps he felt unable to face those struck off the roll by the cotton famine. When the tour was over, Livingstone submitted himself to a medical examination and was advised to have an operation for haemorrhoids, but he refused on the grounds of not liking 'to get my infirmities into the Newspapers', as he told Kirk. This decision, a concession to the strong silent man's vanity, Livingstone would regret agonisingly in the years to come.

Meanwhile he had been exchanging letters with his Kalahari friend Frederick Webb, whom he hadn't seen for over a decade. On hearing that Livingstone was on his way back from the Zambezi, Webb had written to him at Bombay, inviting him, through Mrs Webb, to spend some time at their country residence, Newstead Abbey, in Nottinghamshire. The invitation was repeated to Livingstone at Hamilton. He declined at first, saying that he wanted to have Agnes with him and that she insisted on having a piano teacher. The Webbs told him to bring Agnes, that she would be welcome as would be the boys during the holidays; a music tutor could be shared with their own daughter. (In fact, the Webbs hired the teacher specially, pretending she was the regular governess.) Livingstone accepted; he would not need any cottage Murray might find for him.

Charles now wrote to David from Boston, to which he had returned to join his wife and children after leaving the expedition suggesting that the book for Murray be a joint publication in which the journals which each brother had kept could be incorporated. Charles had written his up into a continuous narrative. In reply on 2nd September 1864, David told him: 'I feel quite willing to do anything in my power to benefit you, but I cannot see how it can be done.' However, after consulting Murray and Livingstone's lawyer friend, Bevan Braithwaite, in London, a formula was arrived at whereby David would receive the royalties from the British edition, Charles from the American, and a legal agreement was eventually drawn up to this effect. David also advised Charles to keep an eye open for a government job: 'You ought to have someone in London to represent your claim in the event of a vacancy in the consular department. Sir Roderick would do it better than I ...' Thus did Charles become the first member of the expedition to join the Barnacles in the queue outside the circumlocution office. Family matters apart, Livingstone spent the first fortnight of September at Burnbank Road preparing his paper for the British Association meeting (his daughter little Anna Mary remembered him seventy years later as 'always writing'); and on the tenth day of the month he was in Bath.

The British Association for the Advancement of Science was in the 1860s, as it remains today, a highly distinguished mass of brainpower. Livingstone could feel honoured to be part of it, even if his address was not expected to be the main attraction of the 1864 gathering. Richard Burton, and his erstwhile travelling companion (and financial crutch) John Hanning Speke, were to provide that with a debate on their rival claims to having identified the source of the Nile and to having solved the world's greatest remaining geographical mystery. On their 1858 expedition Burton and Speke became the first Europeans known to have visited Lake Tanganyika. On the return journey Burton fell ill at Unyanyembe and Speke went off without him to investigate local reports of a large lake directly to the north. After a two hundred mile trudge he arrived on the shores of an immense sheet of water which he named Lake Victoria. Speke believed that this was the source of the Nile, while Burton insisted that the river flowed out of the north of Lake Tanganyika. Both men stuck to their guns and, to reinforce his position, Speke had returned to Africa in 1862, with James Augustus Grant as companion, and had reached the outlet at the north of Lake Victoria which he now declared more categorically than ever, was the source of the Nile.

In 1863 his *Journal of the Discovery of the Nile* had appeared, and the following year Grant published *A Walk Across Africa; or Domestic scenes from my Nile Journal.* Speke was not an aggressive man, Burton was. And with his reputation at stake he was prepared to use every weapon in his rhetorical armoury. The debate promised to be lively, perhaps positively rancorous, but alas it did not take place. The day before, Speke was killed when his gun went off accidentally as he was climbing over a stone wall while out shooting on an estate near Bath. Livingstone attended the funeral.

Livingstone gave his own speech to an audience of two and a half thousand, his attack on Portuguese slavery enraging the Portuguese, his comments on the American Civil War offending the Americans. The vote of thanks was proposed by Bishop John William Colenso of Natal, who spoke fulsomely of the former Kolobeng missionary:

> ... although I have never looked upon his face before this evening, his name has been dear to me for years as a household word; his writings have been studied by me not merely as containing matters of interest with reference to the tribes of South Africa, among whom my own lot is cast, but as being records of the life of a devoted Christian teacher.

Livingstone was highly embarrassed, not by the words, but by their source, for Colenso was a hotly controversial figure. He had been dethroned and declared a heretic by Livingstone's friend Bishop Gray of Cape Town for publishing a treatise which questioned the historical truth of the first five books of the Bible, and held views on the polygamy question as it affected his potential Zulu Christians totally at variance with the teaching of orthodox, monogamist, missionaries (a question of great interest to Livingstone in view of his convert Chief Sechele's decision to lapse rather than give up his second and third wives). Livingstone thought the choice of Colenso to propose the vote was invidious, that he had been placed in a position where it seemed that he was of Colenso's party and against Bishop Gray's (and, indeed, all the churches, Anglican, non-conformist, Catholic). He wrote to his Congregationalist friend Thomas Binney, minister of Weigh House, on 27th October 1864, that a Scottish newspaper had become exercised about the affair, explaining that he did not know that Colenso was to speak until he was on his feet.

Even if the Colenso intervention raised a few ripples in the steady stream of discussion, Livingstone could not have failed to be interested in the unresolved problem of the Nile, given his long-held belief that the Ancient Egyptians and the southern Africans he knew were one people. However, solving the Nile puzzle did not enter his calculations at this time: when he returned to Africa it would be to carry on, in another place, from where he had been forced, so he claimed, by the Portuguese slavers to leave off. As he had told Sir Bartle Frere in a letter of 23rd June 1864, shortly before leaving India for England, there were good prospects for trade between Bombay and east Africa, particularly in tropical hardwoods.

Livingstone's Bath speech was, indirectly, a public excuse for the apparent failure of the Zambezi Expedition. But had it really been a failure? Certainly its ideals came to very little but they had been doomed from the start. On the other hand the expedition, as an experiment, established a number of important material points. This success was recognised by the British Association (if not by the supporters of the UMCA, of the Helmore mission, by those who had expected cotton to flow by the shipload) or else Livingstone would not have been asked to speak at Bath, let alone make a political statement which was sure to annoy Russell. We shall look later at the implications of the Zambezi Expedition in the extension of European power in central Africa but members of the British Association, once they reached beyond Livingstone's fulminations against the Portuguese, would have found considerable value in many phenomena which the expedition brought to light: the first tenuous hints, for example, of a connection between mosquitoes and malaria (and Charles's observation that it is the female that carries the 'poison'); the efficacy of Livingstone's quinine-based treatment for fever; the shape of Lake Nyasa, so similar to that of Lake Tanganyika (described by Burton) and Lake Albert, of the Red Sea, suggesting some unique geological structure which with Kirk's Galilean fishes perhaps, links the Shire to the Jordan valley. Then there was confirmation of the existence of coal and copper in the interior, not to mention the first generally accurate maps of the Zambezi-Shire-Lake Nyasa system.

After giving his speech Livingstone, consular cap on cranium, accompanied Murchison on a geological trip to Clifton, where he saw Kirk. But his mind was on his book. On 24th September 1864 he wrote to tell Murray that he had been detained by a visit to Lord Taunton but, that complete, he would go to Newstead to begin work in earnest. Charles's journal had arrived from Boston.

Livingstone went to London to collect his papers and then on to the Webbs (to begin work after so much play, as he told James Young) to live in semi-seclusion behind a phalanx of 'top people' for eight months. Newstead is a hundred and twenty miles north of London but, thanks to the railways and the postal service, he was able to do as much business as if he had been in Sloane Street, where he had written *Missionary Travels* in 1857.

One piece of business that was to occupy Livingstone for over a year was getting a job for Kirk who, since returning to Britain, had been spending a considerable time with his mother, elderly and ailing, in Edinburgh. Livingstone told him that no description of Kirk's own researches would be included in the *Narrative of an Expedition to the Zambezi and its Tributaries* (as the work for Murray was to be called), leaving the way open for Kirk to publish a book of his own. He wrote to Kirk on 21st October 1864:

I am purposely avoiding anything like scientific description, having said in the introduction that it is hoped that you will give the botany and natural history of the Expedition (in the way that Darwin did of the *Beagle*'s voyage). . . You may see what can be done . . . by Routledge's 'Natural History'.

Kirk, however, who by now had left Edinburgh to work without pay on research at Kew Gardens, wanted a government salary for the several years he anticipated it would take to write the book and, even then, he was not confident of the success of the project. Livingstone tried to reassure him: 'Your botanical knowledge is not elementary and I thought Welweitsch's frightfully so.' Kirk was suffering, as we have seen, from the loss of many of his records in the Cabora Basa rapids. Livingstone, however, made a formal application to Russell for Kirk to continue his work on expedition pay, following lines laid out by Dr Hooker of Kew. Webb wanted Kirk to come to Newstead to do his research there, particularly on the mammalia, and suggested that the hunting trophies in the hall would inspire him. Kirk was also tinkering with the idea of going into medicine. Webb pointed out that there were openings for a practice in places such as Nottingham, Cheltenham or York, where there was no good 'medico'.

However, with Russell unforthcoming about the salary and Kirk, we must assume, hesitant about going into practice (who would put up the capital?) Livingstone wrote to him on 7th November 1864:

May I ask what you intend to go in for? If for any situation, I would consider it a favour if you would call upon me to testify to your abilities. My recommendation might do you no harm and it would delight me if it could do you some good.

Having made this offer, Livingstone attended a Royal Geographical Society meeting in London on 14th November, and there must have discussed Kirk's case with Murchison (among others), for on 24th November 1864 he wrote to Kirk again:

What we have to do is get the earliest information of any vacancy that may take place. All feel that you deserve something and I have no doubt it will be secured. Are the clubs likely to afford the information required? Are you acquainted with anyone in the Colonial or Foreign Office?

Livingstone, speaking for the Webbs, then invited him to Newstead so that he might 'make acquaintance with Lord Kinnaird who with Lady

The Livingstone family, circa 1856-7. From left to right: third son William Oswell, David Livingstone, second son Thomas, eldest daughter Agnes, Mary Livingstone, eldest son Robert Moffat.

David Livingstone Centre

THE MISSIONARY'S ESCAPE FROM THE LION

THE TRAVELLING PROCESSION INTERRUPTED

ft Livingstone in his consular outfit, taken by Mayall circa 1852. *David Livingstone Centre*

bove Two of the etchings made by J. W. Whymper for the first edition of *Missionary Travels:* Livingstone's 'consular' cap, with its gold braid band, became his trademark even before he was appointed consul. He had ne caps made by S. Starkey of Bond Street, London, and to an extra one with him to the Zambezi in 1858 s a present for Sekeletu. One of the caps, preserved in the Livingstone Museum, Zambia, indicates the size f Livingstone's head: it is too small to fit any adult on today's museum staff.

Examples of Livingstone's sketches from his notebook of April 1859. *Livingstone Museum, Zambia*

left Dr John Kirk (1832–1922) was medical officer and economic botanist on the Zambezi Expedition.
Richard Thornton (1838–64), on the eve of the Zambezi expedition.   *National Archives of Zimbabwe*

ft Commander Norman Bedingfield, R.N. (1824–94), second-in-command of the Zambezi Expedition
ntil Livingstone dismissed him. Thomas Baines (1820–75), who was chosen for the ill-fated Zambezi
expedition.   *National Archives of Zimbabwe*

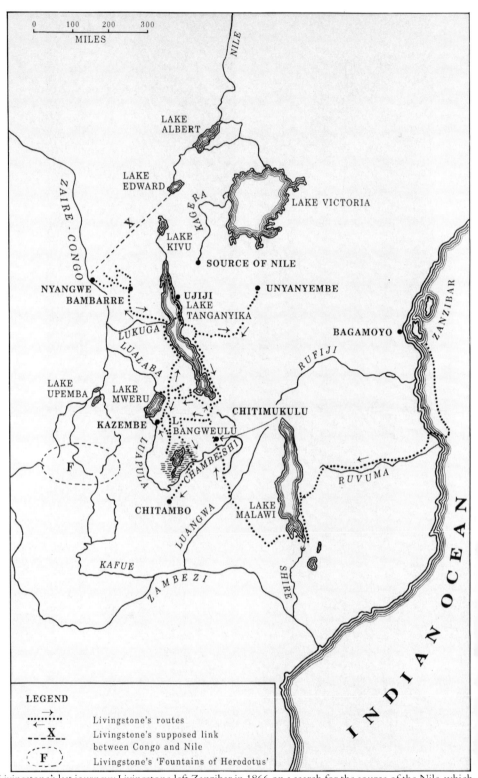

LEGEND

············▸ Livingstone's routes

– – –**X**– – – Livingstone's supposed link between Congo and Nile

⟨ **F** ⟩ Livingstone's 'Fountains of Herodotus'

Livingstone's last journeys: Livingstone left Zanzibar in 1866 on a search for the source of the Nile, which thought to be at F, the Congo being linked to the Nile by X.

H.M. Stanley, who arrived at Zanzibar in 1871 to find Livingstone, who had not been heard of for three years, seen here with Kalulu, his personal attendant. *David Livingstone Centre*

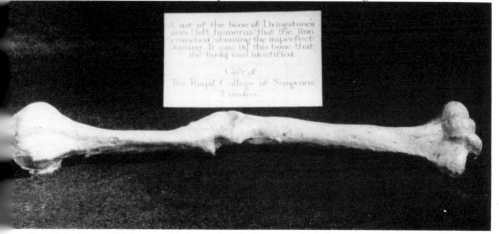

Cast of the bone of Livingstone's left arm that the lion crunched, showing the imperfect joining. It was by this bone that his body was identified. *David Livingstone Centre, Blantyre*

Livingstone's close and faithful servants, Chuma and Susi, surrounded by memorabilia at Newstead Abbey in 1874. They were brought to Britain by James Young to help the editor of Livingstone's journals piece together the last years of his life. It was Chuma who brought the news of Livingstone's death.

Newstead Abbey/City of Nottingham Museums

Livingstone's friends and family at Newstead Abbey, 1874, during the editing of his *Last Journals*. The group includes Chuma, Susi, Horace Waller (the editor), Agnes Livingstone, Mrs Webb, Tom Livingstone.

Newstead Abbey/City of Nottingham Museums

K. are really very good people. He has a great deal of influence with Lord Palmerston.' And the next day he wrote again:

> It occurs to me just now you ought to try to get information about appointments in the East Indies. We may not get all we ask, but we shall get more if we ask much than if we aimed only at a little ... should a good thing turn up in India, I could try to get double influence by asking Lord Russell or some other one to give a note to Sir Charles Wood [Secretary for India]. I would not cast myself away in Kaffraria.

Towards the end of December Kirk went to stay at Newstead for about a month where he had the opportunity to meet Admiral Sir George Lambert and Lord David Kennedy – the latter, according to Livingstone, 'a great Indian hunter, but a very modest fellow'.

In the new year, the quest for the 'situation' continued. There was a rumour that the post in the Comoros might fall vacant and, on 13th February 1865, Livingstone told Kirk:

> Would it not be well to speak to Lord Dalhousie about using his influence with Lord Russell for the consulate. It would keep you before his mind if anything turned up. I stated particularly to Sir R[oderick] 'with sufficient salary'. It is necessary to hold that up, for they might offer a vice [consulship] which is worth nothing. If however the vice c. meant £500, it would be a step to Tananarivo.

Other suggestions are considered: Mozambique (won't do), Bambatook Bay, or perhaps Kirk might replace the profligate Dr Baikie (now dead) on the Niger. The trouble with Kirk was that he wanted a *real* 'Barnacle' position, with light enough official duties for him to be able to pursue his other interests such as botany and hunting. Thus Zanzibar would be unsuitable because he would have too much to do and 'then no scientific results could be expected'. Livingstone wrote to Dalhousie and urged Kirk, repeatedly, to press the noble earl, 'for they will do anything for an influential man like him ... it is only by pressing that anything can be got.' But by the end of April, Kirk was still without a 'situation', while the cowardly and sickly Meller had been given 'a commission and a roving one too to Madagascar, and a good salary.' Livingstone was furious and believed Meller had obtained the vice-consulship solely through the patronage of Russell (Meller kept the job for only a year, then went on to work in the botanical gardens of Mauritius and Queensland and died in Sydney in 1869 at the age of thirty-three). Kirk's suit enjoyed no success in Britain, and when Livingstone returned to Bombay, he tried, through Sir Bartle Frere, to have him made director of the Botanical Gardens there, to no avail. Early in 1866, however, Frere had him appointed medical officer to the British Consulate in Zanzibar where his career flourished, and where we shall meet him again.

Charles Livingstone meanwhile, by joining the queue early, avoiding public controversies or too blatant a demand for a sinecure, had received his appointment before the end of 1864. He was to be consul at Fernando Po (now renamed Boiko) in the Bight of Biafra, a post that David thought might lead to something better, for instance the anti-slavery commissionership with its higher salary, at Luanda. Charles's post had just been vacated by Burton (transferred to Santos, Brazil) who, while there, had stationed his wife at Tenerife. David suggested that Charles do the same with Harriet, even offering him an introduction to Mrs Burton to discuss matters. In the event, Harriet stayed in Europe while Charles went about his duties, one of which, David hoped, would be to refute Burton's sulphurous effusions about missionaries in west Africa. Charles was never promoted from Fernando Po and died there of fever in 1873.

By November 1864, Murchison and the RGS had decided to sponsor an expedition to try to resolve the mystery of the source of the Nile. An offer was made to Kirk to lead it but he declined on the grounds that he was to be married soon. Murchison turned to Livingstone. Until this point his mind had been set on commercial prospects but he had a gnawing feeling that he had to make a fine sum of money soon – for the sake of his own future comfort and to set the children up in life. This he hoped to achieve by opening up east Africa to legitimate trade and he did not want to commit himself totally to the RGS. Murchison told him: 'Never mind the pecuniary matters. . . It shall be my task to look after that.' He told him Kirk was missing a great opportunity by not going and that he would have made a fortune from the book he would have been able to write. These assurances seem to have persuaded Livingstone, and he wrote to James Young on 30th November indicating that he would accept the RGS invitation, adding as a rider '. . . a purely geographical question has no interest to me. I want to do good by opening a path inland north of the Portuguese.' There is a curious ambiguity in this context about the phrase 'to do good'.

At the beginning of January Murchison informed Livingstone that the RGS would put up £500. Livingstone was to investigate the central African watershed and might finish the expedition by settling the Nile question. The sum offered, however, was totally inadequate and Livingstone would be required to give all his notes to the Society (as a further twist to the screw, Livingstone had to give Murchison a full explanation of the Baines affair). Livingstone submitted to these humiliating conditions – which could have owed their existence to the influence of Baines and Burton on the RGS council – and was willing too to use the £800 that had been collected for him at the Cape in 1856. But he would also have to accept Russell's offer of £500. This sum, it was now made clear by the Foreign Office, would be paid only if Livingstone accepted a consulship, and unless he settled in one place it was to 'be understood' that it was not a salary and brought no pension rights. Livingstone was enraged and insulted. He felt he was being treated like a charwoman and asked how he could trace the watershed while sitting in a consulate. However, he agreed to the terms and in March 1865 was appointed consul to the 'Territories of the African Kings and Chiefs in the Interior of Africa' but was not to enter areas claimed by the Portuguese.

Livingstone had very little capital. Even the *Lady Nyassa*, or any sum she might realise, was in a sense mortgaged to James Young. The new expedition, if it were to meet Livingstone's agenda, would cost much more than what had already been placed at his disposal, besides which, money was needed for his family. Once again, Young came to the rescue and subscribed £1000 towards the African journey, producing a total that should be enough for a short expedition. Murray announced in April 1865 that he would be issuing the Zambezi *Narrative* in an edition of ten thousand copies, and Livingstone arranged that Young would handle the royalties account with the publisher, even if this does not imply that Young's £1000 was in any way a loan. Money was much in Livingstone's thoughts during this period and it led to a dispute with John Smith Moffat who had been drawing £150 a year from Livingstone since 1859 for the Matabele Mission. In 1864 Moffat had joined the LMS on salary without letting Livingstone know and had continued, Livingstone alleged, to draw on his account with Rutherfoord in Cape Town. Livingstone demanded that Moffat repay what had been overdrawn. Shortly after receiving these words (written on 20th February and, again on 11th March 1865), Moffat abandoned missionary work altogether to become an official in British colonial administrations in various territories of southern Africa. As for the Thornton business, the unfortunate Richard's brother, George went on arguing about Livingstone's handling of the estate. The correspondence continued from the moment of Livingstone's arrival in London in July 1864 until January the following year when Livingstone, having pointed out that the estate owed *him* money, wrote to say he was having nothing more to do with the matter.

The Zambezi days, however, had not produced only animosity and misunderstanding. Apart from Kirk, Livingstone had made another lasting friend in the person of Horace Waller, the Lay Superintendent of the UMCA, with whom he seems to have enjoyed a mutual scorn for Bishop Tozer. On returning to England, Waller went to Cambridge to take orders, in 1867 becoming Curate of St John's, Chatham, and then moving to serve as Rector of Twywell, Northants, where he ended his days in 1895. At one stage during 1865 Waller seemed keen enough on missionary life for Livingstone to attempt to interest Miss Coutts in supporting a Waller mission to Borneo. He wrote to Rajah Brooke at the same time, but nothing came of the matter. But Waller was to render a notable posthumous service to Livingstone, as we shall see.

Kirk had inspired enough of the confidence of friendship for Livingstone to ask him to join him on the planned Nile expedition, though there was not enough money available to pay a salary. 'I would be delighted,' Livingstone told Kirk, 'if we could be together ... Could Lord Dalhousie not manage a salary for you?' On 13th May 1865, Livingstone explained his proposed line of march:

> I mean to go to Rovuma to where we turned in boats – make Ndonde's a depot for goods – not many for I don't mean to waste them as Speke and Burton did, nor go in grand array ... work quietly west ... We were always in too great a hurry last expedition.

Kirk must have shuddered at the mere mention of the Rovuma, but declined the invitation graciously, not recalling past terrors, saying he needed a salary as he would soon have a wife to support. One stalwart *volunteered* to accompany Livingstone. He was the Reverend Charles Alington, who had been for a while Bishop Tozer's chaplain. One point in his favour was that he spoke some Zulu, the language of the Nguni 'Mazitu' who had migrated into areas Livingstone expected to traverse, another was that he did not want a salary. But Livingstone turned him down and told Kirk, in the same letter of May 1865, 'I would rather go alone than take anyone untried. I suffered too much from Bedingfeld & Co.'

Livingstone never needed the cottage for which he had asked Murray to look. When he was in London he stayed either at Storey's Hotel, Dover Street, or with friends such as James Hamilton, minister of Regent Square Presbyterian Church and editor of the review *Evangelical Christendom* to which Livingstone contributed a thirty-six page article on slavery in Africa. He also gave Hamilton advice on how to introduce the Bible to Angola. But however much Livingstone may have been involved with his friends, with the RGS and with the Foreign Office, his main occupation from September 1864 to the end of April the following year, was the composition of the *Narrative*, and this he did at Newstead, as calm and unwhirling a place as could be imagined.

22

QUIET AMONG FRIENDS

In thee the wounded conscience courts relief
Retiring from the garish blaze of day

These lines from Byron's 'Elegy on Newstead Abbey' could not better express the mood that surrounded Livingstone when he went into retreat at the Webbs' stately home, 'vast and venerable' as Byron described it, standing in the midst of three thousand two hundred acres of good English ground. Byron sold the estate, which had been the family seat since the time of Henry VIII (it was one of the dissolved monasteries) to Thomas Wildman, a Jamaica planter, for £94,500 in 1817, Byron thereby putting an end to his money problems. Webb bought it on sight in 1860, three years married and not having a large enough house on his Yorkshire or Lincolnshire estates for his growing family. Although he claimed not to know it at the time, he was buying a property that rested on one of England's richest coalfields. Tenant farms and small lakes surrounded the house; the estate was served by its own private railway station, and was self-sufficient in many ways. Fresh food and cured meats, butter and cheese, came from the farms, beer and bread from the house brewery and bakery. The enormous kitchen stove burned half a ton of coal a day, there was a plant that made gas from coal to feed the lights.

Livingstone was given an apartment on the first floor of the Sussex Tower, an addition in the Regency style made by Wildman to the main, gothic building. Over all reared the ruins of the original abbey church, stripped and vandalised during the Reformation and the Civil War. During the tenure of the last three generations of Byrons the fabric of the residence had become seriously dilapidated. Wildman spent £200,000 on restoration.

Webb, William Frederick, a giant of a man over six foot six inches tall, was thirty-five when he welcomed Livingstone to Newstead. He had been educated at Eton, had bought a commission in the 17th Lancers, and then given it to his brother Augustus when he grew bored with army life. Augustus died in the Charge of the Light Brigade. Mrs Webb was a beauty who spent a good deal of time collecting Byron memorabilia, while Webb covered every square foot of wall in the mansion with hunting trophies, many of them acquired during the Kalahari trip. Livingstone said that he did not mind people being rich provided they were good. And in both respects he received every possible consideration from the Webbs, besides being saved a substantial sum of money for board and lodging, as he remarked to James Young. It is quite probable that Webb would have died in the Kalahari had Livingstone not rescued him and nursed him back to health at Kolobeng. Now the Webbs at Newstead were providing Livingstone with the care and affection a spirit even as resilient as his needed, to recover from the battering it had received. Agnes too, apart from the piano lessons, was given special attention: 'Although Agnes on her arrival at Newstead,' wrote the Webbs' eldest daughter Alice, 'was an unformed schoolgirl she had in the course of a few months under my mother's care so developed and improved in carriage as to be almost unrecognizable.'

Or as Livingstone himself told James Young in a letter of 4th January 1865:

> Agnes has been dancing like mad, at two balls. A colonel's wife here took her to the first at a neighbouring laird's, and that laird's wife took her to the second.

The boys came to Newstead too, from time to time and slept in the spare room of their father's apartment.

No sooner had Livingstone settled in towards the end of September than labour on the *Narrative* commenced. Agnes became his secretary, Mrs Webb helped with the copying, as Livingstone created a text by transcribing suitable portions from his journals and from that of Charles. Not being near London hardly interfered with the work, the mail cart from Mansfield passed by every weekday, letters would be taken to their destinations overnight. Livingstone was able to issue instructions without stirring from his desk, as this on 8th and 10th October 1864, to Charles, now in London:

> I am getting on pretty well with the work – you have got most of the interesting incidents in your journal and it is a great help [Livingstone later complained that having to incorporate Charles's material was a nuisance] Will you ask Mr Murray who ought to make the map ... I think there is a map in one of the drawers of the Zambezi from Tette upwards. By opening the upper left hand [drawer] you will get a bunch of keys for all the others and one for the wooden despatch box in the same packing case as the flat tin case was taken out of [Charles was at the Fitches', where David's boxes were being stored] – Open up this despatch

box you will get a journal with dark red covers – which please send at your convenience by rail to Newstead ... In the upper left drawer you will find some trinkets of gold which please send with the other things.

Stewart, Waller and Kirk were also enrolled as runners, Stewart in Edinburgh to deliver a message to Lord Dalhousie, Waller to find things out in Cambridge, Kirk to do any number of odd jobs, ranging from collecting government reports, to requests as quaint as this of 12th December 1864:

I enclose a cheque for £10, which you will be good enough to bring in gold when you come. Say to the cashier that I had this cheque book with me in Africa and don't know if any alteration is required to the stamps. Bring please a little black doll, dressed, for one of the little [Webb] girls, for 4 or 5 shillings (and pay yourself out of £10).

Or, again this one of 19th December 1864:

Will you oblige me by bringing a bottle of Hair stuff. I found one called 'Molena' but any kind will do. I bathe all over every morning and the hair becomes very dry after it.

Livingstone took some pride in his hair and told W C Oswell in February 1865:

I am very old and grey – and face wrinkled like a grid iron. A barber offered to dye my hair for 10/6 – I must be very good tempered for I did not fight him.

Livingstone established a routine for the work on the text – at the desk in his apartment solidly all morning (with his assistants nearby) then breaking off for the day at lunch time. During the short winter afternoons he would accompany Webb around the estate, sometimes observing landlordly duties, sometimes shooting or fishing, and helped Webb with a scientific experiment he had started – raising trout from ova stripped from females, fertilised with milt from males, and set to hatch in glass containers: 'We are spawning the trout like mad. We have 130,000 ova down,' Livingstone told Oswell on 8th January 1865. Livingstone was also able at times to act as family doctor, especially after Webb developed a painful complaint in his knee, the result of dislocated gristle in the joint. The religious tone of Newstead is suggested by the daily prayers in the chapel (led often by Livingstone), parish church on Sundays, Agnes being prepared for confirmation (as an Anglican), and strict sabbath observance. Here Livingstone caused something of a scandal – while strolling back from church one Sunday he hauled out a fish trap set in a lake the previous week, found a large pike and started to carry it to the house. His shocked companions wanted him to put it back. 'There is no harm in it', he insisted and took it with him. In this atmosphere it is hardly surprising that Mrs Webb should report that Livingstone took little interest in Byron and could brush the poet off with the remark that 'his character was horrid', as no doubt it was to fervent sabbatarians. Mad, bad, and dangerous to know might Byron have been, but so indeed was Livingstone at times, as Kirk could testify. Whatever the disclaimers, Livingstone did take the trouble to learn by heart reams of Byron's verse, which he was to recite to H M Stanley when they were together in Africa in 1871. There were many aspects of Byron's life that Livingstone would have sympathised with. He was half-Scots and had grown up poor (in Aberdeen); he was a reformer, hated tyranny, abhorred slavery; he was brave enough despite his club foot, to swim both the Tagus and the Hellespont; he was prepared to give, and gave, his life for the freedom of the oppressed. Byron's club foot was the metaphorical equivalent of Livingstone's ill-set arm.

Besides these generalities Livingstone, in the midst of his campaign against the Portuguese, could not fail to enjoy Byron's strictures against them in his vignette of Lisbon:

> But whoso entereth within this town,
> That, sheening far, celestial seems to be,
> Disconsolate will wander up and down,
> Midst many things unsightly to strange ee,
> For hut and palace show like filthily;
> The dingy denizens are raised in dirt;
> No personage of high or mean degree
> Doth care for cleanness of surtout or shirt . . .
>
> . . . Poor paltry slaves, yet born midst scenes,
> Why, Nature, waste thy wonders on such men?
>
> *Childe Harold* I, 17-8

And Livingstone shared the same publisher with Byron:

> Tours, Travels, Essays, too I wist,
> And sermons to thy mill are grist;
> And now thou hast the 'Navy List',
>
> Mr Murray

A personal link with the poet was provided by Livingstone's friend (and for a while fellow guest at Newstead) Lord Kinnaird, whose uncle

Douglas Kinnaird had been Byron's drinking companion and for many years financial and literary advisor.

Livingstone and Agnes were only rarely the sole visitors at Newstead. The Webbs enjoyed entertaining, there was always shooting – at least during the autumn and winter (though we hear nothing of riding to hounds). Guests came not for weekends, but for weeks. Besides those we have already mentioned, others included Murchison (who pointed out to Webb a coal-bearing formation); Sir Henry Rawlinson, decipherer of Assyrian cuneiform, politician, and later to succeed to the presidency of the RGS; Thomas Hughes, author of *Tom Brown's Schooldays* (best-selling novel about Rugby, the school W C Oswell had attended), reformer, and later to be Livingstone's biographer; Edward Denison, speaker of the House of Commons; Mrs Webb's uncle, Colonel Goodlake, one of the first recipients of the Victoria Cross; a party of old Africa hands, including Kalahari hunters. At Livingstone's behest, Kirk, and Charles and Harriet came to stay. A strange incident occurred during the visit of Abraham Hayward QC, a particular friend of Mrs Webb. Hayward had been editor of the *Quarterly Review*, now edited the *Law Magazine* and was political agent of Palmerston, the Prime Minister. Hayward had a reputation for being cold, supercilious, and somewhat pernicious, qualities which few people, except Mrs Webb, were able to break through. He wrote her scores of letters, which she refused to allow to be published because each of them contained a sneering remark about someone she knew. Hayward brought Livingstone a message from the Prime Minister: 'Is there anything I can do for you?' There were a host of things Livingstone could have asked for, given Palmerston's warm feelings for him, and his ideals – pension, support for his family, honours. For, as Byron had said:

> To do good to mankind is the chivalrous plan,
> And is always as nobly requited;
> Then battle for freedom wherever you can,
> And, if not shot or hang'd, you'll get knighted.
>
> *Stanzas*, 1820

Livingstone could not bring himself to ask for anything that might seem to his personal benefit and merely urged Palmerston to have the Portuguese sign a treaty opening the Zambezi and Shire to international traffic. Livingstone later regretted his self-denial, as we shall see. Something in Hayward's manner must have upset him, and writing to W C Oswell on 12th January 1865, he dismisses the incident in two mordant sentences: 'Hayward, one of the Saturday *Revilers* left us this morning. Wasn't I civil – that's all.'

Oswell was one of a few of Livingstone's close friends who does not seem to have visited Newstead, despite repeated invitations (although Oswell and Webb had been in the Kalahari at the same time they had never met, despite Livingstone's wish that they should). Oswell's wife was often ill and once, when he might have come, he had to be put off because the Webbs had colds and sore throats. Livingstone at Newstead, later in London, Oswell at 'Groombridge', Tunbridge Wells, spent no extended lengths of time together, but there was an abiding affection between them. When Livingstone left England, Oswell appointed himself Agnes's ad hoc stepfather, a duty he fulfilled admirably. And while Livingstone was at Newstead, Oswell allowed himself to be enrolled for that most tedious, if invaluable, of literary tasks, proof-reading with, in this instance, a fair amount of revising thrown in. Within two months of starting the *Narrative* Livingstone was sending copy to Murray for setting, knowing that the simultaneous burden of composition, correcting and editing was one he could not bear alone. (When he had finished *Missionary Travels* he had remarked that he 'would rather cross Africa again than write another book'.) Besides Oswell, he roped in Professor Owen, who was to receive the galleys first, make his corrections, then forward them to Oswell. Only the railways made this miracle of communication between London, Tunbridge Wells and Newstead possible.

Before Oswell got started, Livingstone gave him a lesson in the use of printer's marks:

> I shall send you one of the first impression on Monday which will enlighten you on the way to correct. It is for [ordinary] purposes quite simple. | on the side draws attention to everything. ⸲ is Greek δ with the upright line and means *dele* or take out. If you prefer after all to let a word remain you put dots under it *thus* or put stet or simply st on the side ... A line *under* italix, R/Roman and if you want to transpose you do so and put ⌐⌐⌐ on anything to draw attention...

Livingstone ends this letter of 12th January 1865 with Newstead news:

> A pond is running off and we spawn the fish so I am in haste ...

The services of Owen and Oswell were not needed simply to correct typographical errors. These proof readers were what might be called 'creative censors'. Nothing was to be present in the book which cast a bad light on the expedition itself — the names of Bedingfeld and Baines do not appear — and nothing was to be said which would cause offence to anyone except the Portuguese. Owen would keep an eye open for scientific errors (or heresies), Oswell for anything that might upset Victorian sensibilities (his uncle, after all, was Thomas

Bowdler). Where necessary, Kirk, Waller or Stewart could be called in to clear up matters of fact. Murray's literary advisor would chew over the text and make it digestible. There was to be a map drawn by Arrowsmith and, for illustrations, etchings made from Baines's pictures (without acknowledgement to the artist for, as Livingstone said, his work was the property of the Foreign Office), and from Kirk's and Charles's photographs. But Livingstone was not entirely happy with the results, as he tells Oswell on 13th February 1865:

> You will see specimens of the illustrations . . . I can't get men to make blacks like their photographs – take high cheekbones, low foreheads, big lips – mouth from ear to ear – ears like an achter wheel [rear wheel of an ox wagon] . . . that is the prescription of all artists except Argas.

Livingstone wrote to Oswell two, three, four times a week once the proofs started arriving in January. Usually short letters, with opening paragraphs discussing the work in hand, this was followed by some personal comment. These conversational asides gave a glimmer of what his talk must have been like in the strange accent the Webbs remarked upon, no longer Scottish, perhaps part African, but definitely foreign:

> Anything the natives of this country won't understand (the stoopids) you will do me an immense good by throwing light on,

he wrote. Or again:

> I am going insane with this writing – for the Yankee papers have it that I married a lady in Constantinople, which place I never saw . . .

or later in the spring of 1865:

> You are quite right about the Portuguese – like the reformed Quaker in 'Uncle Tom' – I feel like 'a cussing and swearin dreadful' when I think on their villainy . . .

(Oswell had met the author of *Uncle Tom's Cabin* on a voyage from New York and had found her rather formidable.)

The *Narrative* is written in the third person, the author appearing always as Dr Livingstone, Charles by his full name, and runs to just over two hundred thousand words. The introduction gives a brief history of foreign penetration of east Africa from biblical times (and ironically, in the light of future events, declares that the discovery of the 'main source of the Nile' was accomplished by Speke and Grant – probably a jibe at Burton). The final chapter reasserts Livingstone's faith in the potential of the Shire highlands, discusses forms of settlement, blames the Portuguese for the failure of his plans, and calls for the end of Portuguese 'dominion' in Mozambique. The narrative itself is presented in strict chronological order, the 'incidents' of the expedition separated by lengthy prose passages – ethnological, geographical – wonderfully detailed and accurate but, cumulatively, tedious. There is a notable lack of personal element and Livingstone takes care in his handling of the UMCA, anxious to exonerate himself from responsibility for the Ajawa Wars but saying nothing that might harm Mackenzie's memory. Attack on the Portuguese runs like an artery through the text.

On 16th April Livingstone wrote *finis* to his script, though work on the proofs continued for a couple of months more. The book, dedicated to Lord Palmerston, could have been issued in August but delays with the map (for which Livingstone blamed Arrowsmith and Arrowsmith Livingstone) forced Murray to hold back until November, by which time Livingstone had left the country. Murray's edition sold the anticipated ten thousand copies, half of them at a subscription dinner. *The Nonconformist* described it as: 'The most thoroughly enjoyable book that has come to hand for a long time'. Writing to Oswell from Bombay in January 1866, Livingstone comments on other review articles:

> I got the Saturday and Athenaeum Reviews which were favourable enough perhaps too much so – My old antagonist John Crawford of the Examiner not quite so much so but still fair and the Reader by Winwood Reade enough to make me shut my eyes. If it touches up the Portuguese to change their infamous system I shall be content.

In comparison with *Missionary Travels* the *Narrative* made a poor showing, both commercially (it was not reprinted) and as a piece of writing, while Livingstone's excuses for the collapse of the UMCA venture to the interior were not convincing enough to save him from being quietly 'dropped' by the Anglican establishment. His correspondence with Bishop Wilberforce, for example, did not continue beyond 1865. Livingstone's last letter to him on 18th March 1865 asked 'Soapy Sam' for a quotation of Colenso's to illustrate the latter's views on 'bigamy' – hardly an endearing request.

The Portuguese for their part, far from 'dropping' Livingstone, elevated him to the status of a public enemy. In December 1864, two months after the Bath speech, the newspaper *Diário de Lisboa* (which Livingstone called Diarrhoea of Lisbon) published four anti-Livingstone articles by José de Lacerda. These were shortly afterwards translated into English and appeared as a pamphlet in the spring of 1865. The publisher was Edward Stanford of London, the title given to it was 'A Reply to Dr Livingstone's Accusations and Misrepresentations.'

Livingstone's *Narrative*, issued later, did not set the Tagus on fire, but Lacerda was inspired to expand his articles into a substantial tome called *Exame dos Viagens do Doutor Livingstone* (Examination of Dr Livingstone's Journeys) which appeared in 1867, its purpose to discredit Livingstone's claims as discoverer and to subvert his reputation. In many instances, the attack is justified (as we have seen in the shameful manner in which Livingstone treated Sr Cardoso of Tete and his map). In England Lacerda had an ally in Burton, who liked the Portuguese enough to translate the whole of 'Os Lusíadas' into rhyming stanzas, and even to translate and publish works by Portuguese explorers in central Africa. Burton respected Livingstone personally, but could stomach neither his pretensions nor his visionary Christianity. He believed bluntly that Africans were a lesser breed, incapable of understanding, let alone of accepting, High Truths. Livingstone and Burton crossed swords, indirectly, in mid-May 1865. A House of Commons committee was reassessing government policy towards the British commercial settlements along the coast of west Africa. The committee had Baikie's Lokoja debacle in mind, but its scope embraced the whole region from Sierra Leone to the Bight of Benin. Burton, who had just relinquished his consulship at Fernando Po, gave evidence to the effect that missionary effort was an expensive waste of time and should not be supported by the government. The following day, Livingstone was called to testify and attempted to refute Burton (at the conclusion of the hearings, the government decided to leave things as they were). Livingstone was so incensed at Burton for questioning and denigrating everything he believed in, that he broke his self-imposed vow against public speaking and gave a passionate address on the subject at issue to the conference of the LMS taking place at Exeter Hall at the time.

Burton, as we have seen, had founded the Anthropological Society in 1863, and was one of its most vociferous figures. The society had rapidly become the fountainhead of Carlylite radicalism and harboured a group which, according to Livingstone, would be happy to see slavery and the slave trade re-instituted. Lord Stanley, a leading Tory politician, former Prime Minister and destined to hold office again was a member of the group. The Anthropological as Livingstone called it when writing to Oswell, was to play a major part in an affair that had profound effects on the political nation and on Livingstone's attitudes; one of those affairs that bring latent feelings to the surface and make people take a stand.

In October 1865 a riot by land-hungry, one-generation-emancipated former African slaves at Morant Bay, Jamaica, some thirty miles east of the capital, Kingston, caused a panic among the plantation oligarchy who were conscious as ever of what had happened in Haiti on

the neighbouring island. The governor of Jamaica, E J Eyre, declared
martial law, sent in troops to suppress the rebellion (such as it
was). Four hundred and thirty nine blacks were killed, most of them
hanged after summary military trials: six hundred, including pregnant
women – some of whose wombs were torn open – were flogged with
steel-laced cats-o'-nine-tails (including a number waiting to be put to
death) and over a thousand houses of suspected 'rebels' were burned
down. The Jamaican plantocracy supported Eyre to the hilt, in Britain
opinion was divided, some wanting him to be rewarded with a peerage,
others for him to be put on trial for murder. The latter group was led
by J S Mill, Thomas Hughes, Darwin and Thomas Huxley, and received
heavy support from working people, especially in Lancashire. As for
the former party, Eyre was a member of the 'Anthropological' and the
society rallied around him, forming a defence committee which was
able to count among its members Carlyle, John Ruskin, Dickens,
Tennyson and Matthew Arnold. The issue, of course, was race and
empire or, as the Anthropologists declared at their third anniversary
meeting:

> We anthropologists have looked on, with intense admiration, at the
> conduct of Governor Eyre ... The merest novice in the study of race
> characteristics ought to know that we English can only successfully rule
> either Jamaica, New Zealand, the Cape, China, or India, by such men as
> Governor Eyre.

Eyre was eventually put on trial, acquitted 'because his error of
judgement involved only negro blood' as *The Spectator* said, and
retired on a state pension.

Morant Bay came a decade after the Indian 'mutiny' – suppressed
too with vigorous brutality. Taken together the responses to the two
events can be seen as signals pointing to the aggressive empire-building
that the British ruling class embarked upon in the latter third of the
nineteenth century, and to the concomitant flowering of its master-race
ideology. Livingstone was highly critical of Governor Eyre, as was to
be expected in the light of his feelings a dozen years previously about
Judge Wylde at the Cape. But among Livingstone's friends Murchison
and Webb, perhaps even Oswell, supported Eyre, and he did not hesitate
to tell them how deeply he disagreed with them. Morant Bay happened
after Livingstone had left England, but it is impossible that the attitudes
he condemned had not emerged during the long evenings of talk
at Newstead, Livingstone finding himself once again the outsider.
Webb's quip that if Livingstone had not been a missionary he would
have made a good poacher, coming from the owner of an estate not
far from Sherwood Forest, has more bite to it than at first meets the

eye. Nor was Livingstone always happy about the social mores of the stately home. On 1st April he began a note to Oswell thus: 'It seems it is wrong to say Mrs O. or Dr L. so I begin to reform on this Allfools day.' Lighthearted as the remark may seem it suggests unease – Livingstone had detected among these friends the snobbery and cant which featured so prominently on the upper reaches of the English social landscape. But this being said, living with the Webbs was a happy and refreshing time for Livingstone. His stay ended on 25 April 1865, though he was to return for two further short visits. Byron's 'Elegy on Newstead Abbey' ends with the lines:

> Hours splendid as the past may still be thine
> And bless thy future as thy former day

Words that apply with equal aptness to Livingstone at this time. He was not going to be 'on the shelf', and whatever the imponderables, he had a chance to win fresh fame in Africa.

From Newstead, Livingstone and Agnes went to London so that he could finish work on the book, finalise his arrangements with the government and the RGS, and start planning his new expedition. Stores could be bought in Bombay or Zanzibar, the main problem was getting suitable porters lined up in advance. Should he take Baluchis from India? Could he get men from the Comoros? The letters moved back and forth. His first public address since Bath (if we exclude a lecture to the Mechanics' Institute at Mansfield, given as a favour to Webb) was made at the dinner of the Royal Academy on 29th April. Livingstone records the event in his journal:

Sir Charles Eastlake, President, Archbishops of Canterbury and York on each side of the chair; all the ministers present, except Lord Palmerston, who is ill of gout in the hand. Lord Russell, Lord Granville, and Duke of Somerset, were on other side of the table from Sir Henry Holland, Sir Roderick and myself. Lord Clarendon was close enough to lean back and clap me on the shoulder, and ask me when I was going out. Duke of Argyll, Bishops of Oxford and London within earshot; Sir J Romilly, the Master of the Rolls, was directly in front on the other side of our table. He said he watched all my movements with great interest . . . The speeches were much above average. I was not told that I was expected to speak till I got in and this prevented my eating . . . My speech was not reported.

A few days later he adds:

. . . This non-reporting was much commented on, which might, if I needed it, prove a solace to my wounded vanity. But I did not feel offended. Everything good for me will be given, and I take all as a little child from its father.

To be *invited* to dinner but *not* told he was to speak! To be slapped on the shoulder like a groom! Little wonder Livingstone could not eat. There is a sad obsequiousness about these journal entries, recognition by a man past his prime that he may never achieve the independence he yearns for and may be forever at the beck and call of those he described as 'snobs'.

Livingstone's four weeks of work in London were interspersed with a great deal of sightseeing, at Agnes's insistence. She was doing it all, he told Oswell, running him off his feet. One target of their attentions was the Crystal Palace, by now removed from Hyde Park and rebuilt in all its glittering splendour at Sydenham. They spent a few days with the Oswells at Tunbridge Wells, though Livingstone and Oswell met frequently in London to deal with the final proofs. Livingstone saw Waller and was pleased by his remark that the Anthropologists were 'Icebergs, floating down the warm stream of humanity, chilling all who come near them', as he wrote to Kirk.

Towards the end of May, Livingstone and Agnes travelled to Hamilton where his mother was 'sinking gradually and not long for this world'. They stayed in Scotland for seven weeks, except for a brief visit Livingstone (believing his mother was not in danger) made to Oxford at the invitation of Dr Charles Daubeny, the Professor of Chemistry. Livingstone was offered the Sheldonian theatre for his address, but chose instead Daubeny's small lecture room. He was hoping to speak at Cambridge too but cut short his stay in England when a telegram came announcing that his mother had 'felt the touch of the grim king'.

23

TO START THE WORLD ANEW

Livingstone's mother had expressed the wish that her head would be laid in the grave by one of her 'laddies', and the wish was granted, for Livingstone was in Hamilton to bury her on 23rd June 1865, giving thanks that she had 'died in the Lord' and reflecting on his own fate – thoughts made more sombre by the death of Abraham Lincoln a few weeks before, which had struck him to the heart. Livingstone found the manner of his mother's departure, as he told Oswell on 27th June 1865, 'interesting . . . inasmuch as I may possess the same physical organization and the close of my career may be with the same collectedness, but it is not likely that I shall live long.'

On the day after the funeral he told James Young:

> I was very much struck last night in reading a remark . . . in reference to old Dr Thomas Brown and neglect of his body. While waiting for his death he once said '*I have worn myself out in labour which God never required of me, and for which man will never thank me.*' The underlined words are what arrested my attention.

Livingstone's gloom was deepened by the death during the same week of Kirk's mother, and by thoughts of Robert, news of whose transfer to Salisbury, North Carolina, arrived in Hamilton at this time. However, once the family obsequies were over, Livingstone made the most of what little time remained for him in Scotland. He took the children to watch the sea trials in the Firth of Clyde of an 'ironclad' warship built for the Turkish navy, then went to stay with James Young at Limefield for a few days. There, he laid the foundation stone of Young's new oil-from-shale refinery at Addiewell, planted trees in the garden of Young's mansion and gave Young the nickname 'Sir Paraffin'.

The Laird of Limefield, as Livingstone also called him, was now at the height of his fortune. The partnership which had pioneered the petroleum process had been dissolved and Young had formed the Paraffin Light and Mineral Oil Company, in which he took a minority shareholding. Profits of ninety per cent on costs in the previous enterprise had made Young at fifty-four a very rich man and he was now preparing to devote more time to his hobbies – yachting, collecting rare books on alchemy – and pursuing his public interests, particularly the extension of technical education, in line with his belief that only the application of science to industry would ensure the future strength of the British economy. In the 1870s he built, at his own expense, the Young Laboratory for Technical Chemistry in Glasgow. Kirk's brother was working for his company at the Addiewell plant, but Livingstone does not seem to have considered careers in industry for his two younger boys. Tom was now sixteen, Oswell two years his junior and both were doing well at school. Livingstone went to the speech day in early June and was pleased to find that Oswell 'was dux in six classes', that Tom 'got a prize for drawing – the drawing exhibited was very good.' As for their futures, he told W C Oswell in a letter of 9th June 1865:

> The school at which they learn is always very successful in the middle class examinations and seeing they got on, I have been thinking they might prepare for trying the Indian Civil Service examinations, but I don't know anything about them except they are severe, and my boys must fight their own way.

Livingstone was particularly worried about Tom, whose health was not good (blood in the urine suggesting the debilitating tropical disease bilharzia, which he would not have known about). Besides the ICS, Livingstone considered taking Tom to India, finding him a job on one of the tea plantations the British were then establishing to supplement (and perhaps replace) supplies from China, or possibly on the Indian railways. In the event, Tom went to work for a commercial house in Egypt.

Oswell went on from school to study medicine. Little Anna Mary, now six, was to be sent to the Quaker school at Kendal, home of Livingstone's friend Braithwaite, and Agnes was to attend a finishing school in Paris. Livingstone was to take her to France himself. As the future would show, Young had become the virtual foster-father of the children, with access, as we have seen, to the royalties from Murray.

At the end of July Livingstone and Agnes returned to London, went to stay with James Hamilton their Presbyterian minister friend and preparations began in earnest for departure from Britain. With the exception of two short visits to Newstead, Livingstone spent the last month of his stay in London, fretting to get away. Friends tried to persuade him to remain for a few months longer – the *Narrative* was to be published in November but as he told Young on 8th August 1865:

> I have carefully considered all that you and Sir Roderick urge ... it would be agreeable, but I think I shall be better employed in India

trying to enlist the sympathy of the Bombay people – and to see about the Lady Nyassa ... until I have her disposed of I have a great deal on my mind.

In spite of Murchison's promise that he would see Livingstone right financially, in spite of Young's undoubted loyalty, thoughts of money persisted. There is a dash of sourness in his report to Young on 25th July 1865 of Augustus Grant's wedding, which Livingstone attended:

A nice lass with a frank open countenance – £2000 a year and a house in London is the tocher [dowry] and in addition they have the good wishes of all their friends.

£2000 was the magic figure within which he was expected to complete his expedition.

At times, Livingstone was ashamed of being a 'poor relation'. When eventually he sold the *Lady Nyassa* he found himself unable to admit publicly that he was doing so to raise money. He suggested it was because she could not be sailed at that time of year – November – from Bombay to Zanzibar since the monsoon was blowing in the wrong direction, a palpable lie as the north-east monsoon, the right wind for that journey, starts in that very month. Livingstone had to keep his mask of imperturbability in place and removed it only for close friends like Young to whom he wrote on 8th August 1865:

I don't expect salary from Wee Johnnie [Russell]. I can see his reason for saying in his Aberdeen speech 'that I spoke of the slave trade policy as Lord Palmerston's policy.' He was angry because I had not given him more credit than he deserves. It will all come right some how and we need not wish the little man in Heaven any sooner than is right.

It was not only shortage of money that nagged at Livingstone. The conditions, or instructions as to how he was to perform his geographical work, which were attached to the grant from the RGS, made him feel demeaned, as if he were being treated like a dimwit, as if he were – with Russell's 'let it be understood' – a sweeper of outstanding incompetence. If Livingstone utters time and again the words 'All will come right', it is merely his hope that if his expedition were successful all would be restored.

Besides Grant's wedding, Livingstone's social round in London consisted mainly of farewell visits to friends and well-wishers. Luncheon with Miss Coutts, where he met Queen Emma, devout Anglican wife of King Kamehameda of Hawaii; time spent with Oswell; a visit with Webb to the London Zoo (founded by Stamford Raffles); dinner with

John Murray; a trip to Maidstone to see the Dowager Duchess of Sutherland, opponent of slavery (but instigator of Highland Clearances), friend of Harriet Beecher Stowe (supporter of the Clearances). Then, in his parting letter of 8th August 1865 to James Young he says:

> I must now say farewell and wish blessing on you and yours according to your need from the ever present friend. Many thanks for all your kindness to me and mine. We start on Monday at 10 from Charing Cross for Dover etc.
>
> I enclose a statement of accounts from Mr Murray at his desire after I had looked at it. He will pay you the amount . . . Agnes and I write in kind love to Majames and all the family.

(Livingstone was leaving with Young ideas for the manufacture of a wood preservative extracted from the shell of the tropical nut he called vitex. Tests had been made and large supplies of the raw material were needed.) The Webbs travelled to London to bid farewell, Mrs Webb in tears, saying they wished he were coming rather than going, Livingstone scarcely able to contain his emotion. From Charing Cross Waller and Kirk accompanied him and Agnes to Dover. There the packet-boat sailed, and Livingstone left the British Isles forever.

The finishing school to which Agnes was going in Paris catered especially for British Protestant girls and was run by Mme Hocédé, niece of the Reverend Prosper Lemue, who had officiated at Livingstone's wedding at Kuruman in 1845. The Moffats at Kuruman, and the French evangelical missionaries at Motito nearby, had been on good terms from the outset, a reflection of the close ties between Scottish Congregationalism and the Huguenot revival in France. Agnes was being placed among friends, even if Mme Hocédé's fee was £150 a year. After saying good-bye to his daughter, Livingstone told W C Oswell:

> I think Agnes is all right. Revd M. Calliatte, the father of her instructor is a nice old protestant minister and rather clever as a writer of reviews in the *Revue des deux Mondes* in association with M. Guizot [the most prominent French Protestant public figure of the day], and he lives principally in a village near Dreux called Marsauceux. Agnes is with them here for a month or so during the vintage. Mrs Calliatte is Miss Lemue whom you remember at Motito. Mr Moffat lived with them a week when he was in France and all their belongings [relatives] are religious people and thoroughly Protestant. Mrs Hocédé is about 30 – lost her husband after 11 weeks of married life by scarlet fever when she was only 19, seems clever – is certainly a good musician and Agnes likes her.

(Livingstone does not give another interesting detail of Mme Hocédé's life – she had been governess to Queen Victoria's younger daughters at the time of Albert's death. Letters to her family describing what had happened were 'leaked' to the press, Victoria was furious and sacked her.) This letter of 19th August 1865 to Oswell ends:

> [Agnes] poor thing was very cut up by parting from me. She was much attached to poor Bob whose name I fear must be heard no more – and I felt rather alone in the world. Hold her. I told her to write to you in any case in which she required counsel as I am sure that you would give her wise hints for her guidance. We sail hence tomorrow 20th.

Livingstone sailed from Marseilles aboard the P & O liner *Massilia* – the company had given him a free ticket to Bombay. The ship called at Malta, ended its leg of the journey at Alexandria. From there the passengers went overland to Suez at the head of the sweltering Red Sea, and at Cairo crossed the Nile, the river that was to become Livingstone's obsession. Work had started on the Suez Canal, it would be open in four years. But now the journey to India proceeded in a second liner. While at sea, Livingstone made friends with William Stearns, a thirty year old Massachusetts merchant, partner since 1857 in the Bombay firm Stearns, Hobart & Co. He stayed with Stearns for most of his time in India, Stearns giving both hospitality and help in getting the expedition together. They arrived at Bombay on the morning of 11th September, Livingstone hoping to leave for Africa in November, but his timetabling was, as usual, far too optimistic.

A few days after installing himself with Stearns, Livingstone travelled inland to Poonah, a military town in the uplands, to see Sir Bartle Frere. He reported the visit to Kirk when writing to him on 20th September 1865:

> The Governor is very willing to do what he can for my next trip, I am at his house now and very kind he is in the way of aiding my arrangements for the future of my own work.

And looking forward to being where he longs to be, adds:

> Bombay is very hot just now but the air up here is cool and pleasant. The slopes of the Ghauts are splendid and covered with jungle and grass, which look very much like some African scenery.

Whatever Livingstone's Frere-assisted arrangements might be, they could not include the *Lady Nyassa*. He did not have, or expect to have, enough money to man, fuel and provision her and finally put her definitely on sale, with the excuses and the results we have seen. What agreement he had come to with Young we do not know, possibly the money raised to form part of the shareholding of any commercial venture Livingstone launched. Certainly commerce – with all its Livingstonian concomitants – was the prime consideration. Livingstone was pleased to find a substantial Scottish element among the foreign merchants of Bombay (and in Calcutta too, for that matter), men who were 'clannish' (helpful to fellow Scots), making money and wanting to make more. Livingstone addressed meetings of these merchants. A Bombay paper, the *Friend of India* reported his gist:

> Sailing up the Rovuma ... he expects to find highlands suitable for an English settlement ... What the missionaries have done on the West Coast [of Africa] creating a trade of 3 million sterling a year ... he hopes to do on a grander scale, in time, on the East coast.

On the strength of prospects like these, the Bombay merchants raised a subscription of £645 – Livingstone had hoped for £1000 – which he placed with one of their number named Tracey. Livingstone confirmed his intentions to Waller. He was going to select a site on the highlands up the Rovuma, proceed inland to do what the RGS had commissioned, then return to the place that would become his 'establishment'. A few weeks after his letter to Waller of 26th October 1865, Livingstone wrote to Russell (the first time he had done so since reaching India) telling him that the £645 had been deposited in Bombay until it could be used at his establishment. He promises that the instructions he has received from both Russell and the RGS will receive his earliest attention. For this we should read a warning between the lines, that Livingstone expects the promised consular salary to be paid once he has settled.

The Bombay merchants, that is to say the British and Americans, would certainly be happy to increase their share of the east African trade – ivory and cloves in particular – then carried in the dhows of Indians and Arabs. Livingstone could be a valuable ally in this expansion, especially as he was on excellent terms with Governor Frere and might be able to persuade him to pursue more active policies than those in operation at that time. 'His Excellency,' Livingstone told Oswell on 24th September 1865, 'is a first rate man and enters into my project with great heartiness and goodwill.' Frere was an almost exact contemporary of Livingstone, and unlike most British colonial governors, had 'risen through the ranks', having joined the Bombay civil service in 1834 at the age of nineteen as an employee of the East India Company. He was appointed governor in 1862 and remained in that post until 1867, when he was given wider duties. Frere was as interested in seeing the end of the east African slave trade as

Livingstone was himself, and gave his support in a number of practical ways.

In getting his expedition together Livingstone's first task in Bombay was to assemble his personnel. While in Britain he had discussed with Oswell (the former 'India hand') and with Rigby, British consul in Zanzibar, the possibility of recruiting a team of Baluchis to act as porters, Livingstone not wishing to be dependent on the slave porterage agents in Zanzibar. When he raised the matter with Frere, the governor immediately put at his disposal a platoon of twelve sepoys, under the command of a corporal (or havildar) from the Marine Battalion, men who, in Livingstone's words, had roughed it and would be suitable for service with the expedition. 'The Govt. ensures their pay, pensions, allowances as if on actual duty for the state,' Livingstone told Oswell on 29th September 1865. He was also given permission to recruit from the church-run but government sponsored school for young freed African slaves at Nasik, near Bombay, and from there he tells Oswell:

> I have got eight Africans, some of whom have a knowledge of carpentry and smith work, and they may be interesting if we try to build up a canoe for navigating Tanganyika.

From the Church of Scotland mission where he had placed them, Livingstone retrieved James Chuma and Wakatini, the two youngsters he had left there in 1864 – they had both been baptised. He completed his Bombay enrolment with Susi and Amoda, the two 'Shupanga men' he had found work for in the docks on the previous visit. To increase his complement he hoped for recruits from the Comoros and wrote to Sunley, the consul there on 31st December 1865, for help:

> I will feel much obliged if you can engage six good boatmen at five dollars per month, the sixth being headman to have more . . . If a dhow were coming to Zanzibar before February that would do to bring them.

Livingstone thought he would need sixty men, planning to engage the remainder of the party on the mainland. As he was unwilling to hire professional porters – whether slave or free – in Zanzibar, as Burton had done, he had no alternative to the hotchpotch he was putting together, and in the case of the sepoys had a precedent in the platoon of Griquas loaned to Speke by the governor of the Cape for his second journey to Lake Victoria.

Livingstone knew only too well that the greatest impediment to any settlement like the one he proposed on the highlands – or anywhere else in the interior of Africa he had visited – was the transport problem. And, as a result, he had decided to undertake an experiment which he hoped would go some way to providing a solution. He had observed that the African buffalo was not affected by the tsetse 'poison' – the disease known today as trypanosomiasis – so he bought eleven Indian buffaloes in Bombay to use as pack animals and told Oswell in that same letter of 29th September 1865:

> I think there is a good chance of them being able to withstand the poison of the tsetse. They are wonderfully like the wild nyaris [buffaloes in Tswana], I have seen horns with the genuine curves. They are surely more than half brothers, though the males have not the horny forehead.

The Sultan of Zanzibar paid an official visit to Bombay while Livingstone was there, and was persuaded to ship the animals to Zanzibar in his vessel.

By mid-November Livingstone had completed his arrangements in Bombay, and was anxious to move on. He was expecting passage in a Royal Navy man of war but no word came from the authorities. On 15th November he was driven to ask Kirk (in London) to go to the Foreign Office to have orders telegraphed to Bombay, adding: 'I don't like to go by dhow, it would be *infra dig*, or I should go tomorrow.' Fortunately, Frere came to the rescue. The Bombay government was presenting a ship, the *Thule*, formerly in service with the British fleet off China, to the Sultan. Livingstone and his men could have free passage with her to Zanzibar and they sailed a few days after New Year. One of Livingstone's last acts in Bombay was to give Frere a personal (and private) assessment as to Kirk's suitability for the post of medical officer in Zanzibar. Frere was satisfied, and immediately telegraphed Kirk confirming the appointment.

Between 1861 and the time of Livingstone's arrival in Zanzibar at the end of January 1866, the island's total trade with the African mainland and with overseas markets averaged £1.2 million a year, and was set to move to a higher level with the end of the American civil war and the resumption of a previously flourishing commerce with the United States. Zanzibar's principal exports were ivory, cloves, gum copal, sesame, and coconut products. Its imports were textiles, beads, wire, firearms and ammunition.

The external trade in slaves, that is, export to territories outside the Zanzibar empire, was no longer of great importance in strictly commercial terms – perhaps, fifteen per cent of the total imports of some twenty thousand. Eighty-five per cent of imported slaves were being absorbed in either Zanzibar itself or deployed to satellites such as Pemba, Lamu or Mombasa, producing or processing the empire's agricultural exports. Kilwa, south of Zanzibar, half way between the island and the mouth of the Rovuma, was the principal port of entry for slaves from the African interior. From Kilwa the slaves were tran-shipped to Zanzibar slave market, customs duty being paid on each. Livingstone saw from seventy to three hundred slaves a day 'exposed for sale ... the majority are Manganja – their prices when I was in the market were from 7 to 20 dollars,' as he told George Frere, the anti-slavery commissioner at Cape Town in a letter of 17th March 1866. Livingstone goes on to accuse the anti-slavery commission of hypocrisy, on the one hand condoning domestic slavery, on the other by operating patrols at sea only at times of the year when because of the monsoon there was no northward traffic, thus allowing, too, the trade to the Middle East. In addition, he thought that the refusal to stop the traffic between Zanzibar and its satellites was monstrous and wanted a much firmer British policy as he states to George Frere again:

> It is said that without a fresh importation of slaves into Pemba and Zanzibar these islands would soon become depopulated – to people these wretched sinks we allow the depopulation of hundreds of square miles of Manganja and Lake Nyassa country.

(Though he concedes that the circle of hell for these domestic and plantation slaves was far less infernal than it would have been, for example, in the old southern United States.)

Livingstone's observations on Zanzibari slavery at this time reveal once more that frequent inability or unwillingness of his to take his analysis of phenomena beyond the obvious. For him, slavery and particularly the trade were evil. The anti-slavery campaign, all who supported it and the factors that strengthened it, were good. He could accuse George Frere's department of hypocrisy and inefficiency, but he does not see – or if he does makes no comment upon – the conduct of British anti-slavery patrols when they were in action. Time after time he sees only what he wants to see, brushing out of view any flaws in the image. As far as Zanzibar was concerned, the fact of the matter was that it was an independent state which Britain wished to bring to its knees, not because it was a slave state, but because to do so would benefit Britain in terms of global naval strategy and of commercial expansion. In the 1860s the anti-slavery patrols were being used to destroy Zanzibari shipping in the name of suppressing an export of slaves to the Middle East at a time when that export had all but ceased to exist. Thus between 1861 and 1863 thirty-eight of forty-three dhows captured were not carrying slaves. In 1862 a dhow carrying no slaves, merely a cargo of spices and rice, later valued at over £5,700, was destroyed. In 1868 and 1869 ninety-eight dhows were destroyed, whether they were carrying slaves (and that does not mean domestic slaves) or not. A further ten dhows were destroyed off the Somali coast even when the first British ship to inspect them found them free of export slaves. Acts of official piracy were aggravated by the practice of paying bounties to British officers who captured 'slave ships', and by the unofficial looting of dhows by the personnel of British warships. Captain W C Devereux of the *Gorgon* (the ship that had brought the *Lady Nyassa* to the Zambezi), he who had had words to say about Livingstone's bungling and whose crew had had such a roistering time at Shupanga, remarked, in his book *A Cruise in the Gorgon*, of the anti-slavery patrol off the coast of east Africa:

> Fortunately within the last few years captains have been appointed whose private fortunes have needed a little repair; at all events not deterred them from making a little more prize money.

The more vigorous the captains, the sooner would Zanzibar's ships go to the bottom, the sooner would Livingstone's Bombay merchants be able to move in.

In 1866, British control over Zanzibar was far from complete, though the Sultan, Majid Ibn Said (who owed his throne to British intervention during a dynastic dispute), found that his finances – including the customs revenue from slave imports – were controlled by Indian merchants who were *de jure* British subjects and susceptible to British pressure. These 'British' Indians were forbidden to own slaves themselves, but profited enormously from the internal (and legal) slave trade. At the time the total population of Zanzibar was about 100,000 of whom probably seventy per cent were slaves. 'The slaves swarm here,' Livingstone told George Frere, 'and the majority are Manganja,' and the British were content for them to go on producing the cloves and carrying the ivory.

Sir Bartle Frere had delegated Livingstone to present the *Thule* to the Sultan on his behalf. One of Frere's reasons for inviting Majid to Bombay the previous year was 'to give him some new ideas', and by way of a new idea he had brought back with him a brass band which enlivened the ceremony with renderings of 'God Save the Queen' and 'The British Grenadiers'. 'This,' Livingstone remarked to Agnes when he wrote to her on 22nd January 1866, 'was excessively ridiculous, but I maintained sufficient official gravity.'

Although Majid was a slave owner and the chief beneficiary of the system, he had forbidden Zanzibari traders on the mainland to raid for slaves – they were permitted only to purchase. Livingstone convinced himself that the Sultan was a crypto-abolitionist and hoped to draw him into his plans: 'I shall confer with him as to getting supplies by way of [Kilwa]', he had told Oswell on 22nd September 1865 and mentioned to Kirk on 1st January 1866, that he would like to get 'an Arab settlement near the mouth of the Rovuma, positively free to all and without slavery.'

Nothing came of these ideas, though Majid gave Livingstone one of his houses for the duration of his stay in Zanzibar, and when he left, a *firman* (laisser-passer) valid throughout his dominions. The Zanzibar empire, makeshift as it may have been, extended from the Rovuma to Mombasa, from Lake Nyasa to Lake Victoria and as far west from the coast as Katanga and Lake Tanganyika.

In Zanzibar itself, Livingstone had to make his final arrangements. Nine of his buffaloes had died 'of some plant', he told Stearns, and asked him to send replacements from Bombay. They could not arrive in time, so he bulked up his train of pack animals with six camels, four donkeys, two mules, all to undergo the tsetse experiment. He also had a dog, a poodle he named Chitane (the French cook at Newstead had had a poodle and Byron, whenever possible, kept a dog). As for manpower, Sunley in the Comoros had been unable (or unwilling) to send any men, so Livingstone recruited ten Comorans in Zanzibar, their leader a man called Musa who had worked for Livingstone – unsatisfactorily – on the Zambezi. To make up the sixty men he required, Livingstone would have to hire on the mainland. A Somali guide would lead the caravan up along the Rovuma, 'Nassik boys' (as Livingstone called them) Comorans, Sepoys, piece-work porters, Susi, Chuma, Amoda and Wakatini, these men Livingstone hoped would see him through as well as Sekeletu's Kololo had done. As for supplies, little basic food would be carried, but a large stock of trade goods to buy meal and meat (when hunting did not fill the pot) along the way. Only items like sugar, salt, tea and coffee need be taken from Zanzibar, with Livingstone's little luxuries such as cheese and brandy. And goats to provide him with milk would be found on the mainland.

Livingstone planned to ascend the Rovuma valley to the highlands to the east of Lake Nyasa, head north to Lake Tanganyika, make his investigations and then return. So as not to run short of supplies, he commissioned a Zanzibar Indian chandler, Ludha Damji, to send a replenishment consignment – which was to include medicines – to Ujiji, the Zanzibari trading town near the northern end of Lake Tanganyika, and with the consignment were to go new buffaloes ordered from Stearns in Bombay. Murchison had wanted Livingstone to go first to Lake Tanganyika, establish whether there were a northern outlet to the Nile and only then, if there were, find the watershed from which rivers flowed into Lake Tanganyika: these rivers which would be the southermost sources of the Nile. Livingstone, however, put less store by the 'purely geographical question' than by his own plans for a settlement, besides which, to do as Murchison wished would entail taking the caravan route to Ujiji and find himself following in Burton's footsteps – unthinkable. And even if his own route were half as long again, Livingstone was confident that it would not take any more time than his money and the manpower and supplies it paid for allowed. The geographical task would be completed within two years, then the real work could begin.

On 19th March 1866, having spent six weeks in Zanzibar, Livingstone and his men sailed for the Rovuma in the Royal Navy ship *Penguin*, towing a dhow which, with its cargo of Livingstone's menagerie, could not have failed to look, as it sliced the waves, like Noah's Ark on its way to start the world anew.

'I trust that the Most High will prosper me', prayed Livingstone. Great that trust would need to be.

Part Six

1866–1874

Towards the City of God

24

WE HAVE BEEN VERY SLOW

Now that I am on the point of starting another trip into Africa I feel quite exhilirated. When one travels with the specific object in view of ameliorating the condition of the natives any act becomes ennobled . . . The mere animal pleasure of travelling in a wild unexplored country is very great. When on lands of a couple of thousand feet, brisk exercise imparts elasticity to the muscles, fresh and healthy blood circulates through the brain, the mind works well, the eye is clear, the step is firm, and a day's exertion always makes the evening's repose thoroughly enjoyable . . . The effect of travel on a man whose heart is in the right place is that the mind is more self-reliant: it becomes more confident of its own resources.

With these words in an entry of 29th March 1866 in his journal, Livingstone launched himself on his last journey. On 6th April he left the coast for the interior. Alas, the exhilaration is to be short-lived, at best returning momentarily to relieve the misery of long painful marches, of long days, weeks and months of illness. At the very start it was clear that he had made a mistake in deciding to land at the mouth of the Rovuma, despite the fact that he had been there twice before. No place could be found to disembark the menagerie from the dhow. The ships had to back-track up the coast and dock at Mikandani, forty miles north of the river, where everything could be put safely ashore. Porters were hired, as planned, and then when the party marched back to the river it was clear that Livingstone had made yet another mistake, even greater than the first. Unlike most of the coastal lowlands, the Rovuma valley was so densely forested that a special path had to be cleared in advance of the caravan to enable the camels and buffaloes to pass. Livingstone hired villagers along the route as woodcutters, but progress was slow, the weather oppressively hot. Soon the animals began to lose condition, partly as a result of overloading and maltreatment, partly no doubt because of disease: the camels were completely out of their element, the Indian buffaloes without immunity to African infections, whether tsetse-borne or not. When the animals started to die off, Livingstone blamed rough handling; though he had seen them being attacked by tsetse he could not admit that his experiment had been a waste (early white settlers in central Africa went some way to overcoming the problem of draught animals in tsetse areas by training zebras to pull carts, but this option was not available to Livingstone). The death of the animals increased the loads the porters had to carry, but even before this became a factor, Livingstone began to realise that, with a few notable exceptions, he had made a bad choice of men, but could not admit that he had been rash in assuming that the animals would do service. In some of the 'Nassik boys' he detected what he called the 'slave spirit' – dishonesty, laziness, unreliability. It became obvious that the sepoys would be no good at all, that the Comorans were of doubtful quality. However, he was not going to treat his men as Burton had done, at the outset of the journey he wrote hopefully in his journal:

> Our sympathies are drawn out towards our humble, hardy companions by a community of interests and, may be, of perils, which makes us all friends. Nothing but the most pitiable puerility would lead any manly heart to make their inferiority a theme for self-exaltation; however, that is often done, as if with the vague idea that we can, by magnifying their deficiencies, demonstrate our immaculate perfections.

But there did not exist here (except in the case of Chuma, Susi, Amoda and Wakatini) those common interests which had bound Livingstone and his porters together on the transcontinental journeys, when all of them were in one way or another subjects of Sekeletu. Only the four we have named would find anything to look forward to in fulfilling Livingstone's highlands dream – the others were hired hands, the sepoys reluctant servicemen, afraid for their skins, concerned to get home alive with their pay in their pockets. Livingstone, for all the steely side to his character, was not a disciplinarian, hated regimentation (Burton had drilled his porters in army fashion before leaving Zanzibar for the mainland) and trusted his men to do what was expected of them as if by nature. He was sadly disillusioned by the men's slackness, but did not take as simple a step as keeping the caravan together. He allowed the sepoys, for example, to take three weeks to cover ground he had travelled in one. At one stage he became so infuriated that he caned one of them but was so ashamed that he resolved never to do so again and henceforth punished them by making them carry loads, but to no avail. They still malingered, abused the animals (while they were still alive), stole, hired villagers to do their work for them and demanded that Livingstone pay. Matters in general became worse rather than better as the party advanced. Although the ground conditions improved when it began to emerge from the valley, there was a severe shortage of food, the area being crossed having been raided by the Ngoni and left desolate. Livingstone feared actual starvation, but was able to buy just enough grain, and the occasional fish, to keep the caravan on its feet. When at one juncture the sepoys refused to move at all, Livingstone dismissed them but the next day, moved by the pleadings of the havildar, he took them back. On 11th June, after nine weeks of travel and still less than two hundred miles from the coast, the twenty-odd men Livingstone had recruited at Mikandani decided to go home. They were afraid of attack by the Ngoni, afraid that they might be taken into slavery, for the party was now on the slave route between Lake Nyasa and Kilwa. Livingstone had no alternative but to release them and redistribute the loads among the men who remained. Loads made all the heavier since every pack animal was now dead, and heavier still when one of the Nassik boys, Richard, died of fever, the first human casualty of the expedition. The situation was made more depressing by constant reminders of the slave trade – slave-sticks discarded by the path, abandoned captives lying shot dead or tied to trees to perish of thirst or starvation. Thus did an impatient slave trader deal with the weak, the ill or the slow.

On 3rd July, Livingstone and his men arrived at the town of a Yao chief named Mtarika and, lecturing him on the evils of 'selling his people', was told in reply to preach that to all the other chiefs. Mtarika was unruffled by Livingstone's moralising, supplied him with meal, pork and vegetables, discussed his plans with him and advised him not to take the north-westerly route to Lake Tanganyika because of the danger presented by the Ngoni raiders in the region. The only other way to get to the lake was to make a wide detour west, crossing Nyasa and approaching Tanganyika from the south, a route which would add two hundred miles to the journey. Whether or not Livingstone himself was afraid of the Ngoni, his men certainly were. He had no choice but to change course and, on 5th July left Mtarika, heading south west. It is unfortunate that this decision was forced on Livingstone. For one thing, it complicated the journey and gave it, as we shall see, a dimension of suffering he had not anticipated. For another, it deprived him of 'discovering' the highlands that flank the north east coast of Lake Nyasa, an area so perfect for his 'establishment' that he would have felt himself to be 'Stout Cortez . . . silent upon a peak in Darien', a place where the range of altitude between the lake shore, 1500 feet above sea level, and the high plateau at over 8000 feet, would make it possible to grow every conceivable crop, tropical or temperate.

Livingstone proceeded from Mtarika's to Mataka's, a hungry march which lasted a week. There he rested for a fortnight. The chief's town lay on the southern flank of the highlands, and even here Livingstone had a taste of the Darien he was missing. On 24th August 1866 he wrote to Adam Sedgwick:

The number of running rills [this was the middle of the dry season] in the mountainous district is quite astonishing, the land rises up to 3400 and even 4000 feet. This elevated region is just Magomero magnified, and to this poor bishop Mackenzie hoped to extend his mission – I had to wear my thickest flannels – The water though only 61 degrees felt much too cold to bathe in – cattle showed that no tsetse exists, and large patches of English peas in full bearing showed how English vegetables could flourish.

As, desperate for food, Livingstone was approaching Mataka's, he was accosted by a Kilwa slave merchant named Sef Rupia and by him presented with an ox for slaughter and a bag of meal: the gift was quite unsolicited. Livingstone hesitated before accepting it, unhappy at being helped by one of his sworn enemies. He then rationalised his acceptance on the grounds that he could not do God's work if he starved to death and transformed Sef into 'our friend in need'. Rupia led Livingstone to Mataka's, introduced him to the chief and, when he resumed his journey (with his eight hundred captives) to Kilwa, took Livingstone's letters and had them delivered to the consulate in Zanzibar. With them he took the second of two despatches to Lord Clarendon, once more Foreign Secretary (the first despatch had been entrusted to the Somali guide when he left the party a short distance up the Rovuma). In these despatches Livingstone analyses the Zanzibari slave economy and suggests how more efficient use of the Royal Navy could stop the trade between the mainland and the island. Once that had been done, he believed, the domestic and plantation slavery of Zanzibar would die out. The 'depopulation' of the interior, and especially the Lake region would be halted, as would the social and political disruption caused by slaving – then missions like the UMCA could resume their work. Whether the slave trade was in fact 'sweeping the country clean of people' is debatable – drought and famine were a more serious factor, as Livingstone had seen – and a case can be made that the slave trade was an important element in promoting social and political stability (if not individual happiness) insofar as it increased the authority and power of rulers such as Mtarika, Mataka and others we shall meet.

Sef Rupia was the first actual slave merchant from whom Livingstone had taken help, and would not be the last. His abhorrence of slavery never diminished, but he now began to make a casuitical distinction between the evil and those who perpetrated it, a process that had begun with the Sultan. As he had said about Webb, 'I do not care how a man gains his riches, provided he is good (to me)'. Sef had told him that a hundred Kilwa traders had died in the interior during a recent bad year. Livingstone saw some of the graves and used this statistic to belabour Tozer for withdrawing the UMCA from the Shire to Zanzibar where it had become 'no more than a chaplaincy to the consulate'. If slave merchants were prepared to die in pursuing their business, how much more willing ought missionaries be to sacrifice themselves for their cause.

During the final stage of the march to Mataka's, the behaviour of the sepoys had become so intolerable that Livingstone dismissed them and hoped that the Bombay authorities would take action against them. The havildar, however, was allowed to stay on. The caravan was now reduced to twenty four men, and with them Livingstone pressed on towards Lake Nyasa. He arrived there on 8th August, hoping to hire a trader's dhow to ferry him across to the west coast. Livingstone was left helpless and frustrated when the shipowners refused to help, but the very arrival at the lake raised his spirits:

> It felt like coming to an old home to see Nyassa again and dash in the rollers of its delicious waters – I was quite exhilirated by the roar of the 'inland sea'.

But after taking four months to struggle up from Mikandani, Livingstone realises that the overland route to the Lake is impracticable, and continues in his letter of 24th August 1866 to Sedgwick:

> I was very much delayed by wanting provisions and by the laziness of some sepoys whom I had to dismiss, but the easy boating of about three weeks to Magomero will bear no comparison to the four months hard toil we had in coming here [Can Livingstone really have forgotten the tribulations with the *Ma Robert* and the *Pioneer*?] ... wherever a path [to the lake] may be found I can conceive of none superior to that by the Shire.

The words are Livingstone's farewell to his establishment on the highlands, to the entrepôt at the mouth of the Rovuma, to his fondest dream. He still believed, however, that 'Africa must be Christianized from within', where the people were friendly, not corrupted by slavery as was the case, he thought, along the coast.

As he could not hire a boat, Livingstone attempted to travel north along the shore of the lake. He found the route impossible, however, turned around and made south, overland. The sight of the Shire flowing from the lake filled him with memories:

> Many hopes have been disappointed here. Far down on the right bank of the Zambezi lies the dust of her whose death changed all my future prospects; and now instead of a check being given to slave trade by

> lawful commerce on the Lake, slave-dhows prosper ... it is impossible
> not to regret the loss of good Bishop Mackenzie who sleeps far down
> the Shire ... but all will come right some day though I may not live to
> participate in the joy, or even see the commencement of better times.

Thus he wrote in his journal on 13th September 1866 on arriving
at the head of the river.

Livingstone called on chiefs in the area whom he knew from previous
visits. He was received well and helped with food and canoes to carry
him and his party across to the west bank and then across the southern
toe of the lake to the foot of the escarpment – Kirk's Range as he had
named it in 1864. A short while after crossing the Shire, Livingstone
said goodbye to young Wakatini, freed slave, Mackenzie's favourite,
who had found the village from which he had been abducted and
had decided to rejoin his family. Chuma now became Livingstone's
personal attendant, seeing to his accommodation, his meals, looking
after his private possessions. Livingstone was sorry to see Wakatini go
and wished him well, hoping that marriage would end his skittishness,
which he had begun to find annoying. Livingstone had no regrets, however, when the havildar also took his leave; 'he had never been the least
use'. The party had now lost two more men, and a fortnight later, as it
approached an area where the Ngoni were reported to be active, Musa
and his Comorans decided that they too had had enough and were
certainly not going to face the 'Mazitu' which was the Bisa word for
the Ngoni and meant 'those who come from nowhere'. Thus, they too
deserted en bloc. Livingstone was left with Susi, Chuma, Amoda and
the Nassik boys – less than a sixth of his original complement.

Musa and his colleagues made their way back to Zanzibar where,
in order to be able to claim their pay, they reported that Livingstone
and the rest of his retinue had been killed by the Mazitu at the northern
end of Lake Nyasa. Seward, the Consul, and Kirk, by now at his post,
believed the story, as did the Sultan. All the flags in Zanzibar were
flown at half mast. When Murchison in London heard the news, he
wrote to *The Times*:

> If this cruel intelligence should be substantiated, the civilized world
> will mourn the loss of as noble and lion-hearted an explorer who ever
> lived.

Two men, Waller and Lieutenant E D Young of the *Pioneer*, who
both knew Musa from Zambezi days and mistrusted him profoundly,
did not accept the report. The RGS was persuaded that a search party
should go out and £1200 was raised for it. The government, with
Livingstone's sympathiser Clarendon at the Foreign Office, agreed to

second Young to lead it, and provided all the support that he needed. (Much more money was being spent to find Livingstone than had been provided to send him!) Young and his men steamed up to the Shire cataracts. Arriving in August 1867, they carried up to the lake a river boat brought out in sections, assembled it, launched it and cruised along the coast stopping at villages to ask about Livingstone. Within a few weeks, Young established beyond doubt that Livingstone had passed along the south shores (many people remembered the poodle, Chitane) had gone on in safety westwards, and that the Comorans had deserted him. By the time Young returned to the Cape, letters written by Livingstone after Musa's defection had reached Zanzibar. Although by this time Livingstone had once more 'disappeared' into Africa and had abandoned hope that there would be any 'establishment' on the lake highlands in his lifetime, Young's expedition had proved that Livingstone's plan to 'force steamers up cataracts' was perfectly feasible, given proper backing.

After waiting ten days at the foot of Kirk's Range for porters (who did not turn up) to replace the Comorans Livingstone hired a few more-or-less willing villagers and set off again. At the end of September he ascended to the Dedza plateau, an upland of some 4000 feet, fertile, well-watered and cool. An area as suitable for a settlement as the Shire highlands, the Dedza upland stretches to the north, forms the watershed between Lake Nyasa and the Luangwa river. The actual watershed is marked by a line of hills like the knuckles of a spine, the rest of the upland sloping gently towards the eastern and western escarpments, is in its natural state covered with light miombo forest, which at the time Livingstone was there would be in new leaf, a tapestry of brilliant fresh colours, greens and ochres and reds. Livingstone took a zig-zag course, from one village to another as his local porters directed him, partly to avoid platoons of Ngoni, partly to be able to meet as many chiefs and headmen as possible. This six weeks of leisurely marching was a delight, as he told James Young on 10th November 1866:

> . . . and we got up Kirk's Range, and among Manganja not yet made slave sellers. This was a great treat for like all who have not been contaminated by that blight they were very kind, and having been worried enough by unwilling sepoys and cowardly Johanna men [Musa and company] I followed my bent by easy marches among friendly generous people to [whom] I tried to impart some new ideas in return for their hospitality. The country is elevated and the climate cool. One of the wonders told us in successive villages was that we slept without fires. The boys having blankets did not need fires, while the inhabitants being scantily clad have their huts plastered inside and out.

This brief interlude was to be the last bit of pleasant wandering Livingstone ever made. As he and his party approached the western stretches of the plateau, they came into an area where the depredations of the Ngoni had made food difficult to obtain and had made it impossible to hire carriers. Livingstone, in fact, passed near the present residence of today's Paramount Chief of a section of the Ngoni, Mpezeni IV, his traditional authority extending over a large part of the plateau. The Ngoni arrived in the area from the south after crossing the Zambezi in 1836, more or less when Sebitwane entered Barotseland. Like Sebitwane's Kololo, the Ngoni had been caught up in the centrifugal turmoil of the *mfecane* in south Africa and had migrated to escape from Shaka's Zulu empire. Cousins of theirs, the 'Landeens' of the lower Zambezi, were held in awe by the Portuguese. For several decades the Ngoni raided far and wide across east-central Africa, one group reaching the south of Lake Victoria, another the headwaters of the Rovuma, as we have seen, but an attempt to conquer what is today northern Zambia was defeated by the Bemba, whom we shall soon meet. During the 1870s the Ngoni who were raiding across Livingstone's path finally settled as farmers, built up large herds of the sturdy indigenous cattle known today, appropriately, as the Angoni breed. In their heyday they were fearsome people, their regiments in the Zulu pattern irresistible by the scattered villages of the plateau, but they did not generally raid for slaves. They absorbed any youngsters they captured into their number, to become either warriors or wives.

Towards the end of October, when Livingstone left the upland and began the descent to the Luangwa valley, he was stepping into a nightmare from which he would only fitfully emerge. The friendly villages lay behind, no porters would go with him and his little team. The country he was entering was wild, rough, escarpmented and, at that season, stiflingly hot. Guides were unobtainable and Livingstone's companions had to move the supplies forward in relays. It took five weeks to cover fifty miles when they arrived at a village named Kande near the valley floor. There Livingstone was able to hire two escaped Yao slaves as porters. The going through the open mopane forest of the broad, flat valley was easier, ten days of following game trails took the party over a further fifty miles to a crossing point on the Luangwa. During this march Livingstone was for the first time since leaving Mikandani so ill that for a day he could not move at all. The rains had now begun, bringing even greater difficulty. Travel becomes additionally tedious and, more important for the Livingstone party, much of the game leaves the floor of the valley near the river and scatters to feed on the new grass of the upland flanks. The only food that villagers would part with (December is when food is scarcest) was finger millet, which Livingstone found totally indigestible. To make matters worse, Livingstone's small flock of goats disappeared. On 1st January 1867 he wrote to James Young:

> We have had precious hard times and I would not complain if it had not been for gnawing hunger for many a day, and our bones sticking through as if they would burst the skin. When we were in a part where game abounded I filled the pot with a first-rate rifle given me by Captain Frazer [a sugar planter on Zanzibar] but elsewhere we had very short rations of a species of millet called Maere [amale (Bisa)] which passes through the stomach almost unchanged.

Matters did not improve when the party climbed up the western side of the valley, the Muchinga escarpment, on to the upland. (The Luangwa flows along a rift valley, the escarpment rising so abruptly 1500 feet above that from the floor it is for all purposes a range of mountains, and precipitous at that.) Livingstone was now in the territory of the Bisa, for generations the greatest long distance traders between the Lunda empire of Katanga and Lake Nyasa, though by the 1860s their commerce had been substantially reduced by the changing pattern of trade routes. Livingstone crested the escarpment on Christmas day, 1866, but without much joy, as he told Sedgwick on 1st February 1867:

> A hungry time we had in passing through the dripping forests of the Babisa country – no animals to be shot and the people had no grain to sell – Mushrooms in plenty, but woe's me, good only for exciting dreams of the roast beef of byegone days – no salt either. This causes the gnawing sensation to be ceaseless, but we got through by God's great mercy – sugar we have forgotten all about, and roast a little grain to make believe it is coffee.

The only thing that cheered Livingstone was his confidence that he had reached the central African watershed. He knew that somewhere to the north-west lay two large lakes, Bangweulu (which he had heard about, under the mistaken name Bemba during his final inland tour at the end of the Zambezi expedition), and Mweru, which had been reported by the Portuguese, the two lakes linked by the Luapula river. He told Sedgwick in the same letter:

> I have been a long time in working up to what is probably the watershed I seek – 4500 feet above the sea, and the Luapula in front.

Nothing stimulated Livingstone more than to have something 'in front'. On New Year's day 1867, Livingstone wrote in his journal:

> May he who was full of grace and truth impress his character on mine. Grace – eagerness to show favour; truth – truthfulness, sincerity, honour – for His mercy's sake.

He was now at the village of the Bisa chief Chitembo, and here the party rested for a week, enjoying what little food was available – the stomach-passing millet with, for protein, the flesh of the short-tailed, beaver-like rodent, weighing 10–14 lbs called locally *insenshi*, in English, cane rat, which is, according to W F H Ansell, 'good eating and much esteemed by Africans for this purpose.' Livingstone probably found some salt, for it was one of the main items of Bisa trade, extracted from the ash of a grass that grows around the marshes in the area. 'I am not a dreamer' Livingstone remarked in his journal, but with his 'healthy highlands' behind him (in both senses) and the Luapula in front, the New Year saw new outlines forming and dissolving in his mind.

From Chitembo's, the crest of the watershed – between the Zambezi and Zaire (Congo) drainage systems – falls away to the broad valley of the Chambeshi. Livingstone appreciated the importance of this large river which the Portuguese believed to be the upper reach of the Zambezi (the two names are etymologically identical, meaning 'great water'). Livingstone believed it fed into Lake Bangweulu, making it the source of the north-flowing Luapula. To establish this would confirm indisputably the position of the central watershed and, at the same time, show up Portuguese ignorance and deflect some of their attack on his reputation as a discoverer. Believing that Bangweulu was Lake Bemba (in fact a small stretch of open water just east of the Chambeshi's mouth into the large lake), Livingstone decided to march from Chitembo's to the capital of the Bemba king, Chitimukulu Chitapankwa, one hundred and fifty miles to the north and departed on 6th January. He was now in an area of very high rainfall, and had to cross the wide Chambeshi basin, low in relation to the watershed and the plateau on the other side. In its natural state, the land in this region is covered by tall, dense forest interspersed with wide grassy plains. These plains, known as 'dambos' are in fact water drainage lines and, soon after the onset of the rains in October turn into vast marshy sponges, on lower ground into actual swamps (the habitat of, among other creatures, the cane rat). By January the rains are at their height, the sky often clouded over for days, even weeks, at a time. The landscapes, the forest, the wild flowers may be beautiful, but the going is very difficult, even if Livingstone is able to make light of some of the dangers. On 12th January 1867 he notes in his journal:

> Sitting down this morning near a tree my head was just one yard off

a good sized cobra, coiled up in the sprouts of its roots, but it was benumbed with cold; a very pretty little puff adder lay in the path, also benumbed; it is seldom that any harm is done by these reptiles here.

Not long after leaving the village, the first serious accident of the expedition occurred. While negotiating a slippery ravine, the porter carrying Livingstone's instruments lost his footing and fell, twice, dropping the case to the ground. One of the chronometers was damaged, with the result that from this point onwards, Livingstone's observations gave longitudes which were wrong by twenty miles eastwards. As the chronometer did not actually stop working, Livingstone did not realise that it was faulty. If he had suspected he could have checked it by returning to where he had made his last readings but, unfortunately, the occasion did not arise.

Once off the watershed, the route to Lubemba lay through mile after mile of forest, of marsh and swamp interlaced with streams and small powerful rivers. Nine days after the accident to the instruments, as the party was struggling waist deep through a swamp at the head of a small lake, Livingstone's little dog disappeared, drowned or taken by a crocodile. Livingstone was greatly upset, the dog had been a souvenir of happier times. He tried to commemorate the lost pet by naming the lake 'Chitane's Water', but the name did not survive. Nor did another, 'Lake Young', given in memory of a later colonial official Robert Young – its appellation today is the original Bemba 'Shiwa Ngandu' (Lake of the Crocodiles). A few days later a real disaster occurred: the two Yao freed slaves taken on in the Luangwa valley defected. Why they should do so at this stage is not clear, perhaps they were worried to be approaching Lubemba, a slave kingdom, perhaps like the Comorans they saw no prospects ahead. However, they took with them clothing, plates, dishes, two guns and powder, and most ominously of all, Livingstone's medicine chest – a gift from Apothecaries' Hall, Glasgow, fully stocked – and with it all the expedition's quinine and other remedies. Livingstone's men went in pursuit of the runaways, but in the thick forest, with footprints obliterated by the rain, it was a fruitless chase. Livingstone told James Young on 1st February 1867:

> This loss with all our medicines fell on my heart like a sentence of death by fever as was the case with poor bishop Mackenzie – but I shall try native medicines and trust in Him who has led me hitherto to help me still.

Livingstone had no intention of turning back, and a week after the defection, a week of little food and much effort getting through the swamps, sometimes up to the neck in water, the party crossed the

Chambeshi. Three days later they arrived at the Bemba ruler's triple-stockaded town on the upland overlooking the wide valley. Chitimukulu Chitapankwa was friendly and welcomed Livingstone with the gift of a fine slaughter ox. As he told Sedgwick on 1st February 1867: 'We have got to a land of plenty and are going to have our Christmas feast tomorrow'.

It had taken ten months to travel seven hundred miles inland as the crow flies. 'We have been very slow,' Livingstone told James Young.

25

THERE IS A RIVER...

Livingstone was the first European to come to the lands of the Bemba, and his visit coincided with the arrival at the Chitimukulu's of a small party of traders in ivory and slaves from Zanzibar. They had used a new route from the coast to the interior, starting at Bagamoyo and taking a south-westerly course to pass the high ground between the north of Lake Nyasa and the south of Lake Tanganyika. Livingstone claimed that he had heard nothing of the route while he was in Zanzibar, and it may well have been secret then as it promised a new line of Zanzibari penetration of the mainland. Besides any advantages it may have brought to Zanzibar, this new route had a considerable effect on the development of the Bemba, enabling them to capture the trade originating in Katanga and the Lunda kingdoms from the Bisa, whose routes led to Lake Nyasa and Zumbo at the Zambezi-Luangwa confluence (the present Zambian town at this point used to be called Feira – Portuguese for market). The country of the Bemba straddling the great plateau of what is today the Northern Province of Zambia covered some 20,000 square miles, with a population approaching one hundred thousand. The kingdom was a family federation of chieftainships, each with its specific territory, ruled by a member of the dominant clan, the Bena Ngandu (the people of the crocodile). The Bemba's supreme ruler was a sort of pope-king known as the Chitimukulu (the great tree), his own county (to use an anachronism) called Lubemba. The soils of Bembaland, leached by the heavy rainfall, are not generally fertile, slash-and-burn shifting agriculture the practice, and of other natural resources such as metals there were few, though the Bemba were sophisticated craftsmen in iron and copper, both imported. A speciality of theirs was the manufacture of very fine copper wire, the metal being drawn through a succession of reducing dies. The Bemba rulers depended on raiding and trade to maintain their position, and the new route gave them the edge over their rivals, enabling them to acquire the firearms which made them a formidable force. They were, like almost all rulers in central Africa, slave holders, and the raiding provided them not only with cattle and ironware, but with slaves and ivory for export. By Livingstone's time, the slave trade was becoming central to the Bemba economy, with all which followed from that.

The Zanzibaris Livingstone met at Chitapankwa's were on the point of returning to Bagamoyo and not unfriendly towards him. If he had wanted to go to the coast to replace his medicines and lift the 'sentence of death' he could have accompanied them or simply taken their route: Bagamoyo was a mere six hundred miles away, and from there he could have made for Ujiji. Instead, he decided to go straight to Ujiji from Chitapankwa's, a distance of less than four hundred miles, and there replenish his supplies with the consignment sent from Zanzibar in 1866. Whichever way he went, he would be equally under sentence, so it was better to make the shorter journey. However, he took the precaution of writing to the consul in Zanzibar to send more medicines to Ujiji, as well as trade goods and provisions such as coffee, cheese, port, sealing wax and candles. The Zanzibaris took this letter with them, together with others he had written or was writing and agreed to wait a day while he finished, on a promise that the consul would pay them for their trouble when they reached Zanzibar. The letters were delivered (and confirmed Lieutenant Young's report that Livingstone had not been killed by the Ngoni), the traders received their reward.

In the letters to James Young and Adam Sedgwick which we have been glancing at, Livingstone is worried about his children, especially the education of the boys:

> I have several times recollected a remark made by the Dean of Ely in your house that he might be able to do something to promote the education of my children. I did not think about it at the time but it has since struck me that if I had the opportunity I would tell him that I shall esteem it a great kindness if he in any way remembers them ... I have one son at Glasgow College sixteen years of age – Another at a private school in Hamilton about ten years of age ... The Dean may have nothing at his disposal but I do not value his kindly feelings the less ...

Livingstone hoped that the Dean might find university scholarships for Tom and Oswell, but nothing, apparently, came of the approach through Sedgwick. The rest of the correspondence is straightforward description of the journey and comment on the slave trade, though a paragraph to James Young reveals that Livingstone was using the journey to subject commercial propositions to practical trials:

> I am sorry I could never write to Dr Stenhouse about his invention. The sheet his agent gave me to place on the ground beneath my bed has been [as] invaluable as a tent overhead. He offered me a covering of a lighter kind and I regret exceedingly not having accepted it. The

Mackintosh sheets I have tried are not to be mentioned in comparison. This black sheet is lighter and lasts wonderfully while the India rubber sheet so glues itself together that you soon tear it to pieces in drawing the folds asunder. The first pair of shoes have lasted during a five hundred mile tramp, often over tough stony soil and in the driest hottest season. I gave away the first pair not because the uppers were broken or the soles worn out but because the inner seam had given away at the toes and the heels were gone. I ought to have had a pair *not* Stenhouse to try against the others. I am now putting a second pair to severe test – daily wet outside and then exposed to a broiling sun. If they last long at this I shall let the Dr. know. I think his invention really very valuable, and I wish you would give him this extract as a sort of acknowledgement . . .

(Dr John Stenhouse of Glasgow University worked on the application of chemistry to industry, patenting his waterproofing process in 1861: he does not seem to have used Livingstone's name to 'promote' his inventions.)

But on the subjective side the letters are signs that Livingstone was beginning to feel neglected and hard done by – a niggling complaint to Young about the deficiencies of the locks on his boxes, an aside to Sedgwick:

> . . . again and again I have been left in the lurch – one mentions some new and interesting book 'I would have sent it' he adds 'but you have so many friends I am sure some one must have sent it', so with news. They are sure some of my 'many friends' must have given all.

Livingstone was at Chitapankwa's for three weeks. The Chitimukulu was a good natured and generous man who gave Livingstone a tusk when he received him in audience and, besides the ox, supplied grain. Livingstone reciprocated with a gift of cloth and lectures on Christianity illustrated with the pictures in Smith's *Dictionary of the Bible*. He had hoped to use his new magic lantern to this end, but an acquaintance in Bombay had failed to supply the slides he had promised. Livingstone had not wanted to stay for so long, but Chitapankwa would not let him leave until a misunderstanding over the exchange of gifts had been sorted out. It had arisen as a result of poor interpretation by two of the Nassik boys, Livingstone not being familiar with Cibemba though he was learning Swahili. Towards the end of the visit Livingstone had a recurrence of the rheumatic fever that had afflicted him in Angola, but though he was not well, he resumed the journey as soon as Chitapankwa would allow, accompanied by an escort, and, taking with him the king's parting gift, an iron knife in a carved ivory scabbard. At the insistence of his men, Livingstone made a courtesy call on Mwamba, the second most important Bemba ruler then headed north, receiving a present of goats on the way, and reached the southern shore of Lake Tanganyika on 1st April. Livingstone had been ill ever since leaving Mwamba's:

> ... every step I take jars in the chest and I am very weak; I can scarcely keep up the march, though formerly I was always first.

In spite of his sickness, he descended the 2000 foot escarpment to water level, calculated latitude, longitude and altitude (though he could manage only one set of observations) and had hardly climbed back up to the plateau than he was so prostrated with fever that he could scarcely move. He was unable even to keep up his journal. There is a gap of nearly a month, until 30th April, when he describes his illness:

> After I had been a few days here I had a fit of insensibility, which shows the power of fever without medicine. I found myself floundering outside my hut, unable to get in; I tried to lift myself from my back by laying hold of two posts at the entrance, but when I got nearly upright I let them go and fell heavily on my head on a box. The boys had seen the wretched state I was in, and hung a blanket at the entrance of the hut, that no stranger might see my helplessness; some hours elapsed before I could recognize where I was.

This attack marks the first serious crack in Livingstone's constitution, his illnesses from now on become progressively worse. But it also marks the beginning of the extraordinary bond of love and loyalty which tied four of his companions – Susi, Chuma, Amoda and the Nassik boy, Gardner – to him for the rest of his life and beyond his death, even if Amoda did once desert him.

When Livingstone had recovered sufficiently, he went back down to the lake from his camp on the plateau, and wrote:

> This is the southern end of Liemba, or as it is sometimes called, Tanganyika . . . The nearly perpendicular ridge of 2000 feet extends, with breaks, all round, and there, embosomed in tree covered rocks reposes the lake peacefully, in a huge cup shaped cavity. I never saw anything so still and peaceful as it lies all the morning. About noon a gentle breeze springs up and causes the waves to assume a bluish tinge. Several rocky islands rise in the eastern end, which are inhabited by fishermen, who capture abundance of fine large fish, of which they enumerate about twenty-four species . . . After being a fortnight at this lake it still appears one of surpassing loveliness. Its peacefulness is remarkable, though at times it is said to be lashed by storms. It lies in a deep basin whose sides are nearly perpendicular, but covered well with trees; the rocks

which appear are bright red argillaceous schist; the trees at present all green; down some of these rocks come beautiful cascades, and buffaloes, elephants and antelopes wander and graze on the more level spots, while lions roar by night . . . In the morning and evening large crocodiles may be observed quietly making their way to their feeding grounds; hippopotami snort by night and early morning.

(Part of the lake described by Livingstone is now one of Zambia's National Parks, the 'surpassing loveliness' hardly altered.)

Livingstone now planned to proceed northwards along the west flank of the lake, making for Ujiji, but had scarcely begun the journey when the country he had to cross burst into war – the Tabwa chief Nsama and a party of Zanzibaris were fighting over the spoils of the slave trade. On 15th May Livingstone turned south to visit a Zanzibari encampment some fifty miles away to get information about the conflict. The leader of the caravan was a merchant named Hamis wa Mtoa (to Livingstone, Hamees Wodim Tagh); he advised Livingstone to stay where he was, as they were on the fringes of a nasty little war in which the chief actor on the Zanzibari side was a well armed caravan of seven hundred people led by Tippu Tib, the most ambitious, persistent (and successful) Zanzibar imperialist of the latter half of the nineteenth century. Livingstone was forced by the war to remain with Hamis for more than three months, a providential interlude for without Hamis's kindness in all things – including food and shelter – and the enforced rest it is doubtful whether Livingstone would have been able to undertake, let alone survive, the toils he would soon be submitting himself to. His stay with Hamis was the beginning of a close association with Zanzibari traders that was to stretch over four years. Hamis's hospitality restored Livingstone to a semblance of health; in the near future, other Zanzibaris would save him from certain death. If Sef Rupia on the Rovuma leg of the journey had been 'our friend in need' the men he travelled with now were veritable saviours. They treated him, except in one or two minor instances, with kindness, courtesy and respect – and without a touch of patronage. No doubt the Sultan's *firman* helped Livingstone, and he tried to place the relationship on an equal footing by promising to pay for the services he received. In July 1868 he wrote to James Young that he needed more money:

> . . . for I give the Arabs, who have been overflowing in their kindness to me, agreed return in presents. If I had good but not very expensive guns and good watches they would serve me a deal.

Livingstone could see and hear that he was in the midst of what he regarded as evil (after his first day at Hamis's he wrote: 'A slave in a slave stick burst into a loud cry last night ... a few switches from his master quieted him instantly'). Yet his acquired ability to distinguish the man from the deed made it possible to see these Zanzibaris as good men. Not long before, however, the thought of supplying them with firearms would have filled him with horror.

By the end of August, Tippu Tib had forced a settlement on Nsama, and Livingstone was able to move again. Only one misfortune had befallen him at Hamis's: in early July there had been an earthquake one night, and the chronometers had been damaged again, compounding the errors that were being caused by the first accident this time giving readings at fault by fifty miles, making Livingstone's longitudes seventy miles off true. Once again, he remained in ignorance of this. Tippu Tib was about to travel west, and Livingstone decided to join him in the hope of reaching Lake Mweru, rather than go north to Lake Tanganyika and Ujiji on his own. On the way west, the party visited the now quiescent Nsama. He appears to have started the fighting by ambushing and stealing from caravans such as Hamis's, and Livingstone seems, in his reference to the chief as 'the Napoleon of these countries', to confirm this. While at Nsama's, Livingstone heard good news from travellers from the north that his goods had arrived at Ujiji.

On 8th November the caravan reached the north of Lake Mweru, and Livingstone learned that a large river, the Lualaba, flowed out of it towards the equator. He deduced, correctly, that he had identified an important watercourse, beginning with the Chambeshi on the central watershed, flowing through Lake Bangweulu to form the Luapula, and thence Lake Mweru and the Lualaba. The thought of the Luapula 'in front' had stirred his heart on the Muchinga watershed. Now a much more elaborate 'line of drainage' began to etch itself into his mind. Livingstone set himself to find out more, parted company with Tippu Tib, who was going on to Katanga, headed for the capital of Mwata Kazembe, king of the eastern Lunda, in the Luapula valley, south of Lake Mweru.

In visiting Kazembe's territory, Livingstone knew that he was not breaking new ground, since the Portuguese had been there before him, attempting to open a transcontinental route from Tete and Zumbo to Kasanji and Luanda. The Portuguese failed despite the encouragement given them by Kazembe. Meanwhile, co-incidentally, Kazembe's wealth and power had been declining as the Bemba took control of trade with Zanzibar. The King gave Livingstone a public welcome, and once the two men had overcome their mutual reservations – Kazembe's suspicion, Livingstone's distaste at the king's show of authority in the form of his executioner and his mutilator standing on either side of the throne – Livingstone and his party were given housing and food. In 1867 the king was Muonga 'Sunkutu', Mwata Kazembe VIII, who had usurped the throne in 1862 and thrown the country into a prolonged spell of inter-tribal warfare, in which the Zanzibaris joined when it was to their advantage, eventually helping to restore the rightful king. Kazembe VIII ruled by terror, Livingstone did not arrive at a happy time.

Livingstone stayed at Kazembe's for more than three weeks, and apart from long conversations with the Mwata about the river systems, made friends with a further two Zanzibaris, residents in the town, named Mohamed bin Saleh and Mohamed bin Gharib (Livingstone called him Bogharib). The former had lived at Kazembe's for twenty-five years, a prisoner he said, and Livingstone persuaded the king to release him. Livingstone's search for geographical information did not prevent him from spending a good deal of time with a centenarian named Perembe investigating the history of the kingdom – an offshoot of the Lunda empire of Mwata Yamvo further west. But his main interest lay in the geographical venture, he had decided to devote himself fully to the RGS commission, though on his own terms. As if to confirm his resolution, he now wrote for Lord Clarendon a seventeen page report on the topography, geology and resources of the lands between Lake Nyasa and Lake Mweru. The 'geographical task' may have become an end in itself, but Livingstone was in no position to carry it out until he had replenished his stores, which entailed going to Ujiji. As the newly freed Mohamed bin Saleh was heading there, Livingstone decided to go with him.

By mid-December, when they left Kazembe, travelling conditions had deteriorated with the rains and it took three months to make the distance to the north of Lake Mweru which in the dry season had taken three weeks. The plains and shallow basins of the plateau had become quagmires aptly described by the local name for a vast stretch of land they passed through: Mweru Wantipa, Lake of Mud. Once they reached the north-east corner of Lake Mweru, Bin Saleh decided to spend some time with his son, who lived there. Livingstone pressed on to Pweto, arriving in mid-March at the point where the Lualaba pours out of Mweru in a mighty stream, and where, he discovered, the Zanzibari Said bin Habib whom he had met fifteen years before at Linyanti had, after crossing the continent in both directions, settled down in what Livingstone could only call 'a very pretty spot among the mountains.' He gave Webb's name to the Lualaba, then returned to Bin Saleh, hoping to proceed to Ujiji. But Bin Saleh was unwilling to move until travelling conditions had improved, and that would not be for several months, depending on how long the rainy season persisted.

Livingstone with his timetable mind was often infuriated by the slow pace of Zanzibari travel, the need to stop to trade, the need to consult the Koran or wait for the correct phase of the moon. He did not know it but the traders he gave his letters to at Chitapankwa's took twelve months to cover the six hundred miles to Bagamoyo but Bin Saleh was quite right to wait. Livingstone had a sort of instinctive urge to keep moving and, despite the pleas and warnings of Bin Saleh, keep moving he did. He decided to go, not on to Ujiji, but back south to Kazembe and then to Bangweulu, back through the stinking marshes and the leech-infested swamps. When Livingstone announced this decision to his men on 20th April, they went on strike. Always on the alert for an ulterior motive, he accused Bin Saleh of trying to lure them away from him, but it is more than likely that, if he did advise Livingstone's companions not to go, it was to save him from his own foolhardiness. Besides, there had been signs of indiscipline before among the Nassik boys – one, Baraka, had deserted, some of the others had begun stealing from Livingstone to pay the Zanzibaris for sexual access to their female slaves. Livingstone, however, persuaded six of the men to return to work and set off. Amoda defected the next day, but Livingstone continued, with Susi, Chuma, Gardner and two other Nassik boys, Abraham and Simon. As it happened the going, though sticky at times, was not as bad as might have been expected and the party reached Kazembe in three weeks.

The Mwata was cordial, provided food, gave Livingstone a laissez-passer through his dominions along the Luapula and undertook to provide guides. Livingstone, to his annoyance, was kept waiting for a month but cemented his friendship with Mohamed Bogharib, with whom he shared meals. Having now spent a year with the Zanzibaris, Livingstone was able to speak Swahili fluently. Bogharib was also going south and on 11th June – with Kazembe's commendations and, at last, the guides – they set off and stayed together for some weeks. Bangweulu is little more than a hundred miles from Kazembe's, but there were delays on the way – difficulty getting new guides, warnings to beware Ngoni raiding parties, rumblings of the impending civil war, some bad, swampy ground – and it was not until 18th July that Livingstone reached the north-western shoulder of the lake, near the present town of Samfya at 28°33′ east longitude. Because of the faults in the chronometers, however, he thought he was one degree, about seventy miles, further to the west – an unavoidable but (as events five years later would show) dire misapprehension.

Livingstone's Bangweulu expedition (for that is what his journeyings had been since he joined the Zanzibaris) and his own conclusions about the connection between the Chambeshi and the Lualaba were his greatest, if not his only, contributions to geographical knowledge. But by the time he made them, at the age of fifty-five, his past sufferings in body and spirit were beginning to take their toll. In body, his exertions and fevers had left him debilitated. His upper front teeth had now come out, forced from their sockets by gnawing at cobs of maize and no doubt, too, because of general deficiencies in his diet. He made a joke of it saying his mouth looked like that of a hippo, but he must have presented an unusual sight as he passed, with his lined face, wild hair and emaciated form. As for his spirit. . . Approaching Lake Bangweulu, with paper borrowed from Bogharib, he used one of the many delays to write a batch of letters to friends and a despatch to Lord Clarendon. The latter is a carefully worded explanation of the climate of the watershed region with particular attention paid to the seasonality of the rainfall, relating that to the annual flooding of the Zambezi and the Nile. There is also an account of the vegetation in which he explains the phenomenon of the 'dambos', or as he calls them, 'sponges':

> The places where the sponges are met with are slightly depressed valleys without trees or bushes, in a forest country where the grass being only a foot or fifteen inches high, and thickly planted, often looks like a beautiful glade in a gentleman's garden in England. They are from a quarter of a mile to a mile broad, and from two to ten or more miles long. The water of the heavy rains soaks into the level forest lands; one never sees runnels leading off it, unless occasionally a footpath is turned to this use. The water descending about eight feet, comes to a stratum of fine white sand, which at its bottom cakes so as to hold the water from sinking further.

Livingstone checked the depth of the seepage by examining the ditches dug for defence around villages; the economy with which he explains the formation of the 'dambos' could not be bettered. He ends the passage with the laconic words, 'These sponges are a serious matter in travelling.'

Livingstone now believed that the central watershed was 'undoubtedly the primary or ultimate sources of the Zambezi, Congo and Nile' and that his travels had brought him within reach of what would be his greatest geographical feat. Immediately after compiling his despatch to Clarendon, he wrote to W C Oswell on 8th July 1868:

> I hope I am not premature in saying that the sources of the Nile arise from 10° to 12 South [the latitude of Bangweulu] – in fact where Ptolemy placed them. The Chambeze is like the Chobe, 40 or 50 yards broad . . . it runs west into Bangweulu – leaving that lake it changes its name to Luapula – then into Lake Moero. On leaving it the name Lualaba is assumed.

Livingstone goes on to speculate about the destination of the Lualaba. One possibility, he says, is that it flows west of Lake Tanganyika and then swings north east to join Lake Albert and thence the Nile. The other possibility is that it enters Lake Tanganyika, which itself empties northwards through a river called 'Loanda' into Lake Albert and thence once again into the Nile. If either of these suppositions were correct, the sources of the Nile lay indeed at 10°–12°, and Burton, Speke and Grant would be proved wrong; and as Livingstone was genuinely the first European to link the Chambeshi with the Lualaba, he would not face the embarrassment suffered by James Bruce of Kinnaird when it was pointed out that his 'discovery' of the source of the Blue Nile in 1770 had been anticipated a century and a half earlier by the Spanish Jesuit Pedro Paez. Livingstone's theories at the time were not as untenable as they appear to be today largely because it seemed to observers unlikely that the Lualaba could be the headwaters of the Congo (or Zaire), since that river enters the Atlantic from the north-east, whereas the Lualaba lies south-west of the mouth. In fact, the river describes a vast arc stretching from Mweru, half encircling the equatorial lowlands, before debouching. Livingstone never dismissed the idea that the Lualaba might be the Congo, rather he suppressed it, though the thought that it might not be the Nile joined the legion of worries that inhabited his mind. However, from the instant he wrote this letter to Oswell he devoted all his energy to proving his theory, to solving the great mystery of the age, realising that if he did so, and survived, his fortunes would take on a new lease of life in all respects.

He now began to find the conditions attached to the £500 grant from the Royal Geographical Society more and more oppressive, both because the work they demanded was irksome and because to surrender his notes to them would deprive him of the 'scoop' which he expected to present to the world. Thus he writes to Oswell:

> I have suffered much needless annoyance by two blockheads, the busy-bodies on the council [of the RGS] writing 'instructions' for my guidance and demanding all my notes '*copies if not originals*'. Because the society pays one fourth part of my expenses, I am to sit down as a slave and copy for it the only property I shall have left. If I were to get £2000 after finishing instead of nothing after finishing the £2000 I would not be annoyed by snobs asking memoranda, though I think few English gentlemen would have done it. Speke preferred to burn all his notes and observations too to submitting them to the busybodies of the council.

Livingstone's feeling of estrangement from Britain is intensifying, the Zanzibaris have been more considerate to him than the RGS, he states his preference in his journal on 26th June 1868:

> We came to a grave in the forest; it was a little rounded mound as if the occupant sat in it in the usual native way; it was strewed over with

flour, and a number of large blue beads put on it; a little path showed that it had visitors. This is the sort of grave I should prefer: to lie in the still, still forest, and no hand ever disturb my bones. The graves at home always seemed to me miserable, especially those in the cold damp clay, and without elbow room . . .

He feels that by devoting his life to duty he has deprived himself, and in this sad vein concludes his letter to Oswell of 8th July 1868 with:

I hope you are playing with your children instead of being bothered by idiots. In looking back to Kolobeng I have but one regret and that is that I did not feel it my duty to play with my children as much as to teach the Bakwains. I worked very hard at that and was tired out at night. Now I have none to play with. So my good friend, play while you may. They will soon be no longer 'bairns'.

The children are a constant worry, particularly Tom. In a letter to James Young sent at the same time as that to Oswell, Livingstone writes:

. . . now I send a note to Sir Bartle Frere who will willingly assist Tom as he did Kirk on my petition. Tom had better be well prepared for examination. I think that some of the ministry [the government] would help him on. . . I need not say to you my friend, help Tom to get a good education – though he may have chosen another line the education is indivisible.

And Livingstone now deeply regrets that he let the opportunity at Newstead slip by, when Hayward asked if there was anything that Palmerston could do for him:

Lord Palmerston sent [a] gentleman to ask me what he could do for me . . . It never occurred to [me until] I was out here that he meant anything for myself or for my family. [I] thought only of my work in Africa in which from private notes I knew he took a warm interest . . . I was not selfish enough, and perhaps that was best.

Sentence after sentence of this letter (which was badly torn and had to be reassembled from scraps) runs with regrets, and with gall; gall against the RGS, far sharper than the words used to Oswell; gall (yet again) against Baines, 'I had to dismiss him afterwards not so much for his theft as for getting hold of the store book and forging entries'; gall against a man now seven years in his mausoleum, 'Prince Albert was our enemy and hand in glove with the Portuguese.' But even if being far from any 'beautiful glade in a gentleman's garden in England' put Livingstone in this frame of mind, even if he feared that he would never see Newstead again, he believed that all would come right, that he would get the better of his enemies, real or imagined, and Bangweulu would help him.

The Lake was (and is) by African standards a relatively small sheet of water, oval in shape, about forty miles long and twenty-five across, its longer axis lying north-east by south-west. Livingstone approached the lake from the north-west and as the adjoining land is flat would have been unable to get an accurate idea of its size except that it stretched beyond a horizon broken by low-lying islands. He hired a canoe, paying for it with his last remaining fathom of cloth, but the crew would take him no further than Mbabala Island, approximately in the middle; they would not go further in any direction because they had stolen the canoe and were afraid of being caught. From Mbabala, Livingstone was able to see the south-eastern shoreline, but could not examine it, nor could he circumnavigate the lake. He had thus to construct his picture of Bangweulu from his own limited observations, and from what he was told. The stretch of coast where he had arrived, and which he could examine on foot, is a 'normal' shoreline, terra firma meeting the water by way of sandy beaches. Livingstone assumed that the entire shoreline was like this. Answers to his enquiries as to the extent of the water led him to calculate that the lake was about fifty miles wide and a hundred and fifty long, lying oval on an east-west axis. Perhaps because of difficulties with language, he thought that this area of 7500 square miles (the size of Wales) was an open stretch of water dotted with islands whereas, in fact, most of it (Livingstone got the area right) apart from the 1000 square-mile lake itself and a few contiguous lakelets, consists almost entirely of swamp, networked with channels that can be used by canoes, though only by persons who know the terrain intimately. (Woe betide anyone who gets lost in the swamps! The Zambian civil aviation authorities forbid light aircraft to fly across them as survivors of an emergency landing would be unrescuable.) Livingstone, through no fault of his own, made two fatal errors about Bangweulu. He placed it in the wrong position on the map, and he thought its full 7500 square miles was open water.

At the end of July, after about a fortnight at the Lake, Livingstone headed back north to rejoin Bin Saleh. It was a slow journey, not because travelling conditions were bad – the dry season was well established, the weather cool – but because of the campaign being waged by Kazembe against rebellious subjects, and involving some Zanzibaris and Ngoni. It took Livingstone ten weeks to cover one hundred and fifty miles, but he made successful rendezvous with Bin Saleh, found the porters, including Amoda, who had deserted, and were now asking to be taken back. Livingstone re-hired them, forgave them, confessed that he was not without faults himself. The Zanzibaris were assembling themselves into a single enormous caravan, the better to secure themselves from attack – though on one occasion at least it was they who, to Livingstone's disgust, started the fighting. Mohamed Bogharib from Kazembe's joined the party and by December a mile-long procession of Zanzibaris, their servants and slaves carrying ivory, copper bars and provisions was heading for the south-west coast of Lake Tanganyika. At first Livingstone marched with it, but on Christmas day 1868 he fell so ill with pneumonia – the rainy season was under way and he was constantly wet – that he collapsed, too weak and in too much pain to move. His agony was made worse by an infestation of subcutaneous maggots, the larval stage of the putsi fly, which lays its eggs on damp clothing where they hatch. The grubs boring into and feeding on the flesh cause acute pain. One day alone Livingstone extracted twenty of them from his limbs. Bogharib saved his life by having a litter made for him and, on this borne on the shoulders of slaves, being jolted over rough ground, being burned by the sun (he was too weak to hold a shade over his face) he lay for ten weeks until the canoe port on Tanganyika was reached. On 14th March, after being paddled along and then across the lake, he arrived at Ujiji.

The Zanzibaris found him somewhere to stay. His goods had come up from Zanzibar, as he had been told, but the consignment had been plundered. Sixty-two of eighty pieces of cloth (each of twenty-four yards) had been stolen, there was no mail; and the medicines, wine and cheese had been left, he heard, at Unyanyembe, two hundred miles to the east. Livingstone was not only desperately ill, and grievously disappointed, but he was also virtually penniless with no trade goods except the remains of the cloth. Even the buffaloes ordered from Stearns in Bombay to replace those that had succumbed in Zanzibar had died.

But in front lay the Nile.

26

. . . THE STREAMS WHEREOF SHALL MAKE GLAD THE CITY OF GOD

Livingstone spent four months in Ujiji. For the first fortnight he was too ill to move around, but on 28th March he reported in his journal that he had walked half a mile. Although he had no medicines he was able to buy food with the remains of his cloth; he could get milk, and a friend who worked for the P & O Company had sent him a parcel of tea. It was not long before he felt well enough to continue his 'work'. A less determined man would have repaired to Zanzibar, even if temporarily, but Livingstone would have none of that. Ujiji was to be his base. He wrote to the governor of Unyanyembe about his missing goods, and rented one of the square Zanzibari-Arab houses that were a feature of Ujiji, standing in geometric contrast to the round huts of the African inhabitants. Livingstone did not like Ujiji nor its Zanzibari residents. He wrote to Kirk on 30th May 1869 and told him:

> The people here are like the Kilwa traders, haters of the English. [The] Zanzibar men whom I met between this and Nyassa were gentlemen and traded with honour. Here, as in the haunts of the Kilwa hordes, slaving is a series of forays . . .

At the time, Ujiji, on the north-east coast of Lake Tanganyika, was the most westerly of the Zanzibari trading towns, at the head of the seven hundred mile route from the coast. Two hundred miles to the east lay Unyanyembe (today known as Tabora), the most important Zanzibari town in the interior, a hub from which trade lanes radiated north to Lake Victoria, north-west towards Uganda, south-west to Bembaland and Kazembe's, west to Lake Tanganyika. In Livingstone's time a great expansion of trade was taking place through Ujiji as the Zanzibaris penetrated the rich ivory and slaving grounds west of the lake, extending their commercial empire into what is now Zaire. Ujiji was a frontier town, experiencing the equivalent of a gold rush, for it seemed that Zaire ivory was available in enormous quantities and at ridiculously low prices – particularly important factors when supplies from the Kazembe-Katanga region were drying up as a result of overkill.

Livingstone's sense of isolation from the outside world was relieved somewhat when a parcel arrived from Unyanyembe containing recent sets of his two favourite magazines, *Punch* and the *Saturday Review*, but there was still no mail and he was worried that his own letters would not reach Zanzibar. The Ujijians, he told Kirk, 'dread exposure by my letters. No one will take charge of them.' Livingstone reports that during his 'slow recovery' he wrote about forty letters very few of which reached their destinations. But among those that did were those to Kirk himself, and to the Sultan who was asked to provide an escort for Livingstone's next consignment from the coast and told of the kindness of Zanzibaris such as Bogharib and Bin Saleh. Livingstone told Kirk that he needed 'fifteen good boatmen to act as carriers if required' as well as trade goods – calico and beads – and new shoes (Dr Stenhouse's had presumably worn out at last).

Lack of good shoes were to cause Livingstone serious problems on the forthcoming stage of his travels, which he mentioned to Kirk in that same letter of May 1869 as merely connecting 'the sources I have discovered' with the Nile, and going 'down the eastern line of drainage' to Lake Albert.

> The western and central lines of drainage converge into an unvisited lake west or S.W. of Ujiji. The outflow of this, whether to Congo or Nile, I have to ascertain.

When he was well enough to resume his researches, Livingstone made a careful study of the movement of the surface water of Lake Tanganyika, and when he established that beds of algae moved consistently towards the north he concluded that a current flowed in that direction. This observation strengthened his belief that Tanganyika was a river-lake, flowing into Albert and so into the Nile – such was his 'eastern line of drainage'. Zanzibaris he discussed the matter with told him too (on no better evidence than hearsay) that a river flowed north out of the lake. When Livingstone felt fit to travel, he wanted to inspect this outlet – about a hundred miles north of Ujiji – but, as he told Kirk, he could get 'no assistance in hiring carriers'. He no doubt felt that the Ujijians were conspiring to thwart him, but in fact it was more likely that porters (of whom there was a shortage) preferred the pickings of the ivory trade to promises of pay from an obviously semi-destitute Livingstone. He was compelled to put this planned journey aside for the future, and direct his attention to the Lualaba and the 'western line of drainage'. Fortunately, Bogharib was going in that direction, to the territory called Manyema in the Lualaba basin; he was willing to have Livingstone join him and would keep him supplied. Livingstone's own carriers and supplies would have arrived at Ujiji from Zanzibar by the time they returned in six months or so. Bogharib went ahead to the west side of the lake and Livingstone and his party, after three days in hired canoes, met up with him at Kasanga on 15th July 1869. Livingstone deliberately left his journal behind but took writing materials and his instruments, including the chronometers which had stopped while he was prostrate with pneumonia, and had been reset at Ujiji, the longitude of which he knew from Burton's observations. He took also the Bible, but no medicines for he had none to take. He retained the house he had rented, leaving Amoda in charge. Among the curiosities of his stay at Ujiji is a vocabulary of the Masai language, evidence either of his insatiable curiosity or of his intention, when he had finished his work, to return from Lake Albert to the coast across the highlands that skirt Mt Kenya and Mt Kilimanjaro, east of Lake Victoria, where at the time the Masai were the power.

The crossing of Lake Tanganyika was made some eighty miles south of Ujiji, at the narrowest point, landfall on the west coast being a few miles north of the Lukuga river. This river is the sole outlet from the lake, flowing west to join the Lualaba. Livingstone missed it, heard not even a rumour about it from Bogharib or local people, was deprived by circumstances of an important 'discovery', even if it would have made little difference to his course of action. The only investigation of the lake Livingstone made on this crossing was to try to measure its depth, playing out a sounding line from his canoe. The line broke at 1956 feet; although this is less than half of the actual depth of over 4750 feet, it would be enough to alert geologists to an unusual phenomenon – Tanganyika is in fact the second deepest lake in the world, after Baikal in Siberia.

Early in August the journey on foot to Manyema began. Livingstone enjoyed the well prepared meals that Bogharib shared with him, but he was not really well:

> Any ascent though gentle makes me blow since the attack of pneumonia. If it is inclined to an angle of 45°, 100 to 150 yards make me stop to pant in distress.

This remark in his journal on 10th August 1869, illustrates what a poor state of health he was in: the journey was broken by rests, sometimes to hunt for the pot, sometimes, it would seem, out of consideration for Livingstone, who confessed that he was 'still weak'. The weather was hot and fatiguing – the route lay only a few degrees south of the equator and after leaving the mountains on the west of Tanganyika, descended to the Lualaba basin, a bare 2000 feet above sea level. After a march of one hundred and fifty miles the caravan arrived at Bambarre (now Kabambaré) on 21st September, six weeks of travel, and about half way to the Lualaba.

At Bambarre, Bogharib went off on his own in search of ivory, leaving Livingstone to make his way with Susi, Chuma, Gardner and the Nassik boys to the river. Bogharib was only one of many Zanzibaris who had moved suddenly into Manyema, using Bambarre as a staging point for their forays. The area was, as Livingstone remarked, very beautiful, the land fertile, and the people able to raise the variety of crops and livestock to make them all but self-sufficient. Self-sufficiency meant that the people were willing to barter their ivory only for commodities of special value. Even with items as apparently exchangeable as slaves they were fussy, as Livingstone noted in his journal on 11th November 1869:

> The Manyuema . . . would rather let the ivory lie unused and rot than invest in male slaves, who are generally criminals, at least in Lunda.

Although the ivory was, by world market standards, cheap, this Manyema fastidiousness enraged the Zanzibaris (to see a hoard of ivory that people would not sell!) and the result was inevitable. The traders with their armed gangs resorted to intimidation, violence, murder, hut burning, pillage, abductions into slavery. Manyema was ruled by small rival chieftaincies, united opposition to the Zanzibaris was impossible, the situation chaotic. Livingstone once again found himself in a position where circumstances were beyond his control, this time in the no-man's-land between traditional African life and the commercial and industrial civilisation to which he, like the Zanzibaris, belonged.

Once Bogharib had left, Livingstone started to negotiate with other traders for a passage to the Lualaba, offering £270 (on credit) to whomsoever would take him there, but no one was prepared to forsake the ivory fields, even temporarily. Livingstone was stuck for over five weeks before deciding to make his own way west. The frustrating interlude at Bambarre at least gave him time to rest, time to write. His eye for the details of local life was as sharp as ever:

> When the white ants cast off their colony of winged emigrants a canopy is erected like an umbrella over the anthill. As soon as the ants fly against the roof they tumble down in a shower and their wings are instantly detached from their bodies. They are then helpless and are swept up in baskets to be fried, when they make a very palatable food . . .

The fluent prose is deceptive in this journal entry of 18th October, 1869 for on the Manyema expedition Livingstone kept only diary notes, which he wrote up when he returned to Ujiji. His notes had necessarily to be brief, but he was expansive in long letters to his brother John, to Tom and Agnes, and to W C Oswell. He also started letters to Maclear and Sir Bartle Frere which he finished later.

The letter to Oswell opens with a description of Livingstone's theories, which we have seen, about the Nile sources, but takes the matter further by suggesting that confirmation of his ideas is to be found in the pages of Herodotus and Ptolemy – a line of thought to be looked at more closely later. He is confident of being right, but feels he must discredit and run down his rivals; just as he had done (in a letter to Oswell) when he 'discovered' Lake Shirwa; just as James Bruce had done in the case of Jeronimo Lobo, the second Jesuit (after Paez) to examine the source of the Blue Nile.

Thus Livingstone writes to Oswell in October:

> I feel at a loss how to speak about poor Speke's discoveries. If I say nothing about them I shall give offence – if I say that Ptolemy in his small lake 'Coloe' gives a more correct view of Victoria Nyanza than Speke and Grant offence will still more be taken – He affords the best example I know of the eager pursuit of a foregone conclusion . . .

Livingstone's personal resentments rise to the surface:

> I feel a little sorry for Speke's friends, but my regret is lessened by remembering that he went out of his way at a geographical meeting [to say] that the Portuguese crossed the continent before I did and that Dr Roscher discovered the north end of Nyassa before we did the south . . . The meeting had not this subject under discussion but in this and other cases he thought that he was imitating the dashing style of Burton, but for whose evil teaching Speke would have exhibited the qualities of an English yeoman. Grant needs no pity. The sources led to his getting a good wife – £2000 a year, and a London house with her, though he never saw them [the sources].

Livingstone now, to show how much more thorough he is than Speke and Grant, adds another dimension to his itinerary:

> I have to go down and see where the headwaters join – then finish up by going round outside or south of all the sources . . . I don't like to leave my work so that another may cut me out and say he has found sources south of mine. . . I am dreaming of finding the lost city of Meroe, at the confluence of the two branches . . . [Such a feat would put him on a par with Sir Austin Layard, discoverer of the lost city of Nineveh.] [But the] reality reveals that I have lost nearly all my teeth – that is what the sources have done for me.

After several post-scripts, the sixteen hundred word missive ends, exhausted, 'I long sorely to retire.'

In contrast, much of the letter to Tom is taken up with a lecture on what today would be called 'race relations', observations on news and comment which Livingstone presumably found in the pile of the *Saturday Review* and *Punch* he had received at Ujiji. He gives a vigorous defence of the emancipation of slaves in the United States: the Yankees, he declares, have a 'gigantic task laid at their doors', to redress the wrongs that slavery had imposed on four million people, and 'I earnestly hope that the Northerners may not be found wanting in their portion of the superhuman work'.

Livingstone is worried about Tom's health, and is also concerned to prevent him from embracing the racialism which Governor Eyre's Morant Bay massacre and the ensuing controversy – still blazing furiously – had brought to the fore in Britain:

> England is in the rear. Frightened in early years by their mothers with 'Bogie Blackman' they were terrified out of their wits by a riot, and the sensation writers, who act the part of the 'dreadful boys' who frighten aunts, yelled out that emancipation was a mistake. 'The Jamaica negroes were as savage as when they left Africa.' They might have put it much stronger by saying, as the rabble that attended Tom Sayers's funeral, or that collects at every execution at Newgate.

Part of this letter of 24th September 1869 deals with a painful personal matter, recalled after more than twenty-five years, the affair of Catherine Ridley, which left Livingstone deeply wounded and gave him the first powerful hint of the estrangement he was now feeling in the deep interior of Africa. Catherine, Livingstone told Tom, had not turned him down – he had rejected her because she would not have made a good missionary wife.

The letter to Agnes in September 1869 contains large praise for her mother, Mary, and goes on to consider the 'role of women'. Livingstone had been impressed by the exploits of the Dutch explorer Alexandrine Tinné, who had travelled by boat with her aunt (who died of fever) up the Nile from Egypt to find its source, and he mocks the idea that it is only men who can – to use a modern expression – 'achieve'. After all, Livingstone remarks, 'the death-knell of American slavery was rung by a woman's hand.'

Livingstone is calling on his daughter to stand up for herself, not to be subservient to men, not to be pushed around – as her mother had been, both by himself (in the accepted Victorian way) and by the directors of the London Missionary Society. It is difficult not to feel that at this stage Livingstone had come to see the low status of women in

Britain as an aspect of exploitation. Was not Grant exploiting his wife by becoming the owner of her property? With this proto-feminism, with the unambiguous stand on the Governor Eyre issue, Livingstone places himself even more on the margin of the social milieu which he feels has been rejecting him.

On 1st November, after kicking his heels at Bambarre for a month and a half, Livingstone set out with his small band of companions for the Lualaba. He made for the Luamo, one of its tributaries, but local people were suspicious, if not actually hostile – was he not the friend of the Zanzibari invaders? Although he came within a few miles of his goal he could not get a canoe and had to turn back. Besides frustration, Livingstone was suffering from continual bouts of what he called 'choleraic dysentry', bleeding from the bowels. On 19th November he was in Bambarre again, laid up with illness, without medicines. Fortunately Bogharib was there too, back from his foray, and he gave Livingstone opium to relieve the intestinal pain – without effect, Livingstone says, which suggests he took large doses; Bogharib also presented a goat for Christmas.

On 26th December, although he was feverish, Livingstone believed he was once more fit to travel and set out again for the Lualaba, this time in a north-westerly direction, without regard for the wet season in full spate. During this journey, Livingstone was unremittingly ill, his journal reads like the medical report on a patient approaching death in a hospital for tropical diseases – dysentry, anal bleeding, and then ulcers on his poorly shod feet. Villagers refused to act as guides, food was often hard to get. Livingstone was unsure where the Lualaba lay, believed, wrongly, that it swung east to join the Nile. When he was finally given information that killed this idea, he changed direction and headed south-west to a camp called Mamohela, seat of a Zanzibari overlord named Katomba. The going was terrible, rain pouring from the sky, the ground a morass. But in the midst of his selfimposed torture, Livingstone was able to find relief in amazement at natural wonders, just as if he were drawing strength from the arms of the Saviour he trusted was bearing him forward, God and Creation becoming one:

> Indeed if you would know spiritual things, it is to know how the spirit or power of wisdom and life, causing motion or growth, dwells within and governs both the several bodies of the stars and planets in the heavens above; and the several bodies of the earth below, as grass, plants, fishes, beasts, birds and mankind.

This expression of what we can recognise as Livingstone's own anti-hierarchical religious standpoint was given by Gerrard Winstanley, the seventeenth century radical protestant 'independent', deemed a heretic by the established church. 'To know the secrets of nature,' he had said, 'is to know the works of God.' Amidst the mire of a day of misery, Livingstone came across just such a 'secret of nature':

> Caught in drenching rain which made me fain to sit, exhausted as I was, under an umbrella for an hour trying to keep the trunk dry. As I sat in the rain a little tree frog, about half an inch long leaped on to a grassy leaf, and began a tune as loud as many birds, and very sweet: it was surprising to hear so much music out of so small a musician.

His spirit lifted by this little miracle, Livingstone is able to press on:

> I drank a little water as I was faint – in the paths it is now calf deep. I crossed a hundred yards of slush waist deep in mid-channel, and full of holes made by elephants' feet, the path hedged in by reedy grass, often intertwined and very trippy.

And then the blessing of Charity falls upon him when villagers, who had every reason to fear him, take him in, ease his pain, and give him food:

> I stripped off my clothes on reaching my hut in a village, and a fire during the night nearly dried them. At the same time I rubbed my legs with palm oil, and in the morning had a delicious breakfast of sour goat's milk and porridge.

Even when we know that these passages (entered as of 3rd February 1870) were put into final form later at Ujiji, they illustrate a remarkable metaphor of a religious conviction that enfolds God, man, and nature in a single trinity. Small wonder then that Livingstone cared so little about the differences between Christian persuasions. For him, the Trinity was destiny, which perhaps had decreed Christians to differ, decreed that he should continue his work with the help of men engaged in evil.

A few days after the tree frog, Livingstone arrived at Mamohela and was welcomed by the Zanzibaris. Here, apart from one more unsuccessful attempt to reach the Lualaba, he sat out the rainy season. All but one of the Nassik boys – Gardner – had by now had enough, deserted and gone to work for traders, who were always in need of porters. On 22nd July, Livingstone limped back into Bambarre, his only companions Susi, Chuma and Gardner. The sores on Livingstone's feet having turned into tropical ulcers, he went into his hut not to emerge for three months. The tropical ulcer from which, Livingstone says, many slaves in Manyema died (as had a good number of Mackenzie's charges at Magomero) starts with a sore on the skin which does not spread laterally but, as Livingstone says, eats through everything:

> ... muscle, tendon and bone, and often lame permanently if they do not kill ... If the foot were put on the ground a discharge of bloody ichor flowed, and the same discharge happened every night with considerable pain that prevented sleep; the wailing of slaves tormented with these sores is one of the night sounds of a slave camp ...

To the agony of the ulcers, acutely described in that journal entry of 17th August 1870, were added periodic bouts of fever and the pain of haemorrhoids. But Livingstone had reduced attacks of dysentry by boiling his drinking water, a piece of hygiene learned from the Zanzibaris. Then there was the helplessness of being bedridden – even the chronometers were allowed to run down. Livingstone may have been unable to move physically but he could wander mentally, and whether or not he was taking opium, its wanderings described a vision which was to sustain him for the rest of his life. He had always needed a divine purpose, and now a dream infused him, replacing the castles in the air he had constructed with Christianity, commerce and civilisation as foundations.

From his earliest days in Africa Livingstone had believed there to be a continuity between Egypt and the people of the south of the continent. If he could prove that the Nile rose on the central watershed he would become so famous that no one would be able to stop him from putting an end to slavery. Moses had led God's chosen people out of slavery beside the Nile in Egypt. Livingstone, likewise, would lead out of slavery the people of the Nile of inner Africa. We have seen the outline of Livingstone's theory about the Nile sources, but now he becomes quite specific. Having dismissed Speke and Grant – and Burton – now, at Bambarre, he bases the solution to the 'mystery' on his own observations, on information obtained from 'natives and intelligent Arabs', on the *Histories* of Herodotus, on Ptolemy's *Geography* and on quasi-biblical traditions recorded in Josephus. Put briefly, Livingstone now believed that the river, as Herodotus says, rose from fountains lying between two conical peaks called Crophi and Mophi (Livingstone changed the cones into ridges) and that half the waters flowed north to Egypt and half south to 'Inner Ethiopia [inner Africa]'. The 'natives and intelligent Arabs' had told Livingstone, correctly, that two affluents of the Lualaba, and the Zambezi and Kafue, all rose within a short distance of each other – half flowing north, half south. Ptolemy asserted that the Nile rises in two sources in the Mountains of the Moon (which Livingstone transforms into the central watershed), the western source flowing through a Lake Coloe before joining the eastern. Livingstone believed that the affluents of the Lualaba flowed into a lake which he named Lake Lincoln, and that this was Coloe (by a geographical coincidence, the Lualaba system resembles Ptolemy's outline, the lake in question being Upemba in Katanga). From 'Lincoln', this proto-Nile continues north to join the Lualaba, the confluence being the site in Ptolemy's book, of Meroe, from where the river, now the true Nile, flows on to Egypt.

'One of my waking dreams,' Livingstone wrote, expanding on what he had said to Oswell,

> is that the legendary tales about Moses coming up into Inner Ethiopia with Merr his foster-mother, and founding a city which he called in her honour 'Meroe' may have a substratum of fact.

Livingstone believed that if he found the remains of Meroe, he would be confirming the accuracy of the 'Sacred Oracles' as he called them, meaning presumably the Bible and the traditions attached to biblical figures such as Moses. Livingstone's explorations would acquire further divine purpose, he would justify his own ways to God and man. At this time he had constantly in mind the 46th Psalm, the fourth verse of which declares: 'There is a river, the streams whereof shall make glad the city of God'.

This was his river, its streams his 'lines of drainage': when he had finished his work, the City of God, the faith and moral order it represented, would not only be made glad, it would be made stronger against attack by its enemies.

A month after he had taken to his bed, the Zanzibaris gave Livingstone powdered malachite to use as treatment for the ulcers, and shortly after he had begun to apply it in a solution which he painted on with a feather, the sores started slowly to heal. On 26th September he records that the ulcers were clearing up, on 10th October he emerged from the hut, and quoted Ecclesiastes 4.i:

> So I returned, and considered all the oppressions that are done under the sun: and behold the tears of such as were oppressed and they had no comforter.

He was thinking of the slave camps around him, and of Exodus. Zanzibari slaving had developed a rapacity equal only to that for ivory. 'Gentlemanly' trading had been replaced by raiding, enslavement through force of arms. The reason for the change, in direct defiance of the Sultan's code of conduct, was the 1869 cholera epidemic in Zanzibar, when 67,000, most of them slaves, perished. Replacements were needed urgently.

And Livingstone's own 'oppressions' were as burdensome as ever: he had sent W C Oswell a sketch of the 'sources' and on 24th November 1870 he wrote telling him not to pass it around as it is sure to be plagiarised, alleging that that was what had happened with a sketch of Lake Nyasa a copy of which the 'small geographers' of the RGS had 'emblazoned on the walls' and described as 'Dr Kirk's sketch of Nyassa'. He then added:

> It would be unwise in me therefore to let my feelings of affection for you to prevail so far as to place any other observations in your power.

Is he losing trust in Oswell too? Even if not, Kirk is for the first time coming into Livingstone's line of fire, a new grudge surfacing – and still he cannot forget the old ones:

> I sent a sketch of Victoria Falls [to the RGS] and when I wanted it, applied to Mr Bates [the Secretary] and was answered not by him but by old Mrs Baines!!! I had actually to tell the old hag that I wanted none of her son's property but my own.

Much of the letter is in this tone, much of it suppressed in a version published in the biography of W C Oswell written by his son.

Livingstone was desperate to move on to the Lualaba, but could not travel with only three companions. By the end of 1870 he had been stuck at Bambarre for two-thirds of a year and had read the Bible from Genesis to Revelations four times. He believed that if he had had the men he would have been able to finish his work in a few months. Then, at the end of January 1871, as if in answer to a prayer, part of the caravan Kirk had despatched in response to Livingstone's letter from Ujiji nearly two years previously, arrived at Bambarre. Seven men, a letter from Kirk, tea, coffee, sugar, cloth, quinine, copies of *Proceedings of the Royal Geographical Society*.

The Manyema expedition had already taken eighteen months instead of six but now the river and its streams lay in reach, 'in front'.

27

THE IMPRESSION OF BEING IN HELL

Livingstone was enchanted with the landscapes of Manyema. In his Journal he writes of the hills and mountains, the cool clear streams, the forests and the groves of palm, the well-ordered settlements:

> The villages are very pretty, standing on slopes. The main street generally lies east and west, to allow the bright sun to stream his clear hot rays from one end to the other, and lick up quickly the moisture from the frequent showers which is not drained off by the slopes. A little verandah is often made in front of the door, and here at dawn the family gathers round a fire and while enjoying the heat needed in the cold that always accompanies the first darting of the light or sun's rays across the atmosphere, inhale the delicious air and talk over their little family affairs.

He was impressed too by all the signs of a flourishing economy, from the large fields of cassava to the exquisite iron and copperware made by the village smiths (one of the few commodities Manyema imported was copper bars from Katanga). Time and again he remarks 'Many of the Manyema women are very beautiful,' some as lovely as Mrs Webb herself. Some very kind, like the elderly lady who prepared for a sick and hungry Livingstone a platter of sweetcorn patties when he arrived in her village. But no Manenko strides splendidly across the pages. As for the men, Livingstone avers that he would rather dine with Manyema than with members of the Royal Anthropological Society.

Livingstone, heading for the Lualaba, left Bambarre on 2nd February 1871 and reached Mamohela a few days later. There he found more letters, including one from Kirk, one from Agnes, another from the Sultan, and was given the news that his consignment from Zanzibar had arrived at Ujiji. These tokens that the outside world still knew that he was alive may have cheered him, but he was nevertheless in a precarious position, principally because the carriers sent by Kirk were a difficult lot and would only do as they were told after Bogharib threatened to shoot them if they continued to refuse. Kirk, as medical officer in the middle of the Zanzibar cholera epidemic, went to considerable trouble to get any porters at all and these men seem to have been what the Portuguese would call *pretos do ganho* – slaves working on commission for their owners. They told Livingstone that Kirk had ordered them to bring him back to Zanzibar, not to proceed westwards, an understandable lie which expressed their own fears but a lie which Livingstone nursed until it grew into a monstrous libel of Kirk himself, as we shall see.

Although Livingstone had recovered from his ulcers and now had quinine he was constantly ill, if not from fevers then from dysentery and rectal bleeding. However, he had Susi, Chuma, Gardner and Kirk's porters, as well as a small flock of goats to provide him with the milk his system craved, and enough confidence in his ability to go forward to refuse to re-employ his 'Nassik' deserters even when they begged him to do so. One of them, named James, had been killed in a skirmish, his body allegedly eaten (the Manyema were purported to be cannibals though Livingstone never fully believed it, despite what Susi and Chuma said). Whatever the truth of the matter, the greatest delicacy in the Manyema cuisine was the hands and feet of a type of large ape – known locally as the soko – an aspect of near-cannibalism which corresponds to the supposed Russian penchant for the flesh of the bear. When Livingstone first came across the soko he was as horrified by its similarity to humans as Darwin had been when he discovered the structural identity in the physiognomies of snake, vampire bat and *homo sapiens*. On 24th August, 1870 he writes:

> ... the soko, if large, would do well to stand for a picture of the devil. He takes away my appetite by his disgusting bestiality of appearance. His light yellow face shows off his ugly whiskers and faint apology for a beard, the forehead villianously low ... [the Manyema] say the flesh is delicious.

But when at Mamohela Livingstone was given a baby soko as a pet he found it fascinating and loveable. In a letter to Agnes in March 1871, he gives a nice description of this so nearly human, and now endangered, species:

> She is the least mischievous of all the monkey tribe I have seen, and seems to know that in me she has a friend, and sits quietly on the mat beside me. In walking, the first thing observed is that she does not tread on the palms of her hands, but on the backs of the second line of bones of the hands; in doing this the nails do not touch the ground, nor do the knuckles; she uses the arms thus supported crutch fashion, and hitches herself along between them; occasionally one hand is put down before the other, and alternates with the feet, or she walks upright and holds up a hand to anyone to carry her. If refused, she turns her face down, and makes grimaces of the most bitter human weeping, wringing her

hands, and sometimes adding a fourth hand or foot to make the appeal more touching. Grass or leaves she draws around her to make a nest, and resents anyone meddling with her property. She is a most friendly little beast, and came up to me at once, making her chirrup of welcome, smelled my clothing, and held out her hand to be shaken. I slapped her palm without offence, though she winced. She began to untie the cord with which she was afterwards bound, with fingers and thumbs in quite a systematic way, and with being interfered with by a man looked daggers, and screaming tried to beat him back with her hands; she was afraid of his stick, and faced him putting her back to me as a friend. She holds out her hand for people to lift her up and carry her; quite a spoiled child; then bursts into a passionate cry, somewhat like that of a kite, wrings her hands quite naturally, as if in despair. She eats everything, covers herself with a mat to sleep, and makes a nest of grass or leaves, and wipes her face with a leaf.

Livingstone seems to have found, briefly, a substitute for the 'bairns' he had neglected to play with. He sent the little soko with a party of Zanzibaris to await his return to Ujiji, but no more is heard of her.

Many a prospect might please but man in his usual way was vile: Manyema was being devastated by the impact of 'civilization', the route from Bambarre to Mamohela and on to the Lualaba reeked with blood as the Zanzibaris cashed in on the slave shortage on the coast and on 25th March, 1871 Livingstone writes to Kirk of an episode

which happened about a fortnight ago close by the spot where I write. My spirits are beyond measure depressed in writing on such matters for the public and I can only give half statements for fear of letting heartless dawdlers drawl from the club sofas 'exaggeration', 'overdrawing' etc . . . The episode I mention was by [Bogharib's] people, and he being the best man of all who have come to trade in Manyema you may, if you can, imagine the conduct of the worst . . . the heads of the party sent to trade gave the Manyema near the Moene Lualaba 25 copper bracelets worth at Ujiji about 2½ dollars – this was the trap – then went down the river and sold all the rest of their copper for ivory. Coming back they demanded ivory for the 25 rings and began to shoot the men in cold blood and capture women and children . . . They continued their murdering for three days in a densely populated district and carried off an immense number of women and children.

Livingstone could do little to lessen this misery except report to the world and hope that the slave trade would be stopped. Although he told Agnes, 'I have tried to refund all that the Arabs expended on me,' he was still too dependent on the Zanzibaris to make public enemies of them. As he moved westwards, his spirits were so low he felt that even God had abandoned him: 'I doubt,' he wrote in his Journal on 24th March 1871, 'whether the Divine favour and will is on my side.' But his flights of fancy were strong enough to sustain him:

> The central Lualaba I would fain call Lake River Webb, the western Lake River Young. The Lufira and Lualaba West form a lake the native name of which 'Chibungo' must now give way to Lake Lincoln. I wish to name the fountain of the Liambai or Upper Zambezi, Palmerston fountain, and adding that of Sir Bartle Frere to the fountain of Lufira, three names of men who have done more to abolish slavery and the slave-trade than any of their contemporaries.

Thus he wrote in his Journal on 4th October, 1870. And besides the lakes, rivers and fountains, there was Meroe and the possibility of 'the great Moses having visited these parts'.

On 29th March 1871, four months after emerging from his hut at Bambarre, Livingstone reached 'Webb's Lualaba' at the market town named Nyangwe where the Zanzibaris had only recently arrived. Their leader was Dugumbe bin Habib, and to him Livingstone turned for help. At Nyangwe the river is about three thousand yards wide, the only way to cross it (which Livingstone had to do to reach the 'fountains') by canoe. But no canoe was obtainable. The Zanzibaris would not supply one, nor would the local people – they associated him with the slavers and were not prepared to straighten his path westwards. Livingstone was once again stuck. He occupied the first month of his stay building a house, hoping that in due course he would establish his credentials and the situation would change. He spent much time at the great market, fascinated by its liveliness, by the range of produce brought in for barter or sale. And his scientific work continued; he managed to reset his chronometers which had gone dead while he was ill at Bambarre, and he writes in his Journal on 11th July 1871 that he, 'bought the different species of fish brought to the market, in order to sketch eight of them and compare them with those of the Nile lower down; most are the same as in Nyassa.'

His overall sense of frustration, however, was increased by his having run out of notepaper. He wrote letters on the wrappings of parcels, on the leaves of his Bombay cheque book; he wrote his diary across the type of old magazines, on any scraps he could find, using for ink an infusion of roots that produced a red dye. A letter to W C Oswell on a cheque form measuring eleven by five and a half inches runs to over a thousand words; the script, a bare sixteenth of an inch high, lies in absolutely straight lines from edge to edge. The red of the ink has now faded but recipients of letters like these thought they had been written in blood!

When the porters sent by Kirk realised that Livingstone, when he left Nyangwe, had no intention of returning to Zanzibar but would go on westwards they became vociferously mutinous. There was even a rumour that they were plotting to kill him. Livingstone dismissed them but two days later they relented, said they would be 'willing to go anywhere', and Livingstone 'eager to finish my geographical work' re-hired them. But with no canoe he could not move.

Early in July, when he had been at Nyangwe for three months, in a final attempt to buy help, he offered Dugumbe all his goods at Ujiji (worth, he believed, £400) if he would set up a caravan to accompany him to Katanga, to the 'fountains'. Dugumbe hesitated, consulted his colleagues. But before the decision, which would probably have been negative, an event occurred which forced Livingstone into a radical change of plan. On 15th July 1871 he writes:

It was a hot sultry day, and when I went into the market I saw Adie and Manilla, and three of the men who had lately come with Dugumbe. I was surprised to see the three with their guns, and felt inclined to reprove them, as one of my men did, for bringing weapons into the market, but I attributed it to their ignorance, and, it being very hot, I walked away to go out of the market, when I saw one of the fellows haggling about a fowl, and seizing hold of it. Before I had got thirty yards out, the discharge of two guns in the middle of the crowd told me that slaughter had begun: crowds dashed off from the place, and threw down their wares in confusion, and ran. At the same time that the three opened fire on the mass of people near the upper end of the market place volleys were discharged from a party down near the creek on the panic-stricken women who dashed at the canoes. These, some fifty or more, were jammed in the creek and the men forgot their paddles in the terror that seized all. The canoes could not be got out, for the creek was too small for so many; men and women, wounded by balls, poured into them and leaped and scrambled into the water shrieking. A long line of heads in the river showed that great numbers struck out for an island a full mile off: in going towards it they had to put the left shoulder to a current of about two miles an hour; if they had struck away diagonally to the opposite bank, the current would have aided them, and, though nearly three miles off, some would have gained land: as it was, the heads above water showed the long lines of those that would inevitably perish.

Shot after shot continued to be fired on the helpless and perishing. Some of the long line of heads disappeared quietly; whilst other poor creatures threw their arms high, as if appealing to the great Father above, and sank. One canoe took in as many as it could hold, and all paddled with hands and arms; three canoes, got out in haste, picked up sinking friends, till all went down together and disappeared. One man, in a long canoe, which could have held forty or fifty, had clearly lost his head; he had been out in the stream before the massacre began, and now paddled up the river nowhere, and never looked to the drowning.

By-and-by all the heads disappeared; some had turned down stream towards the bank, and escaped. Dugumbe put people into one of the deserted vessels to save those in the water and saved twenty-one, but one woman refused to be taken on board from thinking that she was to be made a slave of; she preferred the chance of life by swimming, to the lot of a slave; the Bagenya women are expert in the water, as they are accustomed to dive for oysters, and those who went down stream may have escaped, but the Arabs themselves estimated the loss of life at between 330 and 400 souls. The shooting party near the canoes were so reckless, they killed two of their own people; and a Banyamwezi follower, who got into a deserted canoe to plunder, fell into the water, went down, then came up again, and down to rise no more.

My first impulse was to pistol the murderers, but Dugumbe protested against my getting into a blood-feud, and I was thankful afterwards that I took his advice . . .

After the terrible affair in the water, the party of Tagamoio, who was the chief perpetrator, continued to fire on the people there and fire their villages. As I write I hear the loud wails on the left bank over those who are there slain, ignorant of their many friends who are now in the depths of the Lualaba. Oh, let Thy kingdom come! No one will ever know the exact loss on this bright sultry summer morning. It gave me the impression of being in Hell.

The bloodshed convinced Livingstone that his position vìs á vìs the Zanzibaris had become too ambivalent to be sustained any longer. While the shooting was still going on he sent his consular Union Jack into the villages to signal a cease-fire, and was able to save thirty or so persons. Livingstone persuaded Dugumbe to free other captives, but the instigators of the massacre went unpunished and tried to blame it on 'the people of the English'. Leaders such as Bogharib and Dugumbe might be 'gentlemen', prepared to abide by the Sultan's slave-trade decree, but their subordinates had no such scruples and were uncontrollable. In the last resort the Zanzibaris would stick together. Livingstone had no doubt that Dugumbe would profit from the massacre by taking captives to Zanzibar for sale, and pleaded with Kirk to put pressure on the Sultan to have the Manyema prisoners released when they were brought through the Zanzibar customs house; with what effect we do not know. Livingstone's reports, however, gave the abolitionists (such as Thomas Hughes) in the House of Commons enough ammunition to persuade the British government to seize the occasion and initiate a course of action, using force when required, which led to the closing of the Zanzibar slave market as we shall see.

Ironically, the massacre gave Livingstone a unique opportunity to fulfil the, by now, abandoned hopes for his 'establishment'. By his efforts to stop the shooting and get prisoners freed, by his open break with the slave merchants he convinced the Manyema chiefs that he could be trusted, and trusted to the extent that they could ask him to apportion new sites for the villages that had been burned down. The significance of this overture would not be lost on Livingstone, for, as he had remarked on 16th October, 1870, '. . . each Manyema headman is independent of the others. The great want of the Manyema is national life.' One result of this state of affairs was that there were frequent inter-village fights from which, Livingstone discovered, women were exempt and went on trading at the market while their husbands were 'at war'. In the face of Zanzibari aggression, the villages had now decided that 'national life' was a prerequisite for survival, and in asking Livingstone to allocate land they were, in point of fact, offering him paramount political authority. Brooke had saved the Dyaks from slave raiders and become Rajah of Sarawak. Livingstone could have become Laird of Manyema, entitled, once settled, to the consul's salary from the Foreign Office. The achievement of a great ambition was offered him on a plate, but he turned it down and did no more than arrange a truce between the chiefs and Dugumbe. He made preparations to leave Nyangwe (Dugumbe gave him supplies) and return to Ujiji, there to restock, recruit new porters, and try again to get to the 'fountains'. He must solve the Nile mystery, prove himself again to the world, make enough money to escape that jibe of the 'respectable': 'He's worse than an Infidel that provides not for his own family'.

In the immediate term, he would be able to accomplish none of these objectives by settling at Nyangwe, besides which the place was too far from the coast to be another Batoka or Shire Highlands, even if Livingstone's Lualaba-Nile was a potential 'God's Highway'.

Five days after the massacre Livingstone and his companions departed for Ujiji. Dugumbe saw him off and gave him a warning, well justified, about the hostility of people along the route. Livingstone, ill, had frequently to stop and rest along the way; attacks by villagers had to be fought off, the gauntlet of ambushes run (he was wearing a red Arab waistcoat given him by Bogharib which made village scouts think him a Zanzibari). His last pair of shoes were worn out, his feet tortured by stones in the paths, there were delays in getting canoes to cross the lake. The two hundred and fifty mile journey took thirteen and a half weeks.

Livingstone was, in his own words, 'reduced to a skeleton' when he reached Ujiji towards the end of October. The Manyema expedition, planned to take six months had lasted over two years and he had used up, or lost, all his small supply of stores and trade goods on the way back from Nyangwe. Then, when he arrived at his rented house he was told that the consignment – £500 or £600's worth – sent up to him by Kirk had been sold off by the chief porter, Sherif, for ivory and slaves on the pretext that he had divined from the Koran that Livingstone was dead. Sherif, and the ivory, were still at Ujiji but Livingstone could find no way to recover his property, or to be compensated. Apart from the few yards of calico he had left behind in safe keeping in 1869, he was destitute.

In letters to Kirk written from Manyema, Livingstone had complained about the quality of the porters sent from the coast (and, incidentally, about the deserting 'Nassik boys' alleging that they had been palmed off on him with fraudulent qualifications by the principal of Nassik). Kirk, in Zanzibar, had used the services of Ludha Damji, an Indian and the best established transport contractor, to have both goods and porters sent up-country to Livingstone. Now Livingstone at Ujiji began, in his distress, to build on his suspicion that Kirk had deliberately acted to frustrate him. He had already suggested that Kirk plagiarized his map of Lake Nyasa and had convinced himself that Kirk had indeed told the porters to bring him back to Zanzibar. Thus for Kirk to have hired a 'Banian' and his slaves to bring up the goods he needed so badly was, in Livingstone's mind a sign only of ill will. He wrote to Kirk from Ujiji outlining his complaints about Ludha, Sherif and the others, insisting that future consignments be brought by freemen. He could not break with Kirk as he had done with, for example, Baines, and his criticism of Kirk was, to a minor degree, at this stage justified, even if it took no account of the cholera outbreak: Livingstone remarked to Kirk on 30th October 1871: 'I feel inclined to relinquish the hope of ever getting help from Zanzibar to finish the little work I have to do. . . I may wait twenty years and your slaves feast and fail.'

But in the time between Livingstone's return to Ujiji and his departure for what was to be his final journey ten months later he convinced himself that there was a solid case against Kirk, and expressed his view with the usual pungency. In a letter of 6th January, 1872 he tells W. C. Oswell that he has been

> sorely bamboozled by my friend Kirk, handing over the matter of supplies and men to a rich Banian slave trader who naturally wishes me anything but success and all his slaves come deeply imbued with the idea that they were not to follow but to force me back . . . then they ran riot with my goods and ultimately sold off all for slaves and ivory to themselves. Well with a loss of these which amounted to £500 or £600 – it is not very edifying to hear that Kirk again took half £1000

sent by Govt. to Ludha again and sent slaves again . . . I feel very sore at this 'companion' of Livingstone Sir Roderick calls him.

To James Young in letters in early 1872, Livingstone is more vitriolic, accusing Kirk of trying to frustrate him so that he himself might emerge as the discoverer of the Nile sources:

> What I say to you confidentially I did not say to [Kirk] that his private self-invitation to share in the honours — his public advice for me to retire and leave the work to others, published to Banians and all others. It is uncalled for mixing up his name with a discovery . . . his lazy indifference in handing off large sums of money . . . his eagerness in writing home 'I have sent off men and goods to Dr L. All Dr L's wants have been supplied' . . . Our friend's conduct [looks] grave. His public refusal to do anything for me . . .

When Kirk learned of Livingstone's complaints, he wrote to him to explain. Livingstone's reply on 2nd June 1972, the last letter he is known to have written to Kirk, opens with a sentence which may have mollified the recipient but which, more than anything, shows the extent to which the writer's mind is fracturing:

> My Dear Kirk, I am sorry to hear by a note . . . that you had taken my formal complaint against certain Banyans and Arabs as a covert attack upon yourself; this grieves me deeply, for it is a result I never intended to produce.

There is no doubt that the venom against Kirk was strengthened by the man (equally vindictive himself) who rescued Livingstone from Ujiji and made it possible for him to continue his work – Henry Morton Stanley.

28

YOU HAVE BROUGHT ME NEW LIFE

In January 1869, James Gordon Bennett, manager of the *New York Herald* (founded in 1853 by his father of the same name) summoned his most intrepid young reporter, Henry Morton Stanley, to his hotel suite in Paris and ordered him to go to Africa and 'find out Livingstone', who had not been heard of for three years. (At the time Livingstone, stricken with pneumonia, was being carried to Ujiji. When the news came through that he had arrived there, Bennett told Stanley to postpone his trip for a year or two to enable Livingstone to 'disappear' again.) There had been little newspaper concern for Livingstone once the dust put up by the disasters of the Zambezi expedition had settled. People in Britain or elsewhere who had Africa in their sights at all could find enough to interest them in the South African diamond rush or the British military campaign against the Emperor Tewdorus of Ethiopia, which Stanley himself reported brilliantly for the *Herald*. That the Bennetts were Scots by origin (the father had emigrated in 1819) may have given them some clannish feeling for Livingstone but their primary interest in 'finding' him was journalistic. It would be a sensational story for a sensationalist newspaper and they gave Stanley a virtual blank cheque to pay for his expedition and to buy supplies for Livingstone.

Stanley arrived at Zanzibar in January 1871 (Livingstone was at Bambarre): he called on Kirk, who at the time was acting consul, and told him that he had come to explore the Rufiji, the large river that enters the sea a hundred miles south of the island. It seems unlikely that Kirk would have swallowed this tale, especially after Stanley asked him how he thought Livingstone would react if he should possibly 'stumble across' him. On hearing the question, Kirk fixed Stanley with 'a broad stare' and said, according to Stanley in his Despatches, 26th December 1871, that Livingstone was: 'a misanthrope, who hated the sight of Europeans; who if Burton, Speke, Grant or anybody of that kind was coming to see him, would make haste to put as many miles as possible between himself and such a person. He was a man also no one could get along with – it was almost impossible to please him.'

Stanley came away with the impression that Kirk was indifferent, if not exactly hostile, to Livingstone (which is certainly not correct), that Kirk was certainly not well disposed towards Stanley. Kirk was a plain dealer, Stanley on this occasion deceitful and bumptious. After equipping his expedition, Stanley crossed to Bagamoyo, the entrepôt on the mainland, where he met Kirk again, supervising the despatch of his second consignment to Livingstone. That the caravan had been idling for over three months convinced Stanley once and for all that Kirk cared not a fig for Livingstone. Since Kirk knew, on the other hand, that his first consignment had been all but completely stolen his delay in getting the second on its way was careless, but this is the only point on which he can be faulted, and even then allowance must be made for his duties at the consulate and as medical officer.

Stanley spent £4000 of the *Herald*'s money in Zanzibar, bought about six tons of supplies and equipment, including eighteen thousand fathoms of cloth, a million beads, three hundred and fifty pounds of brass rings and two collapsible boats (for, if Livingstone had gone down the Congo, he planned to go after and overtake him). He hired 192 porters and two white assistants, Shaw and Farquarson. The caravan left Bagamoyo for Ujiji on 21st March and reached Unyanyembe, five hundred miles inland, four months later — very good time for the march, achieved with generous use of the lash, the fist and the threat of the bullet, and during which Farquarson died of fever. At Unyanyembe Stanley found that the road to Ujiji was blocked by the Mirambo war, a conflict between the Zanzibaris and local people for control of the trade route. Stanley and his men (they had over forty rifles and a great deal of ammunition) joined forces with the Zanzibaris during a Mirambo attack, were beaten and retreated to the town. By deaths and desertions, Stanley's caravan was reduced to barely fifty men, and Shaw, after going mad, died too.

To avoid the war zone, Stanley led his party on a long, semi-circular detour, south west then north west, leaving Unyanyembe on 20th September, three months after arriving, and reached Ujiji on 27th October (a severe bout of fever caused Stanley to lose count of the days, as Livingstone had done at Bambarre, and the exact date of arrival has only recently been calculated, see I. C. Cunningham's *David Livingstone: A Catalogue of Documents*, 1985.) Livingstone's desperation at Ujiji had been somewhat lightened when the bush telegraph told him that there was a white man at Unyanyembe, and his heart positively lifted when he learned that he was approaching Ujiji. As Stanley drew near Livingstone's house, guided by Chuma, who had gone to investigate the approaching stranger, he describes in his Despatches of 10th November 1871 what he saw: '. . .a knot of Arabs, and in the centre, in striking contrast to their sunburnt faces, a pale looking and grey bearded white man, in a navy cap, a faded gold band about it, and a red woollen jacket. This white man was Dr Livingstone, the hero traveller, the object of the search.'

Stanley, immaculately dressed, and standing beneath the Stars and Stripes held aloft by one of his men, doffed his topee and greeted Livingstone with the carefully rehearsed: 'Doctor Livingstone, I presume.' 'Yes,' was Livingstone's answer with, in Stanley's words, 'a kindly smile'. Livingstone added a moment later, 'You have brought me new life' – life in the form of medicines, food, mail (brought from Unyanyembe where it had been stuck) newspapers, trade goods, and conversation in English (until he saw the American flag, Livingstone had feared that his visitor might have been a Frenchman, whose language he would not have understood).

While Livingstone in his misery would probably have given a friendly welcome to anyone – even Burton – bringing supplies, Stanley was a particularly favoured guest, with whom there was never any conflict: quite fortuitously, the two men complemented each other. Stanley, thirty years old, was young enough to be the son Livingstone so wished to have beside him (he had hoped to bring 'poor Bob' on this journey): Livingstone, approaching sixty, was old enough to be the father Stanley had missed having, for he had been born illegitimate with the name Rowlands, and abandoned to a Welsh workhouse. (When he was fifteen he rebelled against the cruelty of the superintendent, fled, and signed on with a ship at Liverpool bound for New Orleans. There he was taken up, and virtually adopted, by a merchant called Henry Hope Stanley. When the merchant died, 'Rowlands' took his name. When the Civil War broke out, he enlisted in the Confederate army, was captured by the northerners, placed in a prisoner of war camp as 'poor Bob' had been, released when he agreed to change sides, and became a 'ship's writer' in the Federal navy. His reports of battle impressed newspaper editors, and when the war was over, Stanley started his career as journalist. In 1868, Bennett offered him a job on the *Herald*, sent him to cover the Ethiopian campaign, and then to 'find out Livingstone'.) Like the old man at Ujiji, Stanley had worked his way up (from even poorer beginnings) like him too, he was prepared to go to any lengths to get what he wanted. He was prickly, as Mrs Webb pointed out: 'I really will never ask people to meet you again,' she remarked when he was visiting Newstead in later years. 'You are always very nice when you are with us alone, but directly a strange face appears you are – well you are a perfect porcupine with all quills out.' And he could be spiteful, as he was with Kirk whose alleged misdemeanours he reported to Livingstone with results we have seen, though Stanley's gossip was not necessary to have set him on the attack.

Apart from these points of contact between the young man and the old other factors cemented their friendship. Once Stanley had found Livingstone he knew that he was sitting on a big story, and one, moreover, that he need not hurry over as he had no competitors. Within reason the longer he stayed with Livingstone the better. He could get to know him well enough to make him the centrepiece of the epic which he knew, after the rigours of the journey from the coast, he was capable of putting together. Livingstone, for his part, realised that he could use Stanley and the *Herald* to put himself across to the world and bury the failures of the Zambezi expedition under a mountain of newsprint. Livingstone did not care that Stanley would make a fortune out of him – his own would come later.

Livingstone was weak and ill when Stanley arrived (just a few days, as we have seen, after Livingstone limped back into Ujiji). The young man immediately set to work making himself useful by preparing Livingstone's meals, making conversation, giving news of the world at large: the fall of Bonaparte the Third's French empire, the death of Lord Clarendon, the opening of the Suez canal, the laying of the trans-Atlantic telegraph cable. Livingstone was able once more to enjoy the sensation of being *au courant* and, thanks to Stanley's ministrations, within three weeks was feeling well enough again to travel. He asked Stanley to accompany him back to Manyema, across the Lualaba and onwards in search of the fountains. Stanley replied that his porters would accept no bribe, no matter how large, to go on *that* journey – (it is unlikely that Stanley would have wanted to go either, he could not have filed his story from Katanga). Instead, he asked Livingstone if he had explored the head of Lake Tanganyika and offered his men and effects for the trip. In mid-November they set out by water for the north of the lake, which they reached on the 27th. There they found that the Ruzizi river which Livingstone had supposed led north to Lake Albert in fact flowed south into Tanganyika. Burton's theory that the lake was the source of the Nile was disproved; Livingstone's belief that Tanganyika was a 'lacustrine river' had to be put aside. He now knew that if the Nile indeed rose on the central watershed, only the Lualaba and its affluents could be the headwaters. (In 1868, Burton and Speke made for the Ruzizi but their boatmen refused to take them close enough to establish the direction of flow.) Livingstone named a group of small islands at the north of the lake the New York Herald Islands and in mid-December he and Stanley were back at Ujiji.

Livingstone went down with dysentery and although Stanley suffered a bad attack of fever (which Livingstone was happy to nurse him through) it was, generally, an uneventful and successful trip. Apart from this journey, Livingstone was spending much of his time during these weeks writing up his journal from the notes he had kept in Manyema. The record of his stay west of Lake Tanganyika is largely experience recollected in tranquillity; influenced by long hours of talk with Stanley.

Livingstone had an excellent memory (Stanley notes, as we have seen that he could recite great stretches of verse by Byron, Tennyson, Burns, Whittier and Lowell) and there is no reason to doubt the accuracy of, for example, the passage about the little tree frog or the account of the Nyangwe killings, though both have the air of set pieces. The journal was for publication and Stanley was to take it to England, sealed with five locks so that the 'blockheads of the Royal Geographical Society' would get no peep at its contents until Livingstone gave permission.

On 7th January 1872 Livingstone and Stanley left Ujiji for Unyan-yembe. The Mirambo war was making it difficult for caravans to get through to Lake Tanganyika from Zanzibar, so it was better for Livingstone to go and intercept his supplies east of the war zone: Stanley of course was going 'home'. They boated a hundred miles along the east coast of the lake, then went overland at a tangent to Unyanyembe, where they arrived in mid-February. Stanley had fever on the way, so badly that at one stage he had to be carried in a hammock but Livingstone's state of health was a greater cause for concern. His piles and anal bleeding were so painful that he could not ride the donkey Stanley had bought for him, and besides, he had now lost nearly all his teeth. When they reached Unyanyembe, Livingstone found that most of the goods Kirk had sent him had been either looted or destroyed by termites while in storage. This seemed to Livingstone yet another example of Kirk's lack of care and added the extra bitterness to the Young and Oswell letters we have seen. Stanley tried persistently to persuade Livingstone to travel with him to Zanzibar, have his health attended to, false teeth made, recruit porters, stock up and only then return to the interior to finish the work. Livingstone refused adamantly. He was not going to face the remotest chance that he might be 'invalided out', that Kirk or anyone else might take advantage of the information he had already gathered and take the palm. Little did he realise that it would be Stanley himself, a bare four years later, who would prove conclusively – as Stanley already suspected – that the Lualaba was the Congo, that Livingstone's Nile sources in the 'fountains' was a dream.

Livingstone decided to wait at Unyanyembe while Stanley recruited porters in Zanzibar and sent up supplies. Then Stanley divided his own stores into two equal portions, giving Livingstone enough to keep him going for four years (including the collapsible boats) and left Unyanyembe on 14th March 1872. Livingstone wanted him to stay a little longer, but Stanley insisted he must move on and said goodbye with tears in his eyes. He took with him Livingstone's sealed journal, his despatches (notably that on Nyangwe for the Foreign Office) and over three dozen long letters. Stanley also took the picture of Livingstone he was to present to the world:

Dr Livingstone is about sixty years old, though after he was restored to health he looked like a man who has not passed his fiftieth year. His hair has a brownish colour yet, but is here and there streaked with grey lines over the temples: his beard and moustaches are very grey. His eyes, which are hazel, are remarkably bright; he has a sight as keen as a hawk's. His teeth alone indicate the weakness of age . . . When walking he has a firm but heavy tread, like that of an overworked or fatigued man. He is accustomed to wear a naval cap with a semicircular peak, by which he has been identified throughout Africa. His dress, when first I saw him, exhibited traces of patching and repairing, but was scrupulously clean . . .

I grant he is not an angel; but he approaches to that being as near as the nature of a living man will allow. I never saw any spleen or misanthropy in him . . . His gentleness never forsakes him; his hopefulness never deserts him. No harrassing anxieties, distraction of mind, long separation from home and kindred can make him complain. He thinks 'all will come out right at last'. . .

His religion is not of the theoretical kind, but is a constant, earnest, sincere practice. It is neither demonstrative nor loud, but manifests itself in a quiet practical way . . . Each Sunday morning he gathers his little flock around him, and reads prayers and chapters from the Bible in a natural, unaffected, and sincere tone; and afterwards delivers a short address in the Ki-swaheli language about the subject read to them, which is listened to with evident interest and attention.

This description in Stanley's *How I Found Livingstone*, published in London in 1872, was enhanced by the letters that Livingstone wrote (for publication) to Bennett of the *Herald*, one of which contains Livingstone's much misquoted plea for the end of slavery: 'All I can say in my loneliness is may heaven's rich blessing come down on every one – American, English, Turk – who will help to heal this open sore of the world.' This was also written into his Journal on 1st May 1872.

But Stanley knew that he was not telling the whole truth about his master. His best-seller, *How I Found Livingstone* – written very fast and described by Florence Nightingale as 'the worst possible book on the best possible subject' – contains not a word that detracts from the image of the saintly father-figure. Stanley's private papers, however, (published, in part, after his death, by his widow in a so-called autobiography) show that he was disturbed, distressed even, by the bile in Livingstone's soul; by the sour discourses on, for example, Baines and Bedingfeld (he of the clicking false teeth that Livingstone now so badly needed); on Bishop Tozer and the others he believed had failed him or made the Zambezi expedition to fail. There is no doubt that Stanley admired Livingstone greatly and probably thought, no doubt, that he must shield him from any further public criticism. Certainly, the effect of Stanley's effusions in the *Herald* (promptly reproduced in other papers), in his book, in public lectures, was twofold. He rescued Livingstone from his limbo of half-forgottenness, brought 'new life' to his reputation, and at the same time gave that reputation a further perspective – that of the saint in the wilderness. When Stanley, in later years, flogged and shot his way brutally across Africa while he carved out a domain in the Congo basin for Leopold King of the Belgians (Queen Victoria's cousin) he was constant in asserting that Livingstone's spirit was his lodestar. Stanley claimed Livingstone as his own and gave the impression that it was he, and he alone, who had saved the saint and enabled him to pursue his work. He made it look as if Kirk had been a complete failure if not worse: 'Does it not appear strange to you,' Stanley wrote in his despatch to the *Herald* published on 9th August 1872, 'Dr Kirk never had a word to say, never had a word to write to his old friend Dr Livingstone all the time from 1st November 1870 to about 15th February 1871; that during this period of three and a half months Dr John Kirk showed great unkindness, unfriendliness towards the old traveller in not pushing forward the caravan carrying his supplies. . .?'

Stanley's vituperation of Kirk was unstinting, but friends of the latter, especially Horace Waller, came to his defence and his reputation, fortunately and justifiably, remained undamaged: Stanley's attacks reflected more on himself than on his victim. Shortly after his return to England, Stanley was a guest of the Webbs at Newstead. As Frazer says, Mrs Webb later described him as '. . . the typical American journalist, almost aggressively so both in accent and behaviour. His eyes were like small pools of grey fire, but the least provocation turned them into grey lightning. They seemed to scorch and shrivel up all he looked at. His whole personality gave the impression of overwhelming and concentrated force – a human explosive.'

Soon after Newstead, Stanley was on his travels again, his immediate assignment taking him to the Gold Coast to report Britain's Ashanti campaign of 1873–1874, to witness the progress of the European carve-up of Africa, and then to the Congo and the Upper Nile. His career as journalist and adventurer, with all its lightning and slashing of human flesh, led him to a knighthood and a seat in the House of Commons. He died married but childless, in 1904, the true loves of his life seeming to have been his slave-boy Kalulu (who drowned in the Inga Falls, near the mouth of the Congo), and Livingstone.

In 1872 Livingstone was not as abandoned by the world as he had led himself to believe. Even while he was with Stanley an expedition sponsored by the Royal Geographical Society was on its way to bring him relief. Stanley met the party when he reached Bagamoyo after leaving Livingstone at Unyanyembe, and when he gave it his news it was disbanded. One member was young Oswell Livingstone, then twenty-one years old and a medical student. He had come reluctantly and was soon persuaded that it was too dangerous for him to proceed on his own to Unyanyembe to see his father, he wrote him a letter which Stanley sent inland with the caravan he was assembling. Unspeakable fury beset Livingstone when he learned that Oswell's purpose in trying to reach him was to urge that he return to Britain and make some money.

As had happened with the 1868 search expedition to Lake Nyasa, the 1872 affair cost more than Livingstone had himself been given for his explorations, though Stanley had brought him at Ujiji a Foreign Office despatch to the effect that his grant had been increased by £1000, news that came at the same time as Livingstone learned that he had lost all his *Lady Nyassa* money in the collapse of the Agra Bank. 'I am sorry to hear of the Bombay affair,' he told James Young to whom he was still in debt, in a letter of 16th December 1871, 'but I shall be able to give you something for I have got salary from Govt., and a most kind despatch from Lord Clarendon, now alas gone from us.'

With the help of some of this money, Stanley did an excellent job in Zanzibar for Livingstone, especially in recruiting on a two-year contract a team of over fifty porters, properly disciplined under a captain, and including half a dozen 'Nassik boys' left over from the abandoned search and relief expedition.

Livingstone knew that he would have a long wait at Unyanyembe: he settled into a small bungalow and established a domestic routine while undertaking whatever preparations he could for the forthcoming journey. He spun a sounding line from cotton thread to replace the one lost in Lake Tanganyika, bought cattle and used the milk to make cheese to take with him. In his household chores he was helped by two young women named Ntaoeka and Halima, the latter the wife of Amoda. Both women appear to have been slaves for Livingstone talks of 'freeing' them. Halima's attentions impressed him so much that he promised to buy her a house and garden in Zanzibar; Ntaoeka was 'a fine looking woman, not to be left unattached' so Livingstone joined her and Chuma in marriage.

Both Burton and Stanley had found Unyanyembe intolerable but Livingstone liked the place. He studied the geology, the flora and wildlife of the district and suggested that the area would be suitable for a missionary establishment. As was his custom, he started to learn the local (Nyamwezi) language, and here made a discovery which caused him a great amount of anxiety since he was also at the time worrying over the nomenclature in Ptolemy's *Geography*. 'If the Victoria Lake were large,' Livingstone notes in his Journal on 15th April 1872, 'then it and Albert would probably be the lakes which Ptolemy meant, and it would be pleasant to call them Ptolemy's sources . . . but unfortunately Ptolemy has inserted a small lake 'Coloe' nearly where the Victoria Lake stands, and one cannot say where his two lakes stand.'

As we have seen, Ptolemy believed that the Nile rose in the 'mountains of the moon', and now Livingstone observed, again in his Journal on 23rd April 1872, that: 'The prefix "Nya" in Nyamwezi seems to mean place or locality ... Banyamwezi means probably the Ba – they or people – Nya – place – Mwezi, moon, people of the moon locality or moonland.'

The territory of the Nyamwezi stretched 250 miles southwards from Lake Victoria. To the east, three magnificent mountains rise from the plains – Loolmalasin, 12,000 feet; Meru, 15,000 feet and Kilimanjaro, 19,000 feet – while to the west, the highlands of Rwanda and Burundi soar to over 10,000 feet. In these highlands lie the sources of the Kagera river, the ultimate headwaters of the Nile. Livingstone remarked that: 'The science in [Ptolemy's] time was in a state of decadence', but could not rid himself of the thought that the proximate existence of a 'moonland', of a lake, and of what could be described as the 'mountains of moonland' was not a mere geographical coincidence – that Speke and Grant might be right, that the Nile flowed out of Lake Victoria. 'I am oppressed,' he wrote on 21st May 1872, 'with the apprehension that after all it may turn out that I have been following the Congo,' a remark he made repeatedly in the months ahead. Stanley, as we have seen, believed that the Lualaba was the Congo.

But Livingstone did not allow this apprehension to interfere with his plans. He had been at Unyanyembe for five months when his caravan arrived from the coast, and he was eager to move and quite clear about the course of his work, which he estimated would take six or seven months – south west to Lake Tanganyika, onwards to cross the Chambeshi east of Lake Bangweulu, around the south of that lake (to check for affluents) to the Luapula, down that river to see the copper mines of Katanga and find the fountains, and down the Lualaba to Lake Albert, back to Unyanyembe (where he was leaving stores), to Zanzibar, to London and, finally, to an apartment near Regent's Park. He was confident that he was fit enough to undertake this journey of more than 3000 miles, for he felt his fortunes had been restored by Stanley, that the importance of his work had been recognised in Lord Clarendon's £1000, by the British government's gift of £300 to Agnes (which he learned of at Unyanyembe). And Livingstone felt at peace again with his God, writing on 5th August, 1872:

> What is the atonement of Christ? It is Himself; it is the inherent and everlasting mercy of God made apparent to human eyes and ears. The everlasting love was disclosed by our Lord's life and death. It showed that God forgives, because he loves to forgive. He works by smiles if

possible, if not, by frowns; pain is only a means of enforcing love.

On 25th August 1872, Livingstone led his caravan out of Unyanyembe.

29

HOW MANY DAYS IS IT TO THE LUAPULA?

Livingstone's last journey took a few more weeks than he had so optimistically estimated. He was determined to complete it, whatever the odds, to erase the failures of the past by what would be seen as a planned, accomplished geographical feat. His worry about the Nile fountains led to no change of course and, as for physical survival, Livingstone was now better equipped than he had ever been on his land journeys thanks largely to Stanley's genius as a quartermaster. The party that left Unyanyembe in the last week of August had the air of a parade: it was not quite a cavalcade, but there were two donkeys, one to carry Livingstone, the other a pack of baggage. There was a herd of nine cattle, a flock of goats, the animals in the care of the new 'Nassik boys'. There were over fifty stalwart porters, some armed with rifles, there were camp followers. Beside Livingstone were Susi, Chuma, Gardner, Amoda (and Halima). The caravan had trade goods, medicines, ammunition, supplies to last for years but the staple foods, meal and meat, would have to be bought (or hunted) on the march.

Livingstone led the party back along the south westerly route, previously used by himself and Stanley, to Lake Tanganyika, planning then to strike south so that he could survey the east coast of the lake (Stanley had sent him new chronometers) but soon after leaving Unyanyembe it became clear that even the best thought-out arrangements could go awry. Livingstone's case of powdered milk had been left behind (milk he needed when he was ill), a cow was lost, and some of the others began to sicken. Livingstone alleged that the 'Nassik' herdsman had allowed them to stray into a tsetse area and had the miscreant flogged by Susi, but did not place him in the slave collar Stanley had sent from Zanzibar to be used on 'incorrigibles'. Then two porters deserted with their loads of calico. These were minor troubles but on 16th September came the first signal of the real weakness of the whole venture when Livingstone developed severe dysentery. The attack persisted for seven days, but Livingstone kept on the march, with brief rests, despite his weakness and despite the intense heat which became more severe as the party descended from the plateau to the lake, which was sighted on 8th October. They had taken six weeks to cover two hundred and fifty miles – very good time in comparison with the three months Livingstone had needed to travel up the Rovuma in 1866. Travel along the foot of the Tanganyika escarpment was agony: 'The sun bakes the soil so hot that the radiation is as if from a furnace,' Livingstone noted in his Journal on 9th November 1872, 'It burns the feet of the people and knocks them up. Subcutaneous inflammation is frequent in the legs and makes some of my most hardy men useless. We have been compelled to slowness very much against my will.'

Livingstone was in haste, for though he knew that the rains, which in November were imminent, were the only relief from the heat they brought their own perils, especially around Lake Bangweulu. After struggling across the coastal valleys of Tanganyika for four weeks, Livingstone led the party back up on to the plateau, hoping the going would be easier and food more readily available. By now the riding donkey had died – 'a great loss to me,' Livingstone wrote – but more serious was the resumption of his anal bleeding which was forcing him to stop for days at a time. However, the party was still making good progress and having covered two hundred miles in nine weeks, arrived at Kampambwe village (to the south of Lake Tanganyika) which Livingstone had passed through on his way to Ujiji in 1867. A few days before his return to Kampambwe he had crossed a small river, the Kalambo, flowing towards the lake: either haste, or faltering curiosity, or sheer weariness prevented him from making the detour of a mile which would have enabled him to 'discover' the Kalambo Falls which, with an unbroken cascade of over seven hundred feet, are the second highest in Africa.

From Kampambwe Livingstone retrod his 1867 route for fifty miles in a south westerly direction and reached the village of Chibwe where a vital decision had to be made. He could either continue on his old trail through Mwamba's to Chitimukulu Chitapankwa's, cross the Chambeshi as he had done in 1867 and then strike west for the south shore of Bangweulu (but there was fighting in the area between the Bemba and their northern neighbours, the Lungu) or, he could head straight on south-west to where the Chambeshi, by his reckoning, entered the lake. The rains had now set in and speed was important if he was to reach this objective before the land became impassably 'spongy'. However, Livingstone's reckoning of the position of Bangweulu was based on the longitudes taken with the faulty chronometers in 1867 and 1868. Meanwhile he was now using accurate instruments and the observations he was taking at this stage did not correspond with those of 1867. Livingstone was worried enough about the discrepancy and by the overcast condition of the rainy season sky, which made accurate observations as difficult as if 'taken through a bunghole' – to hire guides.

The guides refused to go south west claiming, correctly, that the route Livingstone proposed led through largely uninhabited country without food for sale, and he had no choice but to follow them westwards, through a populated area, in the direction of Kazembe and the Luapula. When on 18th December, and fifty miles short of Kazembe, they reached the Kalungwishi river (which Livingstone knew) they turned due south. 'Always too cloudy and rainy for observations,' Livingstone remarked, but the guides knew the way though it was at times difficult to get enough food (hardly surprising since December is the planting season and there were more than sixty stomachs to fill). Livingstone kept his ultimate destination – and his resentments – before his mind. In December 1872 he wrote to his brother John in Canada complaining about Kirk and about young Oswell Livingstone, accused of abandoning the relief expedition, of being improvident with money. But despite the barbs and hackles, the higher purpose is paramount:

> If the good Lord permits me to put a stop to the enormous evils of the inland slave trade, I shall not grudge my hunger and my toils ... The Nile sources are valuable to me only as a means of enabling me to open my mouth with power among men. It is this power I hope to apply to remedy an enormous evil, and join my poor little helping hand in the enormous revolution that in His all-embracing Providence He has been carrying on for ages, and is now actually helping forward.

Livingstone is no longer being carried in the arms of the Saviour, he has become God's (or should one say providence's) partner in the unfolding of history. It was now a mere four months since he had left Unyanyembe and seven hundred miles had been crossed (almost as satisfactory a pace as that of the Tete to Barotseland journey in 1860). Livingstone was justified in his feeling of assurance.

Early in January 1873 the party came to the fringes of Bangweulu (losing one man and the last cow on the stretch from the Kalungwishi). Looking at his records and at the chronometer reading Livingstone was certain he was standing on the north-eastern flank of the lake, though not beside the open water but beside a swampy inlet. All he had to do now was to head slightly south-east, and he would reach the Chambeshi and cross it to the south shore. The guides and local people told him otherwise: the best way to get to the other shore was to go south-*west*, and *there* cross to the south side. If Livingstone had heeded them and gone in the direction they urged, for only five or six miles, he would have found himself at almost exactly the place where he had reached the open lake in 1868, the north western shore, and would no doubt have recognised it. He did, however, know that something was wrong, for he told Thomas Maclear in a letter of January 1873: 'I was at the mercy of guides ... [who] brought us down to the back or north side of Bangweulu, while I wanted to cross the Chambeshi and go round its southern side. So back again south eastwards we had to bend.'

Livingstone always found it difficult to admit his mistakes and could not admit now that his informants here (like the Portuguese with Cabora Basa) might be right. Moreover, he believed that his 1868 longitudes were correct, his 1873 readings dubious: he thought he was seventy miles further east than he really was and, acting on this belief, took his party south-east.

The rainy season was now at its height; all the inlets, dambos, and flat land around Bangweulu flooded, the grass and reeds eight feet tall; there were few, if any, landmarks and in any case they could not be seen except from above the vegetation. Unless a canoe route or channel through the swamps was known, a traveller could only follow the compass, and even then the need for frequent changes of direction to avoid impassible patches would make it an awkward instrument to use. Livingstone thought the swamps formed a narrow fringe around a large open lake that could be navigated easily. In reality, as we have seen, the lake is small, an appendage to the swamp.

From mid-January until the third week of March, Livingstone searched for the Chambeshi. A first, south-easterly foray from his camp was fruitless, and after going around in a circle, he returned to base. He then took the party thirty miles east, partly across dry ground, to the waist of the Luena inlet (it was not in sight of the lake) which he believed from his readings to be directly due north of the Chambeshi. After several abortive forays around the inlet, he headed due south, straight and deep into the heart of the swamp. Canoes had been hired, but all the party's remaining livestock (except the donkey which had to be ferried in a canoe) had died or been eaten. Food was in short supply. A few extracts from Livingstone's journal, taken at random, are sufficient to describe the conditions he and his followers endured: 'It was sore on the women folk of our party', he wrote in March 1873, as they made their way from low island to low island for sixty miles to the Chambeshi:

> It was neck deep for fifty yards, and the water cold. We plunged in elephants' footprints 1½ hours ... Carrying me across the broad sedgy rivers is really a very difficult task ... The main stream came up to Susi's mouth and wetted my seat and legs ... Each time I was lifted off bodily and put on another pair of stout shoulders, and fifty yeards put them out of breath and no wonder ... I lose much blood but it is a safety valve for me and I have no fever or other ailments ... A dreary wet

morning ... It is flood as far as the eye can reach ... One does not know where land ends and Lake begins ... We punted six hours to a little islet without a tree and no sooner did we land than a pitiless rain came down. We turned up a canoe to get shelter ... The amount of water spread over the country constantly excites my wonder ...

But he could cheer himself with the thought that it was 'the Nile apparently enacting its inundations, even at its source.' On his sixtieth birthday, in the middle of the swamp, Livingstone wrote: 'Can I hope for ultimate success? So many obstacles have arisen. Let not Satan prevail over me, my good Lord Jesus.' On 25th March, the party crossed the Chambeshi, an occasion for celebration except for an unforeseen reminder of mortality: a canoe capsized in the current and, as Livingstone records, 'We lost a slave girl of Amoda.' But the sight of the river restored Livingstone's hope. On 25th March 1873, the day after a 'bitterly uncomfortable night,' he wrote: 'Nothing on earth will make me give up my work in despair. I encourage myself in the Lord my God, and go forward.' For Livingstone saw the Lord his God all around him, the 'everlasting God made apparent to human eyes and ears.' If the swamp itself, with its voracious leeches and foetid mud was the God that frowns, enforcing love by means of pain, the God who 'works by smiles if possible' was present too in the 'lion that had wandered into this world of water and anthills and roared all night as if very much disgusted', in the crown and stalk of the papyrus plant which Livingstone lovingly measured, 'it was three feet across horizontally, its stalk eight feet in height' (was not the papyrus reed the means by which the baby Moses and the sacred oracles had been preserved?), in the fish eagle which '... lifts up his remarkable voice ... and seems as if he were calling to some one in the other world ... his weird unearthly voice can never be forgotten – it sticks to one through life'.

He saw God, too, in 'many flowers in the forest: marigolds, a white jonquil-looking flower without smell, many orchids, white yellow and pink asclepias, with bunches of French-white flowers, clematis'. Even in the marvellous physical construction of the red, flesh-eating ants which attacked Livingstone one night while he rested, bleeding, on a half waterlogged islet:

> The large Sirafu have mandibles curved like reaping sickles and very sharp – as fine at the point as the finest needle or a bee's sting. Their office is to remove all animal refuse and they took all my fat ... On man they insert the sharp curved mandibles and then with six legs push their bodies round so as to force the points by lever power.

The crossing of the Chambeshi was not the end of the journey.

Livingstone might be out of the worst of the swamp but sixty miles of seasonally flooded country 'with villages on the "islands"' lay between him and land that was permanently above the water line. This last stage was to take five weeks. That the rains were coming to an end cheered him, but he wrote on 10th/12th April 1873:

> I am pale, bloodless, and weak from bleeding profusely . . . an artery gives off a copious stream and takes away my strength . . . and two days later I was so weak I could hardly walk, but tottered along nearly two hours and then lay down quite done. Cooked coffee – our last – and went on, but in an hour later I was compelled to lie down.

He tried to ride the pack donkey which, remarkably, had survived the swamp but was without the strength to keep his seat and fell off into the arms of his companions who insisted on placing him on a stretcher. Livingstone was 'Very unwilling to be carried, but on being pressed . . . allowed the men to help me along in relays . . .'

He had to endure a terrible pain in the area of his colon, so fierce that he could not bear the pressure of a hand on his lower spine. Lying in the bouncing *machila* the agony was unrelenting. In this fashion he was borne into the village of Chief Chitambo of the Lala (and named by some writers Ilala), forty miles due south of Lake Bangweulu on the banks of the Lulimala river. The chief made them welcome, allowed the building of a small pole and thatch house for the sick man and huts for his followers.

During a stop at a settlement on the way from the Chambeshi, Livingstone had asked the men there: 'Do you know of a hill on which four fountains take their rise?' to which the answer was 'No, we are not travellers.' Throughout the swamp journey, Livingstone had sustained himself with these fountains, had written the draft, with blank spaces to be filled in later, of the Despatch to the Foreign Office announcing their discovery:

> I have the pleasure of reporting to your Lordship that on the
> I succeeded in reaching your remarkable fountains, each of which at no great distance off becomes a large river. They rise at the base of a swell of land or earthern mound, which can scarcely be called a hill, for it seems only about   feet above the general level. . . The geographical position of the mound or low earthern hill may for the present be taken as latitude   and longitude   . The altitude above the sea

But Livingstone was not totally confident that the fountains, when he reached them, would turn out to be the Nile sources, rather than those of the Congo.

Now at Chitambo's, the last entry in Livingstone's journal reads '... knocked up quite and remain – recover sent to buy milch goats. We are on the banks of R. Molilamo.' He was hopeful enough of recovering to instruct Susi to exchange beads for ivory which would be used as currency once they reached Ujiji. But Livingstone was no longer a traveller: the eagle was calling from another world, its unearthly voice summoning him. The way in which he answered the call, a few weeks into his sixty-first year, is best told in the words of Susi and Chuma as they were gathered later by Horace Waller in *The Last Journal of David Livingstone*. On 30th April,

Chitambo came early to pay a visit of courtesy and was shown into the Doctor's presence, but he was obliged to send him away, telling him to come again on the morrow, when he hoped to have more strength to talk to him, and he was not again disturbed. In the afternoon he asked Susi to bring his watch to the bedside and explained to him the position in which to hold his hand, that it might lie in the palm whilst he slowly turned the key.

So the hours stole on till midnight. The men silently took to their huts, whilst others, whose duty it was to keep watch, sat round the fires, all feeling that the end could not be far off. About 11pm Susi, whose hut was close by, was told to go to his master. At the time there were loud shouts in the distance, and, on entering, Dr Livingstone said, 'Are our men making that noise?' 'No' replied Susi, 'I can hear from the cries that the people are scaring away a buffalo from their dura fields.' A few minutes afterwards he said slowly, and evidently wandering, 'Is this the Luapula?' Susi told him they were in Chitambo's village, near the Mulilamo, when he was silent for a while. Again, speaking to Susi, in Suaheli this time, he said, 'Sikun'gapi kuenda Luapula?' (How many days is it to the Luapula?) 'Na zani zikutatu, Bwana' (I think it is three days, Master), replied Susi.

A few seconds later, as if in great pain, he half sighed, half said, 'Oh dear, dear!' and then dozed off again.

It was about an hour later that Susi heard Majwara again outside the door, 'Bwana wants you, Susi.' On reaching the bed the Doctor told him he wished him to boil some water, and for the purpose he went to the fire outside and soon returned with the copper kettle full. Calling him close, he asked him to bring his medicine-chest and to hold the candle near him, for the man noticed he could hardly see. With great difficulty, Dr Livingstone selected the calomel, which he told him to place by his side; then, directing him to pour a little water into a cup, and to put another empty one by it, he said in a low feeble voice, 'All right;

you can go out now.' These were the last words he was ever heard to speak.

It must have been about 4am when Susi heard Majwara's step once more. 'Come to Bwana, I am afraid; I don't know if he is alive.' The lad's evident alarm made Susi run to arouse Chuma, Chowperé, Matthew and Mumyasiri, and the six men went immediately to the hut ... Dr Livingstone was kneeling by the side of his bed, his body stretched forward, his head buried in the pillow.

He was dead: it was 1st May 1873.

30

BORN AGAIN

Eleven and a half months later, on 15th April 1874, Mrs William Cotton Oswell at 'Groombridge', Tunbridge Wells, wrote in her diary: 'William went to London to identify the body of Dr Livingstone. He had been profoundly grieved and silent, doubting whether he should be able to recognise his old friend, but not only was the broken arm unmistakeable but the features were unchanged. He brought back home a lock of the hair, dark brown still, scarcely tinged with grey.'

The day after Livingstone died, his followers elected Susi leader of the party. A plan of action was drawn up and set in motion immediately. For the moment, Livingstone's death was to be concealed from Chief Chitambo, but the body was to be taken back to Zanzibar – more than a thousand miles away – with all Livingstone's belongings and papers intact: on the morning after the death, Jacob Wainwright, one of the 'Nassik boys' sent by Stanley to Unyanyembe, made an inventory of Livingstone's possessions, and then preparations for the return journey began. The body was disembowelled, the viscera and heart placed in an iron box and buried at the foot of a large *mpundu* tree (*parinari curatellifolia*). Jacob Wainwright read the funeral service, then an inscription was carved: LIVINGSTONE MAY 4 1873, with the names of three of his men, SOUZA (surely Susi) MNIASERE UCHOPERE (The tree is long since dead, but the inscription is preserved in the museum of the Royal Geographical Society, London. The site of the tree is today marked by a memorial consisting of a truncated obelisk topped by a cross: funds for the structure were raised by the RGS.)

Before the viscera were buried they were autopsied; in the lower bowel a 'blood clot' was found the size of a fist, without doubt the source of Livingstone's final agonies. The empty corpse was rubbed inside and out with salt, tied to a pole and placed on a rack in an enclosure open to the sky. There, turned slightly every day, it was dried in the sun for a fortnight (the rainy season was over) and when it was ready was bathed in brandy (a beverage which Livingstone had latterly always kept in stock), the legs bent back at the knees and strapped to the torso. The cadaver was wrapped in cloth, placed in a bark cylinder (like those used for the beehives Livingstone had admired in Angola), encased in sail cloth, and waterproofed with tar. Livingstone might have smiled to see himself thus mummified, like an ancient Egyptian on the banks of the Nile.

When Chitambo heard of the death he came to pay his respects and suggested that the body be buried at his place. Livingstone's men insisted they would take it with them (in spite of the dangers its presence added to the normal perils of the journey) and strung it to a carrying pole where it could pass for a bale of trade goods. No doubt the men would wish to prove to the British in Zanzibar that they were not deserters, as Musa and the Comorans had been, but even with the body they could not prove they were not murderers. The meticulous pains they took show, above all, devotion.

Towards mid-May they set off for Unyanyembe. The journey was an epic in itself, but Susi's leadership brought the caravan of men, women, children, the body, boxes of papers and instruments through all the dangers of seven hundred miles of hostile country and suspicious people – the Nyamwezi were waging war through much of the country that had to be covered. In October 1873 the relative safety of Livingstone's old base was reached. Ten people died on the way.

The outside world had not heard of Livingstone since the middle of 1872 when his last letters from Unyanyembe reached Zanzibar. Stanley's reports about the state of his health (and Stanley's lies about Kirk) had alarmed Livingstone's friends and supporters, so that while he was heading for Bangweulu two further search expeditions were set in train. One, paid for with £2000 of James Young's money, and believing that the Lualaba was the Congo (as Stanley had assumed) approached from the west coast. It sailed to Luanda, proceeded to the lower Congo and planned to travel up the river in the hope of meeting Livingstone on his way down. The other, supported by the government, set out from Bagamoyo and made for Unyanyembe (one of the members of this party was young Robert Moffat, the son of Mary's brother: he was dead of fever soon after leaving Bagamoyo). The leader of this official expedition (consciences were writhing after Stanley's revelation of Livingstone the saint) was a Royal Navy Lieutenant named V. Lovett Cameron. While he and the remains of his party were recovering at Unyanyembe from the trials of the march from the coast, and malaria, Livingstone's body was carried into the town. It is possible that Livingstone might have been amused that by 1873 at least six times as much had been spent on searches (even if we exclude Stanley's) than he had been given in 1866, but there is no possibility of doubting what his reaction would have been to what happened next. Cameron behaved in the accustomed Bedingfeld RN fashion, ordered Susi and Chuma to have the body buried immediately – which they refused to do – and then despite protests, which he shouted down, opened Livingstone's boxes and took possession of his instruments. Cameron, who had been hoping for fame as a finder and rescuer of Livingstone, was baulked and took his petty revenge. He did not disband and return to Zanzibar, but continued westwards, flogging his way to the Atlantic in Angola and tried to make his name with a book called *Across Africa* published in 1877. In him, Susi and Chuma saw for the first time the hard face of the new breed of British empire builders; the Cecil Rhodes generation had arrived on the scene.

After a short rest at Unyanyembe, Susi's caravan went on to Bagamoyo where it arrived in February 1874. Chuma crossed to Zanzibar to take the news to the British consul and found that Kirk was away on leave in England, his post occupied temporarily by a deputy, Captain W F Prideaux RN, who immediately despatched a warship named (appropriately some may say) HMS *Vulture* to Bagamoyo to fetch the body and effects. To Susi, Chuma and each of the other men, Prideaux paid the exact amount of wages due, then dismissed them. Livingstone's dear Halima received no money, no house and garden in Zanzibar. Prideaux's excuse for this icy behaviour was that Livingstone's funds were exhausted, that he had to dig into his own pocket. Although this is true – Prideaux had to wait three years to be reimbursed – Livingstone's men were made aware that as far as the Empire was concerned they were, if not slaves, beasts of burden, to be given their rations and then sent back to the dark invisibility from which they had been called. (The following year, the RGS struck commemorative medals for each of them, but by then not many could be found to be given this incongruous reward.)

In early 1874, the British in Zanzibar were glowing with self-satisfaction (which makes their meanness towards Livingstone's men even more noteworthy) for the great slave market in the town had been closed forever. We have seen how for many years British policy towards the Sultanate had been to bring it to submission by usurping its trade and destroying its shipping. We have seen how during the first two years of the 1870s (when Livingstone was in Manyema) the House of Commons had been examining new ways to end the Zanzibar slave trade, and thus bring the Sultan to his knees. By the end of 1872 – Zanzibar had been devastated by a hurricane earlier that year – the British government had decided to force the Sultan (Barghash, successor to Majid, who died in 1870) to accept a treaty of abolition, and appointed Livingstone's friend Sir Bartle Frere to enforce the policy. Frere sailed to Zanzibar with four warships, but the Sultan, refusing to move, considered an appeal to the French for protection. Frere, frustrated, ordered his commanders to seize all Zanzibari slave-trade shipping in Zanzibari waters (an illegal instruction in terms of the earlier treaty; despite the illegality, the British government supported Frere) and, in addition, to blockade Zanzibar; in effect a declaration of war. When Barghash tried to argue that Britain was breaking all the previous treaties and was breaking international law Kirk, as Consul, presented himself to him and declared, 'I have not come to discuss, but to dictate'. The Sultan capitulated. With Zanzibar's population greatly reduced by the 1869–70 cholera epidemic, with the major part of its shipping and its clove and coconut plantations destroyed by the hurricane, his economy was in tatters. Now the new treaty would deprive him of his last remaining source of immediate revenue. Barghash thought of fighting but was too weak to do so. On 5th June 1873, a month after Livingstone's death, he signed the treaty and in effect ended Zanzibar's independence; a fact that became plain when Kirk told Barghash when he wanted to go to London to present his case, that he would not be allowed to leave the island.

It was shortly after concluding this piece of imperial business that Kirk went on the holiday which meant he was away from Zanzibar when Livingstone's body arrived. But Livingstone's death made it possible to attribute to Livingstone, to his despatches from the Rovuma in 1866, his despatch about the Nyangwe massacre (which Stanley delivered) the credit for the closure of the Zanzibar slave emporium, the accomplishment of a great moral victory. The strategists of empire, however, aware of Zanzibar's greater importance following the opening of the Suez canal and the Bombay merchants who had backed Livingstone, had reason for more than moral satisfaction (the British allowed slavery to continue in Zanzibar until well into the twentieth century).

Stanley's reports had prepared the British public for Livingstone the holy man. The end of the Zanzibar slave market and the proposal, announced immediately it had been closed, for an Anglican cathedral on the very spot where it had stood, added to the glow of saintliness. The body was shipped with all possible speed to England, its sole African companion Jacob Wainwright, late of Nassik, his fare paid by the Church Missionary Society which planned to send him on a fund-raising tour of Britain.

When Livingstone's remains arrived at Southampton (where eighteen years before Mary had given him her poem begging him to stay at home), the flag-draped coffin was greeted by a twenty-one-gun salute, by the mayor and the aldermen, by a crowd in mourning, by a military brass band that played Handel's *Dead March*. A procession of carriages escorted the body to the railway station, where a special train was standing steaming to carry it to London where the Royal Geographical Society (but not, alas, Sir Roderick Murchison, he had died in 1871) was waiting to receive it. After the formal identification by Oswell, among others, and the taking of a plaster cast of the broken humerus, the body lay in state for two days. Thousands of people filed past, including the Webbs' daughter Alice, who in *Livingstone and Newstead*, (London, 1913) wrote: 'I was taken by my mother to see the coffin lying in state, surrounded by palms and arum lilies, in the big Council Room of the Royal Geographical Society's old quarters in Savile Row. I do not know who suggested the improvised background of flowers, but it was curiously appropriate and far more effective, I thought, in its simplicity than more elaborate decorations.'

Sir Bartle Frere, a favourite pro-consul of Queen Victoria, arranged with the government a funeral at state expense, and on the morning of 18th April 1874 the coffin was borne in solemn progress through hushed streets lined with weeping people to Westminster Abbey. The occasion, worthy of a great and popular statesman, was graced by the presence of the Prince of Wales, leaders of the government and members of parliament. There, too, was the seventy-nine year old Robert Moffat, retired from Kuruman to England. There stood Livingstone's sisters on their first journey out of Scotland, 'nice, sensible looking elderly women, looking very square and solid in their deep mourning' as Alice Webb remarked. There stood Agnes, and Tom, and Oswell. There stood James Stewart. Mrs W Cotton Oswell recorded her view of the occasion as cited by W E Oswell in *William Cotton Oswell Hunter and Explorer*:

18 April. Warm as summer. William and I set off by the early train for Livingstone's funeral. He went straight to the Geog. Soc. Lady Augusta Stanley [wife of the Dean of Westminster] had sent a message begging me to go to the Deanery [of the Abbey] that she might give me a good place. She took me first to the Leads, to see such a sight as I shall never forget, the sea of heads and the long train of carriages filling the broad sanctuary, representing every grade of life from the Queen to the humblest crossing-sweeper. The concentrated, *cumulated* feeling was, as it always is, deeply moving. And then that wonderful Abbey thronged with earnest men and women dressed in mourning. We sat, or rather stood, in the curious little Deanery pew over the Jerusalem Chamber, and looked down on the black carpet laid for the procession, with one white line for the coffin in the centre of the nave. Very soon the words 'I am the Resurrection and the Life' sounded in the distance, taken up in lovely cadences by the white-robed choir. Then came the coffin covered with a pall upon which exquisite white flowers were heaped. There were eight pall bearers, my husband and his friend General Steele, at the head, Stanley and Jacob Wainwright at the feet. Slowly and solemnly the procession wound its way along the black road until hidden by the choir gates. Back at last to gather round Livingstone's last resting-place – his *first* Canon Conway said in his sermon next day. We all – the whole vast assembly – joined in the single hymn 'O God of Bethel' and the choir sang 'His body shall rest in peace, but his name liveth for evermore.' The poor Livingstone family, my husband and all the mourners who entered

the building in heartbroken sorrow, left it with a quiet look of comfort and satisfaction.

The other pall-bearers were Horace Waller, James Young, John Kirk and Webb. Webb, as his daughter wrote, '. . . was so overcome by his efforts at self-control, and looked so deadly white in consequence that my mother was quite alarmed by his appearance.'

It was Alice Webb who remarked later that there was 'a real parallel between Missolonghi and Ilala'. If Byron, as his biographer Hazlitt commented, had died in the cause of freedom, 'for the last, best hopes of man,' then so had Livingstone, lying not more than a few yards from the Abbey's Poets' Corner, where Byron is honoured.

This memory of Livingstone had to be preserved, not only on the tombstone with its falsified quotation, which we have seen, but in the minds of a more general public than could, or would, visit Westminster Abbey. Stanley had given to Agnes the journal sealed with five locks which he had brought back from Unyanyembe, while the diary Livingstone kept during the last year of his life had come to London with his mortal remains. Neither Agnes nor her brother Tom felt able to prepare the papers for publication – John Murray was happy to take them – so Agnes asked William Cotton Oswell if he would edit them, a task for which his work with Livingstone on the Zambezi *Narrative* would have prepared him perfectly, but he declined. Was he worried by the frenzied tone of Livingstone's last letters to him? Enquiries among other friends of the dead man brought Horace Waller to the fore. He was now ensconced in the comfort of the Church of England rectory at Twywell, a few score miles from Newstead, and agreed to be the editor. James Young stepped in once more to help, and paid for Susi and Chuma to travel to Britain so that they might assist Waller with the work, especially in providing an account of the last few weeks of Livingstone's life, of his death, of the journey with the body to Zanzibar, and in filling the gaps in the record when Livingstone was too ill to write. In terms of their brief, Waller and his assistants did an excellent piece of work, preparing the *Last Journals* as a continuous narrative, with text filling the gaps placed in brackets. Like *Missionary Travels*, the story is told in the first person (except where the words of Susi and Chuma are used), and like that book it contains nothing of the side of Livingstone's character which he himself was happy enough to reveal in the bitter letters (some of which we have looked at) to W C Oswell, Young and others (the Webbs too were recipients of these outpourings but burned them because they were 'too sad'). An attack on Prince Albert was torn out of the manuscript journal itself. Waller worked with speed and the book was published in two volumes before the end of 1874. When he received his copy, W C Oswell told Agnes: 'I have begun to read the book, and the short curt sentences, full of pith, bring the dear old Father so vividly before me that I cannot believe I shall never see him again. The dear old fellow, how quiet and gentle he has grown in these last journals. I do not mean that he was ever the contrary, but though his unflinching courage and determination remain where they ever were, his gentleness seems to have become even more and more diffused through all he did.'

In Britain, Susi and Chuma were what might be called a 'success'. They stayed at Waller with Twywell who, during intervals of editing, took them to agricultural shows, to see the sights of London and the zoo, where they searched in vain for a soko. They stayed with James Young in Scotland and built for him a replica of the pole and thatch hut in which Livingstone died (not much different from a crofter's cottage on Ulva); and with the Webbs (in Waller's company), where they lived in the servants' quarters: 'From our maids,' Alice Webb remarks, 'we learnt that their good manner at meal times and their quickness in conforming to English habits, had impressed the English servants immensely.'

They had long talks in the garden with Livingstone's children, especially Tom, who were guests at the same time. Jacob Wainwright was a visitor to Newstead too and came to luncheon in the company of a Church Missionary Society fundraiser. Wainwright made a 'bad impression', left Webb pale and speechless with fury when he took his place as of right at the dining table. Miss Webb remarks that 'He thrust himself forward in conversation . . . had grown so much above himself and was so conceited' and then compounded the feeling that he was by no means 'the superior type of native' when after the meal he asked for a glass of brandy and soda! When their work in Britain was done, Susi, Chuma and Wainwright returned to Zanzibar. Susi became a caravan leader, Chuma worked for a while for the UMCA missionaries, then also became a transporter, as did Wainwright.

After this visit to Newstead, Tom had only two years to live. He died in Egypt in 1876. Oswell, a 'very nice quiet young man' according to Miss Webb, became a physician, went to practice in Trinidad, married, and died in 1892 at the age of forty-one. Anna Mary, Livingstone's youngest child, was fifteen at the time of the funeral, at school at Kendal: she hardly enters this story at all, but in 1881 married a missionary, Frank Wilson, and lived until 1939, leaving a son, Dr John Wilson, who served for a time with the Scottish mission to the Bemba in what is today the Northern Province of Zambia.

Agnes, true to her father's injunction that women should not under-rate themselves, took charge of family affairs after his death and worked with James Young to sort out the estate. Livingstone would have been pleased to learn that, unbeknown to himself in his last years, he had in fact managed to provide, even if not lavishly, for his children. 'We discovered,' Agnes wrote to Mrs Webb on 29th September 1874, 'some £2000 lying in Coutts' bank, and Mr Young says that with all the sums coming in, there will be about £9000 altogether' (in today's terms, nearly a million). As Livingstone left no will, Agnes decided that the money should be divided equally among the four surviving children. In the same letter Agnes is distressed at a circumstance that would not have surprised her father, the undervaluing of his work: 'Is it not disgusting?' she asks 'My Dearest Mrs Webb', 'Mr Waller has written to Mr Young telling him that there was a sale of Arrowsmith's effects and among them were all Papa's original maps. One of them was bought by Stanford, the map engraver, for a few shillings, if not pence and was the one that Arrowsmith altered to suit Cooley and made Papa so bitter against him.' Livingstone would have been amused too to hear Agnes keeping John Murray up to the mark; her letter to Mrs Webb concludes: 'I have written to Mr Murray asking him why I have not received any more proofs. He has written to acknowledge that the printing of the work, the maps and illustrations are all far advanced and no efforts of his will be wanting to get the book out in good time.'

The following year Agnes married Alexander Low Bruce, the wealthy director of an Edinburgh brewery, had two children and died in 1912 at the age of fifty-five. She, Bruce and other Scottish businessmen, were to raise capital to establish what they conceived to be Livingstone's ideal Darien in the country which soon became known as Nyasaland and is today called Malawi.

When the rectangular slab of stone bearing the falsified quotation finally sealed Livingstone's tomb he became the property not of the people of the lands and lakes he loved – and beneath whose trees he had wished to be laid to rest – but of a British imperial class (aristocrat, gentleman, financier, merchant, proletarian alike) that was to exploit, humiliate, betray and dispossess on a scale undreamed of by any nineteenth-century Portuguese or Arab slave magnate.

The scramble for Africa had begun.

Epilogue

In His Name

EPILOGUE

The conquest of the earth, which mostly means
the taking it away from those who have a different
complexion or slightly flatter noses than ourselves,
is not a pretty thing when you look into it too much.

Joseph Conrad,
Heart of Darkness

In Nyasaland Agnes Livingstone's husband, A L Bruce, acquired an
estate at Magomero, where coffee and then tea were grown for export,
and Agnes visited the place, virtually on the site of Bishop Mackenzie's
failed mission, a few years before her death in 1912. In 1915 the estate
was the centre of an uprising provoked by the abuse of labour
at Magomero and elsewhere. The rebellion was organised by John
Chilembwe, the leader of an independent African church. The revolt,
poorly co-ordinated, was soon suppressed and Chilembwe killed, but
in the first fury the manager of the Bruce estate was decapitated, his
severed head placed on the altar of Chilembwe's chapel. The man, a
relative of Agnes, was named William Jervis Livingstone.

As a result of colonisation during the forty years previous to 1915
the Africans of Nyasaland had lost sixty per cent of their land to
foreigners. The process of alienation had started in 1875 when the
Livingstonia Mission of the Free Church of Scotland (aided at the
outset by James Stewart) obtained a grant of land from the chief
in the area of Cape Maclear at the south of the Lake. The following year the established Church of Scotland founded its own
mission – named Blantyre after Livingstone's birthplace – at the
foot of the Shire Highlands. At the same time, the Livingstonia Central Africa Company was founded (one of its sponsors being A L
Bruce) and grew into the African Lakes Corporation. This commercial enterprise was closely associated with the Scottish missions and
for a while with the British South Africa Company (henceforth the
BSAC). The flagship of the Christian-commercial undertaking was the
steamship *Ilala*, which started service on the lake in 1876. By 1896

there were seventeen ships plying Nyasa, the Shire and the lower Zambezi.

A few years after its initiation, the Livingstonia mission moved to Khondowe, near the north end of the lake, and from there extended its work into the Nyasa-Tanganyika plateau and Bembaland. In 1885 the Universities' Mission to Central Africa returned to resume Bishop Mackenzie's work, not in the Highlands but on Likoma Island, half way along the lake. Meanwhile Livingstone's old employers, the London Missionary Society, had started work beside Lake Tanganyika. The party was led by Roger Price, survivor of the Helmore mission to Barotseland, and had a steamer named *Good News*. In Barotseland itself, evangelisation had begun in 1884 with the arrival – and acceptance by Sebitwane's successor King Lewanika – of the Paris Evangelical Missionary Society led by François Coillard. His wife was Scottish, and the PEMS was close to the London Missionary Society.

By the end of the 1880s the code of conduct agreed by the imperial powers at Bismarck's Berlin Conference to regulate the scramble for Africa was being put into effect, and the presence of the Scottish missionaries in Nyasaland enabled Britain to declare a 'protectorate' over the territory in 1891. In Barotseland, Coillard persuaded Lewanika to sign a treaty with the BSAC, while in Bembaland the French Catholic missionary Bishop Joseph Dupont engineered the submission of the rulers to the Company. Refusing a treaty, the Ngoni of the Luangwa plateau (Livingstone's Mazitu) were crushed with firepower, while Mwata Kazembe of the Lunda was subdued, his capital burned to the ground. The Bemba-Ngoni-Lunda area was named North Eastern Rhodesia, Barotseland and adjacent territories, North Western Rhodesia. The two regions were later amalgamated as Northern Rhodesia under the rule of the BSAC, with the town named Livingstone, close by the Victoria Falls, as capital. South of the Zambezi the BSAC – using the good offices of, among others, John Smith Moffat, founder of Livingstone's Matabele Mission – 'acquired' Southern Rhodesia through treaties with the Ndebele king, Lobengula. As the nineteenth century drew to a close the three territories we have named were firmly part of the British Empire.

The African rulers had lost their independence while the Portuguese, not without protest, lost their chance of linking Angola to Mozambique. (When Silva Porto, the Portuguese empire builder, whom Livingstone had met in Barotseland, learned that the Union Jack was flying over the upper Zambezi, he committed suicide, wrapped in the Portuguese flag, blowing himself up seated on a barrel of gunpowder.) If Britain's thrust into central Africa was powered by the BSAC it had the passive and, in the cases of Coillard and Dupont, active support of the missionaries. One ruler at least, Lewanika, was eager for

British 'protection' which he was led to believe the BSAC was providing.

Chartered by the British Government, the BSAC was given by royal signature the right not only to mine and trade, but to take over land and mineral resources, bring in settlers and rule in the name of Westminster. It was expected to finance itself and return a profit to its shareholders. The founder of the BSAC, Cecil John Rhodes, had made his fortune from South African diamonds, his push north inspired by the prospect of further mineral wealth and the bold dream of a British empire extending from Cape Town to Cairo. Northern Rhodesia and Nyasaland (henceforth Zambia and Malawi) were initially disappointing as far as minerals were concerned but fitted indispensably into the jigsaw of the great empire, as did Southern Rhodesia (Zimbabwe), which was sufficiently rich in gold and contained enough 'healthy highlands' to be suitable for extensive European settlement.

Zambia, the country where Livingstone died, and which he traversed more than any other, covers two hundred and fifty thousand square miles, making it almost three times the size of the British mainland. At the time of the complete BSAC takeover at the turn of the century, the huge territory probably had a total population of barely one million. The BSAC's small, efficient military units, equipped with such modern weapons as the Martini-Henry rifle and the Maxim machine gun, had little difficulty in establishing its new order. Once in power, the company acted forcibly to put a stop to the east and west coast slave trades – the last export of slaves from Zambia to Zanzibar is believed to have taken place in 1898. Freed slaves were usually handed, Mackenzie-Magomero fashion, to the missionaries and formed the basis of their flocks. The government office, the Boma, rather than the chief's palace, became the centre of authority.

The Boma, however, did not exist to disburse humanitarianism, it was an outpost of a capitalist enterprise which was expected to furnish a return on investment or at least, in the early stages, pay for itself. Livingstone had expected his Darien to make profits from the trade created by the export of commodities produced by free African farmers benefiting from the efficient management provided by his small groups of Christian settlers. African farmers, he had stated, had developed systems of husbandry which, in the geographical circumstances, could not be bettered. The BSAC on the other hand, regarded the persons of Africans themselves as commodities, their prime function to become a source of revenue. Soon after establishing its Bomas, the administration introduced the Hut Tax and installed collectors to gather it. The tax, which averaged ten shillings per hut, fell heavily on people who were mainly subsistence farmers with few outlets or markets through which surpluses could be converted into pounds, shillings, and pence. In former slave trade areas such as Bembaland there was, at first, little resentment of the tax, seen by the chiefs' subjects as a benign substitute for slavery, and it was often paid in kind. But, as the BSAC's demands for cash grew, the tax became more difficult to gather and the chiefs were enrolled as collectors. The tax became inescapable so that even villagers who had dispersed into scarcely habitable areas (like the Bangweulu swamps) were drawn into the net. Defaulters had their homes burned down and, if caught, were imprisoned. Tax rebellions were suppressed by force.

By the early years of the twentieth century, Zambia had been propelled into the world economic system. The BSAC had, in a formal way, healed what Livingstone called 'the open sore' but had found itself with very little in return. Gold had not been discovered in economic quantities, the only workable minerals seeming to be small deposits of copper (all located beneath pre-colonial surface mines) and a lead and zinc prospect at Broken Hill (now called Kabwe). To the north how-ever, the copper mines of Katanga (part of the Belgian crown's Congo Free State) had proved to be of immense value. In Southern Rhodesia, settler mining and farming had expanded after the 1896–7 suppression of the Ndebele and Shona rebellions against foreign rule, while railways were penetrating the continent. Rhodes dreamed of a spine of line from Cape to Cairo, its first stages were under construction.

Rhodes's treaty with Lewanika had given the BSAC authority over the vaguely defined territories subject to the Lozi throne, stretching as far east as the Batoka, as far north as the central watershed, but preserved the position of the king and the Lozi proper along the upper Zambezi. When the railway from the Cape reached the Victoria Falls in 1903 the BSAC decided to extend it, at least as far north as the Broken Hill mine. A bridge, still in use, was built across the Zambezi a few hundred yards below the Falls. It was now that Livingstone town was laid out. As the capital of Northern Rhodesia, every BSAC diktat could be prefaced with the phrase 'Livingstone says. . .'

After failure to raise £1 million in debentures, BSAC financed the construction of the railway northwards, by bank loans, offering the proceeds of the hut tax as amortisation, to be paid in instalments. The distance from the Falls to Broken Hill is about four hundred miles and the line was laid at speed. But it did not generate enough traffic to make it profitable. The BSAC acted to remedy the blot on the balance sheet by settling white farmers along its length. Taking advantage of the loose wording in the agreement with Lewanika, the company alienated land to a width of fifty miles on either side of the railway (an area the size of Denmark) divided it into blocks and sold it for pennies an acre to any settler who could, or would, produce freight. The Africans on this land –

some of it the finest in the country, Livingstone's Batoka Highlands for example – had either to leave or become serfs. Large alienations took place, too, in other parts, notably on the Nyasa-Tanganyika plateau and on the Luangwa plateau, where the Ngoni were dispossessed. In fact, with the exception of the Barotse heartland on the upper Zambezi, Africans in Zambia could claim no single square inch of land as their own. The BSAC interpreted its royal charter as giving it sole ownership of all land in the territory, its occupants being there on sufferance, and acted accordingly.

The hut tax, which returned an overall profit, was used not only to produce capital, but to supply labour to the new economy (exemplified in the railways) being established. Able-bodied males, from the age of fourteen upwards, who defaulted on the tax were forced to work, at first, as Boma prisoners. Later, when the expansion of mining and the opening of transport routes could be sustained only with great amounts of manpower, it was common to see whole enterprises in Southern Rhodesia, even South Africa, dependent on labour from as far north as Barotseland and Bembaland. On the Kimberley diamond fields in the Cape, 'northern' labour was in great demand as these men could be paid one shilling a week instead of the much higher local rate.

White labour agents from the south roamed Zambia, recruiting young men at naked gunpoint, or by bribing chiefs, to work on mines, farms and railways, hundreds, if not a thousand, miles from their villages. Conditions of travel, conditions of work were appalling, mortality from disease or starvation was as high as thirteen per cent over a six month contract. On returning home, survivors might have a few trinkets, but usually found they had earned hardly enough to pay the hut tax, the exigiencies of which had sent them on their journeys. It is impossible to calculate the number who died, but it is estimated that more than 20,000 men, forcibly recruited as porters for the British forces in the East Africa campaign during the 1914–1918 war, perished of disease or debilitation.

Looking back to the early days of the present century an elderly Zambian remarked in 1954 that there had been benefits at first from European rule – the suppression of the slave trade, the ending of the Ngoni wars, for example – but the whites had replaced past evils 'with a very bad form of slavery, that of recruiting people into forced labour.' The sjambok and the chain gang were much in use, and a recruiter was regarded as generous if he took only fifty per cent of the able-bodied males from a village. The effects, accumulated over decades, of even that reduction in the village manpower of a subsistence economy have not been overcome to this day. In 1946 it was estimated that sixty-six per cent of Zambia's rural manpower was away from the villages, many of which were inhabited solely by women, children and the aged. Like the Highlands of Scotland, the countryside of central Africa suffered its own form of clearances, the very thing Livingstone had wished to prevent.

The colonised people in all the tropical territories Livingstone knew could not escape from the conditions imposed on them, they remained subject to slavery in all but name, in varying degrees of intensity. Even the mouthpiece of the white settlers in Zambia, the *Livingstone Mail*, admitted in November 1911 that, '[slavery] is what forced labour comes to.'

The missionaries' attitude to forced labour was ambivalent, with a conflict between the Protestant ethic, epitomised in Coillard, which called for the 'natives' to be taught 'the need to work', and a realisation that the system was draining the creative life-blood of the countryside. (An early BSAC administrator on tour, had one day to have the broken pedal axle of his bicycle welded and reshaped by a village blacksmith, who used home-made iron and home-made tools. The job was done perfectly, the official commented that it was a pity such ingenious people were destined only to become the servants of the white man.) In time some missionaries, by no means a majority, came to oppose openly the more repressive and exploitative aspects of government policy, but the missionaries knew that in the last resort they relied on the goodwill and ultimately the protection of the administration. In Barotseland, in the first decade of the century, the Coillard mission was seriously threatened by the rapid growth of an independent, purely African church (such as Chilembwe's in Nyasaland). The BSAC saved the situation for the missionaries by expelling the new 'Ethiopian' church's leader from the country.

In 1923 the British Colonial Office took over the government of Zambia from the BSAC, paying the latter £3,750,000 as compensation for the expenses it had incurred, while allowing it to retain all mineral rights. That is to say, the BSAC received a royalty on every grain of anything mined in the country. It was the intention of the directors to build a small fortune of £200 million. This ambition was by no means unattainable for, by the end of the 1920s, Zambia's enormous deep-lying deposits of copper were being developed at a rate which would soon make the country one of the world's principal producers of the metal. When the BSAC surrendered its rights to the Zambian government at Independence in 1964, it received a further £4 million 'compensation'.

In 1935 the colonial government moved the capital from Livingstone to its present, more central site, Lusaka. The Copperbelt mines, and the industries growing up around them, with their rigid colour bar affecting the large labour force, the birth of a trade union movement, and, to some extent, the experience of Zambian troops serving the Allied cause abroad during the Second World War, all created a new political climate. In spite of pass laws which inhibited free movement of Africans to the towns, the country was fast becoming urbanised. Nationalist currents, which had their source among the first generation of 'mission graduates' in the 1920s, gathered force, the trade unions grew in strength, political movements became coherent and articulate. Power and protest confronted each other across the colour line – a line weakened to a small extent by the presence of a handful of settlers and clergymen supporting the African cause.

After the war, stormy days lay ahead for the country, especially when the British government, without African consent, created the Central African Federation in 1953, placing Zambia at risk of being exploited and dominated by the white settlers of Southern Rhodesia. The risk turned into a reality. Hundreds of millions of pounds worth of copper profits were siphoned to the south, a settler leader there could declare that Zambia was Rhodesia's 'milch cow'. The largest, most impressive – and most elegant – skyscraper built in the federal capital, Salisbury, Southern Rhodesia, during the period was erected by a mining company, Rhodesian Selection Trust, waxing fat off Zambian copper. The building is hallowed with the name 'Livingstone House'.

The creation of Federation was greeted with the appearance of a number of substantial books concerning Livingstone. J R P Wallis produced *The Zambezi Expedition of David Livingstone 1858–63*, published in 1956; in 1955, Jack Simmons's *Livingstone and Africa* appeared, and Frank Debenham's *The Way to Ilala: David Livingstone's Pilgrimage*; and in 1957 Michael Gelfand's *Livingstone the Doctor: His Life and Travels: A Study in Medical History*. Three of these volumes had their publication subsidised by the BSAC, or one or other of its siblings.

At various points in the preceding chapters there have been summaries of what appeared to be Livingstone's achievements in broadening the range of human knowledge. The intention of Gelfand, and of Debenham is to show that Livingstone's researches laid the base for the beneficent civilisation which the Federation purported to be. In the preface to Debenham's admirable work, the colonial governor of Northern Rhodesia, Sir Arthur Benson, contemplating in 1954 the hatred for Federation which beset the people he ruled, declared from Government House, Lusaka:

> We who work in Northern Rhodesia strive to work in the spirit and with the motives of Livingstone, and because of Livingstone our work is made easier than the same work elsewhere. For him in this country the trumpets will always sound.

Even if Livingstone's name was being used cynically to disguise the essential nature of the empire in central Africa, the very use of the name of a man regarded as a saint could not fail to have a mitigating effect on the nature of British rule once it had been consolidated. That the initial imposition was violent or treacherous, or both, cannot be denied, but what followed, replete as it may have been with hypocrisy, exploitation, and the humiliations of racial discrimination and paternalism, bears little comparison with what had succeeded the contemporary German occupation of Namibia, or the earlier British settlement of Australia, regarding the native inhabitants.

Although the ethos of colonial rule in central Africa was a far cry from Livingstone's putative Darien, he could not but have approved the Colonial Office's declaration once it had taken over from the BSAC that African interests were to be paramount – albeit at some unspecified time in the future. But despite this statement of good intentions, resistance to foreign rule was all but universal, even when it had in many instances replaced the tyranny of monarchs financing themselves by rapine or the slave trade.

Many Africans today, and with good reason, regard Livingstone as having been a spy. But he was more than merely that; he was the forward, and far from secret agent, of a new culture, the industrial capitalism which by a turn of the wheel of history came to dislodge Iron Age civilisation. Livingstone did not implant the new culture himself but, as far as central Africa is concerned, he established the preconditions for its advance. And, at the present time, this Africa is embracing the new culture wholeheartedly, ridding itself of that post-colonial recrudesence of the Iron Age monarchy, the one-party state ruled by regal dictatorship.

Before Livingstone's transcontinental journey the only account of the interior of central Africa that had appeared in English formed part of Daniel Defoe's story *Captain Singleton*, published in 1720 and reprinted continuously. So authentically did the book read that as late as 1864, during the Burton/Speke Nile controversy, Singleton is credited with having visited the source of the river during a journey which took him across central Africa from east to west at approximately the same latitude as Livingstone's trek. Before Singleton reached the deep interior he came across features which resemble Cabora Basa and the Shire Cataracts but, after ascending the escarpment, he leads us into a realm of pure speculation decorated with two lakes which might well be the Portuguese Zachef (or Maravi) and Ptolemy's Coloe.

Livingstone, while in the middle of the Bangweulu swamps remarked in his Journal that Singleton had come across no such watery wilderness. Singleton's inland plateau was, for hundreds of miles, a totally uninhabited 'desart', of blistering sand.

[350]

These were the two all-important misconceptions of which Livingstone disabused his British public, opening central Africa to the gaze of the empire builders. This was the geographical triumph which Sir Roderick Murchison remarked. Taken together, Livingstone's journeys neatly capped Jonathan Swift's satirical comment on the armchair-experts:

> So Geographers, in *Afric*-maps
> With Savage-Pictures fill their Gaps,
> And o'er uninhabitable Downs,
> Place Elephants for want of Towns.

Equally important today is the record Livingstone left of the people he met on his travels and the events he reported. No account of the pre-colonial history of central Africa is possible without close attention to his writings.

Livingstone's dreams for these lands were his in-bred expression of a wish for self-fulfilment. They were also an example of the utopianism which spread as the full implications of the Industrial Revolution became apparent. He lived through a period when a new economic order was replacing the hallowed patterns of the rural past with incipient new rigidities – the railroad for the village path, the production line for the croft.

He hoped to create a regime of justice in his imagined Africa, but there were forces at work more powerful than his ideals, forces producing worldwide challenges which generated visionary responses, sending men and women in longing pursuit of sacred certainties: Wagner's Siegfried, for the Holy Grail; Marx, for the earthly paradise; Livingstone, for the perfect Darien. For each of these seekers, and for many others, an idea existed beyond mere matter. If they failed in their quests, became icons for people who perverted their memory, the fault lay not with themselves.

Trumpets still sound for Livingstone today. Mutedly, but for better reasons than those of the colonial governor. The huge statue, even if erected to deodorise a regime Livingstone would have detested and fought, stands yet by the Victoria Falls, the sweet-smelling Smoke-that-Thunders rising in billows about it. Christianity in manifold forms has become part of the culture of Africa from coast to coast. Livingstone belongs no longer to the Men of Empire who used his name. If he may have been wrong in believing that the Ideal could be achieved by the single Man of Destiny, wrong in seeking to belittle and crush those he thought stood in his way, he was right in his wish to see people free.

The ground by the great waterfall is trembling insistently, and

the largest curtain of falling water in the world, like a living thing,
is moving grain by mineral grain towards a new horizon.

Waterfalls, like human names, hold no fixed position, for

> All the rivers run into the sea; yet the
> sea is not full; unto the place from whence
> the rivers come, thither they return again.
>
> Ecclesiastes, I, vii

SELECT BIBLIOGRAPHY

David Livingstone: A Catalogue of Documents by G.W. Clendennen and I.C. Cunningham and its *Supplement* (Edinburgh National Library of Scotland for the David Livingstone Documentation Project, 1979 and 1985) lists all material available at the time. Letters, journals, notebooks, etc. are listed in chronological order, the letters being summarized under recipients, essential facts about whom are given. Some material that came to light after 1985 is contained in Holmes (see below).

The provenance of David Livingstone letters quoted in the present volume may be established by reference to the above. The *Catalogue* also contains an extensive bibliography.

Ansell, W.F.H. *Mammals of Northern Rhodesia*, Lusaka, 1960

Axelson, E. *Portugal and the Scramble for Africa*, Johannesburg, 1967

Azevdeo, A. *O Mulato*, ed. Ática, São Paolo, 1986

Bach, D.C., ed. *La France et l'Afrique du Sud*, Paris, 1990

Barnett, Corelli. *The Audit of War: The Illusion and Reality of Britain as a Great Nation*, London, 1986

Bennett, L. jnr. *Before the Mayflower*, 5th ed., Harmondsworth, 1984

Best, G. *Mid-Victorian Britain 1851–1875*, London, 1971

Blaikie, W.G. *The Personal Life of David Livingstone*, London, 1880

Boucher, M., ed. *Livingstone Letters 1843–1972*, Johannesburg, 1985

Burton, R. *The Lake Regions of Central Africa*, London, 1860

Butt, J. *James 'Paraffin' Young: Founder of the Mineral Oil Industry*, Edinburgh, 1983

Buxton, T.F. *The African Slave Trade and its Remedy (1839)*, 2nd ed., 1 vol, London, 1968

Camões, L.V. de. *Os Lusiadas*, Porto, 1974

Campbell, R.J. *Livingstone*, London, 1929

Caraman, F.P. *The Lost Empire: The Story of the Jesuits in Ethiopia 1555–1634*, London, 1985

Carlyle, T. *Essays*, London, 1967

Chadwick, W.O. *Mackenzie's Grave*, London, 1959

Chambers Encyclopedia, Oxford, 1966

Chinyanta, M. and C.J. Chiwale. *Mutomboko Ceremony and the Lunda-Kazembe Dynasty*, Lusaka, 1989

Collis, M. *Raffles*, London, 1966

Conrad, J. *Heart of Darkness*, London, 1902

Coupland, R. *Kirk on the Zambezi: A Chapter of African History*, Oxford, 1928

Coupland, R. *Livingstone's Last Journey*, London, 1945

Darwin, C. *The Origin of Species*, London, 1872

Darwin, C. *The Voyage of the Beagle*, London, 1839

de Lacerda, J. *Reply to Dr Livingstone's Accusations and Misrepresentations*, London, 1865

de Selincourt, A., tr. *Herodotus: The Histories*, Harmondsworth, 1972

Debenham, F. *The Way to Ilala: David Livingstone's Pilgrimage*, London, 1955

Defoe, D. *Robinson Crusoe*, London, 1972

Devereux, W.C. *A Cruise in the Gorgon*, London, 1869

Dickens, C. *Bleak House*

Dickens, C. *Little Dorrit*

Du Bois, W.E.B. *The World and Africa: An Inquiry into the Part which Africa has Played*, New York, 1947

Du Plessis, J. *A History of Christian Missions in South Africa*, London, 1911

Duffy, J. *Portuguese Africa*, Harvard, 1961

Engerman, S.C. and E.D. Genovese, eds. *Race and Slavery in the Western Hemisphere: Quantitative Studies*, Princeton, 1975

Foskett, R., ed. *The Zambezi Doctors: David Livingstone's Letters to John Kirk*, Edinburgh, 1965

Foskett, R., ed. *The Zambezi Journal and Letters of Dr John Kirk 1858–63*, Edinburgh, 1965

Frazer, A.Z. *Livingstone and Newstead*, London, 1913

Fryer, P. *Staying Power: The History of Black People in Britain*, London, 1984

Furneaux, R.S. *William Wilberforce*, London, 1974

Gelfand, M. *Livingstone the Doctor: His Life and Travels: A Study in Medical History*, Oxford, 1957

Genovese, E.D. *From Rebellion to Revolution: Afro-American Slave Revolts in the Making of the Modern World*, Baton Rouge, 1979

Gosset, T.F. *Race: The History of an Idea in America*, Dallas, 1963

Guimarães, B. *A Escrava Isaura*, Ática, São Paolo, 1985

Haldane, A. *Memoirs of the Lives of Robert Haldane of Airthrey and of his brother, James Alexander Haldane*, London, 1852

Hall, R. *Stanley: An Adventurer Explored*, London, 1974

Hall, R. *Zambia*, London, 1965

Hammond, R.J. *Portugal and Africa 1815–1910: a Study in Economic Imperialism*, Stanford, 1966

Hastings, M. *Sir Richard Burton: A Biography*, London, 1978

Healey, E. *Lady Unknown: The Life of Angela Burdett-Coutts*, London, 1978

Hill, C. *The World Turned Upside Down: Radical Ideas During the English Revolution*, Harmondsworth, 1975

Holmes, T., ed. *David Livingstone Letters and Documents: The Zambian Collection*, London and Bloomington, 1990

Huggett, F.E. *Victoria's England as seen byPunch*, London, 1978

Jeal, T. *Livingstone*, London, 1973

Ki-Zerbo, J., ed. *A General History of Africa*, vol 1, London, 1981

Koss, S. *The Rise and Fall of the Political Press in Britain*, vol 1, London, 1981

Krapf, J.L. *Vocabulary of Six East African Languages: Kisuaheli, Kinjka, Kikamba, Kipokomo, Kihiau, Kigalla*, Tubingen, 1850

Kumar, S.K., ed. *Captain Singleton*, Oxford, 1990

Lau, B., ed. *A.J. Andersson – Trade and Politics in Central Namibia 1860–64*, Windhoek, 1989

Listowel, J. *The Other Livingstone*, Lewes, 1974

Livingstone, D. and C. *Narrative of an Expedition to the Zambesi and its Tributaries and of the Discovery of the Lakes Shirwa and Nyassa 1858–1864*, London, 1865

Livingstone, David. *Analysis of the Language of the Bechuanas*, London, 1858

Livingstone, David. *Missionary Travels in South Africa*, London, 1857

MacPherson, F. *The British Conquest of Northern Rhodesia*, London, 1976

Maitland, A. *Speke*, London, 1971

Marchand, L.A. *Byron*, London, 1971

Marques, A.H. de O. *History of Portugal*, 2 vols, New York, 1972

Martelli, G. *Livingstone's River: A History of the Zambezi Expedition 1858–1864*, London, 1970

Martineau, J. *The Life and Correspondence of Sir Bartle Frere*, 2 vols, London, 1895

Marx, K. and F. Engels. *Collected Works*, vol 14, Moscow, 1980

Marx, K. and F. Engels. *The First Indian War of Independence 1857–1859*, London, 1960

Melville, H. *Moby Dick: or, The Whale*, London, 1946

Melville, H. *Three Stories*, London, 1967

Miller, J.C. *Way of Death: Merchant Capitalism and the Angolan Slave Trade 1730–1830*, London, 1990

Mitchison, R.A. *A History of Scotland*, London, 1970

Moffat, R. *Missionary Labours and Scenes in Southern Africa*, London, 1842

Monk, W., ed. *Dr Livingstone's Cambridge Lectures*, London, 1957–58

Morrell, W.P. *British Colonial Policy in the Mid-Victorian Age: South Africa, New Zealand, the West Indies*, Oxford, 1969

Mudenge, S.I.G. *A Political History of Munhumutapa 1400–1902*, London, 1988

Nabudere, D.W. *The Political Economy of Imperialism, its Theoretical and Polemical Treatment from Mercantilist to Multilateral Imperialism*, London and Dar es Salaam, 1977

Naipaul, V.S. *The Loss of Eldorado: A History*, London, 1969

Omer-Cooper, J.D. *History of Southern Africa*, London, 1987

Oswell, W.E. *William Cotton Oswell, Hunter and Explorer*, 2 vols, London, 1900

Pachai, B. *Malawi: The History of the Nation*, London, 1973

Pachai, B., ed. *Livingstone: Man of Africa*, London, 1973

Payne, R. *The White Rajahs of Sarawak*, Singapore, 1989

Pedraza, H.J. *Borrioboola/Gha*, London, 1960

Pendle, G. *Paraguay: A Riverside Nation*, 3rd., London, 1967

Prebble, J. *Culloden*, London, 1973

Prebble, J. *The Darien Disaster*, Edinburgh, 1978

Prebble, J. *The Highland Clearances*, London, 1963

Raffles, T.S. *Memoirs*, London, 1864

Ransford, O. *Livingstone's Lake*, London, 1966

Ritchie, J.E. *Life and Discoveries of David Livingstone*, 6 vols, London, 1876–79 (also 2 vols, National Library of Scotland)

Roberts, A. *A History of Zambia*, London, 1976

Robinson, R. and J. Gallagher. *Africa and the Victorians: The Official Mind of Imperialism*, London, 1961

Rotberg, T.I. *Christian Missionaries and the Creation of Northern Rhodesia 1880–1924*, Princeton, 1965

Schapera, I., ed. *David Livingstone: Family Letters 1842–1856*, 2 vols, London, 1959

Schapera, I., ed. *David Livingstone: South African Papers 1849–1853*, Cape Town, 1974

Schapera, I., ed. *Livingstone's African Journal 1853–1856*, 2 vols, London, 1963

Schapera, I., ed. *Livingstone's Missionary Correspondence 1841–1856*, London 1961

Schapera, I., ed. *Livingstone's Private Journals 1851–1853*, London, 1960

Seaver, G. *David Livingstone: His Life and Letters*, London, 1957

Shepperson, G. and T. Price. *Independent African: John Chilembwe and the Origins, Setting and Significance of the Nyasaland Native Rising of 1915*, Edinburgh, 1958

Shepperson, G., ed. *David Livingstone and the Rovuma*, Edinburgh, 1965

Sheriff, A. *Slaves, Spices and Ivory in Zanzibar: Integration of an East African Commercial Empire into the World Economy 1770–1873*, London, 1987

Smiles, S. *Self-help: with Illustrations of Conduct and Perseverance*, Harmondsworth, 1986

Smout, T.C. *A History of the Scottish People 1560–1830*, London, 1969

Stanley's Despatches to the New York Herald 1871–72 and 1874–77, Boston, 1970

Stanley, H.M. *How I Found Livingstone: Travels, Adventures and Discoveries in Central Africa, including Four Months' Residence with Dr Livingstone*, London, 1872

Storrs, A.E.G. *Know Your Trees*, Ndola, 1979

Stowe, H.B. *Uncle Tom's Cabin*, Harmondsworth, 1981

Tabler, E.C. ed. *The Zambezi Papers of Richard Thornton, Geologist to Livingstone's Zambezi Expedition*, London, 1963

Thompson, L. *A History of South Africa*, New Haven and London, 1990

Tinhorão, J.R. *Os Negros em Portugal*, Lisbon, 1988

Varian, H.F. *Some African Milestones*, Bulawayo, 1973

Waller, H. ed. *The Last Journals of David Livingstone in Central Africa from 1865 to his Death, continued by a narrative of his last moments and sufferings obtained from his faithful servants Chuma and Susi*, 2 vols, London, 1874

Wallis, J.P.R., ed. *The Zambezi Expedition of David Livingstone*, 2 vols, London, 1956

Whitten, D.G.A. and J.R.V. Brooks. *The Penguin Dictionary of Geology*, Harmondsworth, 1972

Wood, A. *Nineteenth-Century Britain 1815–1914*, London, 1982

Woodward, Sir E.L. *The Age of Reform 1815–1870*, 2nd ed., Oxford, 1962

INDEX

abolitionism 14, 15, 30–1, 310–11; DL's convictions 14, 191, 211, 263, 326; 302–3 (Moses); Exeter Hall Meeting 22–23; in USA 14, 71–3, 82–3, 134 *see also* racism; slavery
Ajawa *see* Yao
Amoda 261, 288, 292–3, 321, 334
Analysis of the language of the Bechuanas. An (David Livingstone, 1858) 40–2, 67, 135, 155
Anderson's College (Glasgow) 10, 11, 13, 16
Angola *see* slavery: in Portuguese possessions (Angola and Brazil)
Anthropological Society 251–2, 254
ape 306–7
Argyll, George Douglas Campbell, 8th Duke of xv, 26, 153, 234, 253
Arrowsmith, John (1790–1875) 118, 249, 250, 339

Bagamoyo (port) 281, 315, 320, 334
Baines, John Thomas (1820–75): chosen for Zambezi Expedition 150–1; dismissal 179–82, 240, 248, 291; first paintings of Victoria Falls, 181, 249, 304
Bakwena 48, 57, 61; Boers 67
Bambarre (Kabambare) 296–7, 300, 301–4
Bangweulu (lake) 277, 278; DL reaches (1868) 288; gets bearings wrong 292, 325–6; returns (1873), wanderings 326–9
Barotseland *see* Kololo: territory
Barotseland Mission 132, 170, 183, 344
Batoka (plateau) 61, 182–3; DL's hopes 102, 146, 157, 159, 171
Bedingfeld, Norman Bernard (1824–94); second-in command, Zambezi Expedition 148–9; quarrels begin 159–60; dismissed 166–70, 216, 248

Beecher Stowe, Harriet 249; *Uncle Tom's Cabin* 71–3, 83–5
beehives 124–5
Bemba 281–2, 283–4, 286, 325, 344
Bennett, *Sir* James Risdon (1809–91) 20, 49, 51
Blantyre: Scottish National Memorial to David Livingstone 3–4
Boers 30-3, 51, 67
Bogharib, Mohamed 287, 288, 289, 295–6, 307; saves DL's life 293; forces DL's men to continue 305, 306
Bombay 227–8, 259–62
Botletle (river) 54, 55, 61
Braithwaite, Joseph Bevan (1818–1905) 151, 178, 235, 256
British Association for the Advancement of Science (1864) 235–7
British government: dealings with DL 75, 98, 108, 247; Zambezi Expedition 132, 136–7, 141, 147–8, 164–5; continuation and UMCA 186, 200, 231, 233, 241 *see also* consulships; funeral: Westminster Abbey; Royal Academy dinner
British South Africa Company 101, 343, 344–9
Bruce, Alexander Low 339, 343
BSAC *see* British South Africa Company
Buchanan, Andrew (1798–1878) 13, 151, 207, 220
buffaloes, Indian 262, 265, 269–70, 293
Burrup, Henry de Wint (1831–62) 198–9, 200
Burton, *Sir* Richard Francis (1821–90) 111–12, 117, 175, 240; Lake Tanganyika with Speke (1858) 235–6, 317; racism 128, 251

Cabora Basa: DL's failure to explore (1856) 93, 97, 173; unable to navigate upriver (1858) 171; recklessly

endangers men 185–6
Calvinism: and racism 51, 82–5; predestination 14, 46, 60
Campbell, George Douglas, 8th Duke Argyll xv, 26, 153, 234, 253
cap, consul's xiv, 137, 237, 315, 319
Cape Colony 30–3, 65; Sechele refused redress 67
Cape Town 31, 63, 99, 139, 157–8; Barotseland Mission 183; Robert 209–10
Cardoso, Candido Jose da Costa (c. 1800–90) 173–4, 188, 251
Carlyle, Thomas (1795–1881) 108, 111, 114-16
Cassange 78, 81, 86
Chambeshi (river) 278, 288, 290, 327–8
Chibisa (Chief, Manganja) 174–5, 195, 200, 216
Chilembwe, John 343
Chipping Ongar (Essex) 18–20, 129
Chitambo (Chief, Lala): gives DL refuge 329–31; DL dies in his village 330–3
Chitembo (Chief, Bisa) 278
Chitapankwa, (King of the Bemba) 278, 281–2, 283
Chobe (river) 57, 59, 174
Chonwane 36, 48, 50
chronometers: damaged 279, 286; readings at Lake Bangweulu wrong 288, 292, 325–7
Chuma 284, 288, 297, 301, 306, 324; freed from Yao (1861) 196; sails with DL to Bombay 227; rejoins DL 261; becomes his personal attendant 274; marriage 321; DL's death 330–4; brought to Britain, helps Waller, returns to Zanzibar 337–8
Clarendon, George William Frederick Villiers, 4th Earl of (1800–70) *see* British government: dealings with DL
cloves 191, 260, 264, 335
coal 97, 174, 185, 237
Colenso, John William (1814–83) 236
consulships: DL's first (1858) 132, 137, 141, 182; actions not in accordance 164–6; terminated (end 1863) 225; new consulship 241, 260, 310
Comoros (islands) 194, 227
Congo (river) 80, 290, 295
Congregationalists 8, 14, 18, 30, 71; DL member and minister 8, 20, 121, 231
copper 70, 95, 237, 348–9; Bemba wire 281
cotton 133–4, 136, 232; DL's hopes 147,

149–50, 153–4, 176–7, 227
cotton mill 3-6

Darien Scheme 26, 147, 200
Darwin, Charles (1809–82) 112, 193; *The descent of man* 128–9; *The origin of species by means of natural selection* 114–15, 139, 195; *The voyage of the Beagle* (DL and Darwin compared) 117, 124–9
Dedza (plateau) 275
Defoe, Daniel 9, 26–8, 350
Descent of man, The (Charles Darwin) 128–9
Dick, Thomas 8, 38, 126
Dickens, Charles (1812–70) 16, 23, 132, 137–8, 252
Drummond, Henry 17, 32
Dugumbe bin Habib 308, 309–11
Duncan, John 156, 160
dysentery: boiling of water 76, 302; Thornton 222–3

Edwards, Rogers (1795–1876), 35–6; Mabotsa 45, 46, 48, 50
Edwards, Samuel 49, 184–5
Eyre, E. J. 23, 115, 251–2, 299

Fleming, George 67, 68, 73, 74, 99
Fountains of Herodotus 69, 302, 308
Frere, *Sir* Bartle 227–8, 259, 260-1, 264, 291; Zanzibar 334–5; arranges DL's state funeral 336–7
Frere, George (1810–78) 217, 226, 263
frog, tree 301
funeral of DL: journey from Africa 332–5; lying-in-state, RGS 335–6; Westminster Abbey 336–7

Gabriel, Edmund 78–9, 80, 98
Galilee (lake) 198, 237
Gardner (Nassik boy) 284, 288, 301, 306, 324
George (barque) 26, 28–30, 227
Gharib, Mohamed bin *see* Bogharib, Mohamed
Glasgow 14, 15, 136, 279
Godinho, Manuel: quoted 188, 190
goats 277, 284, 306, 324, 327
Grant, James Augustus (1827–92): Lake Victoria 235, 322
Gray, Robert (1809–72) 139, 236
Great Zambezi Meeting (1859) 192
Grey, *Sir* George 139, 146, 157, 192, 202

Gutzlaff, Karl Friedrich Augustus von 10, 21

Halima 321, 324, 334
Hamilton (Scotland) 5, 16, 64, 233, 254
see also Independent Church, Hamilton
Hamis wa Mtoa 285
Hannan, James 151, 207, 220
Helmore, Holloway 183–5
Highlanders 4, 15, 26; DL 91–2, 118–19, 258
Hottentots see Khoi
Huguenot (French) missionaries 37, 117, 184, 344, 348; Prosper Lemue 45, 258

Independent Church, Hamilton 8, 9, 17, 121 see also Hamilton (Scotland)
iron-working 38–9, 70, 281, 348
ivory 70, 74, 95, 163, 191; DL and 98, 178, 217, 260, 264; Zaire 294

Jesuits 81–2, 147, 221, 290
journals see Livingstone, David, journal

Kafue (river) 91, 92, 153
Kalungwishi (river) 326
Kande 276
Kazembe VIII, *Mwata* (Lunda) 286–7, 292, 344; help to DL 288, 326
Kebra Basa see Cabora Basa
Khoi 30, 32, 81; rebellion 65–6
Kirk, John, later knighted (1832–1922): medical officer, botanist and zoologist, Zambezi Expedition (1858) 150, 152, 153–6, 198; explores Shire with DL 174, 175, 177; has to act for DL over Baines and Thornton 180–1; research notes lost through DL at Cabora Basa 185–6; Galilean fish 198, 237; DL irrational at the Rovuma 217–18; ill but stays to tend DL, gets away (May 1863) 223; DL names escarpment 226; through DL is posted to British Consulate, Zanzibar 237–8, 262, 314–15, 320; finds DL porters despite cholera 305–6, 312–13, 316; away when DL's body reaches Bagamoyo 334–5; pall-bearer 336–7
Kirk's Range (escarpment) 226, 274, 275
Kolobeng 49, 51, 157, 291
Kololo 34, 60, 89–90, 344–5, 346; centuries-old trading network 70; territory 61, 69, 145 see also Barotseland Mission; Sebitwane, King

of the Kololo; Sekeletu, King of the Kololo
Kongone (river outlet, Zambezi delta) 190; found 160; navy patrols 168, 175, 180; UMCA 199–202, 204
Kru seamen 156, 166, 169, 175
Kuruman Mission 35, 121–2, 136, 183 see also Moffat, Robert
Kwena see Bakwena; Sechele (Chief, Bakwena)

Lacerda, Jose de 250–1
Lady Nyassa (DL's steamer): arrives (1862) 199–201; Shupanga and the Shire 214, 220, 224, 225; DL sails her to Bombay (1864) 227–8, 257; sold at a loss 219, 224, 228, 321
Lala see Chitambo (Chief, Lala)
Landins see Ngoni
Last journals (David Livingstone, edited by H. Waller, 1874) 330, 337–8, 339
Layard, *Sir* Austin Henry (1817–94) 158, 189, 231
Leadwood 161–2, 195, 197, 199
Linyanti 60, 61, 87, 183–5, 197
lion 45, 137
Livingstone, Agnes (daughter, 1847–1912) 206–7, 299–300; early years 64, 151, 205; Robert 211, 212, 259; accompanies DL (1864–5) 233, 244, 245, 248, 254; finishing school, Paris 256, 258–9; DL's funeral 336–7; Waller and last journals 337; DL's estate 338–9; marries 339; at Magomero 343
Livingstone, Agnes (mother) 4–5, 64, 212, 233; death 205, 254–5
Livingstone, Agnes and Janet (sisters) 5, 9, 64, 212, 336–7; DL home 233, 254
Livingstone, Anna Mary (daughter, 1858–1939) 170, 205, 233, 254, 255; Quaker school 256, 258
Livingstone, Charles (brother, 1821–73) 5, 9, 65, 71; chosen for Zambezi Expedition 149–50; foments trouble 166, 180; attacks DL and porter 185; leaves DL and Kirk at Cabora Basa without food 185–6; raids village (1861) 196; ill, leaves 223; co-authorship (1864) 234–5, 237; observation of female mosquito 237; appointed consul, Fernando Po 235, 240
Livingstone, David (1813–73): dedication to abolition of slavery 14,

191, 263, 302–3, 326; economic vision 22–3, 134–5, 146, 176–7; faith 21, 119, 300, 328;

life:

1813–29

Highland ancestry 4, 91–2, 119; child worker, cotton mill 3, 5, 6; religious conversion 7–8, 21;

1830–9

medical training interrupted 9, 11, 16; missionary training 18–20, 121, 129; voice constricted 18, 67; Catherine Ridley 24–5, 42, 122; meets Robert Moffat 22

1840–9

completes medical degree 20, 21; ordained (Congregationalist) 20; studies navigation 30; at Kuruman 35; left arm disabled by lion 45; marriage 45, 122; quarrel at Mabotsa, moves to Kolobeng 48–9; Sechele and the Bakwena 48–51, 61, 67; he and Oswell discover Lake Ngami (1849) 37–8, 53–4, 86, 124;

1850–9

infant daughter dies (1850) 59; King Sebitwane befriends DL but dies 58–60; Kololo help continues, he and Oswell map Upper Zambezi 60–1, 75, 86; sends Mary to Britain 63; Boers raid Kolobeng 67; seeks trade route westward, at Luanda (May 1854) 75–9; refuses to leave Kololo men 86; DL sees Victoria Falls (1855) 87–9; unaware of Cabora Basa 93, 171–2; reaches Quelimane 95–9; Mary's verses of welcome (December 1856), 104; RGS Gold Medal 112; *Missionary Travels* 116–30; Cambridge lectures 134–6; grant from Parliament 136; Queen Victoria 136–7; consulship 137, 141; funds John Smith Moffat 145; chooses Zambezi Expedition members 148–51; Expedition sails (10th March, 1858) 156; Cape Town, Mary left 157–8; the Pearl unable to navigate Zambezi inland from delta 160; Bedingfeld dismissed 166–70; paddle steamer blocked at Cabora Basa 170–1, 173; Shire River 173; Murchison Cataracts and Lake Shirwa 174–5; Lake Nyasa (1859) 176–7; Baines and Thornton dismissed 179–82, 240

1860–9

east from Tete 182; Barotseland Mission tragedy 183–5; endangers men's lives at Cabora Basa 185–6; Portuguese doubt his claims 187–90; Expedition's support renewed 186, 192, 193; DL meets first UMCA party and steamer Pioneer (1861) 194; second UMCA party, Mary and DL's steamer, Lady Nyassa 199; UMCA culminates in deaths of Mackenzie, Scudamore and Burrup (1862) 198–200; Mary dies 202–5; Robert 206–12; Government ends Expedition (1863) 224–5; Sails Lady Nyassa to Bombay, arrives London (1864) 227–8; Addresses British Association 236–7; accepts RGS invitation to seek Nile source 240–1, 242; at Newstead Abbey, *Narrative* (1864) 233, 234, 243–51; Palmerston's indirect offer 247, 291; Royal Academy dinner (1865) 253–4; In Bombay recruits non-slaves, to Zanzibar 260–1; RGS Expedition departs (March 1866) 265–6; animals cannot disembark on Rovuma 269; war blocks route to Lake Tanganyika 271, 272; reaches Lake Nyasa after four months 273; Dedza plateau and Luangwa valley 275–6; Muchinga escarpment 277; chronometer damaged, medicines stolen 279; turns in order to pick up supplies at Ujiji 282; fit of unconsciousness 284; route blocked by war, Hamis wa Mtoa gives refuge 285–6; turns west, travels with slave traders 286–7; Lake Mweru 287–8; Lake Bangweulu, chronometer damage causes wrong longitude reading (1868) 288, 292; travels east again, has pneumonia and putsi fly maggots 293; Ujiji (early 1869) 293, 294–6; west with Bogharib, reaches Bambarre (Kabambare) 296–7;

1870–3

ill, foot ulcers, fails to leave 300–1; stores arrive 304; reaches Lualaba, but no canoe to cross 308; Nyangwe massacre 309; returns to Ujiji 311; new supplies looted, destitute 312–13; Stanley arrives (27th October, 1871) 315–16; he and DL prove Lake Tanganyika not Nile source 317; farewell at Unyanyembe (Tabora)

318, 321; DL travels south west inland again (August 1872) 322–3; revisits Lake Bangweulu, incorrect readings of 1867 cause sufferings in swamps 326–9; DL is given refuge by Chief Chitambo and dies at his village (30th April, 1873) 329, 330–1; journey of body 332–4; state funeral 336–7

Livingstone, David, journal 184–5; quotations 60 (Sebitwane, 1851); 77, 81, 86–7 (1854); 88 (Victoria Falls, 1855) 202 (Mary's death, 1862); 146, 227 (1864); 211, 253 (1865); 269 (1866); 277–8, 278–9, 284–5, 290–1 (1867); 308 (1871); 327–9 (1873)

Livingstone, David, published works: *An analysis of the language of the Bechuanas* (printed privately, London 1858) 40–2, 67, 135, 155; *Missionary travels and researches in South Africa* (London, 1857) 93, 117–30, 171–2; 60, 92, 188 (quoted); *Cambridge lectures*, edited W. Monk (1858) 135–6; *Narrative of an expedition to the Zambezi and its tributaries* (London, 1865) 93, 233, 234, 243–51; *Last journals* (edited H. Waller (1874) 330, 337–8, 339

Livingstone, John (brother) 5, 9, 151–2, 212–14

Livingstone, Mary (1821–1862): marries DL (1845) 45–8; Mabotsa, Chonwane and Kolobeng 48–51, 53; journey by ox cart, death of infant daughter 58–9; sent back to Britain with children, wanders in poverty (1852) 62–4; reunited (1856) 103–4, 113, 116; verses of welcome 104; sails with DL (1858) 151, 156; pregnant, left at Cape 157; Anna Mary born, returns to Britain with her and Oswell 202–3; travels to Zambezi delta with second UMCA party, dies at Shupanga (27th April, 1862) 202–5, 220

Livingstone, Neil (father) 4–5, 6–7, 8, 64; death 102; name 91–2

Livingstone, Robert Moffat (son, 1847–64) 49, 151, 205–8; American Civil War 209–12, 233, 255

Livingstone, Thomas Steele (son, 1849–76) 58, 151, 205, 299, 336–7; DL's visits 233, 244, 255; health 234, 256, 291, 338

Livingstone, William Oswell (son, 1851–1892) 61, 151, 157, 205, 206, 336–7;

DL's visits 233, 244, 255; doctor 256, 321, 338; RGS search party (1872) 320–1

LMS *see* London Missionary Society

London Missionary Society: interviews DL 16–17; training, medical studies 18, 20, 21, 120, 121; Mary 64; travels cause conflict 58, 98, 102; DL resigns (1857) 137; Barotseland Mission (1859–60) 132, 170, 183–5

Lozi 61, 62, 76, 185

Lualaba (river) 76, 286, 287, 288; DL's Nile speculation 289–90, 302–3; deduces relation to the Chambeshi 290; misses the Lukuga 296; reaches Lualaba but cannot cross 308

Luanda 75, 80, 126

Luangwa (river) 92, 101, 276, 347

Luapula (river) 76, 93, 277, 278, 286

Lunda Empire 76–8, 80, 93, 191, 344; DL (1867) 286–7

Ma Robert (naval paddle steamer) 148–9; hull 148, 173, 182, 186; inadequacies 160–2, 197

Mabotsa 43, 44, 45, 51

Macgregor Laird 148, 162, 170, 210

Mackenzie, *Miss* 194, 199, 200

Mackenzie, Charles Frederick (1825–62) 194–200, 250, 274

Maclear, *Sir* Thomas (1794–1879) 67, 118, 157, 208, 343; brings DL to Russell's notice 75, 108; Helmores 183

magic lantern 75, 283

Magomero 196, 200, 301–2, 343

malachite 178, 303

malaria: quinine 237

Malawi (lake) *see* Nyasa (lake)

Mambari traders 61–2, 73

Mamohela 300, 305, 307

Manenko (Lunda princess) 76–8, 126

Manganja 96, 188, 197, 263; Chief Chibisa 174, 195

Manyema 295–311, 317; DL describes 305

maps 339; Cardoso's (1856) 173–4, 189–90, 251; Lake Nyasa (1859) 237, 244, 249, 250, 312; Upper Zambezi (1853) 61, 75, 118

Mariano 162–5, 191, 197

Marx, Karl, quoted 110, 133

Mataka, *Chief* 271

Mauritius 99–100

Mbame 216, 222–4

Mburuma, *Chief* 93, 141, 145; murdered 182
Mebalwe 25
medicine chests xiv, 200, 279, 330
Meller, Charles 216, 218, 224, 233, 239
Melville, Herman 73, 112–13, 167, 217; 160, 162, 171 (quoted)
mfecane 34–5, 57–8, 96, 162, 198; Ngoni 276
Mirambo war 315, 318
Missionary travels and researches in South Africa (David Livingstone 1857) 93, 117–30, 171–2; 60, 92, 188 (quoted)
Moffat, John Smith (1835–1918) 127; DL funds mission 145, 157, 183, 241, 344; son dies seeking DL 333
Moffat, Mary *see* Livingstone, Mary (1821–62)
Moffat, Robert (1795–83) 35, 36, 158, 336; meets DL 22; *Missionary labours and scenes in southern Africa* 35, 117; Mzilikazi 58; Setswana Bible 35
Mokhatla 50
Monk, William 135
Monteith & Company 3, 4, 5, 16
Morumbala (mountain) 174, 188, 224–5
Moses 51, 302–3, 328
Moshoeshoe I, King of the Basuto 32, 57–8
Mozambique 95–7, 162–3
Mpende, *Chief* 93–4
Mtarika (Chief, Yao) 271
Mtoa, Hamis wa 285
Murchison, *Sir* Roderick Impey (1792–1871) 98, 252, 253; book agreement 102; introduces DL (1856) 112; negotiates consulship 132; recommends Thornton 150, 180–1; DL names falls (1859) 174; UMCA aftermath 200, 231; proposes RGS expedition (1864) 240, 265 *see also* Royal Geographical Society
Murchison Cataracts 174, 194, 198–9
Murray, John (1808–92) 102, 116, 118, 223; *Last journals* 339; *Missionary Travels* 129, 137; *Narrative* 233, 250
Murray, Mungo (1802–50) 53–4
Musa 265, 274, 275
Mwamba 283–4
Mweru (lake) 277, 286, 287, 290
Mzilikazi (King of the Ndebele) 34, 57–8, 96
Moore, Joseph 23

Narrative of an expedition to the Zambezi and its tributaries (David Livingstone, 1865) 93, 233, 234, 243–51
Nascimento, Belchior do 216–17
Nassik boys 261, 265, 274, 297; unsatisfactory 270, 283, 288, 301; second recruitment 324 *see also* Gardner; Jacob Wainwright
Natal 62, 100–1, 114, 208–9, 236
native agency 36–7, 48, 83–4, 343, 348
Ndebele 34, 58, 96, 344, 346; mission 145
Newstead Abbey 234, 237, 243, 253; Stanley 316, 320
Ngami (former lake, now dry) 37–8, 57, 59, 174; DL, Oswell 53–4, 124
Ngoni 96, 165, 276, 344, 347; migrants 34, 162, 242; wars hinder DL 198, 270–1, 274, 276
Nile (river): source 322; Lake Tanganyika debated 235, 295, 302–3, 317, 318 *see also* Fountains of Herodotus; Ptolemy
Nsama (Chief, Tabwa) 285, 286
Nunes, *Colonel* 98, 182
Nunes, Jose 165
Nyamwezi 321, 322, 333
Nyangwe 308; massacre 309–11
Nyasa (lake) 97, 98, 174, 275, 281; DL reaches 176–7 (1859), 197–8 (1861), 220, 224, 226 (1863), 273 (1866); Jordan link 198, 237; Portuguese claims 187–90

Origin of species by means of natural selection (Charles Darwin) 114–15, 139
Oswell, William Cotton (1818–93) 52–3; Lake Ngami (1849) 53–4, 113; map of Upper Zambezi (1850–1) 58–61, 65; DL's family expenses 63, 64–5; proofreads (1864) 248; identifies DL's body 335; pall-bearer 336–7
Owen, *Sir* Richard (1804–92) 20, 38, 112–13; instructs Kirk 154–5, 191, 198

Palmerston, Henry John Temple, 3rd Viscount (1784–1865) *see* British government: dealings with DL
Park, Mungo 8, 15
Pearl (naval ship) 162; Zambezi Expedition to Cape 156–7; to Zambezi delta 158–69
Peto, *Sir* Samuel Morton (1809–89) 139–40, 160–1, 163, 168

Philip, John (1775–1851) 30–2, 66, 117, 126

Pioneer (naval paddle steamer) 186, 194–5, 198, 225, 227; runs aground 199, 222 see also Leadwood

polygamy 38, 67, 236

poodle 275, 279

Porto, Silva 73, 74, 87, 344

Portugal 96–7, 190–1; and Britain 81, 140–1; explorers 187–92, 250–1 see also slavery: in Portuguese possessions

Prentice, Thomas Lomas 24–5, 42–3; DL letters 25, 28–9, 29–30, 38 (1841), 32, 37, 43 (1843)

Price, Roger 183–5, 344

Proctor, Lovell 194, 200

Ptolemy 175, 289, 302, 321–2

Quelimane 95, 97–8, 163

racism 27–8, 71–3, 113–16; British Israelites 149, 167; Calvinism 14, 46, 51, 82–5; Catholicism 82, 165; Eyre 251–2

Rae, George (1831–65) 174, 180, 203, 205; engineer, Zambezi Expedition (1858) 149; assembles Ma Robert 160; prevents Bedingfeld's cowardice 163, 169; Lady Nyassa 177–8, 200; Mary's coffin 204; with DL at Lake Nyasa 224; farewell (1864) 227

rainy season 76, 93, 87, 170–1, 327–8; crop sowing 326; 'sponges' 278, 289, 327

Reis, Joaquim Moreira 82, 86, 97, 220–1

RGS see Royal Geographical Society

Rhodes, Cecil John (1853–1902) 345, 346

Ridley, Catherine 24–5, 42–4, 299

Royal Geographical Society: Gold Medal to DL 54, 65, 112–13; Baines recommended 150–1; DL funded to seek Nile source (1866–73) 240, 265–6, 274–5; Lake Bangweulu 288–90, 292 (1868), 325–9 (1873); Lualaba 302–3, 308; DL and Stanley show Lake Tanganyika not Nile source 317; DL disaffected 290, 318; lying in state 336 see also Nile (river) source

Rovuma (river) 96, 190; DL's plans 242, 260, 265; not navigable 194, 225, 269

Ruo (river) 174–5, 199, 200

Russell, Lord John, 1st Earl (1792–1878) see British government: dealings with DL

Rutherfoord, Howson Edwards (1795–1862) 53, 67, 209–10, 241

Ruzizi (river) 317

Sa da Bandeira, Marques de 187–90

Said, bin Habib 287

St Ana, Jose de 173, 182

Saleh, Mohamed bin 287–8, 292–3

Schutz, Alfredo 86, 87

Scudamore, Henry 194, 195, 200

Sebitwane, King of the Kololo 57–60 see also Kololo; Sekeletu, King of the Kololo

Sechele (Chief, Bakwena) 48, 53, 57, 58, 236; Boers 67; move 61

Sedgwick, Adam (1785–1873) xiv–v, 135, 146, 282; DL letters xiv–v, 13, 271–2, 273, 277

Sehamy 46

Sekeletu, King of the Kololo 69, 145–6, 183, 185; 27 men, oxen and supplies for DL's Luanda journey 75–6, 87; 200 men and supplies for DL's journey to east coast (1855–6) 87, 175, 182; tragedy of LMS missionaries 183 see also Kololo; Sebitwane, King of the Kololo

Sekwebu 97; suicide 99, 123

Sesheke 60–1, 62, 87

Setswana (language) 30, 34, 35, 40–2, 122–3

Shamo 164, 189

Shinde (Chief, Lunda) 76–7

Shire (river) 198, 237; Cabora Basa forces DL east 173–4, 175; Portuguese claims 97, 173–4, 187–90, 222 see also Universities' Mission to Central Africa

Shirwa (lake) 174–5, 195, 237

Shupanga: inland river post 166, 200–1, 215, 222; Mary 202–5, 220

Sicard, Tito Augusto 94, 97, 131, 165–6; sings 167; slaves 195, 197

Silva Porto 73, 74, 87, 344

Sinbad (ox) 75

Slavery 191; in Central African kingdoms 22, 89, 196–7, 281–2, 297, 70–1 (tsetse fly); in Portuguese possessions 73–4, 80–1 (Angola and Brazil), 95–7 (Mozambique); in USA 71–3, 83–5; in Zanzibar 262–3, 303, 334–5; involuntary labour 99–101, 347–8 see also abolitionism; racism

Speke, John Hanning (1827–64) 235–6, 290, 298, 317, 322

'sponges' (dambos) 278, 289, 327
Stanley, Henry Morton (1841–1904) 314–20, 336–7; meets DL 316
Steele, *Sir* Thomas Montague (1820–90) 51–2, 75, 336–7
Stenhouse, John 282–3
Stewart, James (1831–1903) 199, 203, 204, 244, 336–7; disillusioned 226
Stowe, Harriet Beecher 249; *Uncle Tom's Cabin* 71–3, 83–5
sugar 80, 101, 191, 227
Susi 261, 301, 324, 327; DL's deathbed 330; leads funeral journey 334; in Britain 337–8

Tabwa 285, 286
Tagh, Hamis Wodim 285
Tanganyika (lake) 296; Burton and Speke 175, 235; DL's plans 261, 265, 271, 284–5, 295; he and Stanley disprove as Nile source 317
Tete: DL 94, 97 (1856); 160–1, 170, 174, 179, 180–1 (1858–9); 186, 194, 216, 221 (1860); Kololo porters 97, 182; local war 162–3
Thornton, Richard (1838–64) 223; Murchison's protege 150; geologist, Zambezi Expedition 157, 158, 164, 166, 167–8; surveys Tete coalfield 174; dismissed by DL 180–1; he continues, explores Kilimanjaro 181, 215; DL re-employs (1863) 215–16; death 222–3, 241
Tippu Tib 285, 286
Tswana 35, 36, 38–9 *see also* Setswana (language)
Tsetse fly: and slavery 70; DL links to cattle deaths 59; Vardon's specimens 52

Ujiji: DL at 265, 282, 285 (1867); 293, 294–5 (1869); 311–13, 315–18 (1871–2)
ulcers, tropical 301–2; powdered malachite 303
Ulva (island, Scotland) 3, 118–19, 234
UMCA *see* Universities' Mission to Central Africa
Uncle Tom's Cabin (Harriet Beecher Stowe) 71–3, 83–5, 249
United States of America 71; Civil War 210–12, 232, 316
Universities' Mission to Central Africa 138, 164, 192–201, 220–1, 344; DL at Cambridge 135–6, 192; forward party

embroiled in warfare on the Shire 194–6; deaths of Mackenzie, Burrup and Scudamore (1862) 200; Tozer withdraws Mission 224, 226–7
Unyanyembe (Tabora) 293, 315, 318, 322–3; Burton 235

Victoria, *Queen* (r. 1837–1901) 89, 136–7, 156, 259
Victoria (lake) 235, 321–2
Victoria Falls 87–9, 183, 186
Vincent, Rupert *see* Livingstone, Robert Moffat (son, 1847–64)
Voyage of the Beagle (Charles Darwin) 117, 124–9

Wainwright, Jacob 332, 334, 335, 336-7, 338
Wakatini 196, 227, 261, 274
Waller, Horace (1833–96) 194, 200, 245, 254; resists Tozer 227; takes ex-slaves to Cape 227; becomes rector 241–2; disbelieves report of DL's death 274; pall-bearer 336–7; edits DL's last journals 330, 337–8, 339
Wardlaw, Ralph (1779–1853) 14
Washington, John (1800–63) 147–8
Watt, David 37–8, 45
Webb, William Frederick (1829–99) 61, 287; DL at Newstead to write *Narrative* 234, 237, 243–53, 256; Stanley there 316, 320; pall-bearer 336–7; reunion 338
Weigh House (church) 231, 236
Welwitz, Federeich 86, 156
Whately, Richard (1787–1863) 136, 138, 193
Wilberforce, Samuel (1805–1873) 139, 192, 193, 250
Wylde, *Sir* John (1781–1859) 66, 126

Yao 196, 197; slave traders 191, 271; Yao escaped slaves 276, 279
Young, E. D. 274–5, 282
Young, *Sir* James (1811–83) 12–13, 129, 225, 337; recommends Rae 149; trustee 151, 178; John Livingstone 212–14; the Lady Nyassa 224, 228, 240; DL visits 233, 255–6; large gift to DL's RGS Expedition (1864) 241; pays for search expedition (1872) 333; pall-bearer 336–7; he and Agnes settle DL's estate 338–9

Zaire (river) 80, 290, 295

Zambezi (river) 57–61, 87 *see also*
  Cabora Basa; Victoria Falls; Zambezi
  Expedition
Zambezi Expedition (1858–63) 145–82,
  192; the Pearl unable to navigate
  Zambezi inland from delta 160; the
  Ma Robert 160–2; Bedingfeld 166–70,
  216, 248; DL blocked at Cabora Basa
  171, 173; Lake Shirwa 174–5; Lake
  Nyasa 176–7; Baines and Thornton
  179–82; government support

continued 186; first UMCA forward
  party 194–7; second UMCA party,
  tragedy on the Shire 199–202;
  Expedition ended by government 224
Zanzibar 192, 262–5; cholera 303;
  closing of slave market 264–5, 310–11,
  334–5, 345
Zomba (mountain) 174, 189
Zumbo 96, 127, 162–3, 182; at river
  confluence 92–3, 281; fossil trees
  126–7